Krause, Elliott A

The sociology of occupations [by] Elliott A. Krause. Boston, Little, Brown [1971]

xiv, 398 p. 24 cm.

Includes bibliographical references.

1. Occupations. 2. Professions. I. Title.

THE SOCIOLOGY OF OCCUPATIONS

THE SOCIOLOGY OF OCCUPATIONS

ELLIOTT A. KRAUSE
Northeastern University

LITTLE, BROWN AND COMPANY
Boston

LIBRARY OF CONGRESS CATALOG CARD NO. 79–146305

FIRST PRINTING

Published simultaneously in Canada
by Little, Brown & Company (Canada) Limited

PRINTED IN THE UNITED STATES OF AMERICA

FOR THEO, CAROL, AND ANDY

ACKNOWLEDGMENTS

Many people have helped in the different stages of the evolution of this book. First, I would like to thank my students for their initial encouragement. The staff of Little, Brown helped at every stage: Woody Chittick, who suggested the idea as a formal project; Al Browne, College Editor; and Marian Weil, Assistant Editor, who saw the manuscript through to publication. Several colleagues were helpful with their criticisms of the manuscript: Alex Inkeles, Everett Hughes, Blanche Geer, Stephen Schafer, and Ted Ferdinand. The staffs of the reference divisions of the following libraries were especially helpful: Widener, Social Relations, Countway, Law School, Littauer, and Andover-Newton libraries of Harvard University; the Boston Athenaeum; and the main library of the University of Chicago. Morris Janowitz and the office staff of the Department of Sociology at the University of Chicago were gracious hosts during my stay in their Ph.D dissertation library.

I would also like to thank the people of the Patisserie Française in Harvard Square and the Marengo Street Co-op in New Orleans for their coffee and hospitality during the writing of the first draft of some of these chapters. Luck brought me some fast and able helpers: Jean Hurley typed the first draft of the manuscript; George and Winifred Parker the final draft. Sharon Jermyn prepared the indexes. My wife and children, to whom this book is dedicated, made the difficult task of writing just a little more bearable.

E. A. K.

TABLE OF CONTENTS

PART THREE

FUTURE RESEARCH

CHAPTER FIFTEEN

THE SOCIOLOGY OF OCCUPATIONS

INTRODUCTION

WHY STUDY OCCUPATIONS?

SOME BASIC ISSUES

In an era of political action and rapid social change, when all institutions of society are being reexamined, it is only natural that the central institution of work should come under scrutiny. Occupations and professions are among the main mediators between the individual and society. Yet they have seldom been systematically examined as dynamic, as a process, or as change-oriented. The forces which individuals and occupations bring to bear on one another, and the consequent role which occupational and professional groups play in the political life of the nation, will be a major theme of this book. In pursuing the interactions between individuals, occupational and professional groups, and the wider society, several basic questions will be asked. They will concern the historical development of present occupational and professional groups, the relations of individual to occupation and occupation to wider society, the role of the occupation or profession as mediator among the aims, goals, and needs of the individual and those of society, occupational and professional groups as the target of broad social changes, and the needs for change in the area of work to bring about a more humane and rewarding life for all.

A basic question throughout the book is: What changes have there been in the historical roles of major occupational and professional groups? There is no reason to assume that a particular occupational or professional group performs the same function from one period to the next. One can consider the history of any social elite. Pareto postulated that in most societies there is a circulation — a rise and fall from power — of the governing elite groups. As he expressed it, "History is the graveyard of aristocracies." [1] In some cases, history is also the graveyard of occupational and professional groups. As needs and technology change, some tasks evaporate and some originate from the new developments — witness the fall of the lamplighter and the rise of the laser specialist in engineering. More basically, the mandate and power of rather permanent groups are seen to be affected in basic ways from the perspective of history.

Changes in the broader organization of society may lead directly to a change in career opportunities and job recruitment patterns for the newest generation of workers. In Puritan Massachusetts, from 1640 to 1660, the first graduates of Harvard College went into the ministry to provide spiritual and intellectual leadership for the new parish settlements. Nearly 80 per cent of the graduates from 1645 to 1660 went into the ministry. In the late 1600s and early 1700s Massachusetts changed rapidly from a Puritan church-state to a wide-open Yankee trading state. The percentage of Harvard graduates going into the ministry dropped rapidly, whereas those going into business rose at the same rate. By the time of the American Revolution, most Harvard graduates were no longer going into the ministry.[2] The society of the day had successfully revolted against the political power of the clergy, and with the help of the King of England had effectively limited it by 1700. The role which the clergy had played as moral authorities and power figures in the early church-state was replaced by that of the businessmen, who clearly saw that the Puritan mystique was bad for business. Those in the new college generation had the newer values and saw that the future did not lie in the ministry, but in law, medicine, and especially commerce. Thus the difficulty ministers encountered in finding bright new recruits was closely related to the changing nature of the society and to the opportunities for "success" in given occupations and professions as viewed by the recruits of the time. Such a loss of mandate by occupational and professional groups had made it harder to recruit competent people for the future, leading to a further loss of mandate as less skilled people did a poorer job in the occupation.

Societies differ in the developmental history of occupational and professional groups, and in the following chapters we will be observing more than twentieth-century America. The role of factory workers, for example, varies considerably in America, France, and Japan, both in present and past history and in the kind of political action being taken to change the situation in the future. Therefore, as we study occupational and professional groups, we will regularly carry out a comparative analysis.

A second major question to be considered is the following: What is the individual's relationship to his occupation or profession? This relationship is complex, some dimensions of it being conscious and others unconscious. Some occupations are essentially very mundane; in others the departure from routine makes the work unique — abortionists, high steel workers, professional revolutionaries. These occupations involve something beyond the ordinary idea of putting time into a specific place in a specific organization.

One cannot understand the relationship of the individual to his work without understanding individuals, and thus the issue of human nature is involved. Writers as different as Karl Marx and Max Weber have attempted to understand the relationship between man and his work by opposing and comparing the basic needs of man to the basic needs of society. Sigmund Freud stated that men, in order to live in society, are doomed to be frustrated in that which they want more than anything else, gratification of their instinctual impulses. But Freud also said that the man who is most successful in realizing his potential is he who can love and work (*lieben und arbeiten*). And through work, though not through all work, he claimed, man can sublimate unfulfillable needs and in so doing contribute to society.[3]

Modern sociologists have seldom been as subtle in their understanding of the relationship of man to his work as Everett Hughes, a sensitive analyst of the nuances of the meaning of work and the relationship of persons to institutions. We shall refer to his work directly and indirectly in the coming chapters.[4] But his approach is not typical. Most sociologists think of jobs or occupations as categories, roles filled by individuals. Thus many of the problems frequently studied have been essentially of a mechanical nature: Does *this* type of man fit into *this* role? Does *this* role fit into *this* society? Industrial psychology often takes the same static approach toward the relation of men to work. Besides being politically conservative in its unstated premises, this kind of approach is usually more concerned with the functioning of the system than that of any individual in the system.

But the relationship of the individual to his occupation or profession is a two-way street. In each case, we must ask if the individual is taking a major part in creating his own occupation or whether the occupation or profession is bearing down on him to the point where he is made over in the image of the occupation. Obviously, answers to this question will differ, depending on the occupation or profession under consideration and also on the particular time in history. At one point, men may *create* a kind of work, a new type of function for a society, and, once created, this work becomes a mold for future generations to fit into or, perhaps, to break as other occupational molds have been broken in the past. Therefore the concern throughout this study is with the relationship of individual to occupational role not only in the traditional sense of socialization into the role, but also in regard to the individual's effect on the role, on the training process, and thus on the occupation or profession itself.

A third major question concerns entire occupations and professions as actors: What is the nature of an occupation's or profession's relation to the overall society? What function does the occupation or profession perform in the society? Again, the question has to be asked both from the point of view of the occupation and from that of the society. From the point of view of the society (or those in control of it), what functional need does the occupational or professional group serve for the society? In simple terms, what wouldn't get done if these people weren't on the job? How central is that job or occupational activity to the ongoing existence of the society? This, incidentally, may not necessarily coincide with the traditional prestige system of the society or with its scale for monetary reward. Some groups which a society needs desperately are not necessarily rewarded by that society with equivalent salary or prestige. For example, take the crisis in any major city when the policemen or the garbage collectors go on strike. The city cannot function without these groups, and yet they are not at present rewarded accordingly — precisely the reason for their action as a group against the society. In the following analysis, we will need to consider the activism of occupational groups as sources of social change as well as the present function of the occupations and professions in contributing to the present order and its division of labor.

A fourth question is in many ways another aspect of the previous ones and becomes highlighted in answering them: How do occupational and professional groups mediate between the individual and the wider society? Are they primarily a means of committing, engulfing, and coopting the individual to fulfill a role in maintaining the present social order and its inequities? Or can the involvement of individuals in occupations give individuals powerful leverage to change the system, should they desire to do so? At the turn of the century, Émile Durkheim observed that France was in a state of disorganization. Though this was hardly unique for France, Durkheim's proposed remedy was interesting. He suggested the creation of occupational and professional voluntary associations, which would serve as a focus for a man's loyalty, as his source of social identity, and as his location for voting instead of his geographical area. Occupations and professions were to become a purified and ethical set of political groups through which the individual could feel a sense of belonging and fellowship. Durkheim believed that the society of his time was characterized by anomie, and that the individual was helpless and lost against the impersonal forces of the overall society.[5] He was not a political radical. He did not see these occupational and professional groups combining into large superfactions, or Marxian class conflict groups, to change the society by revolution and restructuring. Nor did he see occupational and professional groups as agents of change. In fact, he believed that the ethical codes of existing and developing occupations could be strengthened and "societalized" to create a way of keeping the populace safe from radicalism, and supportive of the status quo. He failed to show how this could be possible, but he introduced an idea which will be one of the main interpretive themes of this book — the intermediary role of occupational and professional groups between the isolated individual and the wider society.

The mediator role, as we shall see in several chapters to follow, is a conflict-laden one precisely because of the pressures from both sides. Durkheim viewed only one side of this relationship: the role of the occupational groups in preserving the existing system. In a stable society, as represented by the guild system of the Middle Ages, the role of the occupational group is to provide the individual with his station, role, and identity in life. To some extent, it still is. But as we approach the present, when conflicts between powerful and powerless groups escalate, when identity is forged in action as well as in station, we observe increasing political activism in the occupational and professional groups themselves. The occupational group is becoming a place to organize for political action. The big question, which is critical to understanding whether we are observing change or only pseudo-change, is *political action for whom?* For the have-nots or just for the occupation's members? The answer to this question will determine how significant the occupational group's action is in "mediating" between individuals and the society.

This point demands further elaboration. As a group begins to organize to change a society, and as all groups do so, the present division of labor, the existing interrelationships in which "I do this" and "you do that" and "we do this for each other," may change in the process of the political action. In this way, the entire division of labor in a society could change. The big question then becomes: To what extent will the groups campaign for changes of a similar nature, or to what extent are they creating through the medium of occupational and professional groups precisely what Durkheim was trying to prevent? As the groups head off in all directions pursuing self-interests, they could tear apart a society through occupational activism, instead of improving it. Does the goal of improvement and increased welfare stop at the boundaries of the specific occupational group? If it does, the political action will lead to chaos or to the further increase of present inequities and oppressions. Only if there is coordinated action between groups, or deliberate action by an occupational or professional group on behalf of another group of less fortunate people can the activism produce what most would call a constructive or humane improvement over the present. Different subdivisions of occupational and professional groups are on different sides of this issue, as we will see in the coming chapters.

Occupational socialization — the training of the individual by the occupation — can be viewed as the primary post-adolescent pathway for fitting individuals into the present society. Society provides very few avenues outside the occupational and professional realm for a structured involvement. But the essentially political phenomenon is that individuals and groups are increasingly refusing to accept the present boundaries of the division of labor and the present role and goals of their occupation or profession within it. A national business magazine recently devoted an entire issue to the dilemma of the American corporation — the increasing rejection of business careers by the elite graduates of the elite colleges of the country. Ten years ago, when a career recruiter came to a college campus to interview students, the corporation recruiters would dictate the terms of employment, including such things as dress codes which were to be standard in the company. Today, in some of the largest corporations in the country, the recruiter may have a beard or some other clearly visible sign of nonconformity in style to symbolize what he will often say — that corporations are trying to get students to believe that youth's point of view is respected in the corporation, and that the corporation is active on behalf of the poor.[6] The amount of actual change, as compared to public relations activity, will be considered in a later chapter. But it is unquestionable that the corporate positions need to be filled, and the potential power of a unified, activist segment of the youth to boycott these organizations also exists. The fact that this boycott is only in its early stages does not mean that it cannot be realized, and even the stated goals and the ways in which corporations describe themselves to the community are under pressure to change. The effect of the new recruits in many occupations and professions is still minor, but the leverage of the recruit is now understood as a factor in the situation. Another illustration is the radicalization of a segment of trainees no society such as ours can do without — the medical students. They are forcing older professors and the administrations of medical schools to reconsider the goals of medical training, the generally conservative position of the profession in attitudes toward Medicare, the relationships of medical professors to the drug industry, and the social role of the profession as a whole. Some changes are evident even now. In October of 1969, the dean of Harvard Medical School, the director of Massachusetts General Hospital, and 300 other Boston physicians passed out antiwar postcards on Boston Common. They were asking public action for their position, that of influencing the government to spend less on war and the military-industrial complex and more on health.

This book has a focus on change. Most sociological studies of occupational and professional institutions in societies tend to concentrate primarily on the structure and function of the institution, and secondarily on the changes in the structure which have been described, and highly idealized in the process. But it is no longer possible to write a static description of the role of occupations and professions in society without totally ignoring the reality of life in these times. On the contrary, it is precisely the forces causing change in occupations and professions which are the main topic of this analysis. The strategy of the book, even when we take a systems approach, is that of Bucher and Strauss, the study of occupations and professions *in process*.[7]

Two final questions are concerned with the issue of social evolution beyond the control of men and that of social evolution directed and initiated by men through political action. The first social evolution question can be phrased in this way: What can this study say which will help to give a general insight into the direction in which Western societies are headed, regardless of the actions of individuals and occupational or professional groups? The stress of this book, far more than others in this field, will be on the actions which individuals take to make changes within their occupations and the actions which occupations and professions take in attempting to change the society. But in this work we will need to assess these attempted changes in relation to the broader, supra-occupational trends such as bureaucratization, the growth of technology, and the militarization of international politics. It would be inaccurate to infer that a change intended by an activist group was brought about by the group's desire, if independent conditions were in fact what made the change possible. It is true that Lenin organized the Bolsheviks in Russia just before the October Revolution, but in Lenin's own words, "Power was lying around in the streets; we just picked it up."

The final question concerns the political action of informed citizens: What can the analysis say to a new generation, and to other generations, in a revolutionary age, and of what use can this analysis be to them in their future actions? If this book can contribute to constructive political action aimed at the development of an increasingly rich and meaningful life experience for more people, without penalizing the rights of legitimate minorities, if it is used by citizens in their role as participants in community government and social planning to gain a better idea of the forces acting upon occupations and professions, which will help them in their attempts at change, then a major purpose of this book will be served.

THE STRATEGY OF ANALYSIS

In the complex and ever-changing field which is the subject of this book, a clear analytical strategy is important. Otherwise, the complexity in the phenomena may be confused with the complexity of the approach to the phenomena. The organization is threefold: the first section presents general concepts, the second applies these to a series of occupational and professional families, and the third reconsiders the results of the application and draws together the major themes, looking to the future as well as the past and present.

The first section of the book will present four general analytical approaches to be used eventually for every occupational and professional family. These approaches are the historical, the biographical, the functional, and the conflict-of-interest. A chapter is devoted to each one, including the major relevant concepts and issues. They are not considered as mutually exclusive approaches, but rather as complementary, as walking around a statue and viewing it from four standpoints is more satisfying and thorough than approaching it from only one direction.

Chapter One, "A Historical Perspective," will consider the role of occupational groups in society through a selection of key historical eras, each of which introduces an issue concerning the role of occupations and professions in society. The aim is not a comprehensive history of work, nor a history of the meaning of work such as Tilgher's, but a historical review showing how a series of present issues and present divisions of labor developed out of those of the past. The uses of the historical approach will be made clear.

Chapter Two, "The Biographical Approach: Work as Experience," will consider what could be called biographical issues in the sociology of occupations and professions. Biographical approaches involve asking what the meaning of the activity is to the individual and the ways in which the individual interacts with the institutions in which he exists. Socialization — the process of being trained in the values of an organization, an occupation, or a society — is the key sociological idea. Therefore the concepts which illuminate the intricacies of training and indoctrination in occupational and professional roles and the ideas which consider individual motivations and reasons for choice, for accepting or rejecting the values of the roles and the groups, are of central importance. Resistance to the process, the rejection of present occupational and professional values and models and the creation of new ones, has a place in this approach. The career — the life cycle of an individual as it interacts with the work cycle of a society — is a major aspect of the biographical approach to occupations and professions.

Chapter Three, "The Division of Labor: Structure and Function," introduces what we will call the systems approach to this topic. Here a consideration of Durkheim's concept of "division of labor" and the major issues concerning the world of work as an ongoing system will be introduced. The comparative perspective will be used briefly to illustrate the difference between Western technological principles of organization of work and other systems. A set of issues relevant to the systems approach will be introduced: the nature of the labor market, occupational categories and prestige rankings, occupational mobility, work in the bureaucratic setting, and the issue of the professions as a special case.

A companion chapter to Chapter Three goes over the same ground, but with a different approach, characteristic of a different way of analyzing the field of occupations and professions. Chapter Four, "The Division of Labor: Conflicts of Interest," presents the conflict-of-interest approach to occupations and professions. Power, occupational and professional organization and political activism, the roles of technology, greed, and idealism in conflict situations are of general importance. A modified Marxian perspective, used here, will approach each occupational and professional group from the perspective of the following questions: Who benefits? What role do individuals play within the group? Is the group, or subdivisions within it, a set of haves or have-nots within the wider society? On whose side are they found, as a group, in situations of wider conflict over the future of the society? In Chapter Four we introduce conflict-analysis concepts such as occupational consciousness, for use in each succeeding chapter. These will allow us to ascertain, at least in part, the role that the different occupational or professional groups play in supporting the status quo, with its obvious inequities, or, conversely, the pressures from concerned individuals, segments of occupational groups, or changes in the wider society that will bring about a new situation.

In the central section of the book, we consider a set of occupational and professional families important to the life of any society. A *selection* is necessary rather than one chapter per occupation — unless we wish to have 25,000 chapters. Since this is an analysis rather than an annotated occupational telephone book, a selected set of occupations and major professions will be analyzed in terms of their historical development as families, biographical aspects of the roles played, the presently existing division of labor (comparatively with other nations), and finally, the stake which the occupation and its subgroups have in maintaining the status quo or in acting for change. Each chapter will conclude with a brief summary, exploring the potential future of each occupation.

Chapters Five through Eight are concerned with the classical professions: "The Health Field," "The Legal Profession," "The Clergy," and "The Military." Blue-collar, white-collar, and executive occupations will be discussed together in Chapter Nine, "Business and Industry: Occupational Aspects." The creative occupations — the pure scientist and the artist — are paired in Chapter Ten, "Science and the Arts." Chapter Eleven, "Illegal Occupations," presents subtypes within this group. Another important family of occupations, those involved in education, has a separate chapter, "The Field of Education," because of their central significance to the functioning of the society and the increasing importance of political activism within these occupations. "Public Service Occupations," growing in size and importance every year, are the focus of Chapter Thirteen. We will choose a representative set of occupations, from diplomat to policeman to garbage collector, for a comparative analysis in depth of this critical group. The final chapter in the central section of the book, "The Career Activist," deals with three major subtypes: politicians, reformers, and career radicals.

In the third section of this book, the patterns and parallels which have emerged from the analyses of the occupational families will be brought together. Chapter Fifteen, "The Politics of Skill," summarizes the themes of systems function and interest conflict and asks basic questions concerning the political meaning of the division of labor itself, as well as summarizing the trends that are appearing as more and more occupations enter directly into the political arena. The role of youth will be considered and the themes analyzed that have emerged out of the existential dilemmas which the young and other change-oriented people confront when they encounter the present occupational and professional structure with its vested interests. Questions of responsiveness and resistance to change are highlighted here — a topic of relevance not only to the young but to all those concerned with the next generation's aims and goals at work. The future of work will be reconsidered by returning to the historical perspective which is a strong dimension of the overall analysis.

PART ONE

FOUR PERSPECTIVES

CHAPTER ONE

A HISTORICAL PERSPECTIVE

Over the centuries, the role of occupational and professional groups in mediating between the individual and society has changed dramatically. Selected historical periods can show the different modes of relationship, the main themes in the relation of individuals to institutions. A selection of key periods up to the Industrial Revolution shows the importance of a historical approach. And as this book centers on American occupations and professions (with a comparative perspective on other nations), we will take the more recent periods for inspection from the American historical record. In general, the historical perspective allows comparison between past experience, past struggles involving individuals and institutions, and the parallel though not identical issues of the present.

HUNTING AND GATHERING SOCIETIES

For much of the time that man has lived on the earth, he has existed by hunting and by gathering wild fruits and grains. Lenski summarizes the common features of hunting and gathering societies as follows: "primitive and inefficient techniques of food production (in terms of product value per unit of expended energy), an undeveloped or rudimentary technology and tools, a small population size, a nomadic way of life, and limited specialization of an occupational sort." [1] Two occupational specialties were commonly found in hunting and gathering societies: the political head or chief and the shaman. But the usual form of government, the informal tribal council, and the job of the headman itself, did not provide full-time occupations for anyone in the typically small band. The need for subsistence and the uncertainty of life made specialization impossible. Even the shaman, or "medicine man-priest," could be considered a role that was dependent upon personal qualities rather than being an established occupational specialization of significant size and permanence. As Lenski summarizes:

> In primitive hunting and gathering societies, power, privilege, and prestige are largely a function of personal skills and ability. Inheritance only provides opportunity; to be of value to the individual, confirming actions based on personal qualities are required. Where these are lacking, the possession of an office is of little benefit. In this respect hunting and gathering societies differ greatly from more advanced societies.[2]

In comparison, the development of agricultural societies led to the creation of more efficient technologies, which involve a more efficient use of energy.[3] The increase in population size and in food-producing efficiency made possible free man-hours for the specializations in government, war, and religion which were characteristic of agricultural societies.

In such societies organized occupational and professional groups per se do not exist, and thus cannot "mediate" between the individual and society. The rule of custom, the organic place of work as embedded in the existence of all, makes the analytical scheme we are using superfluous. This in turn reminds us that not all individual existence, even in highly bureaucratized and occupationalized modern societies, involves work. The mediating role of occupational or professional groups must be compared with forces relating individuals to society *outside* this pathway.

CLASSICAL GREECE: THE CASE OF ATHENS

Athens in the fifth century B.C. has been regarded as one of the cultural high points of the Western world. It was also a classic case of a society whose division of labor was based on the exploitation of man by man. The social structure of Athens contained three distinct classes: the full citizens, the resident aliens or *metoikoi,* and the slaves. At the time of our inspection, estimates agree that there were three or four slaves for each household, for both citizens and metoikoi.[4] The citizens had the equivalent economic and political rule of shareholders in a closed corporation — the Athenian city-state; the metoikoi were not shareholders and could not vote. The primary mark of the citizen was his leisure. Choice of vocation — the division of labor in the citizen elite — was by talent and by intrinsic interest of the citizen. One did what could gain one the most honor in the contest system of social competition for prestige. Another main function of citizens was to fight in the army. Slaves were prohibited from fighting because of the risk of desertion and because of the honor-bestowing functions of battle, an opportunity that could not be offered to slaves.[5]

The slave in this society had no legal rights and could rarely gain his freedom; freedom did not mean citizenship, in any case. The majority of slaves were female and sexual exploitation as well as economic was common. The resultant children were usually denied the status of citizens. The slaves worked not only at domestic service, but also at large mines and non-mechanical factories, increasing the wealth of the large slave-owners as the Negroes did in the American South.

In contrast to Athens, where the slaves were taken captive in battle or were the wives or children of slain enemies, Sparta had its *helots,* members of a subjugated tribe who had originally ruled in the land governed by the Spartans.[6] The anonymity of the Athenian city and the lack of kinship among Athenian slaves led to fewer slave uprisings than in Sparta, in spite of the fact that Sparta was a militarized and bureaucratized state.

The division of labor in Athens and its cultural glory were bought at a severe price. In addition to the misery of exploitation, there were effects on the exploiters. There was the fear on the part of each Athenian — the certain knowledge, in fact — that if the city should lose any of its battles, the men would be killed and their women taken into slavery. Gouldner argues that this division of labor between a leisured elite, who defined "work" as the activity of slaves, and the needs of the social system for slaves to keep it going, created a vicious circle:

> Maintenance of a cheap slave supply requires large areas of social disorder between the city-states; it requires kidnaping, piracy, privateering, and above all, war. Slavery is thus one of the major inhibitants to the spread of a peaceful international order in Hellenic civilization. Conversely, international disorder is actually useful for the maintenance of Greek slavery, because it allows those outside the basic political unit, the *polis,* to be preyed upon and to be subjugated as slaves. And without the slaves there can be no citizen elite.[7]

The Athenian example is critical in our review of the relationship of the individual to occupation and society because it shows why the political power dimension is basic to understanding the relationship. To the slaves, work was existence because of their power relation to the state; to the citizen, the choice of leisured preoccupation was based on personal interests, and occupational or professional role did not define status or income. Historically, then, man has not yet reached an ordering of society that is inherently occupational, though he has a clearly established division of labor and leisure.

THE MEDIEVAL PERIOD

Walter Ullmann presents the medieval situation, and the role of the individual in this situation, as involving the clash of two theses, an abstract one and a practical one.[8] The abstract thesis was that the "citizen" did not exist and all rights of *subjects* came from the Church. This thesis provided a theological justification for rule from the top and was the ideology of the Church and the rural feudal nobility. The practical thesis was the recently documented existence of local self-government and partial guild autonomy in the villages, towns, and cities. Each thesis, each mode and justification for living, governed a segment of the society more thoroughly than it did the whole. Together, they made up the warp and woof of the medieval social tapestry.

The abstract thesis — that God had ordained the present social structure and that man, as manorial lord and serf, should accept his station — was the official ideology of the Church as it had developed over the years since the fall of Rome. In this Christian cosmological order, every man had been called (vocatus) to fulfill specific tasks: *Unusquisque maneat in ea vocatione in qua dignoscitur vocatus.* (I Cor. 7:20) ("Everybody should abide in that calling to which he is known to have been called.") [9] The primary beneficiaries of this rule were the lords of the feudal manor. Their serfs could be sold with the land if occasion necessitated. As Bloch describes this division of labor, the feudal system

> meant the rigorous economic subjugation of a host of humble folk to a few powerful men. Having received from earlier ages the Roman *villa* (which in some respects anticipated the manor) and the German village chiefdom, it extended and consolidated these methods whereby men exploited men, and combining inextricably the right to the revenues from the land with the right to exercise authority, it fashioned from all this the true manor of medieval times. And this it did partly for the benefit of an oligarchy of priests and monks whose task it was to propitiate Heaven, but chiefly for the benefit of an oligarchy of warriors.[10]

Since the university began, it has been essentially the base of the professions. But Carr-Saunders reminds us that the Church governed the medieval university, and that the faculty of arts and the schools of medicine, law, and theology *all* gave ecclesiastical degrees.[11] Thus all learned professionals were churchmen, by definition, and the trained practice of law and medicine, in the early and central Middle Ages, was a monopoly of the Church, and thus of the power elite of the time.

As Ullmann presents it, the second thesis — the practical thesis — involves the fact that not all groups necessarily acted as if the ideology were in force. The village and the city residents took for granted that individuals had the very rights which the abstract, descending-power thesis of government denied them.[12] The rural villagers of the Middle Ages, as Homans pointed out, conducted village self-government as the "natural" way of doing business. The ancient Roman idea concerning village operations, that "what touches all must be approved by all," was in force, and the villagers elected their own officers such as reeve, hayward, and blacksmith.[13]

In village and city life in the medieval period, the role of the craft guilds was critical. The guilds, based on a division of labor by occupational skill (butchers, carpenters, tanners, bakers, etc.), became the primary organizing bodies of the medieval town. Indeed, in many towns and cities, the council consisted of one representative from each major guild. Self-governing within themselves — and with governmental license and approval — the guilds were another aspect of Ullmann's practical thesis.[14] But they were not a force for change; they were integrally important in maintaining the economic and social status quo. As Pirenne states:

> The guild system thus secured the independence of the individual through strict subordination of all. The privileges and monopoly which the members of a guild enjoyed had as their counterpart the annihilation of all personal initiative. No one was allowed to injure another by improving the methods of production in such a way as to allow him to produce more rapidly and at less cost. Technical progress was seen as disloyalty. The ideal was stability of conditions in a stable industrial organization.[15]

Throughout most of the Middle Ages, then, a man's estate — as churchman, noble, guild member, or serf — was his primary way of relating to the overall society. The Church stood at the apex and presented the governing ideology. The countryside lords of the manor and the serfs accepted it directly, with the self-government of the towns under the mutual cooperative control of the guilds. *Within* a guild a man might have some rights as a citizen, but the guild's function as an anti-individualistic, anti-progressive, and anti-capitalistic institution made for an essentially static town situation, matching that of the countryside. Again, the Church integrated the countryside and the town. Life and time did not evolve; they existed in an ever-recurring cycle.

From this historical period, several themes originate which are strikingly relevant to present issues in occupational and professional life. First, it highlights the role of ideology in maintaining a socio-political status quo and the ways in which occupational and class groups accept or reject the ideology if it serves or does not serve their purpose. Second, the cleavage between the social system of the city and that of the countryside, as well as the nature of occupational roles in these settings, is brought into clarity. A third theme of relevance is the contrasting loyalties, legitimacy, and values of the professions (established, sacred, prestigious, elite) and the guild crafts (informally self-governing, middle-status in the society). This contrast between the "special" callings and the more mundane work in crafts is of major importance. Finally, in this period we again have a major exploited group, and thus an exploitive social order, where the exploiting group and the order itself is legitimated by a higher authority. In terms of our overall model of individual-occupation-society relationships, society, through the Church, prescribed the role of the estates, which then prescribed the role of the individual. The initiation, at each level, was from "above." And, in the medieval period, God stood at the ultimate end of the chain of command.

THE RENAISSANCE AND REFORMATION

The onset of the Renaissance can be typified by changes in the relation of men to institutions: the rise of individualism and the rise of capitalism and a money economy. The first — the reassertion of the individual as an entity in the face of larger organizations and offices — can be seen most concretely in the world of art, in the changes from the Middle Ages. In portraiture and sculpture,

> the hitherto stereotyped and typified form gave way to an individualistic and natural portrayal. If you look at, say, Giotto's or Giovanni Pisano's products, you perceive a concrete image and a human personality in all its individuality. The mere abstract image, which depicted no one individual personality, became a realistic image of human proportions with an infinite variety of personal individual traits. . . . Sculpture and portraiture began to represent the individual qualities of the human person.[16]

The second major change was the development of a money economy. As Von Martin points out, an economy based on the hereditary possession of land is static. Money, however, can be acquired, hoarded, pyramided, lent at interest. In a situation where the group with the money has the power, an opportunity is created for exploitation of resources through trade, investment, and credit finance — in a word, capitalism.[17] And since the feudal lord had his wealth in land, as the merchant economy grew, the merchant prince became a figure of power and the lord of the manor a background figure, a hangover from an earlier era. The action of *individuals*, in pursuit of power for monetary gain, or seeking monetary gain to acquire power, or both, took place outside the entire estate system of medieval times; it brought about the Renaissance, and, partly in consequence, the Reformation as well.

A series of consequences followed the rise of individualism and capitalism. First, the restraining force of the old moral order was revealed when the naked pursuit of power became commonplace. The new merchant capitalists, as individuals or as organizations of businessmen (upper guilds, *Arti maggiori*, guild merchant) aimed at the seizure of control in town and city government and at the crushing of the power of the medieval craft guilds. Von Martin summarizes:

> The great merchants and moneyed men regard the rules of the guild as so many fetters, and they know how to rid themselves of them. . . . An elite of capitalists was forming itself; it no longer took part in manual work, but was active in the sphere of organization and management, standing apart from the remainder of the middle class and the working proletariat.[18]

They took immediate political action in their own interest:

> The wage-earners — excluded from the possession of the means of production and from all political rights — were ruthlessly exploited and even deprived of the right of association. But the mercantile and industrial capitalist elements also asserted their power over the master craftsmen. . . . Not the "people," but the monetary power of the upper guilds defeated the feudal aristocracy, and the middle class represented by the lower guilds was for all intents and purposes excluded from power.[19]

The trading associations of merchants, capitalist in nature, sponsored colonization and controlled international trade. The Hanseatic League of merchant trading associations and the Spanish merchant guild of Seville were essentially trade monopolies that *bought* the monopoly rights from the royal governing families of the time or from the Church in the Catholic south. As Parry notes of the merchant guild of Seville, "By an elaborate series of fictions, merchant houses all over Spain became members by proxy of the Seville guild, consigning their cargoes in the name of resident Seville merchants." [20]

The Spanish *conquistador* was a form of mobile Renaissance entrepreneur. From 1520 to 1550,

> a few thousand down-at-the-heel swordsmen, themselves the product of the tradition of the Moorish wars, possessed themselves of most of the settled areas of both Americas and established the first great European land empire overseas.[21]

As a further consequence of the loosening of the social order, the concept of upward social mobility through changes in occupation became a relevant one for the populace. Those in the middle levels of society pushed the process of secularization and the breakdown of the old order through their desire to change old forms to new ones.[22] Escape to the city from the still feudal countryside became a common phenomenon, epitomized by the saying *Stadtluft macht frei* (flight to the city means freedom).[23] The craft guilds of the Middle Ages, conservative and order-preserving in older times, began in the Renaissance to act analogously to the modern labor unions. Guild members too wished to be modern Renaissance men — to increase their income — and the formerly cooperative relationship of guild to city government disintegrated into a series of power struggles between craft guilds and city governments now in the control of merchant princes. In France, during the late thirteenth and all of the fourteenth centuries, the mason's guild engaged in bitter conflicts with the King of France and the Mayor of Paris over the amount of money to be paid per brick, the amount of free time available during the winter and summer months, and the number of working hours.[24] All the classic signs of labor negotiation issues were present, and records of these negotiations exist from as early as the last third of the medieval period. By the fifteenth century, at the height of the Renaissance, the action of these "labor groups" in Paris and elsewhere had been so disruptive to the governments that a completely new set of regulations was passed to penalize the craft guilds for their actions.[25] The state, acting in the name of the new capitalist groups, crushed the power and the mobility aspirations of a whole estate that had caught the monetary fever of the Renaissance. Of course, the merchant associations kept *their* monopolies. As we have illustrated, one of the prime consequences of the Renaissance was the creation of a new group to replace the Church in its position of power over the butchers and bakers of the world.

The professions gained in independence as a consequence of the secularization of the society. As they maintained their prestige as specialists in the needs of men, the legal and medical professionals capitalized on the free scholarship of the Renaissance, on the searching of the past and the entertaining of new ideas. The law schools introduced the corpus of Roman law — Corpus Juris Civilis — to the curriculum, for it was Roman law that was needed in commerce, and the merchant princes needed trained house counsel.[26] Basing their inquiries on Arabian medicine and treating man as "animal naturalis" rather than sacred, medical schools in Holland and Italy began to teach the study of anatomy and soon became the centers of a new science of physical man.[27] With Machiavelli a new political social science was born, based on observation. Da Vinci, as an "architectus," a combined architect and contractor, designed bridges, calculated their stresses, and built them. In his time, he was known as a famous engineer-architect who also painted.[28] The birth of the technological profession of mechanical engineering is amply documented as a Renaissance phenomenon by William Barclay Parsons. The rediscovery of Roman techniques, a developed medieval technology, and the expanding needs of the great Renaissance cities created the mandate for a major group of technological experts.[29]

Individualism in art, letters, and science was the cultural hallmark of the Renaissance. The discussion of the content and significance of these cultural productions — the work of Botticelli, Raphael, Cellini, Erasmus, Machiavelli, Rabelais, Copernicus, Vesalius, Galileo, and many others

— is the province of whole worlds of scholarship and cannot be considered here. But the significance of the Renaissance for understanding the role of creative occupations and professions lies in its parallel to modern times: a change in man's ideas, combined with a change in his social structure, may indeed create the conditions, as well as the market, for new points of view from the creators. The Renaissance, as both economic and psychic revolution, spread northward like a slowly burning flame, and as it dimmed in the south it began to hit its peak in the north. As it did so, a reaction set in against the new power relations developed between the Church and the merchant capitalists. The revolt took an overtly theological tone and was epitomized by Luther.

The concept of work as holy in itself, as a form of worshiping God, was part of Luther's revolution against what he felt was the corrupt power of the Renaissance Church. What the common man did, rather than the idle churchman or merchant prince, had dignity in Luther's eyes.[30] Max Weber suggested that the "Protestant Ethic" of Luther and Calvin accelerated the rise of capitalism.[31] But the historical record, as summarized by Von Martin and Swanson, and as sketched in above, relegates this idea to a supplementary role at best.[32] The Catholic south brought about the Renaissance a century before Luther, and it was precisely the ties of the Church with the merchant capitalists that Luther protested. After the establishment of Protestantism in northern regions, the new upwardly mobile classes found it harmonious as an ideology with what they already knew about the development of capital. Swanson summarizes his own extensive research on this issue:

> One may find that Protestant entrepreneurs, like the great merchants of Catholic lands, were generally content with their gains, and that the whole economy was moved forward by efforts of the still disadvantaged men of rising classes. One may find, however, that the rising classes in Protestant countries had the special advantage of being upwardly mobile in a society that legitimated the pursuit of economic gain.[33]

Von Martin, following Sombart, goes even further and suggests that both Catholicism and Protestantism hindered capitalism's development in its earliest stages.[34] But once the economic and social revolution was moving, the new leaders found they could use both the Pope and the teachings of Luther and Calvin to advance their interests.

The Renaissance and Reformation carry lessons of critical importance for an understanding of the role of modern occupations and professions. First, the action of individuals in challenging institutions is based on their disengagement from the integrated world of medieval times and their action, as occupational and economic interest groups, in changing the status quo. The rise of the cash nexus and the fall from legitimacy of the total all-encompassing value system of the Church led to action by merchant princes, conquistadors, and other entrepreneurs. Old elements of the feudal system itself, such as craft guilds, were transferred into economic interest groups that began to strike against the city for higher wages. The location of work is again seen as a factor in its future. The entire countryside production system of manorial lords and serfs became economically less relevant; at the same time the flight to the city for upward social mobility in wage-earning positions began in earnest. The relation between new ideas about work, on the one hand, and the action of work groups, on the other, is critical to understanding their actions in political and sociological terms. In an abstract sense, the medieval Church and the more zealous Protestant sects were anti-capitalist. But the actual cooperation of the Renaissance Church with the capitalists and the use of Protestant theology by rising Protestant businessmen meant that the religious institutions did not hinder the development of capitalism in the long run and may have accelerated it after it was under way. In contrast to the medieval period, this was an age when individuals influenced the future of occupations and professions and an age when occupational and professional groups acted to change the direction, nature, and goals of the society.

PURITAN MASSACHUSETTS

One of the consequences of the Reformation was the formation of several militant Protestant sects. Walzer indicates that the early history of the Puritan sect reveals it as one of the first politically radical movements.[35] By this he means that the theology of this sect was used as a radical *political* ideology, as a means for the creation of a social movement. Unsuccessful in England, the Puritans gained a liberal charter from the King and set out for Massachusetts. John Winthrop called the Massachusetts Bay Colony "a City upon a Hill." [36] He referred not to the physical geography of Boston, but rather to the utopian experiment which the colony represented in 1630.

Puritan society was not strictly a *theocracy*, since the ministers did not govern, but was an aristocracy of Puritans, since the right to vote was restricted to the members of the Puritan church and the legal system operated with ministers as consultants to the judiciary.[37] As one Puritan divine put it, approvingly, "We are a speaking aristocracy, in the face of a silent democracy." [38] Only about a tenth of the population were members of the church, in the first thirty years, yet all were compelled to attend services.[39] Any laxity in attendance or any opinion expressed against the church was punished with a dual trial by secular and sacred ecclesiastical courts, followed by expulsion from the colony.[40] A rigid class system was constructed from the start. Under the dual leadership of a small landed aristocracy and the Puritan clergy, there was a middle class of businessmen, a class of craftsmen, and, at the bottom, common farm and urban laborers. (Slavery was not illegal but was quite limited.) The values enforced by the two governing groups — landed aristocracy and clergy — were essentially medieval in the area of commerce. The doctrine of Justum Pretium — a just, moral, and stable price for all goods and services — was resurrected from the Middle Ages.[41] In a sense, therefore, the Puritan experiment gives us a chance to view a replay of the transformation from a medieval type of economy and division of labor to a mercantile era. The role of the major professions — their mandate to practice — will be an issue of central concern to us in the inspection of this period.

By the turn of the century, in 1700, the Puritan state had almost vanished and the old economy with it. Perry Miller sums up the consequences:

> When the businessmen themselves, including many professing Christians, divided into hostile armies, the clergy . . . had to stand helplessly by, begging both factions to remember charity. As times grew hard and prices rose, Increase [Mather] wistfully wondered whether the government ought not to revive the old law "that no merchant should ask above Four Pence, or Six in the Shilling, for what he sells"; when that code had prevailed, the clergy had been the economic arbiters, but in 1719 Mather merely sighed that he could no longer "meddle" in these affairs, and advised sufferers to seek consolation in prayer.[42]

The changed role of the clergy was caused in part by broad-scale economic factors, in part by its own actions, and in part by a mandate struggle with the legal profession. There were three main periods in the struggle. From 1630 to 1640, the early period, the English village self-government plan of the feudal period was followed. But a major difference in Puritan Massachusetts was that the appointed officials were under the supervision of the clergy when decisions of any importance were made. There were significant consequences for the construction and administration of law. The ruling group decided, illegally according to the laws governing English colonies, that there would be no appeal to the King. They decided that any law which was made "contrary to the laws of God" was "not law, but an error." [43] The *clergy* decided what the laws of God were, for they were the colony's experts on the Bible. No decisions of court cases were recorded in this period, for these decisions could set precedents and could thus constitute a growing body of law which might restrict the discretionary power of the magistrates and the clergy. No lawyers were wanted in this system, and lawyers were made quite unwelcome in the colony.[44] Not only were they unemployed (not being allowed to practice in the court) but their concept of law, based on legal technique rather than the Bible, was anathema to the clergymen.

The middle period, from 1640 to 1684, saw the development of major conflicts between the clergy and an embryonic legal profession. The first major code of laws in the modern Western sense, the Body of Liberties of 1648, was drafted by a minister who also had legal training.[45] The existence and acceptance of this code meant that the code and not just the Bible was a source of authority. Miller suggests that four factors resulted in a restriction of the mandate to the clergy, limiting its acceptance as an expert in broad areas of a non-theological nature. First, there was a controversy over land titles in the colony which led to the realization that clergymen were sadly limited in many areas of the law. Second, Charles II eventually discovered the colony's lack of franchise for non-believers and by a royal decree in 1665 he ended the Puritan monopoly on political power by extending voting rights to all freemen. Third, a non-Puritan church formed and survived as the Baptist denomination, and there were revolts against the ruling elders within the Puritan church itself. Coming in the same decade as the royal decree, these developments marked the beginning of the end of religious orthodoxy. Finally, the Puritan clergy's persecution of Quakers was stopped by order of the King of England, an action which certainly lost the clergy a measure of authority.[46]

At the same time when the actions of the clergy led to reaction against them, the international commerce which was at first a small part of the colony's economy became a major factor. By 1680, Boston mechants were open and active in their opposition to the clergy. They stated, both in Massachusetts and in England, that the restriction in immigration was leading to a restriction in their business opportunities. They viewed immigrants as potential customers or employees, and preferred customers to orthodoxy.[47] As the role of the clergy in the administration of the state declined, that of the legal profession arose. Lawyers began to practice in the late 1640s and the early 1650s. Although there was no professional bar in this middle period, there was official recognition by the government, from 1656 on, that lawyers could practice in the courts.[48]

Finally, the third period, from 1684 to the turn of the century and then on into the pre-revolutionary period, saw the nearly total collapse of the power of the clergy and the rise of lawyers to form a professional bar. The commerce of the Boston port demanded legal expertise, and the courts now excluded ministers from positions as legal consultants. The secularization of the state occurred through a change in governing values and ruling occupational groups, with the mandate in the legal area being lost completely by the clergy and given to a professional bench and bar, with lawyers in appointive and elective positions in the government.[49] In the first period, the morality of lawyers was questioned by the clergy, for in Biblical terms there was only one right side to an argument, whereas the lawyer would argue either side of any case for a fee, and indeed considered his professional ethics on this issue as a positive or desirable aspect of his profession. In the last period, the lawyers functioned essentially in the way that Parsons suggests they do today: they represented conflicting interests, mediating the otherwise direct conflict through a legal system where rules existed for settling the conflict peaceably. The legal system, then as now, was secular in nature.

The role of Harvard College, founded in 1642, mirrored the change in mandate of the clergy. From 1642 to 1684, the percentage of graduates going into the clergy diminished from 75 per cent to less than 50 per cent, and the largest post-graduate occupation in the latter period was commerce. After 1700, as many graduates went into law, medicine, and teaching as went into the ministry, and commerce became the most common frequent post-graduate career. In addition, several who had originally entered the ministry left it, adding to the trend to a secular career for a majority of graduates in the first decades of the eighteenth century.[50]

Another instance of the changing nature of the professional mandate came during the smallpox epidemic of 1721. A position was taken against the use of a new technique — vaccination — by the best educated physician of the time, Dr. Douglass, but Zebediel Boylston, a folk practitioner of good repute, and Cotton Mather, the prominent minister, were in favor of vaccination. It should be noted that Boylston and Mather based their argument on articles in the journal of the Royal Society in London, which was quite full of fanciful speculation at this point in its development. As history records, Boylston and Mather guessed right, but Douglass and caution were against them. More important, the reputation which the Puritan clergy had built for narrow-mindedness, bigotry (the persecution of Quakers), and accessory to murder (the illegal Salem witch hangings) meant that the entire population of literate Boston — except the Puritan clergy — opposed vaccination precisely because Cotton Mather was for it.[51]

Puritan Massachusetts was as much an idea as a society and as much a throwback historically as a progression toward utopia. It was the momentum which the early capitalist developments created that doomed this society to a short life-span and assured the ultimate expansion of the mandate of secular professions at the expense of the mandate of the Puritan clergy. This fact raises the general issue of the way in which broad social trends influence struggles between groups over the mandate to perform a given social function. Both a change in the group performing a given social function, as shown here, or the growth of a new need and a new group are possibilities in most historical periods. The Puritan situation of a reciprocal change, where the legal profession gained what the clergy lost, is a different process from the growth of a new occupation or profession that does not involve, at least initially, political struggles between existing occupations and professions. A second issue introduced in this period is the role of the university in the changing mandate of occupational and professional groups. The career choices of the graduates reflect the changing opportunities perceived by the individuals in this elite status. A third issue is the historical reputation of a profession, as with the Puritan clergy in the smallpox crisis. Past group actions can affect a profession's capacity to act in the society at a later time, as well as their capacity to gain new recruits. Finally, the Puritan period continues the theme of the exploitation of a large mass of unskilled workers by powerful groups, a theme which characterized many previous eras. In the cities, the poor and the common laborer of Puritan Massachusetts experienced the same change in masters without change in opportunities that similar groups experienced in the transition from medieval society to the Renaissance. They went from a bottom position in a sanctified status quo, under the authority of a clergy and an all-encompassing religious ideology, to a situation of exploitation by an unrestricted and essentially amoral mercantile group.

JACKSONIAN AMERICA

When Alexis de Tocqueville visited America in 1831, he encountered the social ferment of the Jacksonian era and was impressed by what he called the most egalitarian society of his time. But it was a rough society, a period of frontier manners. When a lady visitor from England arrived, she found that

> Cincinnatti men in their shirt sleeves, reeking of onions and whiskey, thumped their feet in theater boxes; even that stately Hall of Representatives which Morse had painted a few years before was filled when she saw it with men who sat in the most unseemly of attitudes with their hats on and spat with a fluency which decency forbade her to describe.[52]

As Calhoun states, hostility against the professions had always been a part of anti-aristocratic sentiment in the English-speaking world. Professions, by their central skills, were potentially in a position to exploit people, and could do them harm if they were strongly organized. It was also a fact that the leaders of the ministry, the bar, and medicine did in fact come from precisely the aristocratic families and groups that Jackson ran against in his anti-elitist campaign for president. Thus Jacksonian America became important to the history of occupations and professions, because it was a period of active *deprofessionalization* through political action by the aroused masses who voted the licensing laws for lawyers and physicians out of existence, combining at the same time to break the remaining power of the regular Protestant clergy in the countryside. The issues this period raised are still with us today.[53]

The frontier legal profession was a close-knit one, and perhaps precisely for this reason it drew the suspicion of the people who had to deal with it. In the Kentucky of Jackson's time, judge and lawyers rode the circuit, traveling as a troupe from town to town:

> Travelling together, rooming in the same inns, drinking together, the lawyers, the attorney general, and judge all came to know each other intimately. Since they were all one big family of high-spirited gentlemen, they were not always a happy family; but their disputes reflected the tone of their intimacy.[54]

Lawyers would gang up on a judge who was traveling with them, judges would fine a lawyer for ungentlemanly behavior, and barroom quarrels within the profession were sometimes settled with duels. The mistrust of the professions was combined at that time with a "natural right doctrine" claiming that any man had the right to practice any profession. In the period from 1830 to 1845 this claim led, throughout the United States, to the abolition of the requirement of legal training for practice as a lawyer in the courts or the community. As Griswold notes, it was not until the third decade of our present century that the legal profession was able to reestablish these restrictions in many states.[55]

The fate of the medical profession was similar. Because of the extreme shortage of trained physicians, their actual lack of scientific knowledge (bleeding by leeches was common), and the high fees they often charged to all, the Jacksonian era was ripe for an alternate medical professional movement. A major one was the Thomson medical sect, which came out of New Hampshire as a combination herbal folk medicine technology and political movement. The followers of Thomson sided with the poor and suggested that each man and woman could and should dose himself. Kett comments on their politics and their relation to orthodox medicine:

> Thomsonians viewed themselves in alternating perspectives. At times they saw their movement as wresting medicine from the doctors and completing the great revolution which, beginning with the Reformation, freed government from the lawyers and despots and religion from the priests; at other times as intimately involved in a mighty reformation in which there was still much to be done to secure to the common man his rights in *government* as well as medicine. In their latter role Thomsonians throughout the thirties attached themselves to a wide range of political and social reforms.[56]

By the end of the Jacksonian era, the restrictive and in fact unrealistic medical licensing laws had been repealed throughout the United States. Massachusetts was one of the few states where the law was not overturned, but this state's law was not restrictive, but facilitative, in that it "commended" the trained practitioner and urged all those not so trained to use the orthodox practitioners as consultants. The Thomsonians and their political allies were successful in repealing medical and legal license laws because of the unpopularity of the professions at the time, because of the Jacksonian ethos of the day, and, in the case of the medical profession, because the herbal practitioners were actually much less dangerous to the public than the orthodox physician, a fact known to a considerable segment of the public.[57]

Jacksonian America was thus a frontier society where, in ideology and occasionally in successful action, the masses had power. But as Abramson documents, Jackson's cabinet appointees and his nominees for other government posts were from the educated elite, although not to the same extent from the hereditary aristocracy of the nation. Another reality was the continuing existence and partial monopoly of the medical and legal profession, licensing repeal or no. Nevertheless, the issue of professional mandate and political ideology was raised critically in this period. The ideology of the people and of their president was anti-aristocratic, and the people struck out at the intrinsic functional "aristocracy" of the classic professions of medicine and law and made tenure nearly impossible for the orthodox clergymen as well. Yet the degree of corruption sometimes present within these professions and their lack of developed skills at this time led to some justification for the public's protecting itself against unwarranted monopoly. The need of a society for its professions and its concomitant need for regulating (or unregulating) them are seen as inherently political issues, since regulation involves legislation in government, a political process. We have not considered other issues in this historical period, such as the aristocratic philosophy and brutal reality of the slaveholding South, or the elitism of new capitalists such as Biddle, who tried to buy the United States Treasury. These important (and familiar) themes are also relevant to the Jacksonian era. But the power granted to needed occupations and professions, precisely because they are needed, and the subsequent political implications for the entire society are issues highlighted in this era, and ones that we will find constantly recurring in the analysis of present situations.

THE INDUSTRIAL REVOLUTION IN AMERICA: 1860–1900

The Jacksonian era had been a devastating one for American professional groups. The last half of the nineteenth century saw a slow rise in their desire to organize and combine and a major transformation in American universities. At the same time, the Industrial Revolution hit America. In later years, the universities and the industrial world would come together in the form of technological, scientific, and business training. At the time of the Industrial Revolution, it is possible to discuss them separately, for Veblen's Captains of Industry who tried to run the university from the corporate board room were really more a development of the early twentieth century than a factor at the beginning of the industrial change-over.

During the Middle Ages the professions were all located in the university, but this focus changed in later centuries. In medicine and law in England and America, the professions were outside the university. Professions were learned through the apprenticeship system in this country until the time of the Industrial Revolution. Jencks and Riesman sum up the changes that occurred in the last decades of the nineteenth century, changes which would determine critical aspects of the role of today's professions. In their opinion, the modern American university itself dates from the 1880s, when Johns Hopkins and Clark were founded primarily as *graduate* universities, when Eliot at Harvard introduced the elective system and gathered a highly specialized scholarly faculty to staff it.

> The 1890s saw further progress, with the founding of Chicago, the reform of Columbia, and the tentative acceptance of graduate work as an important activity in the leading state universities. This was also the period when national learned societies and journals were founded and when knowledge was broken up into its present departmental categories ("physics," "biology," "history," "philosophy," and so forth), with the department emerging as the basic unit of academic administration. Medicine and law also became serious subjects of graduate study at this time, with Johns Hopkins leading the way in medicine and Harvard in law.[58]

The Industrial Revolution began, according to many historians, with the introduction of a series of machines for the weaving of cotton in England. The English case has been considered the "classical" one, in that the Industrial Revolution first occurred in widespread form, and transformed the society more completely and more rapidly than any other for some time to come. In France, as one consequence of the Revolution, a large number of peasants held small amounts of land, a situation which Kuczynski thinks was a major factor in their remaining on the farm, thereby delaying the development of industry.[59] In Germany, the feudal order of the countryside blocked the early development of industry, and the middle class opposed it for other reasons. America, which had neither a hereditary peasantry nor a hereditary factory worker group, became a rather special case. The key issues were immigration, mobility, and the Horatio Alger ideology, an outgrowth of the Protestant Ethic. We can briefly inspect these topics in the period between the end of the Civil War and the turn of the century, when in America the Industrial Revolution finally assumed the shape and some of the consequences it had acquired half a century earlier in England.

To begin with, all historical inspections of this period must note the essentially unchecked power of the industrialists, the legislation which in many states made the planning of unions or strikes a crime under the conspiracy laws, and the typical 13–15 hour working day. Still, in comparison to Europe, for groups such as the Irish these conditions represented an improvement. The immigration of large numbers of unskilled workers from Ireland, Germany, and Holland characterized the middle third of the nineteenth century, with the population almost doubling between 1830 and 1860. The Irish were by far the largest immigrant group settling in the industrial northeast. As Thernstrom notes, they were unable to break into factory work in the early years, though by 1880 they constituted the largest segment of factory workers in Newburyport. The census records of the time indicate a significant amount of geographical mobility on the part of the jobless, who wandered from Boston to Lowell, from Lowell to Newburyport, in search of work.[60]

Mobility is a critical issue in the American Industrial Revolution. First it was not true that the Western frontier acted as a "safety valve" for the unemployed in the East in the last half of the nineteenth century. They weren't able to buy the wagons and supplies necessary to go West, and even after the railroad was completed it was still primarily the schoolteachers, marginally successful shopkeepers, and farmers who could save enough to make the trip and start over. Thernstrom, in his important statistical study of social mobility in Newburyport during the industrial revolution, stated that ethnic status (Irish versus Yankee) and time of arrival in Newburyport (the expanding 1850s versus the erratic 1880s) were two critical factors in upward mobility. The Irish had far greater difficulty in getting off the bottom rung and their sons had more difficulty than the sons of native workers. For the native worker, the step was one step up the ladder — from unskilled to semi-skilled or from semi-skilled to skilled — in the course of a lifetime. However, for those who held simple factory jobs steadily, the bank records of the time indicate definite, though minor, property acquisition. The workers could and did eventually buy their own homes on a mortgage and put a few dollars into a savings account. It was this fact that lent enough reality to the rags-to-riches ideology and the Protestant Ethic to make the employed workers, even at the lower rungs, unsusceptible to radicalization. But Thernstrom's study ends two decades before the turn of the century.[61]

In the last two decades of the nineteenth century in America, the rather limited flexibility began to go out of the system. The immigrants kept coming, industry did not expand fast enough to employ them, and the economy on its own, manipulated as well by the robber barons, went through rapid cycles of boom and bust. Early in this process the social utopianism of the nineteenth century — Brook Farm, Oneida — was directed at the workers as well, in attempts to form radical workers' cooperatives. But as Mann demonstrates, groups such as the Knights of Labor were unrealistic in their aims, far too utopian in their approach to practical politics. Thus in 1886, the wage system remained, the days of work were long, and the pay for the six-day week was still very low. Present conditions demanded attention. This practical concern came to a head in the 1893 convention of the recently formed American Federation of Labor, the successor as organizer to the disorganized and discredited utopian groups. At this convention, the members literally voted on the question of whether Marxism would be the base of their approach. Mann recounts the event:

> T. J. Morgan of Chicago . . . forced Samuel Gompers to poll affiliated bodies on direct political action to promote a number of reforms, of which the chief, embodied in Plank 10, was "Collective ownership by the people of all means of production and distribution. . . ." After furious debates, at the Boston Central Labor union, a special state conference of workers, and the Massachusetts Federation of Labor, Frank Foster and his colleagues defeated the Socialists. Plank 10 was voted down.[62]

Thus the American Federation of Labor voted for a share of the present pie, and not for the cooking of a new one. Important for our purpose was the fact that the AF of L was a union of *crafts* — masons, carpenters, painters, plasterers, butchers, and bakers. It was specifically *not* a union of the unemployed, the unskilled, the factory machine operators. Even in the early American labor movement, therefore, no group was predominantly fighting with any success for the truly oppressed industrial proletariat of the nation. The self-interest of the craft union members (as they perceived it) and the power of the Jay Goulds of the time were too strong. The union's compromise, its decision against the formation of a political labor party, its inherently conservative self-interest, and its distrust of the Irish — all would have consequences for the American labor movement for years to come. And in the terrible winter of 1894, Jacob Coxey's army of jobless, desperate, unorganized, and unskilled industrial workers descended on Washington.

The Industrial Revolution introduces new issues and reconsiders old ones. What factors determine whether a group of people "in themselves" — those who can be seen as a *category* of workers — will become as well an organized group, such as the industrialists, professionals, and craftsmen, a group that will fight in its own interest? Is human nature and the fear of strangers such that men will always prefer indulging their feelings to combining with those who might gain a little more than they by the effort? Will the poor always be the last organized? Will upward social mobility, minuscule but real, be always preferred by most to the riskier but potentially more rewarding advance of a whole group? Technology brought about the Industrial Revolution and in reaction fostered in America the organization of the weak, along occupational lines, to combat those who were in possession of the polity, the direction of the economy, and the conditions in the factory. But the combination of *part* of the working class was only that, and did not lead to basic changes at this time.

THE USES OF HISTORY

Each period selected here has carried forward a set of general themes and yet had its own individuality. In general, what are the uses of the historical approach to occupations and professions? The explorations of this chapter seem to provide at least three answers. First, general themes can be discovered which appear relevant to almost all historical periods and can therefore be considered as universal issues concerning the relationships of individuals, occupations, and the wider society. Second, a historical approach provides depth to the analysis of present processes and a check against which to compare conclusions about the present situation. Third, the past acts as a reference point, along with the present, to allow a projection into the future.

Several general historical themes appear in our analysis. The first is the exploitation of the weak by the strong, as this has been codified in the work relations of societies. We recall the slaves of ancient Greece, the serfs of medieval times, the workers for the merchant princes of the Renaissance and for the Yankee businessmen of colonial Massachusetts, the slaves of the Old South, and the "wage slaves" of the early Industrial Revolution. Each had different masters, yet all were exploited in a way that was justified by the ideology of those in power at the time. Thus without understanding the power distribution within a society and the ideology of its powerful groups, it is impossible to understand the reasons for the divisions of labor which existed in the periods inspected. Second, the dual role of ideas and economic-technological factors is seen in each period, and changes in either area are seen as related to changes in the other. Third, the alternation in history between static periods, such as the medieval period and early Puritan Massachusetts, when society, in the name of higher authority, dictated the role of each occupational and professional family and the life of individuals, is seen as alternating with another kind of society — the Renaissance, the Yankee trading state, and Jacksonian America — where individual initiative and occupational activism take the lead and change is the order of the day.

In most periods, the mandates and functions of the professions are seen as consequences of a balance of forces, such as the power affiliations and social rank of the profession's members, the degree of actual skill in the group, and the ruling political-social ideology of the time. In medieval times, all the professions were within the church, but in secular times such as the Renaissance or later Puritan Massachusetts, the secular professions gained at the expense of the sacred one. Jacksonian America, inspired by an anti-elitist ideology, acted to end professional monopoly altogether. In any time, the centrally needed skills of the professions make them critical in an overall analysis of the dynamics of social change. A final major theme in this chapter has been the role of occupational and professional groups as avenues of individual mobility in the system, or, on the other hand, as avenues of group action in the interest of an entire social sector. The review of these periods should demonstrate that such themes must be inspected in each era, if we are to understand the role of occupations and professions in society.

Our second and third conclusions — that the historical approach provides a necessary comparison to the present and a point of origin for a projection into the future — should seem obvious. Yet with certain exceptions, such as Carr-Saunders and Gouldner, and a new school of sociologically trained historians such as Calhoun and Thernstrom, the historical approach is simply not a regular approach to the sociology of occupations and professions. We will be making it one of the main approaches in this book. In order to avoid accepting the ideologies and mythologies of occupational and professional groups as the actual truth, we must have a specific understanding of their origins and the reasons for their existence.

CHAPTER TWO

THE BIOGRAPHICAL APPROACH: WORK AS EXPERIENCE

From the individual's point of view, the meaning of work is constructed out of past experience, present aims, expectations of the future, and those factors in the social situation which support or oppose him in his lifetime search for meaningful work. To consider this aspect of occupations and professions, we will use the biographical approach throughout this book, as one of the regular analytical perspectives. By the biographical approach we mean the analysis of the work experience of individuals from the point of view of these individuals. The *meaning* of this experience is critical, for as W. I. Thomas reminds us, a social situation which is perceived as real is real in its consequences. Work as experience will be considered in six closely related areas: early socialization, the school years as a time of occupational aspiration, expectation, and choice, the career as an experienced continuity or discontinuity, the occupational or professional group as a socializer, the work setting as an experienced reality, and the issue of alienation from work.

EARLY EXPERIENCE: THE BIRTH OF ACHIEVEMENT

In the family setting, the child's slow development from uncivilized "beast" to well-controlled, channeled, and yet lively elementary school student is simultaneously the general story of socialization and the specific story of the development of a young worker. Sociologists, social psychologists, and psychoanalysts view this process from slightly different perspectives, but they agree that the development of the ability to work, to strive and achieve, is a process which starts as an interpersonal one, initiated by parents, and gradually is internalized to become the child's own capacity. Parsons points out that the emotional bond between mother and child acts essentially as a rope with which the mother pulls the child up the cliff of self-control and constructive social behavior.[1] Precisely because the bond has been established, the mother has the leverage needed to frustrate the child's immediate gratifications for longer-term achievements. McClelland, as a social psychologist, has constructed a need theory in which *the need for achievement* plays a central part.[2] Recent research indicates that the desire to strive, and the striving behavior itself, may be taught more frequently in middle-class homes than in the homes of the poor, where the parents have been defeated so many times that they do not want to train their children to strive.[3] In later life, as Scanzoni shows, a general need for achievement is not really distinguishable from a desire to succeed at one's occupation or profession.[4]

Erikson, as a psychoanalyst, reminds us that the critical issue in early socialization, and early experience of this socialization, is the reward of work well done *to the small child,* and the costs to self–confidence and self–esteem if individual capacity and social environment do not constructively interact:

> while all children need their hours and days of make-believe in games, they all, sooner or later, become dissatisfied and disgruntled without a sense of being useful, without a sense of being able to make things and make them well and even perfectly; this is what I call the *sense of industry.* . . . To bring a productive situation to completion is an aim which gradually supersedes the whims and wishes of his idiosyncratic drives and personal disappointments. As he once untiringly strove to walk well, and to throw things away well, he now wants to make things well. He develops the pleasure of *work completion* by steady attention and persevering diligence.[5]

These middle-class virtues and competences learned in early childhood (if they are learned, that is) are of critical importance in schoolwork; to eliminate the sense of inferiority and inadequacy which children may develop in the early stages of "achievement" was the specific target of the Head Start Program of the Office of Economic Opportunity.[6] But Erikson is talking about an earlier period in the child's life, a period as early as the second and third year. The development of the "industry" pattern can be taken back this far. What cannot be established is that *types of personality,* as inherited and as a consequence of early experience, predispose a child to a later type of occupation; Roe states that the evidence does not support this hypothesis.[7] Neither are the early *vocational* ideas of the small child much more than fantasy and the conveyed daydreams and aspirations of parents. And, in observing the viewing habits of children, DeFleur suggests that much portrayal of work on television is limited in scope and highly idealized and romanticized as well.[8]

Thus, to sum up, the early years give the child little *occupational* experience, but do give the experience of early success or failure at work. This experience, combined with social class distinction, will be a strong determinant of the frame of mind with which the child approaches his school, the next step in work experience.

EDUCATION: THE PROBLEM OF ASPIRATION VERSUS OPPORTUNITY

In a general sense, the American educational system can be viewed as the key to the present occupational structure of the society. In the present context, we will be concerned with the following question: How are the aspirations for interesting work and rewarding careers, which characterize the majority of younger students, brought into line with the actual opportunity structure of the society? Since only a minority have professional or executive careers, as the majority are in essentially unrewarding white-collar and blue-collar work, how is the acceptance of this work, and the concomitant restriction in opportunity, brought about? We will need to inspect the natural history of occupational world views, from the original dreams of children, to the idealistic aspirations of adolescents, to the more concrete expectations of what they *really* expect to do, to the choice first made, and finally, to the actual career or job, if any.

The problem can be introduced with Ginzberg's early study, which showed the progressive narrowing of aspirations in a group of middle-income children, from the fantasy stage of about six to eleven, to the tentative stage of adolescent vacillation concerning choice, to what he called the "realistic" stage after this time.[9] The important theme is not simply the narrowing of focus, but also *the lowering of sights*. Kuvlevsky's panel study — one of the few which has actually followed a group from their high school days of "hoped for" jobs to a period ten years later — documents what we know must be the case generally, given data on ideal job choice by the majority of lower-class and blue-collar workers' children, as compared to the actual opportunity structure of the society. Over 75 per cent of the respondents did not attain the level of occupational status that they had originally aspired to. More specifically, the ones who were clearly professionally oriented as sophomores in high school managed to achieve a status more in line with their original aims than those who did not aspire quite so high. Those who began with only a moderate aspiration level fell short of even this level.[10]

In inspecting this process of the lowering of sights, we will need to consider how several factors in the experience of the youth bring about this process: the family, the peer group, the school setting, the region and nation-state, and the general social class membership of the individual. At the start, we must reiterate that the research literature, until quite recently, did not clearly make the distinction between *aspirations* (dream choices, wish fulfillments in many cases), *expectations* (what one *really* expects to be working at), *choices* (the first job attempt), and *career* (the actual sequence of jobs — the actual occupational history). The studies briefly considered here did take the necessary care to make these distinctions.

The family, as just considered, is the early proving ground for work capacity. Social class differences in child rearing practices, such as those discussed by Sears, Maccoby, and Levin, do concern themselves with training for achievement.[11] Of equal importance, as Psathas points out, the sex-role aspects of occupational stereotyping — what girls ought to want to be — begin in very early childhood.[12] Dale and Griffith, in a study of the relation of the family situation to the grammar school student's performance, in England, found that family size and education of parents was closely correlated with changes in the school achievement of the children. The low achievers came from homes with large families, where the mother had little education. The high achievers came from middle-class and professional homes, with educated, achievement-oriented, and schoolwork-sympathetic parents.[13] The American situation is somewhat parallel to this. But the information available about this country suggests that high *aspirations* are conveyed to children, even if the skills are not, in most middle-class homes. In fact, Campbell and Ackerman discovered that the working class (blue-collar workers) share the American middle-class idea that "a college education is the birthright of every American boy and girl." [14] This value and goal is being conveyed to their children. The new militancy of black Americans now suggests that here too the new ideology is being conveyed. It is not possible to find the sight-lowering process, therefore, in the family of the small child.

Although actually it is not possible to separate peer group influences from school influence, analytically we may do so. Three studies would indicate that there are, within limitations, very real influences on the aspiration level and direction of occupational choice by adolescent peers. The classic study was that of Parsons and Stouffer, on the "cross-pressured" boys in urban high schools. Those of higher socio-economic status planned to go to college, regardless of grades and whom they "ran with." Those of low income background and poor grades did not expect to go to college. The "cross-pressured" group — those with high grades from poor families — split on peer associations. If they "ran with" the college-bound crowd, they wished to go to college also. Those who rejected this crowd rejected their aspirations, in spite of grades. The economic factor as perceived by the poorer boys was real, but not sufficient to explain why they didn't aspire to college. Thus a segment of those with the *capacity* will still lower their aspirations to conform with the lower aspirations of friends.[15] Second, Coleman presents data which indicate that the type of school in which peer relations occur is critical: if it is a "college prep" school, academic aspiration will be a factor in the peer group pressure; if not, the athletic achiever will often be found as the only model.[16] In selected instances, peer groups may even have an influence on the *content* of a choice. Haas et al. indicate, in a controlled study, that girls go into nursing as a career in part because of the favorable attitude toward it by their peers.[17]

The school system itself can be viewed as a primary factor in affecting both aspiration and the nature of the performance upon which it is ultimately based. Parsons demonstrates that the elementary school rewards behavior and values as much if not more than actual achievement, and thus the child with the "wrong" values and behavior — non-middle-class — soon learns that genuine work and narrow achievement are not enough, that "effort" counts more than "achievement." [18] For a segment of the poor and the working class, the school route to occupational success thus begins to look remote even in the elementary grades. They somehow feel "out of tune" with the environment — or, more accurately, they are made to feel out of tune.

In secondary school the "tracking system," based on achievement and compatibility in elementary school, effectively closes the issue before many children or their parents are aware it exists, by consignment of a majority of children — in most blue-collar and poor neighborhoods — into non-college-preparatory programs. Of equal importance is the "guidance and counseling" system. The vocational guidance staffs in American high schools, as Cicourel and Kitsuse point out, sometimes unconsciously and sometimes quite deliberately assign students to tracks, interpreting difficulties as important or unimportant, on a social class background basis: the middle-class troublemakers will "shape up in college," whereas the obviously hostile and brilliant poor boy is an "overachiever" and is counseled out of college track programs; if he objects, he is "showing immaturity and unbalanced personality traits." [19] The counseling process, as they observe it, often has class distinction built in:

> Insofar as the high school is committed to the task of identifying talent and increasing the proportion of college-going students, counselors will tend to devote more of their time and activities to those students who plan and are most likely to go to college and whose parents actively support their plans and make frequent inquiries at the school about their progress — namely, the students from the middle and upper social classes.[20]

Friedenberg, in his observations of the high school experience, notes that in mixed (college- and non-college-oriented) high schools, the elite, the college-bound youth, often have official sanction to harass the poorer, and increasingly alienated, blue-collar youth.[21] The critical point here is that with every passing year, the school experience confirms the expectations of the college-bound youth and makes an outside job — any job — more attractive to the others. By such means — the rewarding or destructive nature of the school experience — rather than by any overt vocational planning, the aspirations of upper- and middle-class youth are confirmed while those of the poor are made "more realistic." It is true that an increasing proportion of industries now demand a high school degree; this delays entrance into the labor market and also gives evidence of a capacity to sit passively and attend regularly. Non-college-bound students thus find the degree helpful in getting a job, but for them high school graduation is often the bitter end of a painful process, with the business or vocational courses which they took to pass the time often proving useless at work. As Slocum notes, the structure of the labor market, the union regulations, the government rules, and the schools all join to prevent youth from having an early and meaningful experience in the world of work, and thus they are entering it with lowered hopes, but with no more experience than they had in the early years of high aspiration.[22]

College, rather than high school, is increasingly the dividing point between high and low status occupations. But Jencks and Riesman point out that to the degree that mass higher education and college graduation is made available to all, to that degree will it lose its value as a final qualifier for high status.[23] These authors are explicit in indicating that the primary interest of most youth, their parents, and adults in evening college, is in the vocational *certification* which the college degree provides — the status which can be converted into dollars. And they are accurate in their expectations. Eckland has shown in a followup study of many graduates from a Mid-western state university that the possession or non-possession of a degree is of far greater importance monetarily than the grades received in college.[24]

If the actual achievement for most college students is not closely tied to their later financial success, the time in school does provide the student with a chance to investigate career possibilities. Rosenberg's study of the different values and expectations which college students have — for people-oriented, money-oriented, or self-oriented careers — indicates that the expectations are realistic, since the college graduate does possess enough information and is backed by the system enough to make a realistic choice.[25] The weeding-out process, similar in many ways to the administrator's request to an employee for his "resignation," has occurred before entry to a four-year college. Two-year public junior colleges are seen by Clark, and also by Jencks and Riesman, as a post-high-school aspect of this weeding-out process. Those who persist in academic career aspirations, but who do not have the capacity for them, are often gently urged into the vocational programs of these schools, programs which produce the technicians badly needed today. The top students are selected for transfer to a four-year school.[26]

Region and nation-state are factors in determining aspiration and career choice. Perhaps the most thorough research on the effect of locale has been done on the vocational and career aspirations of rural American high school students. In a series of studies, Haller, Payne, and Burchinal found that youth who plan to leave the rural area do so because of their high vocational aspirations and the urgings of parents.[27] Straus's study modifies these findings: as in the other studies, parental influence was strong, but the reasons that his respondents gave for staying was the probability of success at home.[28] In all cases, the increasing mechanization of farming and the disappearance of the small farmer caused by economic pressures make the desire to leave the rural region realistic for most rural youth.

Comparative perspectives on the dilemma of aspirations in relation to opportunity indicate similar patterns in strikingly different political regimes, although all are industrialized and Westernized. Two studies of Poland, by Nowak and Janicki respectively, indicate phenomena similar to those seen in this country: high aspiration by those whose parents are low in the social structure, increasing realism as a consequence of experience in the school system, and a desire on the part of youth to leave rural regions for the city.[29] In the Soviet Union, Shubkin et al. indicate the same popularity of non-manual occupations, a desire to change (and often improve upon) the occupation of parents, and the fact that the occupational interests and aspiration levels were formed to a large extent as a consequence of school experience.[30] Brazeau reminds us of another factor, one as prevalent in the Puerto Rican barrios of our large cities as in the French Canada which he studied: being a member of a linguistic minority has a basic and early effect on a student's level of occupational aspiration and expectation.[31]

Social class and race, as general factors, are reflected in all the studies we have considered. With the exception of black Americans, who have recently begun in some areas to organize parallel private school systems for their children, the social class positions of parents does not dim the hopes and aspirations they have for their children. Until quite recently, however, they have not organized to have an effect on the main setting that ultimately influences their children's aspirations, expectations, and actual chances: their school system. In the absence of major changes, then, the entire educational system functions for a significant segment of the population as a "cooling out" device — gently lowering these students' early aspirations and hopes while refusing to provide them with the techniques to "make it"; all this is done in a way that makes the experience one that seems self-generated. This system in most aspects functions unconsciously, reflecting the operation of an entire socio-industrial order. It is far too efficient to be the consequence of a plot by a hidden power elite.

THE CAREER AS PATTERN AND EXPERIENCE

From the individual's point of view, "career" is a concept used to encompass past work history, present occupation, and plans or hopes for the future. The sociologist must also look at careers from outside, using a long-range view, as patterned series of graduated transitions and activities which reflect both the actions and the social structure which has made such actions possible. We can approach the issue of careers from three related points of view: objectively, in discussing career patterns, shapes, and the social factors which influence them; subjectively, in terms of the career experience with its common existential dilemmas and crises; and finally, from the point of view of the combined objective and subjective issue of career commitment.

The career is a minority, elite institution in Western society, if by this term we mean a graduated sequence of ever-increasing responsibilities, within an occupation, a profession, or an organization, with recognized and known signposts along the way. But in a less restricted definition, it is possible to speak of blue-collar, working-class careers or industrial careers, in at least the sense of job continuity. Shepard and Belitsky note that the unions to which the skilled workers belong help them, after job loss, to find similar employment in their craft or skill in another situation. But the unskilled are thrown onto their own meager resources.[32] To the degree that a recognized craft or union is involved, it is possible for a working-class career pattern to exist. But, as Treanton notes, the professional and executive career sequences of jobs are *cumulative*, in that previous experience adds value to the career and the future opportunities. This is not the case for most blue-collar occupations, even where there has been continuous employment in a given field.[33] Still, Wilensky notes that job continuity or stability, even outside the classical professional careers, is real enough in its meaning to a large segment of the work force to act as a bulwark against their radicalization, or their basic opposition to a given society. A steady working-class career is something to lose, in the sense that there is nothing so dangerous to a given social order as a group with nothing to lose.[34]

Contingencies on career development are those factors which either characterize the individual or are relevant to him in a way which makes a difference in the development or outcome of a career. Age and sex are critical contingencies; the biology of development and the culture's rules on aging and the role of women remain critical in Western society. With the increasing bureaucratization of the society, and a growing supply of young people, both ends of the career cycle are being shortened. Berger suggests we are creating a whole subsociety of post-adolescent unemployed young people in schools.[35] At the other end of the life cycle, retirement rules are being more strictly enforced, and a major geriatric unemployment problem is created.

The biology of reproduction and the requirements of the nuclear family as presently constituted result in an interruption in the work history of most women. But the sex factor is far more than biological. Sex acts as a discriminatory factor in education, employment, and vocational opportunity. Baruch notes that 43 per cent of all college-educated females were working in 1962, and that today one out of every three workers is female. But the primary occupations of the college-educated female, before or after marriage, remains low-level clerical and secretarial.[36] Age and sex, officially prohibited in the United States as factors for discrimination in employment and in career development, are still quite real determinants. They are basic factors which, along with social class, have to be used as "controls" before discussing other factors.

In the educational years and the early post-schooling ones, a series of factors are basic to future patterns and choices. The professor is a common factor. Gottlieb illustrates how the research orientation of the professors in graduate schools affects the career plans of many formerly teaching-oriented individuals.[37] Hall in his studies of medicine, and Mills in his study of the ministry, indicate the important ways in which senior colleagues can smooth the way in professional training, in practice, or in the executive ranks of management.[38] This "sponsorship" process, for those of the age, sex, race, social class, and ethnic group acceptable to the sponsors, often determines the difference between the "successful" careers and those which do not live up to ideals or expectations common in the occupation or profession. As Becker and Carper note, the relationship between sponsor and sponsored can be a close one; it is mutual and can often be long-term:

> The sponsor is responsible to his colleagues for the performance of the person he sponsors, who is in turn responsible to him for his behavior. When a person is sponsored into a first position in the work world after leaving graduate school, he feels obligated to act as a true member of the occupation and to remain within it, because of the trust placed in him by his sponsor. The creation of the obligation solidifies occupational attitudes and loyalties — the individual feels that he must remain what he has become in order not to let down his sponsor — and this strengthens the identification with the occupational title and ideology.[39]

As the individual progresses in his occupational or professional career, the settings in which he works, the conventions attended, and the work relationships formed along the way become over time what Katz has called an "occupational contact network." This system has its uses in determining personal career decisions, in gaining and maintaining wider informational perspectives, and eventually in aiding the older career man in sponsoring *his* protege.[40]

In most professional careers there are clients as well as sponsors. Braude's study of rabbis, Lawson's of Protestant ministers, and Roth's of nurses' aides show quite parallel observations concerning the significant power that the clients have in some professional occupations. The clients define much of the worker's role, despite the professionals' earlier expectations.[41] Career persistence often requires counter-pressure, or "client education." Bogdanoff and Glass show the ways in which the bureaucratic service worker — in their case social workers — must learn to handle their clientele by "educating them" about professional limitations. Those who cannot handle the clientele, in many occupations and professions, often resolve the problem by a change of career.[42]

A final major determinant of individual careers is the way in which the individual's life cycle intersects with history, the opportunities or oppositions presented by the current state of society as related to the state of his occupational or professional art. Luther, with his particular gifts, temperament, and ideas, had the good fortune to be born at the end of the fifteenth century, when "the time was ripe" for his innovations. Those in many occupational fields at the present time find they are in an age when social change has major and immediate impact on their career lines. Wager notes the way that bureaucratization in airlines lengthens the time it takes for a co-pilot to become a fully qualified flight captain.[43] Early technological obsolescence is a threat to engineers and scientists. Even the famous and creative scientist can be outrun by the field; he may have to settle for only a partly rewarding administrative career in later years.[44] Ferdinand observes that, in engineering, obsolescence is a function of the opportunities for keeping abreast (highest in universities and defense research firms) and the degree of continuing professional (as against administrative) aspirations on the part of the worker.[45]

Careers have directions — up, down, sideways — and points of transition — situations for choice and change which in many cases have associated "rites of passage." Several examples can illustrate the complex aspects of career patterning. Goldner shows that demotion in industry is sometimes camouflaged by ambiguous terminology. Sometimes the demotion may be functional — less responsibility — without affecting the present salary level; sometimes the absence of an expected promotion is a form of demotion.[46] The extreme subtlety here is to give an individual a short, final, terminal *raise* and no work at all to do — "kicking him upstairs." Another complexity is the subjective meaning of the lateral movement — from one setting to another — which can be felt as a form of promotion or demotion. For example, Becker's study of Chicago schoolteachers showed that they viewed a suburban job, with no increase in pay, as a promotion over their difficult ghetto school job of the year before.[47] Careers also have an ideological dimension. One example is the popular myth concerning avenues to promotion in executive circles as this may contrast with actual promotion policy of some corporations. The myth, at least to the public and to many junior executives, is that moving from place to place is a way of getting to the top. But in the corporation studied by Whyte, the data indicated that too much movement after a certain point in the executive's career was not as favorable to his eventual chances as many dedicated years of work in a corporation which is aware of the individual's long-term commitment.[48]

The biographical approach to career patterns shows its usefulness in interpreting another factor — the role of the sojourner, or permanent transient. Siu, in interviewing all of the Chinese laundrymen in Chicago, found that the majority thought their career transitory, useful in order to save money and return to China. It became clear that, in objective terms, the great majority were there to stay. But the *meaning* of the laundryman's existence was the reality which the laundrymen perceived, and it made a facile characterization of these individuals as "marginal men" or "social isolates" basically inaccurate. As Siu put it, "Physically they were in Chicago, but mentally in China." [49] Hodge indicates that the Navaho silversmiths also fall into the career type of "permanent transient." They couldn't make enough selling jewelry to the tourists to retire to the reservation, and yet could barely stay alive in their present place. Those who remained at the job were the ones who, in their own definition, were failures.[50] The tragedy of this can be appreciated by those who value the beautiful handiwork of these native craftsmen. Another aspect of the question of moving is seen in the city planner's career. Floro indicates that the ideal of planned and phased movement from city to city helps to bring independence from each city and enhances the "professional" role image of the city planner. But this too has limits. Sitting in one place and getting little accomplished or moving rapidly as a "jumper" every year results in little career payoff. Conversely, staying for a long time and building or moving at a well-paced speed can be seen as two alternate ways to the top of the profession in terms of reward and professional prestige.[51]

In considering the patterns and directions of career development, and the contingencies which affect them, we have been emphasizing the social structures through which individuals move. But the career of any individual cannot be known at any point ahead of time; careers are always *lived,* and the future remains unknown. An existential-sociological approach must consider these questions: anticipation of the future, the way in which the career is experienced, the handling of uncertainty, and the reinterpretation of career history. Each of these issues is social but at the same time deeply rooted in the individual's point of view.

Anticipation of the future is a central aspect of career behavior. Rosenberg noted that his college students, planning on careers in different occupations and professions, consciously began to act accordingly, adopting mannerisms and values relevant to the occupation, and obtaining the required preparatory training. We are all familiar with the pre-law student with his stuffy manner and three-piece suit, or the pre-med with a deep interest in his roommate's case of flu. Wallace's data on law students also suggests that the desire to become accepted by the central members of an occupational group may lead, first, to an adoption of their values.[52] Tiedemann goes further when he observes that the anticipation can be partly unconscious, or a product initially of daydreaming of the "Walter Mitty" type.[53]

A career as experienced *unfolds;* it is not viewed as a whole by the individual until it is over. Preliminary research indicates that a basic anxiety and uncertainty may consequently affect many in midcareer. Roe took a group in midcareer, expecting to find the "conscious career planning" which those in the vocational counseling field often assume to be present in the moderately successful. But her expectations were not met:

> We found, then, in our sample of 30 interviews, fewer examples of the decision-making process in operation than we had expected. Subjects find themselves reacting to the external influences and contingencies in their lives without much sense of choice or responsibility. Indeed, if they have had some freedom of choice, they tend to emphasize the chance nature of their present position and changes that occurred.[54]

The career crisis of losing one's job is another situation where the experience of the past and individual as well as social resources are of major importance. As we noted earlier, the socially structured supports of union or professional group membership cushion such shocks for the skilled worker and most of the middle class; for the poor, no such supports are available. Morley finds that the acceptance of the crisis *as a crisis* is of major importance to the individual, at many levels. The worker who denies the difficulty may often be in worse shape than the one who "mourns" the previous job, and sets out again.[55]

But one need not lose a job to experience the uncertainty of career transition. Hughes insists that subjective uncertainty may be socially structured into many forms of career experience within organizations of all types, as a consequence of the one-way observability often found in the work setting:

> Management and supervision try to broaden the man as well as judge his technical skills; at the same time these efforts are subject to misinterpretation by subordinates. In most careers a man who is going up is

> always up against a wall of darkness. He knows what people think about him at his own level but he is in doubt about what the people above him know and are saying about him.[56]

Ways of handling career uncertainty and anxiety are numberless; the characteristic approaches involve dependence on peers, seeking of information, blind faith, or retreat. The career in most cases continues, but it may not always live up to expectations. A frequent set of responses was described by Griff in his study of commercial artists who would like to have been "regular" artists. They may *deny* the difference in career ("commercial art is art"), or redefine their original aims ("I always *wanted* to be a commercial artist"), or admit disappointment, or engage — as is most often the case — in a series of redefinitions of self and career combined with a retrospective reinterpretation or denial of that which cannot be explained away.[57]

Commitment, as the existentialist philosopher Kierkegaard defines it, is a consequence of choosing with one's whole self to go in a direction which irrevocably defines that self, from that point on.[58] The conscious *act of choice,* of *deliberately* going past the point of no return, is a true existential decision. The sociological definitions of career commitment vary from this in taking what could be considered as a combined existential and objective point of view. For example, Becker suggests that commitment to a career be defined as that point in the history of a career where more goods and rewards would be lost by leaving the career — including the "incidental" side benefits — than the conceivable or ascertainable rewards of trying a different career. The process may be partially *unwitting* and unintended, the person waking up to find himself committed:

> Commitment to any consistent line of activity occurs when an individual, confronted with an opportunity to depart from it, discovers that in the course of past activity he has, willingly or not, accumulated valuables of a kind that would be lost to him if he makes a change.[59]

Geer adds a comparative perspective here by showing that some careers, such as medicine, offer more rewards and long-term opportunities and as such are attractive a shorter time after original occupational choice than other careers, such as high school teaching. The speed with which one may pile up the benefits is, in this perspective, the speed with which a person may find himself "committed."[60] On the other hand, more classically existential definitions of commitment are presented by authors such as Grusky and Kornhauser. Grusky, interviewing a sample of over 1600 managers, found that his hypothesis was supported: the greater the obstacles the person has to overcome to obtain the organization's rewards, the greater his commitment. Here the act of hurdle-jumping calls out the commitment.[61]

Vocational career commitment may be greater in some lines of work than in others. Take for example the priest's commitment to the Catholic church, or the radical's total commitment to his cause. Kornhauser compares the total life commitment of the career radical to the segmental, part-time political commitment of the liberal:

> The ideal radical (from the group's viewpoint) is one who has all his friends in the party, his wife and children in the party, his job in the party, and the only status that matters to him is in the party. All of his non-political relations mediate and support his political commitment by being centered in the political group.[62]

To sum up, the concept of career must be seen as a device for tracing the patterns of individuals through social structures at given points in social history, as an investigatory tool for understanding the dilemmas of human existence, and as a natural approach to the basically political as well as the more generally social aspects of commitment. Commitment can be to a career whose aim is to change the status quo, as well as to a career which supports it.

OCCUPATIONAL AND PROFESSIONAL GROUPS AS SOCIALIZERS

The process of socialization involves the acceptance of individuals into ongoing groups, as the individual simultaneously accepts the values, standards, and rules of these groups. Everett Hughes has considered several general issues which arise whenever we consider occupational or professional group membership, as compared with, for example, social class membership or informal group membership. First, there is the issue of occupational cultures specific to given occupations:

> In relation to its technique and the interests of those who use that technique, the occupational group tends to build up a set of collective representations, more or less peculiar to the occupation and more or less incomprehensible to the community. The interests, which the occupational group couches in a language more or less its own, are the basis of the code and policy of the occupational group. The code is the occupation's prescribed activity of the individuals within toward each other; the policy represents its relation to the community in which they operate.[63]

Hughes goes on to note that all occupational groups in a society must operate within most of the generally accepted rules of the society. However, there will be variations in the extent of an occupation's license — its ability to do its work unsupervised by others (surgeons and professors as compared to assembly line workers) — and variations in its community mandate — its power to determine its place and function in the community, its relation to the work of other occupations, and its mode of everyday operation.[64]

To learn the occupation's culture demands time, perseverance, and the possession of qualities which make the new recruit at least initially acceptable. General learning tasks are faced by the new recruits. In most occupations — and not only in the professions — there is an overall occupational image, a justification for existence which may approach an ideology. Once this rationale is accepted, the occupation's members find it exceedingly hard to discard and will sometimes maintain the ideology, and the group's identity, in situations where it is quite irrational to do so. Hughes shows how German statisticians in the Hitler era maintained their ideology and appearance of neutrality and objectivity as they calmly began to reclassify Jews out of the human race, or indeed out of existence, as far as their statistical tables went.[65] Along with explicit ideology go the informal mores of the group on issues such as race and sex — the precise extent to which minority racial or sexual group members will be considered acceptable regardless of external or "legal" rules. Learning the mechanisms for group self-protection is another critical aspect of occupational socialization — knowing when to act as an occupational unit, when as individuals. One issue which arises here is that of mistakes at work. The degree to which the group's members are protected from the consequences which might otherwise follow their mistakes is one way of signifying the degree of group solidarity within an occupation. As Hughes suggests,

> there are psychological, physical, social, and economic risks in learning and doing one's work. And since the theoretical possibility of making an error someday is increased by the very frequency of the operations by which one makes one's living, it becomes natural to build up some rationale to carry one through. It is also to be expected that those who are subject to the same work risks will build up collective defenses against the lay world.[66]

Much of Hughes' writing has been on the human, social consequences of the relations between individuals and their personal careers on the one hand, and institutional "offices" and the collective histories and vicissitudes of the occupational groups within which the offices are located, on the other. In a basic sense, the aims of the central chapters of this book will be to explore these general issues, taking for each chapter a given occupational family or professional group, and exploring the *two-way* relations between individuals and occupational groups and between occupations and the wider society. To use multiple perspectives on this problem — the historical, biographical, systematic, and interest-based — is generally in Hughes' tradition, especially insofar as it respects the actual complexity of process in the social world.

Although we will be giving fuller consideration in the rest of the book to occupational socialization in different types of occupations and professions, it is appropriate here to anticipate these fuller analyses by considering differences in the experience of occupational and professional socialization by *type* of occupation. Taking Hughes' classification of types — professions, near-professions, enterprises, missions, arts, crafts, and jobs — one can see different aspects of the experience assuming primacy during the process of training and during the overall career on the job.[67]

The professions have been well-studied at least in part because they show the different authority-groups' impacts on the recruit. Whether one uses the reference-group approach of Merton and Kendall, or the participant-observation approach of Becker, Geer, and Hughes, one sees the distinct series of stages through which the students pass.[68] Becker, Geer, and Hughes note that even the inner value transformations of the students — from initial idealism to cynicism to optimistic realism — can be related to stages in the career. Even the "unofficial" ways of beating the system (more available to the upper-middle-class students in medical fraternities) are aspects of the overall socialization experience.[69] Professional career contingencies, as Hall has shown for medicine, are often well understood by the recruits, with each attempting to plan his career to capitalize on the greatest opportunities.[70] The medical professional experience has been studied so thoroughly that there is even a literature, and quantitative data, on secondary choices within medicine — the work of Beck, Coker, and Phillips — and on the strategy for making these choices — the recent monograph by S. Miller.[71] The adult years of practice in all the major professions have been much less well studied. Freidson and Rhea's discovery of the essential powerlessness of a group of professional equals in the work setting to control deviant colleagues is useful for the contrast which it provides with the rather hierarchical type of relations often found in the professional training years.[72]

Much less can be brought together for the other occupational types in Hughes' classification, as the research is less complete at this point. But the "political" perspective of this book — deeply concerned as it is with interest-based occupational and professional struggles — approaches these groups in a way that will make it possible to fill in some of the details. In the non-central professional occupations, some existential issues are already rather clear. In the "near-professions," which are continually engaged in professionalizing, socialization involves the recruit in an ongoing and changing group. Here entry into any *formal* training process makes one a member of a vanguard; the older occupational group members become an embarrassment and are relegated to marginal statuses under a grandfather clause. In the business world (Hughes speaks primarily of the entrepreneur and small businessman here), the colleagueship experience is one of the uses of social camaraderie — the skills to be developed are found to be those of developing and maintaining "contacts." In the arts, Becker found for jazz musicians what is true for all the creative arts: the experience of becoming and being an occupational member demands continual struggle for mandate and breathing room against the seemingly barbarian, uneducated, unappreciative public.[73] To become the holder of a "mission" involves its own pattern of commitment. The "conversion experience," although certainly not missing in other types of occupations, is critical in the existential career of the missionary or the political radical. The initial commitment to this type of career and its continued maintenance is qualitatively different as occupational experience from that of most other types of occupation.

Finally, the experience of occupational group membership is highlighted in the contrast between occupation-based craft experience and the essentially non-occupational or bureaucratic experience of the assembly-line factory worker. As we indicated in the discussion on the uses of the historical perspective on occupations and professions, the crafts organized politically decades before the common factory workers in the United States, and the crafts — as occupational guilds — have a corporate history going back at least to the Middle Ages. In a new series of studies on occupational socialization and career experience in craft occupations, prepared in collaboration with Becker and Geer, a series of "craft" occupations — such as beauty parlor operator, butcher, high steel iron worker — is being studied along with some business occupations such as door-to-door sales.[74] The preliminary results of these studies, which will be discussed in selected portions of this book, indicate the presence of informal groups with behavior of the type noted by Hughes. The experience of becoming an occupational or professional group member inevitably involves one in the occupational culture of the group.

THE WORK SETTING AS A SOCIALIZER

Occupations and professions do not exist in a vacuum; the work is always carried out in some kind of setting. The basic issue this creates for analysis is that of ascertaining what part of the work experience is due to *occupational* membership and what part is a consequence of working in a particular *setting*, regardless of specific occupational membership. We can inspect the effect of the setting on the work experience in several ways: as an overt or covert struggle between occupation and setting for dominance over lives, as a problem in learning the informal culture of work settings, and as an issue in the sociology of bureaucracy.

The issue of occupational versus organizational loyalty was considered at length by Alvin Gouldner in his discussion of the "cosmopolitan" and the "local" orientations in academia. The "cosmopolitan" professor has an occupational loyalty and career commitment, seeing his career as one of geographic mobility to the "best" departments in his field, with a colleague group of national scope that he wishes to impress. By contrast, the "local" is committed to a place — Centerville — and to Centerville College, and possibly would prefer a promotion into the deanship to moving away for a raise, if he could maintain his home and his settled circle of friends and neighbors by so doing.[75]

The conflict between occupation and setting can become a matter not only of personal choice or strategy but of a struggle for primacy between occupational group and work organization. All outcomes are possible here. For example, as Whyte has shown, the setting and the organization can subjugate the occupation, as industry appears to have done with most non-academic scientists.[76] Conversely, the occupation can rule the setting, as for example the *elite* scientists rule the National Science Foundation or the chief physicians rule the hospital in the name of their profession, or, as Glaser shows, a mutual partnership can arise.[77] The continuing struggle between unions and employees is concerned in part with wages, but is also deeply involved in the issue of whether it will be the occupational group and the union that determine the day-to-day details of work experience, or the management of the industry. If the work provides little personal reward, the coffee break and freedom from surveillance can become extremely important to the worker.

In addition to the potential conflict between the organization's aims and those of occupations working within it, there is the factor of the social class membership of the workers *outside* the setting as this affects their relationships on the setting. Becker and Geer suggest that the "latent culture" of an organization can be based on such class-based or other criteria external to the official aims of the organization.[78] For example, Yankee upper-class decorum and manners may be the latent culture of a Boston bank, working class "boisterousness" and "machismo" the style of high steel workers. Acceptance into the occupational group and its manner of operation within the organization may be determined more by the expectations of the informal culture than by the requirements of *either* the occupation or the organization. Consequently, members of a "one-class" occupation, concerned about members of their class outside the occupation and the setting, may act differently on a setting than members of an occupation recruited from all social class groups, who will thus have their strongest commitment to the occupation itself and will defend it against all opposition:

> One might expect the occupational culture of bankers to reflect upper-middle- or upper-class culture and that of steel workers to reflect lower- or lower-middle-class culture, while that of jazz musicians, who are recruited from all class levels, would not reflect the culture of any particular stratum. . . . Both bankers and musicians, let us say, may find their

clients or customers difficult. The musician's solution to this problem — open hostility — might not be available to bankers because of the restrictions on such behavior in their social class culture.[79]

Settings have their own informal rules which do not exactly correspond with the occupational ideologies of the settings' members, in part because of the need for working out ad hoc compromises between *different* occupational groups in a setting, in part as a way of coping with a lack of any overt structure. Geer and her colleagues speak of this process of initial learning on settings as "learning the ropes" — ropes which may include the way to choose between competing authorities on the setting, the unofficial but actual way that work gets done, and the precise degree to which one must compromise one's occupational ideals to achieve at least minimum accomplishment on a given setting:

> Our data indicate that teachers, books, customers, patients, bosses, subordinates, auxiliary personnel, and machines — in fact, any frequent contact — may become sources of situational learning. Moreover, we may infer that trainees are capable of considerable ingenuity in finding teachers. If their ordinary teacher is not available, they turn to peers; if peers are unavailable, they make use of client subordinates; supplied with groups of superiors and subordinates, they tactfully exploit them all.[80]

Most work in modern American society takes place in some form of bureaucratic organization. Bureaucracies, to some degree independent of given occupations, require from most workers an adaptation of personality and a kind and degree of expected (and measured) performance, including at least some impossible feats. Work on non-bureaucratic settings can be seen as qualitatively different. Max Weber constructed the ideal type of bureaucracy, and the ideal civil servant, as ethically neutral and in an organization which was constructed to maximize efficiency.[81] Merton, as Weber earlier, feared that the consequence of working in bureaucratic settings would be the atrophy of moral sense, since the taking of responsibility is never a matter of individual choice, but rather an example of "obeying orders." [82] The stereotype of the bureaucratic atrocity — achieved in reality occasionally by an Eichmann or an obedient platoon of troops in wartime — is the consequence, at least in part, of such forms of structuring of work. Determining the extent to which this actually occurs is an important subject for future research.

However, the adaptations that people do make to bureaucratic settings usually involve more human compromises than the above description implies. Blau suggests that an informal "colleague consultation" setup is often constructed among occupational equals: the less competent pays the price of deference to his colleagues when he asks for help; the informal expert provides the help and gets the warm glow of self-satisfaction, but often at the cost of not getting his own work done.[83] Another way of coping with the organization's requirements is the development of informal "ethical codes" which protect the group from subjugation. The workers observed by Roethlisberger and Dixon in the bank wiring room of the Western Electric factory evolved the following four-point code:

1. You should not turn out too much work. If you do, you are a "rate-buster."
2. You should not turn out too little work. If you do, you are a "chiseler."
3. You should not tell a supervisor anything that will react to the detriment of an associate. If you do, you are a "squealer."
4. You should not attempt to maintain social distance or act officious. If you are an inspector, for example, you should not act like one.[84]

That the experience of work in bureaucratic settings is nearly universal becomes apparent when one realizes that the above rules can (and usually do) arise on settings where one observes the work of nurses, assistant professors, turret lathe operators, clerks, junior law partners, or secretaries. Their experience can be contrasted with the increasing rarity of the true apprenticeship situation as a way of learning the ropes on the work setting.

The bureaucratic work setting demands at least *some* commitment, in order to maintain its structure and function over time. This creates painful situations for those who do not have alternatives to the particular bureaucracy in which they work, or to those who wish upward mobility within it. W. F. Whyte presents the anxiety of the executive who wonders whether the organization is playing "checkers" with him: Is the next move which he is being asked to make a step up for him, or just a convenience for the organization? If he doesn't want to go further up the ladder, he can remain in the present town. On the other hand, perhaps the next move will not be a major step up.[85]

What if all the executives in the corporate world refused to move on call? (In fact, because of the high cost of housing, this is beginning to happen.) The organization, faced with group unity and failing commitment to its ends, would be nearly helpless. In fact, as Bogdanoff and Glass show, it is precisely those people who do not have a commitment to an organization who are in the most independent position with respect to it. They are, in most cases, those at the bottom rather than those near the top; they are the ones not interested in more than a "job," those who have given up ideas about upward mobility through the ranks. These two authors found that social service workers in a welfare agency often rejected the idea of upward mobility, deliberately acted as free human beings and bargained (illegally in the narrow sense) with their clients. The supply-and-demand labor situation, as well as the common low pay in such bureaucracies, put them in an excellent position.

They were in effect saying, "If they don't like our way, we'll just quit—and we know they can't afford that." [86]

Bureaucracy and the work setting in industry have been extensively studied in those fields known as "sociology of organizations" and "industrial sociology," as well as those interested in the sociology of occupations; here we have simply introduced major issues concerning the role of the work setting as a socializer which will be considered at greater length in the coming chapters devoted to particular kinds of occupations and professions. To sum up, the power struggles between occupational groups and organizational settings over the loyalties and commitments of the workers, the adaptations and conflicts which result, and the formal and informal cultures which are created to cope with these issues color the experience of the individual in the setting in a way that is only in part due to his membership in a specific occupational group. The setting is a factor of its own.

ALIENATION: THE POLITICS OF WORK EXPERIENCE

In his *Philosophical Manuscripts of 1844*, Karl Marx analyzed the condition of the modern industrial worker as something unique in the world. He was detached from the product of his work, for he sold his labor-time to produce an article of no intrinsic meaning to him, while working for those who owned the means of production, the capitalist factory owners. Thus he was *alienated*—estranged—from the product of his labor. He was also, existentially, alienated from himself, in that it was necessary to tune out his natural desires to identify with his work and to have a sense of accomplishment, not weariness, at the end of the day.[87] The concept of alienation, dual in meaning to begin with, became less clear with continued use by polemicists and political revolutionaries. The young Marx felt that the alienation of workers would eventually have political consequences. They would begin to commiserate with each other and, sensing the potential power of a united proletariat, would combine, overthrow the capitalists, seize the means of production in the name of the people, and end the alienation of the factory worker for all time.

In both the United States and Soviet Russia, however, the research findings indicate that the basic issues of the worker do not center so much on the self-alienation of factory work itself as on the monetary rewards for this work and the social conditions in which it takes place. Oversimplifying somewhat, it is still reasonably accurate to state that factory workers do *not* feel fulfilled in the performance of their work, but do for the most part enjoy the social relationships which grow up on the work setting. As Morse and Weiss indicate, the positive aspect of work is this social experience.[88] Roethlisberger's and Dixon's observations of the industrial plant, as well as Homan's observations of the girls in the "cash posting" room of a bill-collecting agency, confirm the questionnaire studies of Morse and Weiss.[89] The studies of the meaning of retirement from factory work indicate that the work is preferred to retirement, not because of the limited work operations, but rather because of the social participation on the setting and the adult, non-pensioner status which work confers. These factors seem to outweigh, for most, the repetitive aspects of the work.

In Marx's sense, then, are factory workers alienated? Yes, in the economic sense of not profiting from their work directly; they do not profit directly in socialist countries either, as they work for (and can be exploited by) the state instead of a private employer. But in the direct personal sense, social groups at work in industry allow a definitely non-alienating experience, unless one is a member of a minority radical group in a setting where the "knitting of the races," to use Hughes' phrase, just hasn't happened.[90] The issue of self-alienation of work is complex. To learn to *tune out* on what one calls work, to perform essentially as an automaton for week after week, year after year, living only at coffee break, lunch, and off hours, must have some human consequences. Friedenberg has some hypotheses as to what these human consequences might be:

> a plurality of those who share the urban Western world spend one-third of their lives doing noisy, repetitive, uncomfortable work at a rate they do not choose and toward ends that they cannot usually envision. In the rest of their lives they insist equally on discipline and familiarity. . . . For such people the test of an experience or a proposition is likely to be its conventionality. Subjectivity would be suicidal; a high level of sensitivity to external reality would be equally so. These people cannot afford to open their senses or their hearts to new perceptions or new sensations. If they ever become simultaneously sensitive to reality and aware of its possibilities, they are done for. Their routines prevent their being overwhelmed with rage, envy, and despair. . . .[91]

As Chinoy has cautioned, not all work in "industry" is the mass-production, assembly-line work which concerns Friedenberg or this author when discussing alienation.[92] But the issue which Friedenberg raises here is an important one. More than a century has passed since Marx wrote, and still the nature of *any* possible political consequences resulting from this work experience is a conjecture. The facile attempts to research this problem to date have only scratched the surface.

Each of the biographical issues related to work which has been previously considered in this chapter can be reviewed in the light of the alienation concept. In early childhood, early success at work in the nursery can be the start of a strong self-identification with accomplishment, or early failure can start the development of a world view that considers work and accomplishment as alien to the self. In the school setting, the social class background of some children and the middle-class bias of the settings create a process that is profoundly alienating to many sensitive children. To add to this, the state laws on school attendance force a segment of the population to remain in the setting against their will, under the penalty of imprisonment for truancy if they refuse. To add to this, both youth in the "non-college" tracks and those who have dropped out at legal age gain at least an inkling of the kind of work they will be asked to do, and this seems to many of them to be a fate far worse than the present alternative of welfare.[93]

Careers take place in given societies, and at some points in history, the norm may be the alienated person in the alienated career. When we compare Kierkegaard's concept of commitment with Becker's, we notice that the sociological description of career commitment, with the exception perhaps of "missions" and some professions, is of a rather alienated form of "commitment." For the sociologist Becker, a person is committed by what has happened to him, not by what he has chosen. In all fairness to Becker, the research on career experience indicates that most people do take a passive, existentially uninvolved attitude toward their own careers, indeed toward their entire lives, except at moments of crisis. The research to date on the usual attitudes toward career experience seem to provide some support for a contention by Erich Fromm. In *Escape from Freedom,* he suggests that the majority wish life to be planned for them and do not wish to choose it. They prefer an externally ordered security to the anxiety which true freedom of choice in an open society can give a person; they are unwilling to risk.[94]

In occupational or professional groups, the emphasis is on including the recruit to give him a sense of membership, but the research also indicates that human prejudices result in the relegation of a significant segment of each occupational group to the sidelines, producing a dilemma for them — a choice between alienated (self-denying) participation or withdrawal and the status of a total outsider. On the work setting, the deliberate attempts of the "human relations" trainers to cool out dissent and to smooth over differences with "group sensitivity training" may in some cases produce yet another form of alienation — a refusal to face the hard facts of authority, responsibility, and power distribution which characterize the majority of work settings. To sum up, the alienation of the self from desires to achieve fulfillment through work is a consequence of early experience, the nature of the schooling process, the vicissitudes of careers, and the opportunities of the social structure. The attitudes of work colleagues and the power structure of work settings also contribute to these effects. The biographical approach to occupations and professions is a natural one for the consideration of issues such as alienation. Here we have only presented the major problems. Marx was correct, in this writer's opinion, in describing the prevalence of alienation in the socio-psychological, as well as the economic sense, but the evidence does not at present indicate that alienation alone makes for susceptibility to radical political action. One might liken it instead to the effects of anesthesia.

THE BIOGRAPHICAL APPROACH: GENERAL QUESTIONS

We have now introduced the second major analytical approach to be used in the book. Perhaps the best way of summarizing our discussion is to make a partial list of the questions which the biographical approach will lead us to ask regularly of each occupational group. First, the question of becoming a worker: How was the work experienced, and what was the early meaning of achievement? Next, the educational experience: What is typical for the occupation or profession, and what contingencies affect the relationship between aspiration and choice? Then the basic issues of career: What are the main contingencies of career development, the typical and atypical career pathways and patterns in the occupation or profession? How is career experience subjectively perceived, and what constitutes commitment to this line of work? What are the precise forms of occupational socialization, and to what ends are they directed? What forms and techniques are used to maintain occupational group solidarity? And how do the work settings of the occupation or profession interfere with or support the needs of the occupational group? How do other allegiances of occupation members affect their performance and aims on the work setting? The biographical approach gives us an important advantage in understanding the human meaning of work, as the careers of individuals interact with the careers of occupational and professional groups at a given point in history. Without a systematic consideration of the experience and viewpoints of individuals in context, the sociology of occupations and professions would be an empty exercise, not a search for deeper understandings.

CHAPTER THREE

THE DIVISION OF LABOR: STRUCTURE AND FUNCTION

In the functional or systems approach, our third major approach to the study of occupations, the division of labor in society is viewed as a structure, a patterned arrangement of relationships persisting over time. The functions of the various occupational groups within the overall system are analyzed. From this point of view, one cannot understand how a particular occupational group operates without understanding its role in the social system of the overall society, in that society's distribution of power, prestige, and monetary reward. We will begin with the consideration of the general principles relevant to the division of labor as a social system. After a brief comparative inspection of these issues, we will consider in detail five issues that are basic to a systems approach to occupations and professions: the nature of the labor market, occupational prestige, occupational mobility, the special role of professions, and the bureaucratization of the work setting. In each case, these issues are analyzed with respect to their relevance to the overall division of labor.

GENERAL PRINCIPLES

When we approach any society and ask why work has been divided as it has, and why the society has agreed to perpetuate the way the work groups relate to one another, we must ask a series of questions. Each of them introduces a general principle into the discussion.

What is the overall unifying principle in a society's division of labor? This problem greatly interested Émile Durkheim, and in his classic work, *The Division of Labor in Society*, he introduced two general principles for organizing the work of a society.[1] The first plan he called "solidarité mechanique," or mechanical solidarity, which was characteristic of the small primitive tribe, in particular the hunting and gathering groups. The rule of custom was so strong, and the lack of specialization so basic, that everyone "mechanically" did the same work, and all automatically obeyed the strong customs and the overpowering moral order of the society.[2] Durkheim theorized that as societies became more complex — and came closer in form to the modern industrialized society — specialization arose and the *division* of labor took place, with each occupational group "doing its thing" for all the others in the society. Here, instead of the society being held together by custom, the dependence of the groups upon one another became the key to understanding the organization of the society. The analogy — a favorite for those using the systems approach — was the human body. Durkheim labeled this form of solidarity "organic," in the sense that the heart needs the kidneys in the human body, and vice versa. So, Durkheim suggested, does the carpenter need the farmer, and the mill owner the factory worker.[3]

But this idea presented a problem to Durkheim. He indicated that the interdependence between the groups in an industrial society should lead to a stronger and more stable social order. Yet, even in Durkheim's time, this was not so. The points of interdependence between groups can become points of conflict if the exchanges between the groups are not equal. As Orwell said in *Animal Farm*, "All the animals are equal, but some are more equal than others."[4] It is true that the mine owner needs the mine workers and they need him, but their relationship is a source of conflict, because of the workers' lack of ownership of the mine and the owners' desire to maximize his profit at their expense. Durkheim believed that specialization would lead to harmony, but it has led instead to conflict between occupational groups, class struggles between owners and workers, and even reactions against overspecialization such as the atomized work on assembly lines.[5] Georges Friedmann contrasts the solidarity of the organization (within the plant, the management and the workers usually cooperate to get the work done) with the solidarity of class or occupational groups, such as unions and professional associations, a solidarity which extends across organizations and is independent of specific tasks being done in the industrial plant. He observes that Durkheim avoided confronting the very important issue of group political action used to change the allocation of wealth or the pattern of the division of labor itself. He ignored the radical potential of an exploited working class.[6]

Why then is Durkheim still important? It is undoubtedly because he did stress the division of labor as a system and, despite the fact that conflicts do arise in the system, the interdependence he singled out exists as well. One important modern example is the dual dependence of management and unions in industrial disputes on reaching a settlement of the conflict. If the union gets "too much," the factory can go out of business as unprofitable; if it gets too little, the union sees no reason to settle. On the other hand, the workers need to eat and usually the number of jobs available is not unlimited. If jobs are open, many local industrialists combine and refuse to hire workers who are striking another company. Thus, short of a successful revolution by a working class which seizes the factory system (and often not even then), the management group and the workers *are* interdependent, and the division of labor as an "organic" model is a basic concept with some value. The conflict-of-interest approach, which Marx stressed and Durkheim avoided, will be the fourth major approach of the overall analysis, and will be introduced in the next chapter.

A second major question is the following: How does the division of labor relate to other aspects of the society's organization and operation? For example, Parsons indicates the ways in which the organization of family social life is related to the organization of work.[7] In modern times, the size of families has often decreased to the nuclear family of father, mother, and child, because the need for geographical mobility has affected blue-collar and white-collar workers' ability to carry their parents with them as they move.[8] Since, as Parsons states, the job is a contract, an economic arrangement between a household and a work organization, any changes in either partner affect the other partner and the relationship. In a sense, viewing the labor force in this way fuses the study of labor market economics and family sociology.[9] Without becoming Marxists, Parsons and Smelser illustrate the complex ways in which the economic ties between groups have a direct political meaning. These authors view the "economy" and the "polity" as subsystems related through the specific occupations which link the individual to the social order. The study of occupational social relations is thus not just a part of the sociology of group behavior. It cannot avoid being a kind of economic sociology and political sociology as well.[10]

Furthermore, following Merton, the *overt* role of an occupational group in the system may differ from its *latent*, long-term, and unintended role.[11] A system operates on many levels. For example, the overt functional role of the clergy in a society is, among other things, to preach the accepted moral behavior for the society. Yet, if a group of parishioners should take them seriously — as some parishioners have been recently taking the radical clergy — they and the clergy can become a source of change if the society does not usually follow the moral prescriptions that are its official ideology. Only a systems approach gets directly to issues involving these types of complex interrelations; what modern systems theorists inherit from Durkheim is the desire to ascertain what principles do govern the complexities of the system.

A third major question on the division of labor is more concrete: What is the specific pattern of the division of labor in a given society at a given time? Perhaps the most complete inspection of this problem, using segments of the economy instead of occupational groups, has been made by Wassily Leontief and his students. In an approach known as "input-output economics," Leontief divides the work of the society into a series of forty to fifty sectors, such as "heavy industry," "grain agriculture," "entertainment," "government service," and calculates in a matrix how much every sector exchanges in goods and services with every other sector of the society.[12] This is an attempt to visually plot the overall division of production, consumption, and exchange. It comes rather close to a concrete model of Durkheim's idea, for each sector can be shown to be dependent on every other sector, and any change at one point reverberates throughout the system. If we used *occupational groups* instead of types of industry we would have a close approximation of Durkheim's model.[13]

The specific pattern of exchange could be — but has not yet been — calculated for occupational groups and their interdependencies. But students of Leontief, and also sociologists who have studied community power structure, can show that the way in which a community does or does not specialize has major consequences for its overall social system.[14] For example, in the one-industry cotton mill towns of the South, or in one-industry cities such as Detroit (auto) or Gary, Indiana (steel), the dominance of one set of occupational groups and the power relations between the groups in these economic sectors will set the tone for, and control the political dynamics of, the entire community. In a one-industry cotton town, therefore, studying the cotton workers' strike is not just studying occupational conflict, it means studying the crisis and the potential disintegration of the entire town. Jacobs suggests, in *The Economy of Cities,* that greater diversity results in greater long-term stability for a city, or for a region, than one-occupation or one-industry specialization; the latter is susceptible to continual cycles of boom and stagnation.[15]

A fourth question is critical to an understanding of the dynamics of occupations and professions in any system: Is the occupational group meaningful to its members? We must contrast here a government's or a sociologist's facility for categorizing groups with the groups' perceptions of real colleagueship among the members. The primary example of this problem is shown by the *Dictionary of Occupational Titles,* published by the United States Department of Labor. This work is an attempt to categorize all the job *titles* in the work field presenting more than 20,000 job descriptions.[16] To state the basic issue here concretely, does a "turret lathe operator" in a factory think of himself as being in a different occupational group from a "boring mill operator," or do the two in fact think of themselves primarily as "skilled factory workers" and members of the local labor union? The divisions analyzed in this book will be categories that have both subjective reality to the participants and objective meaning to the analyst as a group with a discoverable set of functions in common.

A fifth issue to be considered: What occupational and professional groups are more powerful in the division of labor, and why? What is the meaning of "power" as an attribute of the division of labor? The steering wheel of a car, in one sense, is more "powerful" functionally than the right fender, the quarterback more powerful than the lineman on the football team. Two issues are often confused when the topic of power is considered with respect to the division of labor in an ongoing society. The first is the idea of functional importance to the system: which roles are key and which subordinate to the overall functioning of the system? Leontief has demonstrated that sectors of the economy can be dominant, or primary, in the sense that changes in them have greater and more extensive consequences than changes in other sectors.[17] The second idea concerning power and the division of labor comes from Marx: the ownership of the means of production is what gives power in a system in which labor is divided between owners and workers.[18] The owner can set the pay rates, hire and fire, and determine who will do what task, i.e., he can plot the division of labor to suit his own ends. As we have demonstrated in our discussion of the historical approach, exploitation of workers by owners has occurred in many eras. However, as Berlson noted, today there is in most major corporations a split between ownership and management. Owners constitute a propertied class of stockholders; managers, an occupational group that runs industry for the owners. Conflicts are possible, though not frequent, between the conservative stockholders and a progressive, professionalized management of a corporation. As Marx himself admitted, public stock shareholding in corporations, governmental anti-monopoly law, and welfare state measures such as social security, welfare, and public education reduce the directness of the conflict between owners and workers.[19] Marx, however, stated that technological development would eventually cause major problems in this area. We will return to the issues of ownership and conflicts of interest in the next chapter. But for now, we must note that the complexity of modern social systems — socialist as well as capitalist — make the *functional* power issue more directly relevant to an understanding of day-to-day operation than an oversimplified class-conflict perspective. The issue becomes, "What occupational group can paralyze the system *immediately* by refusing to work?" Both centrality and replaceability are important here: if a society's garbage collectors, firemen, and physicians disappeared permanently, chaos would immediately result, but others could be recruited to collect refuse almost immediately. It would take some time to train firemen, and in that week or two, several homes and buildings would burn. But untold thousands would die until physicians could be educated to replace those who had disappeared.

The sixth major question relates closely to the fifth: Given a difference in the degree of functional importance of occupational groups to the social system, are the rewards for the groups (in terms of both money and prestige) in line with their differences in functional importance? Davis and Moore made a well-known statement on this topic:

> One can specify the two factors that determine the relative rank of different positions. Those positions convey the best rewards and have the highest rank which (a) have the greatest importance for the society and (b) require the greatest training or talent. The first factor . . . is a matter of *relative significance*, the second concerns means and is a matter of *relative scarcity*.[20]

The research reviewed in this chapter will demonstrate that, indeed, functional importance and the law of supply and demand do result in an allocation of prestige and material reward that is similar for all industrialized societies. But we do not need to conclude from this, as Davis and Moore do, that social inequality is inevitable (rewards need not *necessarily* parallel functional importance or supply and demand), nor even that within the present system all occupational groups are rewarded along strictly functional or supply and demand lines. Other factors, such as whether one is an owner who profits or simply a salaried worker, or the degree to which an occupational group is politically organized and able to fight in its own interest, are also of great relevance. But the systems point of view does highlight the fact that the *place* which the occupation holds in the overall division of labor will be a factor in the rewards which individuals receive as members of the occupational group.

A COMPARATIVE PERSPECTIVE

A question which arises naturally when considering the division of labor in a modern, industrialized society, is one of international comparison. To what extent do the needs of an industrial and bureaucratic social order impose the same form upon societies that otherwise have major cultural differences? Does the division of labor have the same meaning politically and socially in the Soviet Union as in the United States, or in Japan as in France?

Raymond Aron has suggested that industrial societies share three kinds of complexity: that related to specialization necessary for production, that related to hierarchies of power, prestige and wealth, and that related to internal conflict between the subgroups of the society acting in their own self-interest.[21] Within bounds, all the industrialized societies have a power and prestige hierarchy that is understandable in terms of the functional importance of key groups in this type of society. The managers or owners of the productive apparatus and the professional and technical experts are high on the reward and prestige ladder; the worker and the unskilled are far lower. Inkeles and Rossi conclude for the Soviet Union:

> It seems relevant to state, therefore, that Lenin seriously underestimated the degree to which strong tendencies toward social differentiation inhere in the organization of modern industry and mechanized agriculture. Indeed, Lenin assumed that the development of this complex organization of production, with its attendant rationalization and routinization of function, provided the necessary basis for social equalization. Actually, Soviet experience indicates that the very fact of modern large-scale production, involving extreme division of labor, precise differentiation of function, emphasis on technical competence, and elaborate hierarchies of authority and responsibility, provides a natural basis for the development of distinct social groups.[22]

The more interesting question appears to be the reverse one: In different industrialized countries, what are the *differences* between them in division of labor, and in power, prestige, and reward? To consider this question even briefly, we must inspect, comparatively, the political regime as related to division of labor, the degree of modernization and its occupational consequences, and the role of special occupational and professional groups.[23]

If the United States and the Soviet Union have similar prestige hierarchies and similar patterns of occupational mobility, they still have marked differences in the political sphere. Certainly the United States is not a laissez-faire economy, and partial monopolies as well as government regulation are facts. But the individual and group choices of action with respect to the division of labor cannot be centrally decided upon in the United States. The evolution of the division of labor, and the consequent rise and fall of the status of and need for a given occupational group, is *reacted to*, rather than planned, by government. Ironically, the very efficiency which the Soviet Union can sometimes claim in directing and training manpower is possible only because they have a near-totalitarian control over career opportunities and changes in opportunities or life plans available to the people.[24] If powerful corporations and other interest groups in America can manipulate some economic factors, they still do not have this other power — the power to control the pattern of the division of labor itself. Friedrich Hayek, the conservative economist, stated that in the capacity to dictate changes or stabilities in the division of labor, in control over production and opportunity processes, lies the kind of power which is inherently, if not overtly, totalitarian.[25]

The degree of modernization has direct consequences for the division of labor. Most students of social change agree that industrialization is destructive of the old moral order and its accompanying division of labor. In modernizing societies, the typically characteristic changes are the urbanization of the labor force and the breakdown of caste- or estate-based ways of organizing the division of labor. In India, the *jajmani* system involved hereditary occupational, caste-based relationships. In a given village, Mr. X, a Brahman priest, prayed for Mr. Y, a barber, who cut his hair in return for the prayer. Eventually Mr. X's son would become a priest, and pray for Mr. Y's son, who would cut *his* hair. The onset of industrialization destroyed this intricate and personalized division of labor in the same way it destroyed the relations between the remaining rural nobility and the peasantry in France, Germany, and England.[26] In the American South, the onset of the modern industrial firms of the New South finally broke the caste hold on job opportunity which the whites possessed. And in South Africa, the caste situation may be perpetuated only with grave threat to social order and human dignity as the pressures for modernization conflict with the policy of apartheid. Note here that political power and repressive force can preserve a caste system along with a modern industrial order, but the complex needs of such systems for flexibility and skilled labor work against this as the easiest solution.

The comparative approach highlights the fact that in different nations different occupational groups may hold the key positions in terms of power and influence. For the highly industrialized West and Eastern Europe, Aron is probably correct in singling out the critical role of two kinds of intelligentsia — the technical (the scientific and technical planning elite) and the humanistic (the communication and media experts, ideologists, and propagandists). However, in much of the world, as Janowitz points out, the military cadre of the society — the officer corps — plays a dual role as primary channel for upward mobility for the poor and as scientific and planning vanguard for the nation.[27] Not all military leaders are conservative — the Attaturks who force modernization upon their country militarily contribute significantly to industrialization, either as solo actors or in combination with Western capitalist, colonialist groups.[28] The comparative approach highlights the different functions that the same occupational group may play or the same function as played by different occupational groups in the social systems of different nations. We will use the comparative approach in the five issues discussed in this chapter, issues which are critical in understanding the division of labor as a functioning system: the nature of the labor market, occupational prestige, occupational mobility, the special role of professions, and the bureaucratization of work.

LABOR SUPPLY VERSUS LABOR DEMAND

The division of labor in any society is not simply an abstraction; the work of individuals throughout their lives is involved. From where do the workers come to "fill the slots" in a society's division of labor, and how do changes in the overall pattern of work affect the life chances and opportunities of the individuals in the society? The contrast between who is available for work and what work is available for whom can be considered in four ways: the way changes in the pattern affect the need for workers; the relation of reward to a given supply and demand situation; the role of individual choice in modifying such situations; and the consequences of a given supply and demand situation for different workers — i.e., the female or the black contrasted with the white male.

Blau and Duncan, in their extensive study of the American labor force, found that the process of increasing technological development and urbanization in our society has had a direct effect on the flow of workers into jobs. For example, the growth in numbers of individuals who in their own lifetimes changed into white-collar, technical, managerial, or professional jobs was matched by a decrease in the number who went into farming. When the observations spanned a generation, similar changes were apparent. The farmer's son went into blue-collar work and the blue-collar worker's son into white-collar work; farmers' sons did not go into farming nearly as frequently as their fathers.[29]

With the increase in workers shifting in midcareer or going into jobs unlike those of their fathers, it becomes increasingly important to ask *how* they go into these new jobs. The research to date indicates that different types of jobs are entered in different ways. Malm reports that most manual laborers enter jobs through unions, white-collar and clerical workers enter through public and private employment agencies, salespeople apply directly or are promoted to their new career from within the organization. Most management positions are achieved by promotion from within.[30] Phelps notes the importance of the contractual arrangements involved in these different pathways: blue-collar workers negotiate with the employer through the union, white-collar workers and management on their own. The large employer hires and fires in different patterns from the small and with different effects on the pool of jobs available; the public service occupations have a far longer duration of steady employment than the non-public service sector.[31] Changes in the overall society will thus have different effects on workers who exist in different relationships to their present employers: the civil servant has more tenure, the smaller employer may irrationally (from an economic viewpoint) hang onto workers that a large firm will fire because the small employer knows the individuals personally.

The rewards which come to those in different positions in the division of labor are universal in their patterning in Western society. Regardless of the regime, the managerial and professional groups are better paid than the white-collar and manual laborers. However, within a group there are wide ranges in income, with some overlapping. In the United States, for example, the blue-collar workers who are lower on the prestige scale in American society than their white-collar counterparts may earn more than many of these — the material reward system of a society is not always exactly identical with its prestige rankings.

A factor of interest in the comparison of rewards is the policy which a nation has concerning the relation of these rewards to the division of labor, and the degree to which the nation can *enforce* the policy. For example, the Soviet Union has had periods in which it allowed a wide range of reward to match the spectrum from unskilled to professional and top managerial; most recently they have consciously attempted to upgrade the salaries of the less skilled, as they have intensified their training.[32] The main point here is that in a totally managed economy a wage policy can be translated directly by the government into a change in wages themselves. It is important to note that the citizens of Eastern European regimes expect that difference in wages will and ought to exist, as do most Americans.[33] In neither type of regime does the issue appear to be the general pattern of reward from high to low, but rather the extent of the spread between the wages of the unskilled and the highly skilled.

Since the time of Adam Smith, the factor of individual choice has played a major role in upsetting economists' equations on wage rates. In theory, there should be a relationship between the degree of reward for a job and the degree to which workers are plentiful or scarce — the law of supply and demand. This should make it possible to predict which kinds of people will take up what kind of work or change jobs and regions to take higher paying ones. However, the uncertainties and anxieties examined in the previous chapter, factors which affect individual decisions to change jobs, work usually toward a conservative reaction to change. The desire of workers for security — unless the rate of inflation far outruns the rate of pay — makes wage changes in most societies a rather inefficient way of galvanizing a labor force into action. And, to the extent that education is needed in the new jobs, the time for this education (if it can be acquired) must be figured into the process.

Finally, the "defined needs" of a division of labor system are of two kinds: the basic functional requirements for a job, and the values and prejudices of a society with respect to who ought to occupy that job, regardless of former qualifications. Modern industrialized societies, as they develop toward the present United States model, increasingly narrow the available jobs toward the middle age ranges, excluding the young and the old. Discrimination in pay against the female sex, for those of the same education for the job, was documented nationally in 1967 by the Department of Commerce.[34] Discrimination by sex in terms of hiring policy has been demonstrated by Rossi in science, Miller in personnel work, Fischer and Golde in anthropology, and by the Sociology Liberation Movement in sociology; in general the pattern has not changed since 1900, as Gross shows in an article whose partial title is "plus ça change, plus ça même chose" (the more things change, the more they remain the same).[35] Comparative data on sexual difference in wages for the same jobs are found by Myrdal and Klein for professional women in "male" professions in England, by Forniciari for all occupations in Italy (where a reverse trend toward less female employment is also observable).[36] Leser, in a study of fifteen Western countries, reminds us, however, that female work activity of a paid sort has risen, even if the pay difference is discriminatory.[37] Housework remains unpaid for culturally defined reasons, if done by spouse.

Racial discrimination in hiring and in pay is a well-known fact in the United States. As Bloch notes, this is clear in three main areas: refusal to hire, early release, and no possibility for upward mobility within the organization. Although token progress has been made in the last few years,[38] Bloch's findings are still essentially accurate. Hutchinson's historical findings on the upward mobility of white immigrants is a contrast to this racial situation in the labor force.[39]

The presence of these phenomena makes a purely statistical calculation of supply versus demand an artificial process. Education, a factor to be discussed in greater detail under social mobility, is not the only determinant of the individual's job level; race, age, and sex must also be considered.

To sum up, the division of labor creates a demand for certain occupations and professions. Changes in the division of labor will lead to career and intergenerational shifts in the nature of the jobs that individuals take. The reward system parallels the functional importance and need for the jobs in most cases, but in some political situations the rewards can be altered from a strict supply and demand ratio. Individuals do not always choose rationally in terms of where they aspire to enter the labor force, and the hiring organizations themselves are often irrational in the age, sex, and racial prejudices which prevent them from using a segment of the labor force that could perform the work. "Supply and demand" is a social phenomenon as much as it is an economic one.

OCCUPATIONAL PRESTIGE

Human evaluation of the desirable and the undesirable is highly subjective. The reward and power hierarchies of a society offer individuals some guidelines in this respect, but each individual can work his own redefinitions of a generally accepted order. As Jencks and Riesman observe for lawyers,

> A federal judge, for example, has more power and prestige than almost any attorney, but he usually makes less money on the bench than he would in private practice. The result is that some men prefer to remain attorneys even when offered a judgeship, while others will make enormous efforts to become a judge.[40]

With notable exceptions such as the above, where status and material reward are not parallel, for the majority of the societies of the West status or prestige is approximately in line with money income. Thus, in Hughes' phrase, the "clean work" of the society, as well as the clean work within a given profession or occupation, gives one both more prestige and more reward than the "dirty." [41] In medicine, the surgeon's prestige far outranks that of the honest general practitioner, and both, in the eyes of society, outrank the abortionist. But ranking systems change with respect to specialties, and legalized abortion is becoming a political issue. With time, the outlawed jobs of a profession may become prestigious, if there is a need for them and the state can be made to change its mind. In the meantime, the abortionist collects in income what he loses in prestige.

The modern prestige system of the West, in the majority of its elements, is international. As we noted, the rating or ranking of prestige in general parallels the reward system, which in turn is based upon the functional importance of the work itself. Svalastoga, in his extensive international comparisons of the prestige ladders of societies, remarks that the extensive similarity from nation to nation must be due to the nature of the occupational role and its place in the division of labor, as individual ratings couldn't display this kind of regularity.[42] He goes further, however, to show that the "distance" from bottom to top in terms of ratings may vary from one society to another. In the Eastern European countries the range of ratings of occupations is narrower than in Sweden; this may reflect the consequences of being told year after year by the Polish Communist Party that workers are "as good as professionals." [43] Yet in a previous chapter we have reported a study from Poland in which people approve a wide range of *income* as acceptable for different occupations and professions.

The issue of occupational prestige is an important one precisely because of its subjective nature. The problem it presents for a society is found in those occupations where neither income nor prestige is high and the individual is blocked in terms of upward social mobility. Here there may arise ways of coping with the situation through denial of the low prestige of the occupation. In the lowest rungs of the prestige ladder, the situation can become desperate. As Gold describes the work of a janitor in apartment houses: It is a continual battle to admit that some of the work even belongs to the occupation.[44] Attempts are sometimes made to rename an occupation (stationary engineer for boiler room attendant, realtor for real estate salesman) and begin a professionalization process, which may amount to little more than some community public relations work to burnish the image of the group. Or the group may organize and fight for power and reward, gaining some prestige if it succeeds.

Man does not live by bread alone; the youth movements of the past few years have often displayed a common theme — the rejection of the reward ladder of the society and its judgment of prestige, and the construction of idealistic alternative ways of evaluating an individual, an occupation, and a contribution to society. The wider society has attempted to capitalize on this idealism through the creation of positions of high prestige, with low material reward and no power, such as the Peace Corps, VISTA, and other government programs. The most recent development has been a rejection by some younger professionals and occupational members of the traditional early steps to success in their field, and a turn to the crusading occupationalism seen in young lawyers who follow the actions of Ralph Nader and other "consumer advocates," or fighters for the community interest. However, it is important to remember that all are not always pure of heart, or even if they are, society eventually may change its mind as to what is prestigious, so that an unprestigious job at time X may be reinterpreted and turned into material opportunities at time Y. For example, those who become famous crusaders are often bombarded with job offers, not the least of which come from the ones they are crusading against.

The relation between prestige and material reward must be seen in terms of the whole career. It is true that men leave high paying private industry or professions to work for government jobs of low pay and high power, but a strictly materialist interpretation can be placed on this: the interim gain in prestige may mean a long-term advantage in material terms as well, perhaps far more than if the low pay, high prestige job had never become part of the individual's career sequence.

The term "occupational prestige" has been the basis for an almost endless series of sociological studies of "ranking orders," usually showing how the freshmen at Utopia College rank twenty-three well-known occupations. Each new study seems to restate, ad infinitum, the intricacies in the statistical manipulations that can be made with pencil and paper scoring schemes.[45] To the functional or systems approach, however, the issue is somewhat more general, as well as more subtle. We must know how and why, to the individual and to the society, the prestige system parallels or diverges from the systems of power and material reward.

In conclusion, occupational prestige is subjectively complex in individual cases, and some men will choose a high prestige, low paying job over the reverse. In general, however, the higher the functional importance of the occupation to the society and the higher the requirement for long-term specialized education, the greater the prestige that accrues to the performer of the work. With minor variations, the same prestige ladder is seen internationally as in the United States. Within the system, low prestige jobs call out coping responses, high prestige occupations are often useful in the long run materially as well as psychologically. The prestige issue cannot be understood in isolation, but only in terms of people's evaluations of the desirability of their position in an overall division of labor.

OCCUPATIONAL MOBILITY

Ideology and reality have seldom been as confused as in the area of social mobility. Immigrants came to America as a "land of opportunity"; whether it really was such, or to what degree, is the subject matter for a major field in sociology. Studies of mobility up and down a society's hierarchies of power, prestige, and reward, have often made major assumptions concerning the data they have gathered, and the literature is complex and extensive. Here we will simply present some major theoretical issues as they relate to the division of labor and the study of occupational and professional groups. We will use the findings from one extensive and thorough study to document these issues, and use the historical and comparative viewpoint to set them in perspective.

First, as Bottomore points out, it is necessary to make the distinction between the up-and-down movements of individuals within a given structure and the movement of whole groups, where an entire group supplants an elite and relegates it to an inferior position in the system.[46] Next, it is necessary to distinguish both of these movements, within a given unchanged structure, from a social change in which the entire structure of the society changes, causing opportunities and disadvantages for occupational groups as a result. By analogy, individual mobility is the trend to championship or last place by the team as a team, whereas mobility caused by structural change is the creation of a new game in which striking out becomes the greatest talent needed, leading to major opportunities for the last-place baseball team in the new game. The quantitative studies to date are primarily of *individual* mobility, with attempts to interpret group mobility and change-caused mobility through the careers of individuals. But groups act as groups — the unions strike for higher wages as a group — and their success or failure involves more than the actions of isolated individuals climbing in an unchanged social structure. But even the attempt to separate these three kinds of mobility from one another is an oversimplification. As Geiger insists, the "social structure" is an abstraction which covers a continual series of fluid and related processes: individuals climb or fall in a changing structure, their careers being a composite consequence of where they start, how much initiative and education they have, whether or not they are part of a concerted group action, and whether they are attempting to climb in an occupation which is becoming increasingly central to the changing society or one which is becoming rapidly obsolete. The time dimension is critical in understanding the nature of mobility.[47]

A second issue is the *kind* of mobility involved. Do we mean upward or downward direction in terms of power, prestige, or material reward? Ideally, both individuals and groups should be studied over time in all three dimensions, but there are no such studies to date. And given these complexities, what do we mean by occupational mobility? In fact, being in an occupation, with its position in a present division of labor, almost automatically defines all three dimensions for an individual: what power he has or does not have over whom, what prestige is his by virtue of his work, and to what degree he is rewarded for it. Since occupational and professional group membership is so critical, and since it is usually a fairly easy piece of information to gather, most "mobility" studies are in reality studies of an individual's occupational history and its changes, or the generation-to-generation studies of father's job as it relates to son's job, for a group of individuals possessing different social characteristics (age, sex, race, ethnic group). The assumption is that "occupational mobility" *is* social mobility, or that it reflects enough of overall change in position in a society to serve as a proper index for such change.[48] In later chapters, the internal conflict within occupational groups and the group actions of these occupations against others in the society will illustrate the weaknesses of this assumption. But something can be learned from occupational mobility studies, if these qualifications are kept in mind. What *is* of critical importance is that a representative sample of a nation, over a long enough time span, must be taken.

A third major issue is the question of *whose* mobility. Are we talking of fathers in their own lifetime or of sons with respect to their fathers? The study must always specify whether one is dealing with career mobility (mobility in one's own career) or intergenerational mobility (what level the son reached in comparison to his father's, etc.).

A fourth major research problem is the relation of schooling to occupation, and thus to career progress. This is a chicken-and-egg problem in studies of occupational mobility. Even in the most comprehensive studies, education is treated as a "mediating" factor between the position (i.e., occupation and education) of father and the position of son.[49] But education, a critical component of occupational mobility, is always education in a real school in a real neighborhood, with the existential facts we considered in the previous chapter. One can best get the education needed to "climb" if one is already in the outer suburbs. To what extent then is the degree of education of the children simply another index of the level of his parents and of his own jumping-off place in the race for success? Friedenberg has called the modern university an "anthrodrome" — a place for people-racing.[50] Some groups have talents more relevant to the present anthrodrome than others; these abilities are related to class position and racial group membership and they complicate the effect of social position on "education."

To talk about the similarity or difference between father's occupation and son's is to forget that the place of *both* may be due to their position in the overall social system in part independently of occupation. This "general" position will influence father's occupation, education, and son's occupation, education, and future, far more than each of these factors alone. Again, when a complex world is considered, simplifications must be made. Studies of occupational mobility are primarily studies which use occupational membership as an index of something else, namely progress up or down a stable, or a changing, social hierarchy.

Blau and Duncan, in a major study of American occupational mobility which was published in 1967, reported their findings from a representative national sample of more than 25,000 respondents.[51] First, they confirmed that for the United States at present, father's education and occupation were important factors influencing son's eventual position, but they were outweighed by the son's own education and the status of his first job. They present a social mobility picture of movement "one step up the ladder" — from blue-collar to white-collar, from clerical to professional and semi-professional — for a majority of the population in a generation. A substantial amount of short-length upward mobility is seen from the previous generation to the present generation of adults at the time of the study. Two barriers were found, one specific to occupation of parent and self, and one to race. If a person in his own lifetime climbed from blue-collar to white-collar, or left the farm for city blue-collar work, he very rarely returned to the previous position and its accompanying life style and rewards. It was slightly harder to cross the hurdle out of blue-collar work and harder to climb for ethnic minorities or those with parents of low occupational and educational status, but if such individuals did get the education they tended to go *further* than those with the same education who started higher in the social class system. Overall, the lower fertility of those at the top of the class structure of the society (producing fewer job-seekers) and the expansion of jobs in semi-professional and technical areas made moderate upward mobility possible for most white Americans in their own lifetime and certainly in the position of their sons with respect to their own position.[52]

But the racial barrier was clear. For blacks, the rules did not apply, and education did *not* do for this group what it did for whites. The more education the black man had, the greater the *discrepancy* between his position and that of a white man with the same education. Thus a true underclass is in process of creation:

> Here we see how cumulative disadvantages create a vicious circle. Since acquiring an education is not very profitable for Negroes they are inclined to drop out of school relatively early. The consequent low level of education of most Negroes reinforces the stereotype against the entire group, thus further depressing the returns Negroes get for the educational investments they do make, which again lessens their incentives to make such investments.[53]

The tiny fraction of blacks who are now college students and politically active on campuses is still far outweighed by those with only a high school education or less. And, given the quality of present ghetto education and continuing racial discrimination, Blau's and Duncan's observation is likely to remain accurate for some time to come, unless something significant is done by the society to change it. Poor whites and poor blacks from the same Southern rural background were compared by the authors. Education for the whites from this region had immediate payoffs, for the blacks it did not. In addition, the group that is now the unskilled one — the blacks as compared to last century's Irish — is confronting a technological society which has no place for unskilled labor. No jobs are available for many at their present level of education, and the group understands what Blau and Duncan have proved: getting *more* education is not likely to help, if you are black.

Historically, Thernstrom's study of Newburyport, Massachusetts, from 1850–1880 gives us one of the very few points of comparison. Here the Irish take the place of the blacks, and the same "one-step-up" is noted for the non-Irish, with the exception that for most it was *property* mobility rather than occupational.[54] The factory worker stayed in his job, but bought a small house or a small farm on mortgage, starting a small savings account as well in many cases. The Irish were blocked from any mobility here. But the difference in this comparison is clear generationally. The second-generation Irish were able to increase their mobility rate over the first, and in many communities gained political power over the city government.[55] For blacks, in this century, the rate of mobility for the group appears to have decreased from World War II to the present time.[56] In general, Thernstrom shows that one hundred years ago there was about the same mobility pattern as today, at most levels, or perhaps slightly less.[57] However, for the oppressed minority, technological change offered some opportunities then which are not available now. The nature of the work available to the sons of the oppressed is different now, and race is a strong factor in the present situation. Lipset and Bendix, in their comparative studies on mobility, indicate that the rate of mobility from blue-collar to white-collar jobs is essentially the same for fifteen other industrialized countries of widely different types as it is for the United States.[58] But these studies do not include the groups at the bottom or the top and do not consider the critical question of minority group mobility within these societies.

Occupational mobility, to sum up, is an issue which relates the division of labor on the one hand to the striving of individuals and groups on the other. Occupational membership is used as an index of a person's changes of position with respect to a society's set of hierarchies of power, prestige, and reward. In industrialized societies, the past century appears to indicate that a minor, constant, technology-based predominance of upward over downward mobility has occurred—with individuals going one notch up the ladder. But in the American case, the studies indicate the development of a dual, racially separated society, with mobility rules applying to whites but not to blacks. The consequence of the blocked mobility of whole groups, in history, is usually their combination as a group to fight and alter the system that oppresses them as a group.

THE PROFESSIONS: ARE THEY A SPECIAL CASE?

The history of work, as far back as it goes, reserves a special place for the professions. But in what way are professions special? This question can be considered in several ways: the relation of professional groups to the overall division of labor, their relation to their clientele, and the relation of internal group dynamics to a profession's place in the community or the nation.

Carr-Saunders' and Wilson's central definition of a profession concerns its possession of specialized intellectual skills and a body of theory acquired over a long period by those socialized and trained in it.[59] This type of definition centers on the relation of such groups to others in the overall division of labor. Those groups which are critical and central to an industrialized society are more likely to be professions by this definition. But it is important to note that the occupational groups high on the scale of power, prestige, and reward may not all be professions in terms of this definition with its stress on specialized intellectual skills. A second requirement, in our definition of the term, and one pertaining especially to the classical professions of medicine, law, clergy, and the military, lies in the crisis-relevant functions they perform. This involves their direct relation to individual as well as group human needs, such as health, liberty, and property, the meaning of existence, and national self-defense. Their functional importance is high on the scale.

A second main dimension of the professional type of occupational group lies in the nature of the interpersonal relationship between professional and client. For a professional, as Hughes notes, "The life crises of others are their routine: the daily routine work of the members of the four professions mentioned include heart surgery, defense in murder trials, burial ceremonies, and battle."[60] And in each case, the layman is expected to hand over self-determination in these critical areas for the promise of professional neutrality and expertise in their performance of the needed duty. Hughes also distinguishes between a *profession* and a *learned society*. For example, he prefers to classify sociology as the latter, since the professional model implies exclusion of too many people as well as the self-interest power plays that in his view do not harmonize with the disinterested pursuit of truth. Friedson highlights another aspect of the professional-client relationship when he contrasts the service professional with the scientist in regard to knowledge. A professional expects his client to take his views on faith, whereas a scientist (in theory, anyway) expects to have his views challenged by all, with the test of truth in the proof or disproof of his ideas by another, even a student. This, as he notes, is inconsistent with the nature of personal relations in the major professions.[61] In addition, as Hughes notes, the profession must have the *license* to delve into the personal affairs of others or make impositions on them in ways unacceptable for the ordinary civilian; for these reasons, a profession must have the official backing of the state and the community to do its work without danger to its members.[62]

Another set of dimensions distinguishing the central professions from other occupations lies in two closely related areas: the internal self-regulation of the group and the relation of the group to the overall society. The construction of deliberate ethical codes — standards known to the membership and used to regulate its activity in the community — is both a means of protecting the community from the "quack" and of maintaining a legitimate claim to the expertise involved, a legitimate right to fulfill a certain function in the overall division of labor.[63]

The deliberate attempts of professional groups to manipulate and handle the community are explored by authors such as Hughes, Goode, and Gilb. Hughes relates the community *mandate* of a profession — the community's willingness to allow practitioners to do their work unsupervised — to the degree of license allowed.[64] To a great degree, if the group has no independence from community or organizational evaluation and control, it will also not have the sanction to delve into humanly personal, critical areas. Goode calls a profession "a community within a community" and notes that all power relationships and divisions of labor *within* a professional group should be understood in terms of community consequences. For example, professionals must control their clients, must not refer clients to unauthorized practitioners, should pressure for legislation to enforce standards for the qualified and penalties for practice by the unqualified, and must maintain a united front with respect to laymen at the community or the national level. Conversely, since the central professions do perform central functions, the state's laws are attempts to regulate the profession and diminish its capacity to use "functional power" selfishly instead of in a humanitarian way. The community can reject an individual profession or a whole professional group, and it can also use a profession's elite to regulate its rank and file, through the use of the elite on licensing boards which grant rights to practice. Finally, the community may in some cases construct an alternative to the group, if all else fails, or ostracize the whole group. Gilb, in her study of the complex relation between the professions and government in the United States, and Millerson, in his study of the same issue in England, note that in the licensing issue lies the key to community-professional relations: a truly powerful profession can usually gain control of the state regulatory apparatus and use it to its own advantage and can use its expertise and influence to perpetuate a monopoly on the work.[65] The King of France in 1539 broke the legislatively based monopoly of the mason's guild; it is harder though not impossible for a modern community to do the same with a functionally critical profession such as medicine or law.[66] On the other hand, having the elite of a profession on the licensing board does give the community the advantage of expert opinion in judging the talent of new professionals. The issue of trust is paramount; if the profession loses the trust or support of the community, its elite will become discredited and the license-monopoly will be repealed. Too great a use of functional power for selfish advantage will lead to just this loss of community support. In essence, therefore, the relation between profession and community is one of mutual interdependence, with natural limits set on the extent to which either partner can take advantage of the relationship.

All occupational groups have some of the characteristics of the central professions. We agree with Greenwood that it is their combination and their intensity, rather than their simple presence or absence, that determine where an occupational group can be placed on a continuum from occupation to marginal profession to central profession.[67] How *much* of the following does a group have: extensive skills with a body of theory, independence from and autonomy and control over the layman-client, community position and sanction, an occupational group culture, and self-administered codes of ethics with respect to practice in the community? It should be noted that the theory need not be scientific — witness the professions of law and the clergy.[68] What is necessary is that all five of the above characteristics be intensively present and the skill of the group be relevant to an area of basic human needs. From this perspective, "professionalization" cannot be obtained by the construction of a self-conscious ethical code (the secretaries' ethical code) or a body of theory (books on the "theory of massage"). The group needs the central crisis-serving function, the autonomy and power given by the community, and the capacity to manipulate the work situation, including the laws governing practice, to its own advantage.

Historically, a change in regime or a change in technology may lead to a change in the mandate, the rewards, or even the very existence of an occupation or profession. What is striking, however, is the persistence over two millennia of the classic professions, even with major setbacks such as those seen in Jacksonian America. This persistence must be attributed to their ministering to the needs of individuals and groups basic during almost any period in history. But a technological society develops other needs. The technology-based occupations and professions are therefore presently increasing in size and power, as is the power of the intelligentsia in scientific and humanistic areas. This in itself makes limitation of the term "profession" to the classic professions unwise. However, it is important to note that the classic professions, the central, top-ranking managerial and technological groups, and the two intelligentsias in Aron's sense are critical not by number of individuals but by function in an industrialized society.[69] We must be careful to avoid a governmental — and sometimes sociological — lumping of "professional, technical, and kindred" occupations, a group which has increased greatly, but not primarily because of growth at the top or in the classic professions. Many "technical and kindred" jobs are a highly developed version of blue-collar work — the name "gray collar" has been suggested. These groups do not have as occupations either the political strength of the unionized laborers or the power of an organized profession. By the criteria we have considered, a graduate school trained engineer or a Harvard Business School trained executive is a professional, whereas a computer programmer, a circuit inspector, or an office manager in the same business is not. The first two would in most census categories be included in that "professional, technical, and kindred" groups, but they have almost none of the functional characteristics of professional groups. The lower level, non-specialist manager cannot be considered as a professional by this definition, but the elite universities in the East are beginning to construct graduate training programs and a colleagueship situation which is in recent years approximating a professional group in higher business management.

We will give major, chapter-length consideration to the classic and the newer central professions. In so doing, we will be considering professions as occupations which are like all other occupations, only "more so." All occupations have central skills, an occupational code of ethics, a group culture, some occupational authority, and some permission to practice on the part of the community. But the major professions have all of these to a very high degree, and in addition share two major characteristics. First, they are functionally powerful, or near to key places in the division of labor, and this is reflected in their political power, prestige, and material reward. Second, they are all dealing with individual or group needs of a basic sort, in situations where the absence of their skills spells immediate and long-term crisis for the individuals of the society and for the society itself.

THE BUREAUCRATIZATION OF WORK

One of Max Weber's greatest conflicts was seen in his analysis of social change. He demonstrated the inevitable rise of bureaucracy, but his evaluation of the desirability of that rise was negative in many ways. The machine-like organization of individuals into groups with military-style chains of command seemed to Weber part and parcel of economic development in the West. He could not conceive of any other way that a factory or a large corporation could be run. He feared the creation of an automaton man or a personally irresponsible citizen, one raised by bureaucracies, educated by them, and working in them, never seriously understanding the meaning of individual rights and duties or the meaning of creativity and the need for change.[70] The bureaucratization of work is an issue directly relevant to a systems approach to the division of labor. We can consider three facets of the problem, each of which was of interest to Weber: bureaucracy as a principle for the organization of work, occupational relations within the bureaucratic setting, and the political consequences of bureaucratization.

As a general principle for the organization of work, bureaucracy was not an invention of the Industrial Revolution. But as Weber points out, the importance of the bureaucratic mode of organization at this time and thereafter lay in the extent to which *all* work became or was becoming organized in bureaucratic organizations.[71] Organization by setting is a different principle than organization by occupation. For example, the medieval guilds had occupational and organizational solidarity, but they worked in terms of their occupational group. We can contrast this with the union organization in a typical Western nation: the factory is organized on bureaucratic lines, the union across a set of factories, with its membership in each setting confined to one stratum of the organization. A strike, viewed in these terms, is the assertion of an occupational or an interest-group principle against the bureaucratic principle of organized ongoing functioning of the setting toward its goal. Weber suggested that another characteristic of bureaucracy is its tendency to perpetuate itself as a system even in the absence of its original reason for being. Another aspect of the bureaucratic principle lies in its diffusion of responsibility for decisions. Except at the top, the "buck" can be passed. As Arendt shows, it was passed by Adolph Eichmann, who as the head of the Nazi extermination camps said that he was "only doing his job." [72]

The bureaucratic manner of organizing work must be considered in terms of the relation of a given bureaucratic setting to the state. For example, the worker in a public bureaucracy — under civil service laws — exists in a different relation to his job and his employer than does the worker in a private bureaucracy. This difference can be a disadvantage as well as an advantage, of course. To the degree that all work in the society is socialized (i.e., under the control of the state) as well as bureaucratized, to this degree will an individual necessarily perform work under the direct surveillance of the state. For example, as Field reports for Soviet Russia during a period of intensive industrialization, the physicians were under state orders to discharge only a minimum number of men from the assembly lines for illness. Quota rules were set here by the central government and the physician could get into political as well as vocational trouble for objecting.[73] In many American manufacturing plants, as Nader and his co-workers have discovered, house physicians often ignore professional standards and cooperate with management to perpetuate conditions causing industrial disease for individuals (black lung in miners, asbestos lung, radium poisoning in watch-making plants, etc.).[74] But these physicians, although they might lose their job if they disagreed with the corporate management, would not get into legal or political trouble by so doing. In a later chapter we will look at this problem in detail when we consider conflicts between public employees and the state, as this issue is handled in different political systems.

Not only will the type of political regime affect the nature of work in a bureaucracy, the nature of the culture of the society may have an influence on the way that the bureaucratic setting's informal rules are constructed. Crozier contends that French "national character" and cultural definitions of acceptable human situations have influenced the nature of the bureaucracy in France:

> the French bureaucratic system of organization is the perfect solution to the basic dilemma of Frenchmen about authority. They cannot bear the omnipotent authority which they feel is indispensable if any kind of cooperative activity is to succeed. It can even be argued that this dilemma has been perpetuated by the long tradition of the French bureaucratic patterns, whose strength comes from their meeting two contradictory and equally potent aims, preserving the independence of the individual and insuring the rationality of collective action.[75]

Occupational relationships and the politics of work are inextricably connected in the bureaucratic process. The division of labor on any bureaucratic setting has two realities: the "official" reality, the way groups and divisions are supposed to relate to each other on the organization chart, and the "actual" reality, the informal division of labor or the way that the setting is really operating and the way decisions are really made and work actually done. As Homans observed with his study of the evolving role of an occupation on a bureaucratic setting, to increasingly restrict a group to its formal role may in fact change its function radically within the organization.[76] In the early stages of the business firm he studied, a small group of "design engineers" were informally the management advisory group for the whole organization. Later, as formal "management" grew in size, this group was demoted by being required to practice only according to its formal title.[77]

The role of scientists and service professionals in organizations illustrates another aspect of the close connection between interpersonal relations on a setting and the power struggle between occupations and bureaucracies. For example, the size of the organization or the degree of formal bureaucratization of an organization does not necessarily mean the occupation is powerless with respect to it. As Glaser found, a governmental research institute can be a place where a scientist can be in his element, since the goals of the setting and the goals of the occupational group essentially coincide.[78] On the other hand, as Whyte indicates, the same group, the scientists, in most industrial settings are restricted in their work to profit-relevant research; this causes a conflict between the bureaucracy and the occupation which usually is not won by the occupation.[79] Again, Smigel shows that a law firm, although somewhat bureaucratized, is run by lawyers for lawyers and thus operates as an organization in their interest and does not force them to conform in ways which will reduce their professional effectiveness. In fact, such an organization may provide a "strength in numbers" advantage for a professional group, if we contrast the solo lawyer at the mercy of his clientele with the secure member of a wealthy and established law firm.[80]

In some marginal professions, and in most occupational groups, the size and complexity of the bureaucratic organization do take a toll in the quality of interpersonal relations. The typical hospital is a well-known example, as is the typical large university. The question in the case of each group, with respect to a bureaucracy, lies in the extent to which the occupation can mold or control the nature of relations on the setting. For either deliberate reasons — management's partial control over workers — or undeliberate ones — such as the bureaucratization of medical settings as a function of size and complexity of function — the bureaucracy can gain ascendancy over the occupational group. This leads to a routinized, somewhat depersonalized work experience for many of the workers. For most non-professional occupations, this has become true to such an extent that it may be one of the reasons why some youth are in an anti-bureaucratic vocational revolt, turning to art and craft occupations as a way of constructing a meaningful career.

To sum up, there is a trend in industrial societies for work to be organized in a bureaucratic pattern. The key question becomes, "Is the given setting structured to benefit all the groups within it, some of them, or, as in the case of a highly bureaucratized totalitarian society, none of them?" In each occupational or professional family, the power of the state, the goals of the occupational group, the goals of the formal and the informal organization of the setting, and even the surrounding culture will play a role in defining the meaning of bureaucratization.

THE SYSTEMS APPROACH: ADVANTAGES AND DISADVANTAGES

The systems approach has now been added to the historical and biographical as a major way to study occupational and professional groups. When we choose an occupational or professional family or group of occupations for study, it will be in terms of their relatively distinct function or set of functions in the overall division of labor. We will want to know the obvious and the unnoticed aspects of the occupation's role in the wider society. A comparative perspective will be necessary to observe the group in different societal settings. We will want to know how the occupation recruits its membership and rewards them, the nature of the prestige system within the occupation and its relation to that of the wider society. The issue of mobility into the occupation and within the general society must be considered, especially as it relates to changes in the overall society's need for the occupation's members and their skills. The issues relevant to the professions — the politics of skill, the relation of the work to human needs, and the complex interrelations between group self-regulation and social regulation — must be considered. For each group, we must understand the effects of bureaucratization on the occupation and trends in this direction.

The functioning of the group, internally and with respect to the overall pattern of the division of labor, is as basic to our understanding as a knowledge of the history of the group and the experience of becoming and being a member of the group. But there is one critically important approach we have not considered, an approach complementary to these, which sees the given division of labor as a temporary outcome in a past, present, and future struggle between groups who are interested in the acquisition of power, prestige, and reward even at the expense of others. If this chapter was "Durkheimian" in spirit, the next one will be "Marxian." We do not live in heaven; occupational groups are composed of individuals and organizations which push their interests as far as they can. The systems approach, taken by itself, naturally tends to emphasize the cooperative aspect of the division of labor, showing how the system looks and operates as an interdependent whole. Conflict issues can be considered within this framework, but we will consider them in another way in the next chapter, through the use of a direct, explicit conflict-of-interest approach.

CHAPTER FOUR

THE DIVISION OF LABOR: CONFLICTS OF INTEREST

If the social world can be viewed as a system, it can also be viewed as an arena, where groups compete by fair means or foul for the rewards available. If a temporary outcome of a conflict is reached, we may ask, "Who benefits?" Marx conceived of social change as a dual process of technological evolution and political action, with the end of history being reached when the oppressed industrial workers united and seized the means of production and the power of the state. Technological evolution would prepare the way, as it would inevitably lead to the pauperization of a major segment of the community, and thus make them ripe for revolution.[1] We will return to the problem of technological change after we consider a set of specific interest-based conflict issues: the concept of "occupational consciousness," the role of occupational ideology in group political action, occupational interests in conflict with the overall public interest, and the growth of "occupational altruism." The theme which ties these issues together, including Marx's basic theory, is that in all societies there are conflicts of basic interest between groups in the system; thus an exploration of the conflicts and the interests which underlie them may provide some basic insights about the nature of the overall society.

THE CONCEPT OF "OCCUPATIONAL CONSCIOUSNESS"

Marx began his analysis of class conflict by making a basic distinction between what he called a "class *in* itself" — a group with a label — and what he called "a class *for* itself" — a group of people who were conscious of their own interests as a group, had united as a group, and were fighting as a group to advance their interests. Marx observed that only groups of the latter sort have an effect on history, because in fact anyone can label anything as a group. Only when the group *acts* as a group in the social arena does it possess the kind of reality which has consequences in history.[2] The *Dictionary of Occupational Titles* lists thousands of "occupational groups," but most of these are simply labels. The *real* groups, in Marx's sense, are those that act as groups to advance their own interests. Thus the real questions are these: Does the group have a consciousness of its interests as a group? Is it aware of itself as a potential or actual struggle group? Is it already fighting?

We will use Marx's idea in two ways here: first, showing that it can apply to specific occupational groups and families of occupations as well as to class groups (a wider social category), and second, showing how the *occupational* consciousness of these smaller groups may in fact prevent the *cross-occupational combination* of large numbers of people to overthrow the entire system. The struggling of smaller groups to advance their group interests within the present system can be seen as antithetical to change of the system itself.

The degree to which a group has developed a strong occupational consciousness is the degree to which it is capable of increasing its political power and its material rewards. We can contrast the occupational consciousness of central professions such as medicine, law, and the military, with, for example, office workers such as the secretary. The central professions through their organization as a group and their relations with power groups in and out of government, press for advantages to the fullest extent possible without damaging their image in the eyes of the public. They often have special committees for political action — such as the Political Action Committee of the American Medical Association — or associations of ex-professionals and interested laymen — the Air Force Association, the Veterans of Foreign Wars, the community organizations which support more power for the police. The nature of professional group culture and organization, especially in the classic professions, in management, and among the intelligentsia, makes group consciousness and action in the group's interest a basic aspect of professional life.

OCCUPATIONAL CONSCIOUSNESS AND GROUP SOLIDARITY

We can learn much more about occupational consciousness from inspecting the actions of groups that have very little of it, such as office workers. When C. Wright Mills wrote *White Collar*, the unionization of white-collar office employees in the United States was almost nonexistent. Except for public service occupations, it still is. Mills hypothesized that the desire for upward social mobility into the ranks of management was a factor that held back the office workers from combination into a union to fight management. Conversely, management would promote an occasional clerk or secretary to lend credence to the hopes of all the others. However, as Mills pointed out, since the office workers were not unionized, they had no group power with respect to management and thus were earning salaries in many cases far lower than the unionized blue-collar workers in their own company.[3] They did not have "occupational consciousness" and were not organized for action. *What prevented them from fighting management was their desire to become a part of it.* They had identified with those above them in prestige ranking rather than with those below, who were, nonetheless, making more money because they were organized.[4] In addition, although Mills did not stress this, a great majority of office workers are female and have been socialized into anti-militant values, militancy having been equated by their parents with unfeminine attitudes. Furthermore, the single office girl might prefer the prestige of a white-collar job to the demotion in status involved in joining a union and thereby becoming less attractive (perhaps even déclassé) to the young executive she had her eye on.

The office worker's case brings out another point about occupational consciousness — its relation to the power and rewards of groups in the present division of labor, and the attempts to gain these through "professionalization." Wilensky warns that the term "professionalize" is overly diffuse and often misapplied.[5] The problem can be seen in the case of secretaries, especially in that of a group which has recently formed a "professional secretaries association," and created a new title — Certified Professional Secretary. (This is *not* certification by any state government.) Here the aim is to gain status and reward through the construction of the external trappings of a profession. But the basic issue remains: either the group is performing a critical function which demands extensive training, and thus has "functional power," or, if not, it must be willing to develop a group militancy and *fight* for its gains. That is, either in irreplaceability of function (doctors) or in militant unity (a strong national labor union) lies the power to change position and reward. If the workers in the occupation are replaceable, and if the group wishes to "professionalize" instead of fighting, the workers then become dependent on the group above them to hand them what they want. Here the case of the secretaries is instructive, as management strongly supports the "professionalization" of secretaries, acting even as members of its board of certification, but at the same time opposing the unionization of these same employees.

OCCUPATIONAL CONSCIOUSNESS AND SOCIAL STRUCTURE

The division of labor between groups that stand in a hierarchical relationship to each other is always a source of interest-based occupational conflict. In the perfectly cooperative system, the "lower" occupations in the field accept the ideologies and rewards dictated by the elite group. In the field of health, for example, doctors for years completely controlled the administration of hospitals, telling nurses what to do and dictating near-starvation wages for hospital maintenance workers. The nurses organized and established themselves as an interest group to bargain with organized medicine, and the hospital workers unionized and struck against the hospital.[6] In each case occupational consciousness meant using the existent position in the division of labor as a starting point for either redefinition of the division of work itself (as with nurses) or major change in the reward structure (hospital employees). Interoccupational relations are always negotiated, and can always be understood in terms of the self-interest of the groups involved.

What relationship does "occupational consciousness" have to Marx's more general idea of "class consciousness"? Marx thought that all workers who worked for an owner would develop a sense of "class consciousness," and his political manifestos were written to help develop this cross-occupational class consciousness. As he wrote with Engels, "Workers of the world unite, you have nothing to lose but your chains." [7] Politically, the greater the number of workers gathered together, the more powerful the party. Therefore, splitting up along occupational lines would result in losing the chance for a revolution but gaining favors for a group. But political realities both in Europe and in the United States, especially the latter, led to union organization by occupation first. So we had the development of craft unions ("masons and electricians for themselves") and industry-based unions (the United Mine Workers or "miners for themselves") before we had the cross-occupational combination into the American Federation of Labor (primarily craft unions) and the Congress of Industrial Organizations (primarily groups working at the newer, industrial-technical blue-collar jobs). Only in recent years have we seen the combination of the AFL and the CIO to form a combined, classical worker's group.[8] Thus, there are many steps along the continuum from the organized group consciousness of a distinct occupation — "occupational consciousness" — to a combined cross-occupational class movement acting in its interest — Marx's "class consciousness." Because of the inherent selfishness of groups, and their usual mistrust of other groups, there has historically been much more "occupational consciousness" and occupational group action than cross-occupational combination. As we have noted, the former is essentially preservative of a given social order, with each group asking for a larger piece of the present pie. In the United States (as compared to some European countries) even the cross-occupational groupings in the blue-collar labor area have been conservative in their aims (wanting more dollars for workers) rather than directly political (i.e., constructing a worker's political party such as the Labour party in Britain).[9] It is noteworthy, however, that even in nations which do have a party system based on occupation and class, not all the workers will vote for the labor party. It is estimated that between one-third and one-fourth of all British workers do not vote for "their" party.[10] In addition, when a specific group gains power, as the Labour party did in England, it may be forced into actions in the national interest which are against the goals and interests of the group which first sent it on the way to power.

"Occupational consciousness," therefore, is a code word for the degree to which an occupational group is fighting as a group in its own interest. Not all members of occupational groups, or broader class groups, will "get the message," and thus there are limitations on the extent to which any group, occupation-based or broader, can act in a unified manner. The key professions — new and old — have much less to gain from this cross-occupational combination than do the many blue-collar and white-collar occupational groups, and thus in general are much less likely to choose a cross-occupational path, although they do most definitely fight in their own occupational interest. They will also informally join with other powerful occupational and organizational groups to preserve their privileged positions. In this sense, group occupational consciousness is seen at all levels, with overt cross-occupational action more often seen at the lower levels of the reward system and hidden cross-occupational arrangements, or "complexing," more prevalent in the professions.

The power of the state is always a factor in the fate of occupational group activism. This entire discussion, in fact, is based on an assumption which is not valid for the Soviet bloc nations — that action in terms of "occupational consciousness" is *legal*. As Ossowski emphasizes, such action is not legal in the Soviet Union or Eastern Europe if it goes as far as opposing the state in order to advance the interests of a specific occupational or cross-occupational group.[11] And in the West, where the private corporations have great power in influencing the decisions of government, laws have been passed which set limits on the extent to which occupational self-interest action may be taken (especially by organized labor). Examples of limits include laws against strikes by public service occupations, and laws which limit the *length* of strikes by labor unions, strikes which cause their power to become too great and thus cause a "national emergency" through paralysis of the system.[12]

OCCUPATIONAL IDEOLOGY AND GROUP ACTION

An inevitable part of any group's action on its own behalf is an ideology which summarizes the meaning of its action and gives reasons why others should support it. Since occupations act politically, either in the strict or the broader sense of this term, they use ideologies:

> Ideologies are texts, theories, doctrines, phrases, or concepts which are proposed by an interest group (proponent) with a target group or groups in mind, for the intended purpose of directing, politically organizing, and energizing the target group toward behaving in a manner which is stated in the specific text of the message. This behavior is explicitly or implicitly stated as valuable and desirable as an activity or goal for the target group. Whether it is in fact valuable for the target group is an open question for research.[13]

In these terms, occupational ideologies are used by specific occupational groups to gain the support and action of target groups, such as the occupation's direct clientele (if there is one), other occupational groups with which the group deals, the government, and the general public. Of equal importance, an occupation's rank and file is often a major target for its own ideology, usually propounded by an elite group within its own ranks.

Some examples of the use of ideologies by occupational groups may illustrate the different factors that are relevant to this phenomenon. For example, a professional code of ethics, such as the Hippocratic oath of the physician, can be considered to function as an ideology with respect to the clientele, which believes in the profession's neutrality and lack of greed, and to the government, which gives the profession special protection. The group is bound by its own code, in theory, but as Friedson and Rhea have shown with the medical profession, doctors are rather unwilling to discipline their colleagues for fear of the damage it will do to their ideology as a force in the community.[14] By contrast, a less functionally powerful profession, such as social workers, may have a code of ethics which does not impress or mobilize the community or the government, which often employs untrained workers and calls them "social workers." Yet the code and the future goals of the group may be used as a club to hit the younger generation, who will be expected to live up to the standards. In this sense, in occupations interested in professionalizing there will often be found the most extreme instances of an occupational ideology being used against the occupation itself, in the interest of constructing a greater unity in the future.

The "expertise" of an occupation is often exaggerated for the effect it will have on its publics. If the claims of expertise are extended too far beyond the central training and competence of the group, the function of these statements becomes essentially ideological. In *The Scientific Estate,* Price illustrates how scientists gained access to political power and control over funds by claiming that an issue was essentially "scientific" rather than political and could best be handled by the occupation's elite.[15] This ideology of "total expertise" brought scientific consultants into government service and spurred a tremendous growth in support for the physical sciences. To take a contrasting example, in the medical specialty of psychiatry, a new movement named "community psychiatry" has arisen. Here the psychiatrist claims the role of "therapist to the community" and bases his claim on the expertise gained in individual psychotherapy and in community-oriented psychiatric training programs. Since politicians, sociologists, community organizers, radicals, and citizen's groups still consider the communty as their turf rather than the psychiatrist's, the community psychiatry ideology (and the movement) is not gaining the acceptance that the physical scientists did. The latter were dealing with the United States government at the beginning of the arms, missile, and space technology race with Russia. True expertise, and a moderate degree of relationship between ideology and capacity to deliver skills in a situation of need, are necessary for the successful propagation of an occupational ideology.

The uses of an occupational ideology will vary from one historical period to another. Some ideologies disappear as the group which propounds them vanishes or alters. For example, the robber barons of the late 1800s and early 1900s adopted the social Darwinism of the time — the doctrine of laissez faire — as a group occupational ideology.[16] As the economy of the Western nations became more managed and management of corporations became more professionalized and functionally distinct from ownership, both the robber barons and their ideology became a part of history. Other changes over time can occur when one occupational group uses one message at one time, another message at a second time, and yet another at a third time, although in each case trying to get the same occupational target group to act in essentially the same way. A central example here is the differing ideologies used by management in major industry to convince the workers of these industries that class conflict of a Marxian sort is unwise and undesirable. In the early days of industry management used a straight "survival of the fittest" ideology, and the workers knew that no combination would succeed as long as the power remained centralized in management and the number of workers exceeded the number of jobs so overwhelmingly.[17] The Taylorian era of "scientific management" saw the managers attempting to convince the workers that "science knew best" concerning production rates, although the aim was only to increase production.[18] The "human relations" era, which Friedmann suggests we are now leaving, used group dynamics techniques extensively as a way of cooling out dissent, especially but not exclusively at the white-collar and executive level.[19] But the union movement was almost always able to see that social Darwinism, Taylorism, and human relations were management-initiated ideologies directed at workers for the intended benefit of management at the expense of workers. And, in turn, the socialist and radical counter-ideologies of union organizers, or similar appeals to self-interest, are always attempts to mobilize the groups to act in their own interest, or at least in the interest of the union's managing elite.

There are consequences for both the target groups and the proponents if an ideology is accepted, and differing ones if the offered ideology is rejected. For example, the AMA got its way for many years by convincing the American public that it stood for their health and welfare and was not a selfish organization working for doctors. During that time its power was unchecked. In recent years, however, the AMA has actively campaigned against health insurance and various forms of medical care innovation, through the use of the slogan "preserve the sanctity of the doctor-patient relationship." As a partial consequence of a more critical public and the general "desanctification" of professional images in the nation, the ideology became less effective.[20] This is another way of stating that there are natural limits to the amount of success which an occupation can have with an ideological description of its role in the community. The AMA became too overtly political in its fight against Medicare, and part of its ideology of the disinterested, old-fashioned family doctor who cared for the poor and sick was contradicted by the mass media reportage on its activities as a political pressure group.

If an occupation's set of ideologies is rejected, it has several choices: it can give up attempts to extend domain and power (not a frequent choice), it can construct a more effective ideology, or it can take direct action to gain power without appeal to slogan or ideology. For example, in most Latin American military dictatorships the man presently in command tries to get elected to power on an ideology of progressive expertise — "We'll shape up the country just as we did the army." If this fails, the direct use of force follows quickly. Occupational ideologies, as any other form of ideology, may influence a situation by extending the power of one group at the expense of another. But there are natural limits to the power of ideas if nothing else in the concrete world is congruent with them.

To sum up, occupational ideologies are one way in which interest groups use ideas to advance their influence over others. An ideology may change in its functions from period to period, or it may lose relevance and die, or it may be replaced with a new ideology which serves the same function in an intergroup struggle for power over the rewards and control of a society. It is always important to know the degree of congruence or discrepancy between an occupational group's actual role in a society and the ideology it directs at that society. This will tell us where the group wants to go, or, if it is conservative, where it wants to stay. The degree to which it can get its message across may greatly determine whether it reaches its goal.

OCCUPATIONAL INTERESTS VERSUS THE PUBLIC INTEREST

When an occupation attempts to advance its interests in the society, it almost never admits that this is what is taking place. Instead, claims are made that greater power for the group is "in the public interest." The problem of analysis becomes difficult here in that occupation A may see an advantage to becoming involved with occupation B, and together with occupation C the three groups may form a complex group with great power to advance their interests in the society. When the A-B-C complex gets more power and resources, a significant segment of the general public may indeed benefit because of the nature of their relationship to the A-B-C complex. But at the same time, another segment of the public at large will be disadvantaged by the advance of the A-B-C complex and its benefiting clientele. The nature of the overall social system may even begin to change.

Thus we will need to analyze this problem at three levels: cross-occupational "complexes" which involve the cooperation and combination of different groups in their mutual interest, the relation of occupational groups to technological change, and the role of general broad social groups, such as the middle classes and "outsiders," such as the young, the black, and the poor. First, we can consider occupations and occupational complexes which benefit by the present system and the ideologies which they direct at the general public to keep their position. Special attention must be paid to the military-industrial complex, the rise of "technocracy," and the difference between the interests of the classic professions and the new, technocratic "social engineering" professions. Those who do not benefit by the present system, or who are losing power in it, groups such as labor unions, public service workers, and the non-occupation-based outsiders, can be seen as acting in their own interest also. We will consider such groups and also the reactions of those who benefit to those who don't. One of the major issues will be the ways in which segments of the public support, reject, or remain aloof from the struggles of these groups to gain power and greater control over their destiny.

When C. Wright Mills wrote *The Power Elite*, the military-industrial complex was considered by most to be an exaggerated hypothesis.[21] The events of the past fifteen years have essentially confirmed Mills' hypothesis, and it is now public knowledge that a large segment of the budget of the United States is under the essential control of the military high command, a group of key politicians, and the major defense contractors with their subcontractors. However, since these firms are nationally distributed and employ from 10 to 20 per cent of the work force, depending on how defense-related work is defined, a sizable segment of the electorate itself is dependent on defense work.[22] To cite Pilisuk and Hayden's conclusion, there is not a military-industrial complex which "runs" America, but to some extent America *is* a military-industrial complex.[23] Given this situation, groups such as the military profession, a segment of the capitalist group, professional managers who work in the defense industries, labor unions involved with defense work, and politicians who have made their career in defense-related areas advance their interests through mutual cooperation at the expense of others. The ideologies in use by this complex are several in number and are centrally propagated by the Department of Defense. The targets of these ideologies are multiple: the public at large (through appeals to patriotism or fear of invasion and annihilation), the manpower and human resources professionals (the Department of Defense as a skill developer and schoolmaster) and all of organized labor (the Department of Defense as job creator). Again, some of the ideologies are directed at the complex itself, some externally. But it is impossible to analyze the actions of the military, segments of industrial management and labor, and many national politicians, without considering the consequences of their participation in the military-industrial complex.

A second area where occupation and segmental interests may be opposed to overall public interest involves the role of the expert. Jean Meynaud has considered in great detail the growth of what he calls "technocracy," or the growth of political rule by expert planners and social engineers:

> In politics, the switch from technical adviser to technocrat is accomplished when the technologist himself acquires the capacity for making decisions, or carries the most weight in determining the choices of the person officially responsible for them. The acquisition of technocratic powers does not result from a sudden change in the existing regime, but from a sort of slipping sideways of power.[24]

In another definition, he suggests that technocracy is the fusion of bureaucracy and technology, with the central state bureaucracy using technological devices and procedures to plan for and justify its essentially political actions in the community.

Who are the technocrats? Meynaud presents three basic groups:

> The higher civil service, high military personnel, and the scientific elite. It would be completely wrong to think of all members of these groups as technocrats. Many carry on their professions without seeking to influence the running of the state and the course of politics. By citing these groups, I wish simply to point out that today they operate in a privileged sphere, in which technocratic influence may be won or spontaneously established.[25]

A comparative viewpoint on the functions and power of the technocrat is important. We might range the United States, Great Britain, France, and the Soviet Union on a continuum in this respect. In the United States, the bureaucracy is highly politicized because federal agency heads change with each administration, and direct their agencies to operate in a partisan political manner on issues such as health, education, and the regulation of commerce and finance. The growth of technocracy is primarily seen in relations between large corporations, the elite universities, and the private consulting corporations (e.g., the RAND Corporation), as all of these work with and influence the decisions of high federal administrators and the executive branch of the government. We are approaching, but not yet equalling, the British "establishment," which is a combination of hereditary position and meritocracy; the latter group is sponsored by the former into positions in government or into key advisory posts with respect to it.[26] France is even more centralized administratively; even the Sorbonne faculty are employees of the central government. The bureaucracy is not only very powerful functionally and able to carry out central, long-term economic and social planning, but is often the only continuity in government operation during the changes in political regimes. France has also gone further than most Western countries in giving strong decision-making power to technocrats.[27] Finally, in the Soviet Union the technocrat plans for the state, which is one-party in nature, and he is not in any sense outside the government system, as on occasion he is even in France. In the Soviet Union, the state has the power to compel whatever the technocrat decides.[28] The growth of technocracy is universal in industrialized societies, but the nature of government-citizen relations in general has a major effect on the speed with which this form of social organization can develop unchecked.

Meynaud demonstrates that there are two main dangers to a democratic society inherent in the growth of technocratic power. First, in a democracy the experts and planners should be controlled by the electorate, but in fact the central bureaucratic experts have a widening set of decision-making powers which cannot be influenced by the electorate. Second, the technological rationale and mode of operation — the "expert planner" as a neutral figure — may disguise the partiality of these groups to private clientele, especially the large corporations. Huntington calls this "clientalism" when the central groups are regulating agencies and their heads are former heads of the corporations that the government agency is supposed to be regulating.[29] As McDermott stated, "We may refer to all of this as the disinterested character of the scientific-technical decision-maker, or more briefly and cynically, as the principle of the Altruistic Bureaucrat." [30]

In addition to the loss in power by the general public and the gain in power by the industrial-corporate sector of the society which can use the experts for its own ends, other consequences of the growth of technology are suggested by McDermott: the insistence on conformity to master plans and the suppression of individuality in approaches, a widening gap between the culture, vocabulary, and social knowledge of the managers and the mass, with an overvaluation of the technologist's capacities going almost as far as mystification and hero worship.[31] These, it should be noted, are possibilities, and the counter-forces against these trends will be considered later in this section.

The ideology of the technocrat — as expert planner, scientific consultant, systems engineer, sociologist, and political scientist — has several facets, according to Meynaud, beginning with the following:

> The starting point of this ideology, as revealed through current attitudes, is the high value placed on the technician's methods, especially as they apply to the imperatives of industrial civilization. This optimistic estimation usually goes hand in hand with a critique of the normal machinery of politics, which borrows much if not the core of its argument from traditional anti-parliamentary attitudes. This standpoint makes it possible to advocate that politics be reduced to technics, which is in fact one of the many varieties of anti-political thought.[32]

Since the normal mechanisms of politics are denigrated, it would seem reasonable that politicians themselves would be denigrated, as "unscientific," "compromised," "unobjective," or "incompetent to solve the complex problems of the age." McDermott suggests that one underlying theme in the ideology can be expressed by the phrase *laissez innover*, after the laissez faire of the robber barons. Laissez innover indicates letting the experts solve the problems without any opposition from groups that might disagree with their recommendations.[33] There may be more than one ideology in use, however, and this is an important area for further research.

The functional role of the expert planner is encompassed by the term "technocrat" as used by Meynaud and others. "Technocracy," or rule by technocrats, is criticized for some of the same reasons as the military-industrial complex, and some of the same occupational groups appear to be involved. A comparison would indicate, however, that the differences have to do with the difference between an institutional arrangement of groups for their own benefit, such as the military-industrial complex, and a functionally powerful occupational group in a society used by another group in the self-interest of both groups. In the military-industrial complex, occupational groups are involved as part of the institutional arrangements (military, labor groups, corporate managements, politicians, engineers, and scientists in industry and the universities), whereas in the second situation the "technocrats" are an occupational group, but one which is defined by functional role and power with respect to government rather than by formal training or label as "technocrat." In the second group, for example, we may find economists, sociologists, or engineering systems analysts who are functionally technocrats. They do their work and in so doing advance the technocratic way of life, the corporate interests that they directly or indirectly represent, and their own personal interests. But in most cases they are also members of more standard occupational groups, and they are not working to advance their original occupational group's interests (unless they convince all of them to become technocrats). We may compare the military-industrial complex with the onset of a technocracy in this way: The military profession stands to gain as a whole from an increase in power of the military-industrial complex, whereas a technocratic advance would give more power to systems analysts and consultant planners everywhere, including those at the Pentagon, but would not do much for the average general, who would have to sit on the sidelines of his own profession.

The comparison between the classic professions and the newer technocracy-related professions can be made outside the issue of the military-industrial complex. We may note that the classic professions had their strength, and their leverage, in the functional power that they possessed with respect to individual needs (health, freedom, the meaning of life, self-defense) that were at the same time societal needs. In the technological professions the expertise is primarily system-related. The potential for growth in the power of the technocrat is directly related to the increasing complexity of the society and the imminence of a series of functional systems crises, such as the day traffic permanently stops in Boston or the day the sea is irrevocably poisoned. The mandate for the second group of professions is increasing, although human nature and basic individual needs continue to hand a mandate to most of the classic professions. The important issue for further research lies in the extent to which the technocracy-related professions (including the social scientists) play their role as experts not in a neutral sense, but in order to advance the interests of the very groups that are largely responsible for the problems which the system is having.

In the United States, the reaction of the non-military-industrial, nontechnocratic public to the actions of these groups has been intensifying in recent years. For example, each year the political opposition to the power of the military-industrial complex has increased, as a consequence in part of the war in Vietnam and the increased information finally being made available to the general public concerning the size and nature of military spending. Also, although the technocrat remains in a powerful position in France and the Soviet Union, the "citizen participation" movement and the skeptical attitude toward social engineering and expert planning which is growing in the United States have resulted in a slight strengthening of the political checks upon the free operation of government and consultant planners.[34] The fights against urban renewal and the populist-style campaign against the destruction of the environment are examples of public action in the face of both corporate-government complexing and hired expertise. The concept of "consumer power," advanced but not originated by Ralph Nader, is a further example of reaction against the attempts of these interest groups.[35] Wide segments of the middle class, as well as the poor, are affected by the power and actions of the military-industrial complex and the technocratic elite and by the power of organized medicine and other professional pressure groups. The main difference politically from the situation of a decade ago is that now the public is aware of this. Until recently the mass media and the professional group Aron calls the "humanistic intelligentsia" had not been critical of corporate power and professional self-interest action, but this has changed to some degree. The youth of the society have in addition been exposed to a radical press and even radically oriented news magazines which concentrate on these issues. But if the middle class is better informed, it has not been radicalized by the information received.

There are major groups in American society which are low on the hierarchy of prestige and reward, and which occupy either an inferior or a nonexistent place in the division of labor. They too may be discussed with respect to occupational and cross-occupational group interests. We can briefly consider the interests and actions of three groups, as these relate to a concept of an overall "public interest": industry-based labor unions, public service occupations, and the occupationless — the young, the poor, and the black unemployed.

Labor unions are at present fighting a defensive battle, one which involves holding the line against automation in unskilled and semi-skilled areas. The march of technology has decreased the percentage of the overall labor force in industrial blue-collar work and thus diminished the political leverage which a national labor union can exert. Furthermore, the cost factor tempts many managements to invest in automation for the long run, as the predictability involved (machines do not strike) is considered to be worth the extra cost. The attempts of unions to expand into white-collar areas are often frustrated by differences in status aspirations and life styles.[36] Still, it is far too early to count the labor movement out as a political force. Rather, the main problem seems to be the tendency of an overcooperation between union leadership, management, and the government, at the expense of the interests of the average worker. This is leading to repudiation of union leaders, wildcat strikes and, ultimately, a lack of unity in the labor movement which benefits management and the corporations.[37]

Public service workers, especially those in police and postal work, are an exception. In the case of these two groups and in other critical but underpaid areas such as sanitation, the functional power of the group is much greater than their reward. The ideologies of the past, which offered the public service worker "security" and "an opportunity to serve," are being increasingly rejected and replaced by militant action and far greater unity. In fact, for several decades most European countries have had a unionized public service, but only in the last decade has the United States begun to catch up in this respect. The tricky issue here lies precisely in the *public* nature of the work: a strike by firemen, police, postal workers, or garbage collectors hurts all, not just an exploiting corporation. From the point of view of the workers, they are being exploited by the public, but the bargaining position of the public service worker, although functionally strong, is political dynamite in terms of the number of groups that can be disadvantaged by his actions as part of a unified movement. There are still many citizens who subscribe to Calvin Coolidge's motto: "There is no right to strike against the public interest, by any group, at any time, for any reason." [38]

The occupationless groups — those outside the occupational system such as the young, the poor, and the black — cannot use an occupational group for functional leverage in a struggle to advance their interests. Part of the political desperation of these groups lies in their double dilemma: they are not members of occupations, in a society which suspects and sometimes acts repressively against action that is not occupation-based, especially if it is carried on by an "outsider" group.

Unions in industry, public service, and the outsider groups share another kind of problem: the middle class, which will fight the military-industrial complex, the spread of technocracy, and overly strong professional groups which directly threaten their interests, will not fight either for or against the unions, service workers, and outsiders. But if forced to choose between the haves and the have-nots, most will side with the haves. They can give reasons: public service strikes increase their taxes, the labor unions add to consumer costs and inflationary pressures, and in the eyes of the majority of the middle-class voters, the young, the poor, and the black are insufficiently appreciative of what they already have. As a consequence, the middle class is attempting to *reform* (not demolish) the military-industrial complex, *moderate* technocratic intervention, and *amend* the role of the professions, but will very probably side with such complexes and their component groups against militant action by unions, public service occupations, and the outsider groups.

The public interest is defined by the groups with the power to define it, and by the groups which accept such definitions by default. To define the public interest as the same as the interest of one's group is a privilege of power; only when the direct interests of the middle class appear threatened do they begin to question the ideologies of the corporations and the technocrats. But some middle-class professional groups are beginning to act on concepts of the public interest which are strongly biased in favor of outsider groups and have-nots. It is to this phenomenon that we may now turn.

THE GROWTH OF OCCUPATIONAL ALTRUISM

By the term "occupational altruism" we mean the actions by members of an occupational group directed at the group itself to change the way in which it deals with have and have-not groups. It should be distinguished from attempts to advance the occupation's own interests when the occupation is acting as a unified body. In occupational altruism the issue is that of changing the way the occupation benefits others, whereas occupational consciousness is an issue of pure occupational self-interest. In reformist and radical actions by an occupation's subgroup directed at its own membership, internal conflict is a basic consequence, as conservative is inevitably pitted against radical. Radical and reformist altruism is a relatively new phenomenon within the central professions in the present century, although there were such movements in the past, and in general the reformist spirit is quite ancient. Conservative action by a profession's power elite to preserve the professional status quo and the present relations between the profession and the society is a phenomenon found in all historical periods.

The rise of altruism in the classic professions has been marked in recent years: the medical student activist, the young lawyer engaged in community action work or group action suits in the manner of Ralph Nader, the radical priest, and the draftee rebelling against the Army's legal system and its concept of freedom of speech. In the coming chapters we will consider these movements in greater detail; suffice it to note here that each major profession, including university teaching in the social sciences, has been developing a radical-reformist wing.

The change in political attitudes on the part of a segment of the students in American universities, primarily but not only in the elite schools, has begun to have an effect on their perception of the present interest alignments of the major professions. As they enter training in professions, these youth bring pressure to bear on the university to redirect professional service toward the outsider groups. University faculties of professional schools, although not as radical as a body as most undergraduate faculties, are progressive enough and idealistic enough to be somewhat receptive to many of the proposed changes. Professors are beginning to enter into alliances with graduate student groups and with reform action organizations in order to intensify the changes. An attack is being made on the aims and goals of the professional socialization system by those who do the socialization, in its critical earlier phases, and by those who are being socialized.[39] Changes in recruitment policy are leading to an increase in the number of minority group members within the profession's ranks, and the development of a "non-sellout" minority action group is observable. In addition, racial minority professional organizations, such as the predominantly black National Medical Association, have taken on the militancy of the overall black movement and are now part of an overall action wing of the medical profession.[40] The prime casualty among the young recruits has been the ideology of "professional respectability." This phrase usually meant the pursuit of extensive private gain combined with a visible, minimal, but well-advertised amount of charity work in the poor people's division of a dual care system. The idealism of the younger graduate professional is one major reason for this upswing in activism, but it must not be overemphasized as a factor. The problem of the conservative nature of post-graduate professional institutional settings and arrangements is a major block to rapid change initiated from within professions, as we will see in the coming chapters.

ALTRUISM AS A LUXURY

The difference between occupational altruism and self-interested occupational action can be considered by comparing professional with white-collar and blue-collar groups. The degree of self-interest in the motivation of occupational activists seems to increase with every step down the ladder of present prestige and reward. The public schoolteachers are a group presently in conflict over issues of this sort, and the essentially "professional-style" National Education Association is beginning to work with more radical teachers' unions in an attempt to unify the public schoolteaching group for greater control of the classroom situation, the school administration, and the salary level. This is presented as being "in the community interest."[41] In the case of the firemen and police, the issues are even clearer. A difference is emerging between the self-interested attempts of universities (and the occupation's elite) to "professionalize" these groups, and thus have higher pay dependent on further university training, and the growth of police and firemen's unions with their increasing willingness to use the strike as a way of advancing their interests without the requirement of further education. The issue of altruism here becomes increasingly irrelevant; the less the reward for a group as a whole, the less its interest in altruistic actions. A medical student altruist urges his group to deny the opportunities they have, the teachers' union alternates between altruistic ideologies and self-interested action, whereas the striking policeman makes his position quite clear — he does not feel he can afford altruism at this point. His activism is directed at the rank and file membership against the "coopted leadership," which not only accepts a low pay rate for rank and file members but is silent on the validity of laws against strikes by public service workers. In the public service occupations, the altruistic ideology of "public service" has lost its following.

Reactions to the radical and reformist altruism of the new radical-reformist wings of the profession vary according to the group being considered. The university elite, the home base of professions, has attempted thus far to coopt these movements or play along with them in the hope of moderating their effect. Younger professors often view themselves as very much on the side of change. In addition, the profession's leaders in the university setting are often far-sighted enough to know that a total lack of altruistic behavior in a profession will eventually result in a community and national reaction against the profession, which might both limit its profits and restrict its freedom to operate. The government, especially to the degree that the "technocratic innovator" has any influence on social planning, appears at present to be remaining neutral or to be encouraging those movements that are the least threatening to the ongoing social system or those ideas which would result in a redistribution of resources or services more in line with governmental ideas. In addition, the actual governmental *financing* of the less radical of these groups — such as OEO community health clinics or legal services for the poor — is occurring as the government planners and consultants view professional service reform as a means of preventing open conflict between haves and have-nots.[42]

The mass practitioner — both as an individual and in his domination of the settings of practice, as head of the hospital appointment board, senior law partner, or director of church placement — has ultimate control over the opportunities open to the majority of young professionals, including radicals and reformers, after they leave the university professional schools. As a consequence, he is in a position to force the incipient reformer to choose, in many cases, between starvation (ostracism with honor) or lucrative conformity. Only in the case of settings which continue to recruit from elite schools, where the prestige of the school and the skill of the graduate are of more importance to the setting than his often leftish politics, are adjustments of a minor sort presently under way. For example, the law firm on Wall Street will now offer a day per month, or perhaps even two, for "poverty law" work.[43] The problems of reform seem to hinge in large measure on the ever-present, historically ancient conflict between the university elite of a profession and the practitioner mass. Only because the university can bestow prestige upon the practitioner does it have the leverage it has to effect some changes in community practice. As of now, these changes are minimal, but the power of an entire younger age group to boycott a profession is a growing possibility. So, too, is the construction of alternate institutional forms within which to practice a more altruistic version of the profession.

Occupational altruism, to sum up, is primarily a movement on the part of younger professionals in their early years in training and in practice on the behalf of have-not groups in the society. The opponents of radical and reformist altruism within the occupation have the advantage of influence over the settings where the profession is normally practiced, and thus the altruistic activist must construct new institutions as well as setting newer, non-monetary goals. The latter is the case, of course, because the altruism is on behalf of clienteles who cannot pay for services. But one critical problem remains: doing "for" a group still keeps the power within the profession, and the poor grow more suspicious every year of the altruism of middle-class professionals and corporate managers, whatever their age or announced political sentiments. And without the support of the poor, such an approach becomes rather meaningless. It is much too early to tell, and the picture varies for different occupations and professions, but occupational altruism, without a major change in the overall economic-political system, may be more a luxury for the haves than a solution for the have-nots.

TECHNOLOGICAL CHANGE: WHO BENEFITS?

Occupations and professions have now been seen as self-interested, self-conscious sectors that use ideologies and power inherent in their role and the power developed in cross-occupational combinations. As a reaction, altruistic movements are developing in many fields. But both the haves and the have-nots exist within the same social system. The growth of technology can be seen as producing consequences for all the groups we have considered, adding yet another division to an interest-based analysis.

Marx believed that inherent in the capitalist system were the seeds of its own destruction. Technological change initiated and used by industrialists in pursuit of profit would lead first to the impoverishment and eventual unemployment of the work force and then to its political combination to fight, as an organized force, for the overthrow of capitalism. Yet this has not happened. As Aron has shown, to the extent that a country is industrialized, to that extent it has an organized blue-collar union movement whose marginal share in the profits at least prevents it from becoming a revolutionary force.[44] In fact, blue-collar workers in America, as in several industrialized countries, have many right-wing attitudes or allegiances.

The onset of automation and the beginnings of cybernation — automatic feedback and control of automatic production — has been thought by some to be leading to the eventual long-run proof of Marx's thesis, which was disproved for the working class in the short run. Since the systems approach does indicate a shift from blue-collar work and farming into white-collar work, the central issues seem to concern the political meaning of two groups: the permanent under-class which exists outside the occupational system, and the white-collar worker's potential "proletarianization" and eventual elimination from work because of *office* automation. Will the poor arise? Will the office be automated so that the secretary and the clerk join the ranks of a swelling army of the unemployed? Will this be the eventual dispossessed army which will bring about the revolution, seize the means of production, and proclaim the rule "from each according to his abilities, to each according to his needs"?

The evidence at present, and for the foreseeable future, does not appear to indicate a revolution by the have-nots nor the dispossession of the middle class.[45] Yet there are potential ways in which significant social change in the long run may lead to a greater share for the have-nots, for example, within a state-managed, semi-capitalist Western society. The issue of vocational dispossession of large segments of the middle-class, white-collar worker indicates the extent to which the office is in fact being automated. Evidence at present, by such writers as Hoos, indicates that downgrading of some jobs is occurring in many rather menial forms of office work. But the extent of the difference between the projected needs of society (especially in service areas) and the present supply of workers indicates a potential set of job *openings* in the future.[46] Another factor which argues against massive dispossession and revolution is the hiring of social-technocratic expertise by the government and the corporations. These consultants will no doubt convince the corporations and the government, should technological unemployment rise too fast, to keep a large work force for political stability and for the preservation of a consumer market with money to spend.

In the future, there is a definite possibility of a growth in the power of the technocratic professions, who could work with the corporations to help keep the mass "happy" through shorter work weeks, more extensive mass media entertainment, etc. The so-called "problem of leisure" would then be of greater concern to the planner than the problem of work. If the presently observable trend in this direction continues, a "negative vision" of a technocratic utopia can be seen. Stanley calls this the "pessimistic vision."[47] We might see the development of a permanent two-class society, made up of the enjoying mass, which would include all those presently poor by government subsidy, and the group of "responsible expert managers." Some authors, such as Brzezinski, even suggest that this is a desirable possibility.[48] The great flaw here is that the managers, given the greed and hunger for power that may well be permanent in human nature and all human governments, may not be trusted to act in the interests of all. Furthermore, a politically uncheckable managed society would probably not be intellectually and creatively a free society. If artistic creation and social criticism truly threatened the status quo, and thus the power of the managers, they would not be allowed. The kind of "leisure" one would be likely to enjoy here has more of the quality of mindless gratification in a totalitarian situation than the pursuit of ultimate values.

On the other hand, a growing trend toward increased citizen participation in government may combine with a growing occupational altruism to unite the poor, the young, and the racial minorities with those segments of occupational groups who are working in their behalf. These groups wish to alter power positions of the present elites in occupational groups, to stop the growth of the military-industrial complex, or to check the rise of technocratic power. But the struggle has just begun, most of the middle class is standing aside, and as we have indicated, the groups who possess the resources and the expertise are far stronger and better organized than those who do not.

The impact of technology on society is illustrated by both the pessimistic vision and the anti-technocratic reaction; both highlight the relationship between technological change and political change, particularly changes in the distribution of power and the rise of new interest groups. Marx believed that the primary political consequence of industrialization and industry change would be the rise of a worker interest group that would act as the vehicle of political change. The workers did arise and organize, but have not primarily changed the system. Instead, the primary consequence to date has been the rise of the "technocrat" interest group as a partner of those who own the means of production. This, incidentally, is as true for the Soviet bloc as for the West, for technocrats have as much, if not more, power if the state owns the means of production. Political reactions to a rise in power by this new interest group and to the complexing of older professions with government power are coming in turn from a new set of altruists and an old set of have-nots. No specific one-to-one correspondence can be discovered between technological change and political action, although the rise to power of the technocratic elite is facilitated by the changes. The eventual future of the poor is thus not predictable by technological projections. The controllers of technological institutions in the future might include the poor, in which case the poor could benefit, or the present power groups, in which case the future is dim indeed for any basic improvement over their present conditions. The politics of the *use* of technological innovations, including social planning, must be distinguished from the growth of technology itself.

CONFLICTS OF INTEREST: THE BASIC QUESTIONS

An interest-based approach allows an analysis of occupational and professional group actions which goes beyond description. The *why* of the actions is the basic issue. In this chapter, a series of questions were asked which will be repeated in each succeeding chapter on specific occupational areas. We may review them as a summary of the interest-based approach.

First, there is the concept of occupational consciousness. To what degree is the group organized and fighting in its own interest as a group? To what extent is it benefiting or being deprived in the present division of labor? What consequences does its struggle (or lack of it) have for the social system? And what positions do the government, and the most powerful non-government groups, take in relation to such self-interest struggles on the part of given occupational and professional groups?

Second, how does the group advance its interests politically and, in particular, what occupational ideologies does it use to gain support for its position among related occupations, the clientele, the government, and the public? Ideologies have histories of use, and the history of proponent-target group relations must be ascertained for each area. If ideologies increased, to what degree are they in line with or totally divergent from reality? The reasons for acceptance or rejection of a group's ideology may tell us much about the trend of the group power in the future, the degree to which it can influence its own fate.

Third, what are the consequences for the overall public interest of the gaining or holding of power by limited professional groups, by institutional complexes such as the military-industrial complex, or by financially powerful groups of other types? How may the military-industrial complex be seen as an "occupational complex" and what is the role of government in the perpetuation of such complexes? In the case of the growth of technology, who are the technological experts in each given field of work and how are they functioning with respect to private interest groups and government planning; that is, who benefits from the expert advice and who may not? How does this technocratic type of power vary from one type of political system to another? And who opposes the strong occupational and professional interest groups and the technocrats? What is the reaction of the middle class and the poor in accepting or rejecting attempts by individual occupations, complexes, or technocrats to gain even more power, in each field of work?

Fourth, who is fighting for the have-nots within each major occupational field, and what are the overall have-not fields doing for themselves? In particular, what is the relationship between occupational altruism — a segment of an occupational or professional group working in behalf of have-nots — and the actions of the have-nots themselves? What are the differences between the manifest, overt functions and altruistic actions and the unnoticed, latent, long-term consequences?

Finally, what are the self-interest consequences for the different work groups in the society of long-term, broad, overall processes of social development and change, especially the growth of technology in both the physical and the social science meaning of the term? To what extent are broader processes helping or hindering the advance of the interests of given occupational and professional groups? In this area, as in all the areas considered in an interest-based analysis, we ask of every situation: Who benefits? We ask of every change: Who brings it about? Action by occupational groups, in their own interest, is a basic process and its explanation a task of importance to the overall analysis.

PART TWO

OCCUPATIONAL FIELDS

CHAPTER FIVE

THE HEALTH FIELD

A person's health, or a nation's, is an almost priceless asset. But it is usually a most vulnerable area. Thus it should not be surprising that the group of professions and occupations whose work deals with the preservation and restoration of health should have a long history, that elaborate training and initiation experiences abound, that the division of labor is complex, and that struggles for power within the field, or between the field and segments of the society, are of basic sociological importance. Rather than concerning ourselves with physicians alone, the health *field* will be the unit for study. Only in this way can we understand the relationships between interprofessional struggles (doctors versus nurses, the AMA versus radical activists) and struggles with the community ("doctor power," hospital worker's strikes, citizen participation in health planning). The historical, biographical, functional, and conflict-of-interest viewpoints will allow a general approach to the major issues of the field.

HISTORICAL PERSPECTIVES ON THE HEALTH FIELD

Ancient Egypt had physicians. They practiced the ritualistic, priestly medicine that has been associated with many primitive tribes; the major difference seems to have been the greater organization of the profession, with temples of healing.[1] The hieroglyphics of physician's activities and the bas-reliefs in the temples indicate that auxiliary personnel — aides or students — were present at operations such as trephination of the skull.[2] The birth of medicine as an observational science appears to have been at about the time of Hippocrates (460–377).[3] Primarily noted as the framer of the first major medical ethical code, he is considered more important by medical historians for his accurate clinical observations, and for his teachings on the importance of careful recording of and non-intervention without good reason in the natural processes of the patient. The "Hippocratic school" which he founded had its impact on Roman society and thus on the Roman empire.[4]

If the contribution of the Greeks was the importance of observation, the Romans used their organizational genius in the field of health as in other areas. The first hospitals, with health workers and patients gathered together, date from this time (if we do not count the Egyptian or Greek temples). The Romans were responsible for the first great organized works of public health and safety: the aqueducts with continuous fresh water, the sewerage systems which are still in use in modern Rome, the laws on public health, military medicine, and quarantine.[5] The use of field personnel — "medics" — in the conquest of other nations was a development of the Romans, who discovered that a healthy army and nation was a militarily strong one. The public health of Imperial Rome disintegrated, however, with the fall from power of the Roman state and it was only at the time of the Industrial Revolution that such efforts would be made again.

MIDDLE AGES, RENAISSANCE, AND REFORMATION

The medieval era, as a historical period, was long and complex, but the role of the Catholic Church predominated in medicine as it did in law and theology. The medical schools, as Rashdall illustrates, were one of the three higher or graduate facilities in a university system where the Church controlled all.[6] Charlemagne (742–814) established medical schools at every cathedral, after the model of the Egyptian and Greek temples, as the Eastern branch of the Church had done a century or so earlier in the area of Constantinople.[7] At the time of Charlemagne and for the next two centuries, Arabian medicine arose, following the establishment of the Moslem empire. The early years here were concerned with copying the work of the Egyptians, the Greeks, and the Romans, but at the end of the golden age of classic Arabian culture, in the early Middle Ages of the Christian world, there were great clinicians on the Hippocratic model, such as Rhazes and Avicenna.[8] Thus the body of clinical observations and essentially unscientific theories which constituted the medieval texts on medicine were international, with Egyptian, Greek, Roman, and Arabian origins.

During the period 1200–1500 the great medieval medical schools trained their graduates at such centers at Montpellier, Salerno, Paris, and Padua.[9] The construction of a medical *profession*, based on university training, dates from this period, but the growth of medical *science* has not begun at all, in our sense of the term. This was due in large part to the influence of the Church, which viewed the body, and the healing arts, as sacred, and viewed all dealings with the sacred as under direct theological, scholastic Church rule. As Copeman summarizes, to the Church of the Middle Ages "disease is a function of the wrath of God, healing medicines are the function of His mercy, and the physician is His instrument." [10]

Not surprisingly, therefore, the origin of science in general and the rise of scientific approaches in medicine date from the Renaissance. Copernicus and Vesalius (the founder of modern anatomy) were exact Renaissance contemporaries, and the time of the Reformation was the age of Harvey, whose discovery of the path of the circulation of blood in the human body founded the modern science of physiology. As Copeman shows, the formation of the English and Scottish medical profession — in its tripartite form of physicians, surgeons, and apothecaries — dates from Tudor England. The College of Physicians (1518) dates from this time. In the succeeding century, the Age of Enlightenment in England and on the Continent became the age of the gentleman scientist and led to the foundation of international organizations such as the Royal Academy of Science in England.

THE AMERICAN CASE

During these scientific beginnings of medicine, the European powers were engaged in colonization, and thus the history of the health field becomes complex, divided by nationality and by differences between the Old World and the New. In Puritan Massachusetts, as in most of the colonies of England and other powers of the time, the first health professionals were clergymen, who trained in European medical schools before leaving for the New World.[11] The growth of the colonial population brought with it the development of an indigenous medical profession, one in which new practitioners combined apprenticeship experience in the colonies with travel back to Europe and England for formal training. Thus in colonial America there were men experienced in the training of the time, but there were not, nor would there be for some time, American medical schools. In spite of this, and in the face of a massive shortage of trained or even partly trained health professionals, the American medical profession passed a series of extremely restrictive and unrealistic licensing laws on the practice of medicine. From the start, they were both unenforced and unenforceable, but their existence and the high fees charged by the regular practitioners in the late 1700s and early 1800s identified the medical profession, in the minds of the mass, with the cultured, gentlemanly elite which founded the nation but which was beginning to lose political power as more and more American citizens obtained the vote.[12]

Jacksonian America, the time when mass democratic ideology, if not the masses, ruled the nation, was a difficult period for the medical profession.[13] It was a time of opportunity for the nonorthodox health practitioners, such as the Thompsonian herbalists or "botanic doctors," who identified with the poor. Kett documents the ways in which political action by these groups, with the support of the populace, led to the repeal of the law limiting the practice of medicine to orthodox practitioners.[14] As a counter-reaction to this mass anti-professional and anti-elite action, the orthodox physicians formed a protective political association, the American Medical Association. It would have the roles of setting up an informal licensing procedure, setting up standards of practice, and protecting the medical profession against further political actions.[15] At the time of Jackson, America was in a period of major economic growth and social change.

We can look at the American medical profession in the Jacksonian era in three geographical regions: the urban North, the plantation South, and the frontier West. In the urban North, as Calhoun shows, the major efforts of the profession were in the construction of local and state "academies of medicine" which would be, and in fact still are, the building blocks of the American Medical Association.[16] Problems of membership, qualification, and the handling of deviant fellow physicians were acute; strict discipline was essentially unenforceable because there was no set procedure for getting medical training, nor much scientific knowledge available. In the South, the slave economy created a great demand for physicians. As Shryock states:

> The young Southern physician found in slavery a means to an early start; while at the same time, the slaves found in the system a sort of health insurance. Hence emancipation injured the practice of many doctors, and the health of many ex-slaves, since the former could not afford to attend a poor Negro, once he had become "nobody's nigger but his own."[17]

In the frontier West, the physician was lonely, if he was present at all. The majority of the folk did their own doctoring and the mortality rate (with or without physicians) was high. Two items symbolize this form of practice: the medical saddlebag for the horsebound practitioner and Dr. George Goodfellow's excellent medical articles on the surgery of gunshot wounds, written from his office in Tombstone, Arizona.[18]

The Industrial Revolution, and the onset of the labor-management social conflict, had definite repercussions in the health field. Out of social reform movements and mass action at the turn of the century, the role of government in public health, in welfare legislation, and health insurance was increased from next to nothing in the late 1800s to the major role it played during and after World War II. Modern scientific medicine, and the present relationship between medical education in universities and the practitioner mass, can be dated by three events in the period from 1880 to 1910: the foundation of Johns Hopkins Medical School with a strictly post-college student body and European-trained professors, the onset of efficient and realistic state licensing on medical practice with boards of examining physicians, and the Flexner report on medical education of 1910, which resulted in the eventual abolition of "Class B" and "Class C" medical schools, most of which were little more than diploma mills.[19] We are presently in a simultaneous series of new revolutions: the rise of public health and psychiatry, the rise in bureaucratization and technology in the health field, the rise in government involvement in health insurance, and the rise of citizen activism in the health planning area. These recent trends are still very much with us, and will be considered in the rest of the chapter.

Several major themes are suggested by this brief review. First, the existence of an occupational group — the medical profession — can be seen to antedate the foundation of medical *science* by three thousand, one thousand, or five hundred years, depending on whether one counts from ancient Egypt, from Hippocrates, or from the foundation of the medieval medical schools such as Montpellier. This is a basic point — the mandate of a profession is based on the expertise which it can successfully *claim* in a society, regardless of whether the expertise is real or not in terms of some outside or objective criterion. Second, the history of the health field demonstrates that conditions of practice cannot be understood outside of the historical context, and that therefore the division of labor and conflicts of the present must not be taken as universal for all times and places. Third, opportunities for professional development are related to the achievements and disasters of each period, such as public health in Imperial Rome, anatomy and physiology in the Renaissance and Reformation, and surgery in wartime and the frontier West. Finally, although the history of the health field has mainly been written by physicians and thus centers on this group, in all periods the power of the state, the reaction of the community, and the auxiliary health professions have also played a role in developments. Temples of healing were found in Egypt, Greece, and Rome, as well as in the Middle Ages, and then as now most of the staff were not physicians. Conflicts between the profession and the society are a part of history. Especially now are we seeing a reassertion of the conflict between physicians and other groups — the government, the citizenry, the other health workers — which have been seen before in similar though not identical ways. The health field is not unique here. As part of history, it naturally reflects its main themes.

BECOMING A HEALER: THE CAREER EXPERIENCE

A biographical approach to the health field will necessarily need to consider at least four issues: the special idealism which is said to be part of the world view of health professionals (and its fate), the factors which lead to choices to enter the field, the structure and experience of the careers themselves, and the situational learning process which occurs as the groups confront each other in the health service settings.

THE IDEALISM ISSUE

The layman's view of the work of the health professions and the actual experience of the day-to-day work form a contrast of major proportions. Since all health workers start out as laymen, they must undergo a set of conversion experiences, a set of "rites of passage." In most cases these are gradual, not immediate and direct. As Becker, Geer, Hughes, and Strauss have described in the case of the physician in medical school, health workers must develop a routine attitude toward events that laymen endow with mystery and fear: death becomes a clinical puzzle or a problem of medical and legal responsibility.[20] The early idealism of the incoming student must be supplanted by a practical, technical attitude toward getting the work done.[21] And, as studies of both doctors and nurses in training report, the patient himself is a partial cause for the faltering of the early idealism, as he does not seem either as responsive to advice or as grateful for service as the student had originally expected.[22] In spite of this, much research indicates that there remains a thread of idealism of a more sophisticated sort:

> Medical students enter medical school openly idealistic about the practice of medicine and the medical profession. They do not lose this idealistic long-range perspective but realistically develop a "cynical" concern with the day-to-day details of getting through medical school. As they approach the end of school they again openly exhibit an idealistic concern with problems of practice.[23]

CHOICE OF CAREER

Student choice of a health profession appears to be closely related to family experience (especially to whether a parent or relative is in the chosen profession), to socioeconomic status (considering the expense of training), and to ability in the basic sciences required for entrance into training programs. Rogloff found that the physician-parent was a major factor for a medical student's choice; Thielens found a relative in the profession for about 50 per cent of the students in an Eastern medical school.[24] However, early aspiration by the sons of the working class and even rural youth is not always unrealistic, for a democratization of the social class origins of physicians is seen over the last fifty years by Adams.[25] At least a third have come from homes of average or less-than-average income in recent years. Still, the need for a college degree in American medical training, as a virtual prerequisite, eliminates a sizable segment of the poor and the lower middle class from even considering this profession.

For nursing, the recruiting pattern and the nature of the individual choice vary according to the type of program. The hospital-based programs — 80 per cent of all nurses are trained by this pathway — tend to recruit from the lower middle class; the newer and higher-status college programs from the middle and upper middle class. The generational pattern is seen here as with physicians, with a sizable proportion of nurses being the daughters of nurses or having a nurse somewhere in the family.[26] Men are beginning to enter nursing in small numbers, but Mannino's study indicates that they do so primarily because they intend to become administrators in the field.[27] Dentistry, according to Quarantelli as well as Sherlock and Cohen, could provide an example of a "second-choice" medical career, with medical school not chosen because of its longer training period, its greater expense, and the stiffer competition for places.[28] On the other hand, the usual idealistic motivations are given by dental students, and a specially strong one — desire for autonomy — is singled out by More and Kohn in their interviews.[29] Once in school or in practicc, early misgivings about dentistry seem to be denied by the students.[30]

Little research has been done to date on why people choose to become X-ray technicians, lab workers, or such, or on why those who are in the large and greatly underpaid work force of hospitals (laundry, housekeeping, janitorial, cafeteria, etc.) choose their jobs. Impressionistically, based on the author's work experience in hospitals, the technical workers are only mildly committed to their jobs, which they received through short-term training programs, and the desperately poor — usually the black in major cities — are often the source of the hospital labor force, as the salaries are so far below those for almost any other kind of hard physical labor with long hours. In recent years, the hospital work forces, especially at the lower levels, are becoming unionized, and for the first time reward, rather than lack of other opportunities, may enter the choice for those at the bottom of the health field. In general, therefore, there is a hierarchy of choices which can be made in entering the health field, from doctor to laundry worker, and social class position, health-related family experience, and personal educational and financial resources are much more important in the choice than idealism alone. The lower the level of entry, the less the choice, and the fewer the opportunities resulting from the choice.

CAREER PATHWAYS: THE PHYSICIAN

The career experience in the different health professions varies by group in ways that are similar to the hierarchy of choices available at the time of entry. The greatest information available concerns the most complex set of career pathways — those of the physician. We can begin by tracing the different choice points of the physician's career and the student or physician's attitudes toward them, and then consider comparatively the career patterns and experiences open to nurses, dentists, and other health workers.

The years of medical school have been extensively considered in the classic study of Becker, Geer, Hughes, and Strauss, *Boys in White*.[31] In the typical medical school pattern, the first two years are pre-clinical, essentially academic instruction in basic medical sciences, and the last two are clinical instruction in the hospital setting. Alternative plans have been constructed in recent years, such as the Case-Western Reserve plan which assigns a medical student to a family in his freshman year, with the student assuming more responsibility for care each year. But reforms of the old pre-clinical and clinical separation seem to be limited to the elite medical schools, and even here they do not reverse the pattern, but rather allow more early clinical experience.[32]

From their entry as a class in medical school, the students form a "community of fate," which is destined to share essentially the same general goal and a set of critical experiences, risks, and dangers.[33] One early experience in medical school is the impact on the student of the information and knowledge explosion in medicine; as they soon put it, "You can't know it all." In fact, recent revisions of the policy of education at some medical schools stress this officially for students, urging them to develop the skills of question-asking and researching for themselves, rather than attempting to ascertain what the faculty wants as was common at the time the Becker group did their study.[34]

An experience parallel to the sobering confrontation with medical literature, with its extensiveness and yet massive incompleteness, characterizes the clinical years in medical school. Fox notes that the need to cope with ambiguous reality is a basic aspect of clinical experience, as the patients' distresses often do not follow the textbook description.[35] The high value which is soon placed on direct clinical experience by students is a direct consequence of their confrontation with the reality of the patient and his complex and sometimes undiagnosable ailments. The students are now at the bottom of the hospital staff totem pole, with a lot of busy work to do, and no real legal right to practice medicine, such as even the nurse in the ward possesses. They cope with the work and the need for experience by developing a mild form of restriction of production and by actions designed to help educate each other:

> Students set work norms only in situations where the faculty does not set a qualitatively defined goal, and where limitation of work will not reduce the amount of learning of facts and procedures the students think necessary for practice. Students cooperate to help their fellows avoid making a bad impression on the faculty by doing their work for them on the ward in emergencies and help each other acquire clinical experience by trading off patients or opportunities to perform therapeutic procedures.[36]

The last two years allow the student an exposure to the different specialty areas within medicine. The stress in schools on research and specialization, as well as the student's natural desire to master at least one area in medicine, lead to an overwhelming preference for specialization before the student has even entered internship. Specializations almost always pay much better than general practice, under much more favorable working conditions. Other rewards among the considerations weighed by students when choosing a specialty include the nature and quality of relations with the patients, the opportunity to exercise medical responsibility, and the degree of intellectual breadth in the specialty area. Limiting factors, or general issues also mentioned by students as relevant to specialty choice, may involve the need for a particular kind of personality (psychiatry, obstetrics), an especially long residency (surgery), or the need to live in a large city (for some "micro-specialities" there will not be enough patients outside of a large urban area).

Of critical importance in making decisions are the discussions which students have with their peers; the medical fraternities provide greater access to information at some schools. Also important in decisions are the number and nature of medical contacts (the specialty of father or relatives in medicine) or the specialty opportunities in the region where the young doctor will want to live.[38] In all of these considerations there is a mix between stereotypes of specialties and the actual nature of the work, with some students in possession of more facts and connections than others in this respect. Behind the choice to specialize at all is again the socioeconomic factor. For each additional year of post-medical school training, the student must have so much more financial backing. Although loans are now possible, it is still true to some degree that those in the elite schools, the upper social class brackets, and those with diligent, non-pregnant working wives become the specialists, and the less well-backed students, those from the less-well-known medical schools, and those with a poorer academic record in medical school become the general practitioners for the society. There is presently a new trend toward a community-oriented medical altruism on the part of students of elite medical schools, which sometimes leads them to adopt general practice, but this trend is too new for predictions, and the vast majority of present medical students (over 97 per cent nationwide) are going into specialty practice.[39]

Besides deciding the nature and place of internship, American medical students must also decide the time of their service in the armed forces. A total doctor draft has been in effect since World War II, and each doctor must decide when to serve (before or after specialty training), rather than whether or not to serve. The compulsory nature of this service, combined with the general anti-war sentiment of many young medical students, is leading to career uncertainty and anti-war activism on a scale seldom seen in past years.

INTERNSHIP AND RESIDENCY

The internship year is transitional in modern American medical training and is in many ways somewhat outdated, as its original purpose was to give the student the kind of clinical experience he now usually gets in the last two years of medical school. But legal responsibility and legal status are now his, and he supervises (and often learns from) the medical students and nurses under him and works for the residents and staff who in turn observe him and train him. The *type* of internship, especially the type of hospital at which it is experienced, is critical to the future prospects of the physician, especially if he wishes to become a member of the university medical school professorial elite. If so, as Miller observes,

> . . . for academic careers, the route begins with the obtaining of a university-affiliated internship and continues through the "right" residency to teaching and research positions at medical schools and teaching hospitals.[40]

One such elite internship, during the middle third of the twentieth century, was the Harvard Medical Service at Boston City Hospital. As Miller notes,

> From the Harvard Medical Unit (at BCH) have come twenty-eight deans of medical schools and numerous chairmen of departments at the "name" schools such as California, Illinois, Western Reserve, and Wisconsin. Many executives and members of the Association of American Physicians, the American Society for Clinical Investigation, and other select societies of academic medicine are also alumni of the Harvard Medical Unit.[41]

In general, university-related hospitals — those with close ties to medical schools in which teaching occurs and medical students and professors are regularly present — are preferred for internship and residency. They give the student the maximum number of options: he may go into research and teaching, using the internship as a moratorium or time for further study; he may stay on to get an excellent training for specialty practice in the community, with rights to use the hospital in later years; or he may try out several interesting combinations of the above. But in any case, a prestigious internship is prestigious not because of the amount and quality of the work involved (Miller suggests that elite internships may in fact involve more drudge work than those less desired) but because the young physician is in a place with the correct and desirable sponsorship lines to residencies and future career opportunities.[42] The less capable students, or those who choose general practice, will be more likely to choose a general or a public hospital and leave this hospital after the one-year minimum requirement of most states.

Residency, or post-internship specialty training in the hospital, takes from two to four years, depending on the specialty, and is increasingly common. All the strings of personal influence and professorial prestige are pulled to get young protégés into the right hospital at the right time. Since there is a massive doctor shortage in the nation, the second-rank hospitals, and most public hospitals, suburban community hospitals, and proprietary (profit-making) hospitals must often do without interns or import foreign physicians who are badly needed in their own country. Mumford, in her recent study, indicates that another reason why students of the elite schools avoid the community hospital for internship and residency is not because of poor working conditions — conditions are often better than at university hospitals — but because of the nature of the medical training offered. The student will get more first-hand experience, but he will not get it under the supervision of residents, full-time hospital staff, or teachers, and thus it may be less valuable to him in the long run.[43]

The "minority" types of specialization, both having direct relationship to recent trends in the medical profession, are those in psychiatry and public health. The early years of training in psychiatry demand of an individual the redefinition of the meaning of his interpersonal experience, or as Blum and Rosenberg put it, the professionalization of social interaction.[44] The career in individual psychotherapy or in community psychiatry is quite different from that of the non-psychiatric physician and demands adjustment to relations with a whole set of health professionals — social workers, clinical psychologists, psychiatric nurses — that constitute almost an alternate service world, a world in which the psychiatrist must demonstrate his expertise with considerably more difficulty and much less legal definition than that which separates the surgeon from his scrub nurse. The public health field — a specialty which Back, Coker, Donnelly, and Phillips indicate is often chosen by default or as a rechoice after experience elsewhere — is another specialty with a career pattern deviant from the standard career structure of medicine.[45] Since both groups work in the community or relate to the layman in ways not traditional for the doctor-patient relationship, and since both groups are interested in widening their mandate in the community, they are increasingly involved in conflict situations as specialties in a way that is not characteristic of the other groups. In many ways, the specialty training in these fields is, in fact as well as in theory, training in the handling of conflict situations.

THE LATER YEARS

The medical career in its middle years varies according to social class membership, ethnic or racial group membership, and colleague contact networks. The private practitioner from an elite residency will have a far easier time getting "use rights" at the better hospitals in a community. However, most hospitals in America allow community practitioners access on grounds that are in most cases a mixture of two criteria: social characteristics the hospital feels are desirable (race and religion especially) and the quality of medical training. The first kind of criteria is often more important than the second. Referrals of patients also often follow lines of friendship and social group membership, as Hall pointed out many years ago.[46] As a partial defense against this somewhat irrational system, and for reasons we will go into later involving interest-based conflicts, there is developing a trend for groups of specialists to practice together, preferring group security as well as pooling talents. Younger private practitioners appear to prefer this method.

The twilight years of the physician's career have not been well studied, but from older doctors in medical families this kind of advice is sometimes given informally: "You'll have it hard at first, then you must make hay while the sun shines, because as you get older it will get harder to work those long hours."[47] Again, the safety of some form of group practice and some form of pension plan or the position of professor on a tenured faculty, may look somewhat different to the practitioner in his fifties and sixties than it does to one in his thirties and forties.

In general, the medical career plan is a classical model in the American understanding of the professions. From the point of view of the medical student and young intern, the most talented and privileged have the greatest number of options and thus the best prospects. The factors influencing choice at entry and decisions along the way are increasingly becoming part of the public domain, especially since the television medical series and medical soap operas have become a part of mass experience. In fact, even the interns in real hospitals can be found kidding each other on their "Ben Casey" or "Dr. Kildare" manners. This is simply one index of the great preoccupation of people in complex Western societies, or perhaps people everywhere, with their health and thus with those who bear the central occupational responsibility in the health field.

THE NURSING CAREER EXPERIENCE

The question of career commitment, which is not a problem for a physician because of the rewards for perseverance, is central for the nurse.

The high turnover rates of nurses on hospital settings (from 40 to 70 per cent in most hospitals on a yearly basis) are a consequence of at least two commitment-related issues: the role of marriage in the nursing career and the relation between the image of nursing presented to students and the actualities of work.[48] The commitment problem is highlighted by a study of Strauss' group on two versions of the Florence Nightingale legend, one used in a hospital school of nursing and one in a university-based program.[49] Neither gave a historically accurate picture of Florence Nightingale; the hospital program version stressed the need for humility and submissiveness toward staff physicians and the need to provide practical care, whereas the university program pictured Miss Nightingale as a sort of modern, crusading, administratively oriented professional nurse, years ahead of her time. The problem of commitment is obvious here: Why should students already in nursing schools need inspirational ideologies about their profession unless there are doubts in the minds of both the students and the practitioners about the value and nature of the career experience? In addition, the marriage issue is critical, as surveys of the field indicate that the pattern of interruption for marriage and children seen with female schoolteachers is not the main pattern for nurses, but rather marriage and *desertion* of the career.[50]

The question of ideals as opposed to reality must be considered in terms of the two main settings for nursing training: hospital-based programs and the university. The contrast between an apprenticeship training in hospital work (with some formal courses) and formal academic training by professors of nursing is intensified by the contrast in social origins of the two groups: most hospital nurses are from working-class backgrounds; most college nurses from the middle class.[51] The academic programs aim at the creation of "nursing administrators" and stress social science jargon, whereas the hospital-based programs are more practically oriented. In some cases, when university-trained student nurses are placed in hospitals for "clinical experience," the emnity between the two groups becomes open, especially the resentment of the hospital nurses. The professors of nursing are concerned that the students not become disillusioned by the nature of nursing work in some settings, and the hospital nurses are angry and suspicious of changes in the profession which would give the new administrative jobs to young college nurses instead of those with hospital backgrounds and years of experience. And in fact, the hospital nurses and those with a working-class background appear to be able to stand the stress and strain, the long hours, and the frustrations better than the college nurses, who appear to have higher rates of dropout from the profession. Krueger thinks there may in fact be two groups of nurses in training: a group of "genteel" girls of middle-class background and a group of girls who are "hell-raisers" without this personal style, but with more capacity for stress.[52]

Both types of nurses are finding that the number of auxiliary personnel in the hospital is growing, and their own job is becoming the low-level administration of work that they no longer have to do themselves, such as emptying bedpans, washing patients, or scrubbing floors. In many settings they now carry out medical procedures formerly reserved for doctors.[53] But what they may or may not do, in the case of medical procedures, is not under their command. The primary experience of the nurse in the health field is one of legally defined marginality, blocked upward mobility in the health hierarchy, and institutionalized second-class citizenry. It is perhaps this continual experience of second-class status that is behind the strong drive toward professional organization and "nurse power," and the low present level of commitment of many nurses to their profession and settings in which it is practiced.

LIMITED, MARGINAL, AND DEVIANT CAREERS IN HEALTH

Following Wardwell's distinction, we may distinguish between health careers that involve practice limited to part of the human body (dentistry, podiatry, optometry) which are not specific specialties of the American medical profession, and careers that are essentially peripheral in some way to standard areas (chiropractors, osteopaths), or deviant in terms of scientific understandings of the therapeutic process (faith healers, quacks, Christian Science practitioners).[54] In the case of "limited" practitioners, the career resembles that of the medical profession, with shorter training periods and lower rewards, with the exception of dentists, who approach and sometimes surpass the earnings of general practitioners. The marginal career — that of the chiropractor or the osteopath, for example — is similar in experience to that of the physician in most external respects, especially the doctor-patient relationship, and in the rural regions of the nation such practitioners are often the only ones with any medical training at all. In marginal health professions of this type, much argument exists in the group as to whether they should join the medical profession in an auxiliary role, under supervision, or remain independent with less official status and more real independence. Again, the near monopoly of services which some osteopaths have in some regions, including owning their own hospitals, make a nurse-type relation to medicine somewhat improbable.[55]

The career of the quack, faith healer, or similar practitioners is less well defined, often depending on a "call" as much as any formal initiation of a training period or defined stages of career development. Although one might expect it, there is apparently little persecution or prosecution of such individuals by organized medicine, which is not threatened by them. In the case of religion-related movements such as Christian Science, the group can and does claim freedom of religion as protection for practice. In addition, the Christian Science practitioner and others who use essentially a form of psychosomatic medicine and therapy are not looked on with quite the same ferocity since the onset of the psychiatric revolution. This does not apply, however, to those who have a mail-order "Doctor of Psychology" degree; the clinical psychologists trained by universities are greatly threatened by this type of practice and are attempting to stop it. But practice involving the mind and the emotions is not licensable, nor in fact as policeable as practice involving "intervention" in the human body, although of course psychological intervention in fact can cause consequences which are as severe.

Career experiences in health are almost infinitely variable, but the principles are in general the same ones relevant to all other careers. The differences relate more to position within the division of labor and within the power structure of the present health field than to the actual work done with respect to patients. In most cases, the health workers do not work alone, but in some form of cooperative relationship which requires sharing the work setting. Although each of the groups has been considered in isolation, in fact the career experiences intertwine, and important experience is cross-occupational; it is to this kind of experience that we now turn.

SITUATIONAL LEARNING: HEALTH WORK AS A COOPERATIVE ENDEAVOR

A nurse can put a medical student in his place in many ways. The easiest is simply to tell the patient that that fellow who is puncturing his vein is not a doctor at all, just a student, and pointedly refer to him as Mr. Jones at every opportunity. On the other hand, a nurse who continued to do this would soon find that the student had complained to the training supervisor for the ward and that this physician had raised a commotion with the nurse in charge of nursing at the hospital. As Miller notes, the process of work in a hospital setting involves exchanges of favors and bargaining between the groups, and is essentially a political process.[56] Strauss, et al., found the same kind of bargaining around a simple set of rules; they called this the "negotiated order of the hospital."[57] The conflict between getting the work done and the formal rules always leads to a divergence between official policy and reality, and the career experience of individuals in the health field is in large part learning what corners can be cut and what rules are truly breakable.

Conflict is inevitable when those with *de facto* power do not have *de jure* authority, and this situation is common in the health field. This experience is also gained out in the community, when the practitioner may have to bargain with laymen in situations that simply cannot be interpreted in narrow "medical" terms, yet have direct consequences for health. Each setting has a set of unwritten rules, and the new workers must "learn the ropes," learning from underlings and patients as well as from superiors.[58] Situational learning, the rounding out of the experience of the healer, is an ongoing process for all workers, and each solution will contain some new elements. Perhaps it is the novelty of each treatment problem, rather than each disease, which gives the field its continuing fascination for practitioners, and for social scientists as well.

DIVISION OF LABOR IN THE HEALTH FIELD

No matter how complex, the health field has a single obvious goal — the restoration of health to those who have lost it and the maintenance of health in those who are presently functioning well. Profit and payment issues aside, the goals of the health occupations are humanitarian, and the disagreements in many cases are over means of reaching the goal rather than the goal itself.

Division of labor in the health field can be understood in terms of four related sets of phenomena: *the occupational group* — who the health personnel are and what their skills and actions consist of; *the state of technological development* — the tools and knowledge available for service work at a given time; *the organization of services* — how the groups are distributed across the map, in what types of arrangement; and the *service program activities* — who gets what kind of help from whom, and how it is paid for.

In order to understand even briefly the nature of the division of labor in occupational terms, it will be necessary to consider the state of science and technology used by these occupations, the way they operate in health settings, and the services they provide for the community. It is not possible to describe the field as static, for a major aspect of the American system is the progressive changes in the principles under which the division of labor itself is accomplished. Indeed, it is not possible to speak, except in a very abstract sense, of a single health *system*, which is why the term "health field" is used instead. By considering the four division-of-labor problems in the United States, and then comparatively for the Soviet Union, Britain, Japan, and the developing nations, we might begin to see what principles are generally found to be true of divisions of labor in the health field.

OCCUPATIONAL BOUNDARIES IN THE DIVISION OF LABOR

The division of labor by occupational groups has a history of increasing complexity and specialization, with a decreasing proportion of the occupational field being composed of physicians (from three out of five health workers in 1900 to about one out of ten today). The present complexity of the health field is illustrated by the number of health work groups in 1965. There are at least twenty occupational groups with a significant function to perform in the health field. Of these, the three largest groups are physicians, nurses, and dentists.[59] Although physicians are still more numerous than most occupational groups in the health field, their percentage of *all* health workers (not including the maintenance staffs of hospitals) is diminishing on a yearly basis.[60] This may have major implications for their functional power, given the present trends toward occupational self-interest action and cross-occupational combinations by other health groups, especially nurses. In general, the health occupations are one of the largest and fastest growing groups in the entire society and as such must receive extended attention.[61]

The reasons for specialization in the health area are multiple in origin. In the oldest and largest groups, specialization has proceeded the farthest. The growth of technology and medical knowledge, as well as the increasing complexity of the bureaucratic health settings in which health work is increasingly carried out, are leading to the demand for specialized expertise. The increase in community-oriented programs calls for a greater variety of administrative, technocratic, social-planning skills, a controversial issue to the established power hierarchies in the health field, for although these positions entail power and responsibility, as in the role of hospital administration, for example, in many cases they do not require medical training. The onset of the psychiatric or mental health revolution in the last three decades has led to a major set of specializations in these areas, which complement the new specialties within the general medical profession and the auxiliary groups.

SOCIAL CHARACTERISTICS OF HEALTH WORKERS

The division of labor in the health occupations may also be understood in terms of the classic demographic variables: sex, race, ethnic group, birthplace, and social class standing of parents. In each case a distinction can be made between the medical profession and the auxiliary professions: the female sex is heavily represented in the auxiliary professions but is a distinct minority in medicine; blacks are a minority in medicine, a larger minority in nursing, and are predominant in hospital jobs of an unskilled nature. The quotas on certain ethnic groups are not as extensive as they once were, but evidence is incomplete at present to indicate that these have disappeared. In any case, ethnic and religious minority representation is higher in the auxiliary groups than in medicine. Because of the shortage of physicians, however, the percentage of foreign-trained practitioners has risen in the last decade; this is also true for the other ranks.

In terms of socioeconomic status, as we noted earlier in the consideration of career patterns in health, the length of training in the United

States combined with the minimal amount of scholarship money and the need to attend four years of college before medical school, leads to a stratification by social status of parents, with the vast majority of physicians coming from the upper class and the upper middle class, the nurses and other auxiliary professions from the lower middle class, and the hospital workers from the ranks of the poor. In general, in the health field in the United States, social marginality characterizes the bottom rung occupations, with each step upward represented by groups which possess, as a group, more of the characteristic WASP traits.[62] Since Hughes pointed out this image of the ideal physician, there has been an upswing in minority representation in medicine, and now even the growth of a non-segregated medical training system. But it is still true that the WASP is more likely to have the resources to pursue a medical career than those of most other backgrounds, unless, as for the Jewish group, it is of overwhelming cultural importance as an occupational identity in a group which possesses WASP educational and financial resources.

THE ROLE OF TECHNOLOGY

The degree of technological development in the health field has a direct impact on the nature of the work to be done. In some cases — the myriad newer health occupations such as audiometrist (hearing tester), medical electronics technician, X-ray technician — the skill is precisely the ability to use a new piece of technology. In this sense, the proliferation of new occupations in health is a consequence of the rising use of technology by the central practitioner — the physician — in situations where he either does not want to or cannot operate the machinery. It is important to note that the degree of supervision (as opposed to independent operation of the equipment) in the newer occupations is usually in direct relation to the degree to which the process is critical to the maintenance of life in crisis situations. For example, in the technology-based medical specialty of radiology, the fluoroscope is a valuable but demanding diagnostic procedure with a radiation hazard if misused and a need for a physician's understanding of internal anatomy and pathology. The process of radiation therapy (an emerging subspecialty) involves such dangerous doses of energy that the work must be supervised by the physician, although the technician can turn on the machine after the patient-machine arrangement has been approved. In most cases, the radiologist allows the technician to handle most of the everyday work of the hospital X-ray department, or office, such as the X-rays of the chest and extremities, the abdomen and skull. The *diagnosis* is the work of the radiologist, in all cases.

This type of responsibility-adjusted division of labor in a medical-technological field exists on most health settings. For example, present arrangements between anesthesiologists (a medical specialty) and nurse anesthetists involve the degree of criticality, with the doctors claiming that nurses don't have the expertise to handle crises, and thus ought not to act alone even though they may know how to use the equipment. But the problem is intensified by a combination of manpower and technological factors. The way for technology-based occupations is opened by the shortage of physicians to supervise the different technical operations, so that in many settings the hospital may have to choose between a nurse anesthetist and none at all. In addition, some of the complex electronic equipment now used to monitor operations, including the anesthesia, need skills possessed by neither the doctor nor the nurse, and thus various engineering personnel are becoming members of the operating team.[63]

A great variety of the new technical developments involve diagnostic or information-getting procedures, or are management-related, such as monitoring the environment and the life signs of a patient in an intensive care unit for heart attack victims, and do not involve active intervention in the patient's life process in a way that could be crisis-producing. Thus all sorts of "measurement," "monitor," and "rehabilitation" occupations are arising without causing responsibility problems, although after a certain number is reached they do cause bureaucratic problems concerning patient time and coordination of services. Since extreme criticality is not involved, such jobs as laboratory technicians, supervisors of machinery, and the new therapists, such as "inhalation therapist," may be open to those with less training than the registered nurse.

Field has suggested that technological development creates a moral demand for its use which then leads to its dispersion throughout the medical field.[64] The moral issue is that if we know that the Z machine can save lives, we have no right to refuse to buy one, pay a Z machine operator, and have a Z unit in the hospital. Field notes that since there is no essential end to the number of machines that can be invented, medical technology is labor-intensive, instead of being somewhat labor-saving as in some fields in industry. But the adoption of much of the new medical technology in a health setting is a cost-benefit analysis problem, and involves a decision on the part of the setting to pay for such technology. Since this technology is expensive, usually only hospitals can pay for it. Sometimes a nation may decide to use its limited resources for the development of manpower (training thousands of physicians and nurses) before spending money on the expensive technology. The United States appears to have chosen the route of extensive technological development, and our health personnel are falling behind previous levels, whereas the Soviet Union has deemphasized spending on technology, leading to a somewhat less sophisticated level of care for most groups, but with far greater coverage in terms of health personnel.[65]

In general, the American occupational structure in health has expanded more in the last decade than any other major industry in terms of numbers at work, but much of this is an increase in the technological backup of a limited number of physicians working in complex hospital settings, rather than an increase in the ratio of practitioners to patients and families. We have seen a technology-based expansion of personnel and high-quality service for some, but not an increase in the general level of service available for the have-nots or the typical middle-class person who is not hospitalized.

ORGANIZATION AND DELIVERY OF SERVICES: THE VARIABLES

The third and fourth aspects of the division of labor in the health field are best considered together: the organization of services and the delivery of these services to those in need. In systems terms, the internal structure of the health field and the relation of the health field to the wider society are the two related areas to consider. The occupational groups and the technological tools are in action on *settings* which have organizational forms, delivering certain kinds of *services* as a consequence of these forms of organization and the skills available. We can understand the division of labor in terms of organization and delivery of services by means of a series of oppositions, which in reality are polar extremes on a series of continuums: urban versus rural practice, solo versus group practice, general versus specialty practice, private general medicine versus public health and mental health, community versus hospital-based practice, local versus state and federal organization of services, practitioner-patient versus third party arrangements, and decentralization versus centralization of services.

Rural Versus Urban Practice. In the United States, the health practitioners are more highly concentrated in urban areas than in rural. More specifically, they are concentrated and practicing in the area between the ghetto and the countryside, rather than in either extreme. Although Peterson's study of general practitioners did not find significant differences in the skills of urban and rural physicians, the low ratio of physicans to population in rural areas leaves the way open for other formal and informal practitioner groups such as osteopaths and chiropractors, who have much more opportunity in these regions.[66] Conversely, most physicians prefer the greater facilities of the city area and the "medical environment," which includes numbers of colleagues.[67]

Solo Versus Group Practice: The Medical Network. Whether the physician practices alone or as a member of a group is an important factor. As Friedson demonstrates, there is a continuum ranging from (1) complete isolation, where the client is in control of the doctor's practice by his ability to leave or choose others at will, to (2) a practice where patients are referred to the practitioner by his colleagues, to (3) solo practice of a group of physicians (general practitioners and specialists) working under one roof and sharing rent and janitorial expenses but not profits, to (4) a medical partnership of a group of physicians with the same specialty, such as pediatrics or radiology, where the profits are shared, to (5) true group practice where a large group of different kinds of specialists practice as an organization and share profits and expenses.[68] The medical network, singled out for detailed description by Hall, is usually informally organized in manners related to these different forms of practice.[69] The patient in most cases unwittingly enters a network that will be limited or extensive depending on the degree and nature of contacts of the physician he first sees. The forms of practitioner work arrangement do make a difference for the typical patient, as the greater the number of skills under one roof, the less he must be shuttled around the community. If he is referred, he may discover that many informal contact and referral networks are ethnic, racial, or religious in nature, so that the client of whatever religion who consults a Catholic general practitioner in the Northeast may very well be referred to a specialist who is also Catholic, and if the patient needs hospitalization, it will be at the Catholic hospital at which both the general practitioner and his specialist colleague have practice arrangements.

The group practice arrangement, by itself, can be a convenience for a group of specialists and a travel convenience for the patient, but it may not necessarily be a monetary saving for him, any more than other arrangements are. Unless group practice is combined with a prepaid medical plan involving the practitioners as well as the patient, such as the Kaiser plan on the West Coast, the practice arrangements are simply a business convenience of the medical profession.[70] The other forms of group practice, less strictly defined, are becoming increasingly common, but prepaid group practice is an important occupational conflict-of-interest issue, and we will treat it in further detail in the final major section of this chapter.

General Practice Versus Specialty Practice. Peterson et al. in their extensive study of general practitioners in North Carolina, used physicians as interviewers and observers to check the actual medical diagnostic techniques of the physicians in community practice.[71] They found an extreme variation from excellent standard technique to haphazard and essentially uninformed practice, but they also found — to their consternation — no correlation between the quality of observed medical technique and either the degree of training and performance in medical school or the observed popularity of the physician. The star performers in diagnostic work were not necessarily either the most popular physicians or the ones with the best formal training and grades in medical school. It appeared that the personality of the physician was a major factor in the size of his practice.[72] This is not surprising, however, as the function of the general practitioner is becoming essentially psychiatric in nature now that serious illness is either prevented through immunization or handled by specialists, who are growing in numbers each year.

Field and Friedson both note that the functional role of the general practitioner as a "referrer" is disappearing as his numbers decrease. Field compares the role to the process of triage on the battlefield, where the field physician decides who should be sent back to fight after first aid, who should be treated in the field hospital, and who should be flown back to a rear area hospital. The general practitioner should theoretically provide this function for all patients in their relation to specialists, but since the number of general practitioners is diminishing yearly, the patient must often decide himself which specialist he needs.[73] Friedson notes that the rising level of education itself may be a factor in this, with the patient more capable of making such a decision than he used to be.[74] But if he guesses wrong, he will still have to pay the bill for an office visit to the wrong specialist.

A new role, that of the "specialist g.p.," is beginning to evolve in the field of "internal medicine," one based on clinical diagnostics. We may be witnessing the transformation of the old general practitioner to the new internal medicine man, and the fall in the percentage of students entering "general practice" must be reinterpreted to observe the per cent going into individual or group practice in community-based internal medicine. For children the pediatrician is performing the role of general practitioner. The disappearance of the general practitioner is critical because of the need for a central repository of data and a home base for each individual, with a person — or a group — who can take professional responsibility for orchestrating the services.

Private Practice Versus Public Medicine: The Case of Public Health and Mental Health. The division of labor in the American health field can be considered in terms of the difference between the completely public "public health" system, the primarily public (state and community) mental health system, and the primarily private practice of medicine. Public health medicine, as we noted earlier, arose as a reaction to urban conditions, especially industrialization.[75] The health occupations involved in this sphere — physicians, public health nurses, sanitarians, medical secretaries — are all on public salary, and are thus part of the government in the region in which they practice. Of primary importance here are the local public health units, which offer child care education and clinical services for children, as well as home visits by public health nurses for that segment of the community, especially the home-bound mother and the aged, who have no private physician.[76] The overall inspection-oriented functions of the public health system — sanitation, food inspection, etc. — benefit the entire community.[77]

The division of labor between public and private medicine in the mental health field is closer to that of public health than to general medicine for one important reason: although the majority of the psychiatrists are in private practice, the majority of *patients* are in public mental health hospitals, along with the majority of social workers, aides, and other auxiliary mental health personnel.[78] In this sense, therefore, the psychiatrist in public mental health is usually an administrator of large numbers of programs involving the poor and the lower middle class, while the majority of psychiatrists are in private practice with the upper middle class or the wealthy, or with their sons and daughters in the psychiatric clinics of universities. For all the health occupations except that of physician, the public sphere, especially in federal hospitals such as the Veterans Administration, offers more rewards than the private.[79] The size of the clientele, the resources of the government, and the shortage of physicians afford them opportunities for equal pay at the middle ranks, and with the unionization of mental hospital aides, salaries here are beginning to rise as well. The public sphere offers the reverse situation for physicians, leaving the field either to the reformers and altruists or to the incompetent who could not make a living in private practice.

Community Versus Hospital Practice. There is a marked trend at present among specialists toward a jointly based hospital and community practice, with a companion trend for the hospital to function as the general practitioner for the community, through its outpatient clinics and emergency room.[80] This is true in part because the nature of many medical specialties requires facilities not available in office practice. In same, such as anesthesiology, surgery, and post-mortem pathology, legal restrictions locate the practice at the hospital, and in others, such as radiology with its expensive X-ray machines and radiation therapy units, only the hospital can usually afford the technology. The disappearance of the community-based general practitioner, and his virtual nonexistence in slum areas, is leading to the use of the emergency room and the clinics of the hospital as the general medical advisor and dispenser for all segments of the community.[81] Even in suburban communities, the usual night procedure for general practitioners and specialists is referral of the patient to the particular suburban hospital at which the doctor practices, with the doctor coming himself if the hospital decides it is a true emergency. During the day, therefore, the poor have the public health nurse and the outpatient clinic of the hospital, and the middle class and wealthy have their internal-medicine general practitioners and specialists. At night, the emergency room takes care of all, with the distinction being the location of the hospital: a busy and overworked ghetto emergency room or a clean, quiet suburban emergency room with the specialist a phone call away.

In those metropolitan areas where a medical school exists, the hierarchy of power, prestige, and available medical resources depends on the degree of affiliation of the practitioner with the university hospital. Because of the medical school's connection to the national medical elite, many of these settings have access to sources of funds for research, training, and equipment, usually in Washington. In the more prominent medical areas of the country, the university hospital centers become a set of medical palaces in an otherwise undistinguished field of voluntary, public, and proprietary (profit-making) hospitals in the community. As Elling states:

> the university-based health center has gathered, in most cases, the most elaborate and effective armamentarium of personnel, equipment, and facilities of any organization in the immediate vicinity. To the extent of these occurrences, the university health center has become the power center of the local health system.[82]

As Miller further points out, the medical professors with joint appointments at university medical schools and university-affiliated teaching hospitals form the elite of the profession.[83] We may note further that *some* community practitioners have use rights at the university hospitals (usually the students of the elite medical schools who choose community practice over research and teaching). Others, such as the typical community practitioner, may often not be allowed to use such hospitals, or may be encouraged to take his patients elsewhere. Recently legal cases involving "use rights" and restrictions on practitioners have been fought through the courts and won by the practitioners, but priorities can always be set in terms of admission of patients, with the nod going to the "approved" practitioners with closer relationships to the hospital staffs and the teaching units.

Local Versus State and Federal Organization of Services. The locality of practice has expanded with the increase in the speed of transportation to the point where the services of a famous university hospital are given to a nation or to the world, with the important ailing flown in from everywhere. In general, however, the strong local character of private practice is matched in localization by the informal colleague networks of private medicine. State and federal programs, on the other hand, legally and by definition serve *all* in a given geographical region. In fields such as sanitation and mental illness, and in most rural areas, government services may be almost the only services available. The complexities of the present crisis in medical service in the United States are giving functional power and a mandate to planners and experts in regional and national health. Local medical bodies resent the ideas or aims of such planning groups, and fear, to some degree realistically, that some of their autonomy might be taken away as the result of a regional plan.[84] On the other hand, an increasing share of the revenue of general practitioners and hospitals alike comes out of government funds through Medicare,

Medicaid, and support of hospitals; thus the government is increasingly in a position to add force to plans for organizing services on a wider basis.[85]

Practitioner-Patient Versus Third-Party Arrangements. In the older style of medical practice, the doctor's occupational role had much in common with that of the small shopkeeper, the owner of a family-run store with one employee and a steady clientele from the neighborhood. As costs have increased and as fees have outrun the patient's ability to pay, private health insurance arrangements have arisen in which the doctor is wholly or partly paid by a third party for his services to the insured.[86] This may be by private insurance (Blue Shield for doctor bills, Blue Cross for the hospital), by the federal government (Medicare and Medicaid), or by a health plan with the physicians as salaried members of the staff of the health plan's own hospitals (the Kaiser plan in California). The trend toward third-party purchase of services introduces yet another series of complex organizations into the once simple doctor-patient relationship. Whether this diminishes the value of the doctor-patient relationship, as medical conservatives claim, is a question involving interests and ideology, and will be considered later. It is obvious, however, that any three-cornered exchange of services and goods is different in structure and function from a two-person one. As Simmel once pointed out for small groups, the triangle is one of the world's least stable forms of social relationship; when the third partner is the federal government the instability is complicated immediately by political considerations of a direct sort.[87]

Decentralization Versus Centralization: A Summarizing Theme. Let us consider two "ideal types," each of which is a form of practice constructed out of the extremes considered above. On the one hand, we have a division of labor and an organization of services based on decentralization:

> Rural, solo, general practice, with the physician working alone or with a nurse, private, community-based, local-scope arrangements involving only the doctor and the patient.

This extreme is not only reality in some areas of the nation, it is also an ideologically desirable type of practice to such conservative organizations in medicine as the American Medical Association. This extreme can be contrasted with its many-factored, centralized opposite.

> Urban group, specialty practice, with a complete health team, under public sponsorship with public health and mental health aspects, hospital-based, in a state and federally organized plan which has third-party payment for all patients.

The contrast is almost ideological in nature, yet each variable is real and so is the existence of each extreme. The centralized version above is viewed by some with hope and others with horror. In fact, the organization and delivery of health services, and thus the role of the health occupations and professions in the system, is presently about halfway between the two extremes, with the balance heading in the centralized direction at present. We have many health arrangements at present for each step along the way, as well as the overall trend which is reflected in the *gestalt* above. Thus the organization of services is in process of change, and these changes dovetail with the increasing role of new health occupations in the large settings of practice, using an increasingly complex and sophisticated technology. If one of the ideal types is a view of America's past, perhaps the other is a vision of its future.

HEALTH OCCUPATIONS: A COMPARATIVE VIEW

When the role of health occupations is viewed comparatively, it becomes obvious that the role of central professionals and auxiliary groups depends at least to some degree on the type of social structure and political system within which they are set. To illustrate this fact, we can compare some of the most predominant features of the American situation with those of different countries: the Soviet Union, Britain, Japan, and three developing nations — Peru, Turkey, and India. Following the approach used for the division of labor in America, four issues will be considered: the nature and extent of occupational manpower, the role of technology, the organization of services, and their delivery.

OCCUPATIONAL MANPOWER

In the Soviet Union, recruitment of physicians is primarily from the ranks of the middle and upper class, whose children tend to qualify more frequently for college and university training in general.[88] But information from Hungary indicates that since the sovietization of their health system, the percentage of working-class students in medicine has risen in the period from 1950 to 1965 from less than 5 per cent to about 37 per cent.[89] The size of the medical force in the Soviet Union is larger than that of any major nation, with a ratio of 20.5 physicians per 10,000 population, a ratio higher than that of any other nation in the world with the exception of Israel, a special case.[90] The Soviet Union presently trains three times as many physicians as the United States per year, and more than one out of five physicians in the world today are Soviet.[91] In terms of sex, 75 per cent of all Soviet physicians are female, but Field indicates that the percentage may well be peaking at this point.[92] In terms of all personnel, the health field is overwhelmingly female, almost 90 per cent. The pay for physicians in the Soviet Union is low, at the level of skilled workers or lower level engineers; scientific and Party activities are higher on the rating scale and thus the reward system. The distribution of physicians varies by geographic location as in the West, with the physician scarce in the countryside.[93]

The primary division of labor in the Soviet health occupations is similar to that of the United States, with the addition of one major group — the physicians' assistants, or civilian medics, called *feldshers*. This group tends to replace the physician in the countryside and in some urban settings, but only as a temporary measure. There are enough physicians in the urban centers so that they can be observed giving the kind of individual patient care that in the United States or other nations might be given by nurses, if at all.[94]

The career pattern in the Soviet system is the classical European model — secondary school followed by a six-year medical school program, with the first two years being similar to the American college "pre-med" program. After medical school the graduate is a physician, a *vrach*. The next step for almost all is a three-year period to repay the state for subsidizing the total cost of education by serving wherever the state wishes; this usually means service in the countryside, with a mass return to the city at the end of the three-year period. Specialization, if engaged in, involves a three-year residency at a clinic or hospital. The title "Doctor" is an academic one only, reserved for those who have gone through further academic training to the masters level (in about midcareer) and then taken a doctoral degree for research. The latter degree is necessary for professorships, where the individual may earn three to four times the salary of an ordinary physician. From this group a select few will become academicians — members of the Academy of Medical Sciences — and enter the Soviet elite and incidentally earn five times the salary of an ordinary professor. One final major and very important aspect of the Soviet health career system is its deliberate stress on vertical mobility from one profession to the other. The Soviet Union in 1963 maintained sixty-three evening schools where nurses and feldshers could take the courses that would qualify them as physicians.[95]

In Great Britain recruitment to medicine is also primarily from the upper middle class with a few from the upper class and the lower middle class and minimal subsidies. The size of the health occupational force is smaller than the United States' in practitioner-patient ratios, and it is decreasing absolutely as well as relatively, as the British general practitioners emigrate to the United States, Canada, and Australia, whereas the British population grows each year. The sex ratio in British medicine is similar to that in the United States, that is, the medical profession is predominantly male, with the auxiliary professions being primarily female. The monetary rewards are satisfactory by English standards only for the hospital-based practitioners (consultants) and very poor for all general practitioners. In urban-rural terms the same understaffing of the countryside exists as for other industrialized nations.

The pattern of the division of labor in occupational group terms is standard, with, however, a greater (and historically based) distinction between physicians and surgeons than in the United States. The most important principle for the division of labor — and it is essentially a social class principle as well as a professional one — is between the predominately upper-class Oxford-Cambridge physician who is a consultant specialist based at a hospital and the middle- and lower-middle-class, sometimes ethnic or racial minority physician who practices in the community, shut out of hospitals by custom and by the rulings of the National Health Service.[96] All physicians in Britain work under salary arrangement with the National Health Service, the nationalized system for paying physicians for medical care to patients. The difference between this system and that of the Soviet Union has to do with the fact that the *settings* are not owned by the government and are thus less under control. There is a special difference between the pay rates and privileges of the consultants in hospitals and the general practitioners in the community, with the latter getting a lower fee for their services as well as having poorer working conditions and a lack of practice rights in the hospital setting.[97]

The career pattern for the English physician is the standard European six-year medical school, following secondary school, and is usually taken at a hospital-based medical school; some universities now offer part of the medical education. The six-year program leads to the Bachelor of Medicine degree, after which most get a year of internship. But residencies are scarce and are reserved for those who will qualify as specialists or who will become the medical professors of the future. Increasingly the British medical student is finishing school and internship, facing a low-paying general practice career in the community without hospital rights, and is resolving the dilemma by emigration for higher wages with better privileges. This has become an established subpattern for young British physicians, but the financial difficulties of the British government are making it difficult to raise the salaries for physicians under the National Health Service to the point where they are competitive with American incomes.

In Japan, recruitment is also predominantly from the upper and upper middle class, and from medical families in particular. The doctor-patient ratio is about the same as for the United States at present; there was a rapid growth to this point in the last two decades. The traditional male-female division of labor is also seen in Japanese medicine, which is even more conservative than in the United States because of cultural mores concerning the roles of men and women. The level of pay is not high, unless the physician is a specialist in his own personally owned private hospital, or a senior specialist in an industry-owned hospital, or a medical professor at a leading medical school. General practitioners are very poor, even by Japanese standards. The urban-rural distribution problems are found here as elsewhere, with few doctors in the countryside and only general practitioners or public health clinics with medical staff. But transportation in Japan is good, and since the nation is geographically compact, no countryside is too far from an urban center.[98]

In general, the pattern of the division of labor by occupational groups is similar in Japan to that of the United States, with less subdivision in the nursing area. The most important structural principle in the division of labor in Japanese health is the general practitioner-hospital split. There are no open hospitals in Japan; thus any physician wishing to treat patients in a hospital must be accepted to practice at the given hospital, a possibility in most cases only if he was formerly a student with ties to the medical elite and was sponsored by a professor into a hospital-based position. The career is thus three-directional: all medical students go to the six-year medical school after secondary school, after which most take a one-year research degree — the *gaiku*.[99] The losers go into general practice alone or with a nurse or two; they may have a few hospital beds next to their office. The successful ones will get an internship or residency in a hospital setting, with staff and equipment, or a university post as an assistant. A year or two abroad, if the family of the student can afford it, is very popular, usually to the United States or Germany. These two countries are preferred because of their influence on the Japanese system of medical education: the structure of the university is German and the research approach is essentially American. Sponsorship, which is also a cultural pattern in Japan (*oyabun-kobun* relationships), is critical to the Japanese medical career, even more than it is to the American, where it is very important. The two elite schools — Tokyo and Kyoto — provide the key to professorial openings and appointments to the best hospitals.[100]

In the developing nations, less is known about the division of labor, beyond simple survey data on numbers of practitioners at different levels and practitioner-patient ratios. Most studies indicate, however, that in countries such as Peru, Turkey, and India there is a massive undersupply of the auxiliary health professions in proportion to the supply of physicians. For example, in Turkey there are five doctors for every nurse. This reflects the two-class system, consisting of an urban elite upper class and a rural peasantry, which in the case of Peru or India may be of a different race or caste as well. Medicine is a popular career for the upper-class youth, but the system is underdeveloped and in essence there are two systems, an urban Western profession and a rural folk practitioner group. In Turkey, in 1965, there were 30,000 "needlemen," a few of whom were ex-medics from the Turkish Army, but most of whom had only the ability to use a hypodermic syringe to inject anything and everything into the arm of the unsuspecting peasant. The rural regions are just now being staffed in many of these nations by public health clinic personnel, usually nurses or aides, but at present the primary problems of these nations include the creation of a stable middle class and working class; until this occurs there will probably be a shortage of individuals to fill the auxiliary positions within the present health hierarchy of occupations. The conversion and training of folk practitioners is talked about, but this has met with little real success in most areas of the world at this time.[101]

To sum up, the occupational division of labor in health follows a generally similar pattern in the industrialized countries, with a dual modern and folk practitioner system in the developing countries. In the Western model, rural areas are less well supplied than urban, and in all areas, the physician heads the occupational pyramid. The social class origins of recruits, at the different levels of the health hierarchy, is essentially the same across the board, as is the central role of the university medical school in determining the future career prospects of the student. The differences show up in terms of specific variables. The sex ratio is reversed in the Soviet Union in the ranks of the physicians, and their overall supply of health personnel exceeds markedly the supply for any other industrialized nation. The general practitioner-specialist division is seen in all countries, with the hospital the province (in some countries the *exclusive* province) of the specialist and the university medical professor. In career terms, the post-secondary school, six-year European pattern of training is nearly universal, with additional residency required for specialty practice and additional degrees as well as residency for university positions. The division of labor, in terms of occupational groups and patterns of training, have international variations, but they are clearly variations on a single pattern.

THE ROLE OF HEALTH TECHNOLOGY IN DEVELOPING NATIONS

The use of technology is not as extensive internationally as it is in the United States; this is hardly surprising given the overall higher standard of living and greater resources of the United States. As a consequence, some of the technology-based complications in the occupational field are not as frequent abroad. In the Soviet Union, the lack of much sophisticated technology is due to a deliberate decision of the state to invest in manpower rather than hardware; as we well know, they are capable of making as much technological progress in an area as they decide to. In Japan, as in Britain, there is a difference between the increasing technological sophistication of the hospital settings and the rudimentary conditions of general practice. The Japanese case is especially relevant, as Japan has become a world electronics center and many of the electronics firms have their own major hospitals, stocked with every conceivable piece of medical electronics available.[102] In the developing countries, the sophisticated technology is at present essentially a luxury for the rich; the priority items are those of basic public health technology—sewer systems, the prevention of malnutrition, immunization procedures—and these do not require the complex hardware of modern medicine nor the complicated occupational structure of the technological hospital.

ORGANIZATION AND DELIVERY OF SERVICES

It is in the organization and delivery of services that the different political systems, and the differing political power of the health occupations, show their greatest contrasts. The Soviet system is both completely public and completely centralized under the power of the state, with regional, local, and neighborhood health centers as the main unit of operation. These units take both general and psychiatric cases, and the out-patient mental health program of the Soviet Union, which is work-oriented and community-oriented, is of great interest to those in the "community mental health" division of psychiatry in America.[103] Health planning is centralized and all personnel are directly employed by the government; thus no money at all changes hands between doctor and patient nor between patient and treatment setting. Delivery of services is at least as efficient as that of the Western nations, and is quite popular with the citizenry, being one of the concrete and provable successes of the Soviet system, even to emigrés who have left for political reasons but still rate Soviet health services higher than those of Britain or the United States. The Soviet elite has special facilities, as is true of most elite groups in the Western nations, but the public health statistics of the World Health Organization indicate that the mass is far more completely served for typical illnesses than is the case in Britain, Japan, the developing countries or the United States.[104]

Japan and Britain have the strong contrast between community general practice and closed elite hospital practice, with the public forced to choose between the overworked general practitioner and the hospital. But in Japan the hospitals are closed even to the *patients* in many cases, who must have hospitalization privileges through their physician or a health plan arrangement as part of employment in a factory.[105] The National Health Insurance system is used in both England and Japan, with a large proportion of the income of the average practitioner coming from the government, but there are more variations in this plan in Japan than in England, although the general practitioners were bitterly against the founding of the system in both places and profit less by it in both places than do specialists and hospital-based physicians.[106] In terms of the continuum of public to private service, we can go from the Soviet Union on the one hand, then to Britain, and then to Japan, where the patchwork of public and private clinics and public and private health insurance plans is rather close to the American scheme. The underdeveloped countries are presently still involved in the early stages of health prevention and control of epidemic diseases that are no longer a problem in the more industrialized countries. The elites here, as in the other countries, get the best care. In Peru, for example, this means special hospitals for the large army and national police force. The wealthy have the use of the university teaching hospitals and the best clinics; the poor in both the city and the countryside have public health clinics or folk medicine.[107]

In general summary, the occupational training and manpower, the role of technology, and the organization and delivery of services are seen to have both international similarities and definite variations. The elite groups in all societies considered here, as in the United States, get the most extensive care in the hospital setting. Manpower recruitment is related to the class structure of each society. In terms of overall organization and delivery of services, the role of the health occupations depends on the relationship between the government and the groups involved. In the centralized systems such as the Soviet Union, the health occupations are low in status and power but effective in delivery of services. With each step of increasing independence of government control and government pay systems, going from Britain to Japan to the United States and the underdeveloped countries, comes increasing inequity of service delivered, especially to the poor. In all systems except the Soviet, the hospital becomes the center of power, resources, and quality practice to the exclusion of the community practitioner and the average man in the street. However, in the less centralized system, there is a trend toward increased costs and a growing need for more general planning and more comprehensive insurance programs; thus there is a great impetus toward such programs, regardless of present views. What is profitable to one segment of medical occupations, such as the strong hospital system, may not be profitable to the general practitioner or to the public. In all systems, there are conflicts of interest between the state, the professions, and the citizenry. It is to these that we now turn.

CONFLICTS OF INTEREST: HEALTH AS A BATTLEGROUND

The health of an individual is one of his most basic interests; the health of a nation is a critical resource. Thus those in a position of functional power in the health field possess great leverage and ability to gain their own ends and defend their own interests, sometimes at the expense of the layman. Traditionally the ideology of the physicians, which pictured them as selfless servers of humanity, has not been challenged by any major segment of the general population, except in periods of major social change such as Jacksonian America. Still, the mandate of a profession to practice as it desires is at any given time the outcome of a negotiated understanding that it will benefit those served at least as much as it profits from the payment received. In recent decades, as the process of social change has accelerated and as the American health field has continued to disintegrate organizationally, a series of clear conflicts of interest have arisen between different groups in the health field, and between segments of the health field and the wider society. The basic issue is the conflict of interest between occupational groups in the health field and the public interest in the area of health. The conflicts may be understood as encompassing all the organizational aspects of the health field: the division of labor in work and manpower terms, the role of technology, and the principles of service organization and delivery.

In the past, sociological approaches to the health profession have concentrated on division-of-labor conflicts and on the impact of technological change. These are important issues, of course, yet both can be understood in depth only when related to conflicts between given health groups and conflict between groups in the health field and groups in the wider society. For example, we have already considered the division-of-labor conflicts between the different groups in health: doctors and nurses, general practitioners and specialists, bureaucratic problems inherent in the bureaucratized hospital setting. Similarly, it has not been possible to discuss the role of technology in the health field, as it has grown, without getting into the intramural conflicts between anesthesiologists and nurse anesthetists, surgeons and medical electronics technicians. Though we have not considered it extensively, conflicts regularly exist between the lay administrators of hospitals and the chiefs of each medical department in the hospital over the organization and delivery of services, as the technology of the hospital eats up more and more of its operating funds. Yet each of these issues, important as they might be to a functional approach, do not get at the largest and most basic conflict of interest in the health field: the conflict between those who profit by the giving of health services and those who are the consumers of the services. This area of conflict is changing the very nature of the health field, from an inefficient system to an open battleground where everyone's basic interests, financial and healthwise, are on the table.

THE GROUPS IN CONFLICT

In order to consider the battleground it is first necessary to delineate *some* of the major armies. No listing can ever be complete, and subdivisions of each army can of course be made. What can be done, however, is to briefly describe each major group, some of which are subgroups of a given health occupation (such as the general practitioners among physicians), others are whole blocs (hospital maintenance workers), others are occupational-institutional complexes which operate as a unit on some issues, but act at cross purposes on others. What can be done, after describing the major groups, is to show how they line up on a series of conflict issues, and from this draw some tentative conclusions on the direction in which the health field is heading, at least in part as a consequence of the past and present outcomes of the battles.

The following groups can be identified: "organized medicine," especially the American Medical Association; the medical school–university hospital–federal government research and teaching complex (the medical elite); the private health insurance companies and their lobbyists; the medical-technology drug companies; lower-level hospital workers; the labor unions; the citizen-consumer; and the professional politicians. Each group is a study in itself in the politics of work; here we may simply outline the interests they defend and the ideologies they use in the health area.

The group of physicians known as "organized medicine" are exemplified by the general practitioners who constitute the majority of the American Medical Association. The term "organized" refers to their possession of a specific, financially oriented form of occupational consciousness, and a set of ideologies which range from general political conservatism ("socialized medicine is the first step to socialism") to specific defense of one extreme of medical practice organization, the "decentralized" one which we constructed earlier in the chapter. The ideological stance ("preserve the doctor-patient relationship") is part of a defense of the single practitioner mode against any other form of practice or third-party intervention. The interests they defend are both selfish — their profits — and ideological — symbolizing a way of occupational life.

The medical elite — the complex composed of the leading medical schools, their teaching hospitals and staffs, and the health research and service support branches of the federal government, is a second coherent action group. The interchange of personnel and funds, the exchange of information, influence, and decision-making power makes this group an increasingly important power bloc on the national scene, one which gains in importance with each increase in the role of the federal government in health planning and services. The basic interests to be defended here are control over the direction and change of medical thinking and knowledge, and the defense of privileged access to the financial resources of the general social elite groups and the federal government. Its ideologies are more subtle than those of the AMA, stressing "expertise" and "science," the importance of the "advance of knowledge," and the "university hospital's responsibility to the community." But the medical palaces in which the elite operate are a set of concrete interests to defend, as is their insider role in government.

Two corporate power groups are of central importance. One is the private insurance companies who stand to lose millions if health insurance is directly financed by government; the largest of these include the Blue Cross–Blue Shield plan participants, which include some of the largest insurance companies in the nation. Their power is extensive. The other major group of corporations make and sell the medical technology and the drugs to the health sector and the citizenry. They are active defenders of that business, should it be threatened by a deemphasis by any group on the use of hospitals and post-illness measures and a stress on prevention and health manpower to insure prevention. Their ideologies are classically capitalist and specifically technocratic: "medical progress through science, courtesy of the Acme Company." They spend millions of dollars in subsidizing research of professors in medical schools and in subsidizing a large number of medical journals, which gives them in both instances leverage over segments of the occupation, of a subtle but real sort.

Three groups which have the common property of not being members of the central or "professional" occupations in health are hospital workers, organized labor, and the abstraction which can nevertheless be considered an interest — the citizen consumers. It is only recently that hospital workers have joined with organized labor, and that the citizens have become aware of the political nature of interest-group politics in health. Although these groups do not have specific ideologies in the concrete sense of the other participants, the labor union and hospital worker group uses labor phraseology and rhetoric. Among the Spanish-American and black hospital workers in New York, there was much talk about "La Cruzada de Local 1199." The citizen consumer, in health as in other areas, is just now in the process of organizing, some under the radical rhetoric of activist medical students, more through pressure on elected representatives.

The final group, the general public, like many groups considered, is in reality split into progressive, conservative, and disinterested factions, though the latter group is disappearing as the conflict, and the crisis, escalates. This public includes the politicians, both pro- and anti-change, with a variety of allegiances to all of the groups mentioned, with little inherent power to change the situation themselves but with access to the mass media and sometimes the skills to organize the different factions of the public and the health groups on a given issue.

THE ISSUES: INTERESTS IN CONFLICT

Although we will be able to consider only a limited number of issues in which these different groups are involved, they are among the most important: national health insurance, group practice, "hospital power," pay for nonprofessionals in health, and the issue of citizen participation in health planning.

The first major issue illustrates in almost classic fashion the role of occupational ideologies in conflict situations. The AMA fought a legislative battle on four separate occasions, and with four different bills, against the enactment of government-financed medical care for the aged. The Political Action Committee of the AMA spent more than $7 million in its unsuccessful fight. Although in the short run it could be demonstrated that the groups involved would benefit by the legislation (and the medical profession's income has risen sharply as a partial consequence of the legislation), the AMA feared the long-term imposition of a standard fee schedule by the government and other regulations by federal agencies. In the fight against government-based health insurance, the allies of the AMA included the private insurance companies whose income was threatened by the government funding of such programs (especially the future ideal of insurance for all, not so much for the aged, on whom they did not make money). Those regions of the nation where the AMA was strong found local medical societies and local hospitals alike fighting against national health insurance for the aged. But the medical elite, which had a major role in planning the Medicare legislation, whose interests were not basically threatened, and who would be able to use the plan as a demonstration of "new thinking," were for the legislation. In this they worked with the labor unions and citizens' groups. Politicians who had earlier supported the AMA, found, as citizen support built for the insurance plan, that it would be wiser to change sides and support the new legislation. In the long run, the medical profession as a whole may have lost their "image" as dedicated servants of mankind as a result of the fight against health insurance by one segment, the AMA.[108] In Canada, similar damage to the older image was done by the Saskatchewan doctors' strike, a protest against the onset of government health insurance.[109]

Group practice arrangements — prepaid medical plans involving the consumer as part of a plan in which the doctors are also plan doctors who often work in a plan hospital — have been opposed and supported by essentially the same configuration of forces, with the AMA and the health insurance companies "against," and the medical elite, the labor unions, workers, and citizens "for." Penchansky has documented a long fight against a group plan by AMA-affiliated local physicians in a mining area of Pennsylvania. The group doctors were denied use of local hospitals until they won the right to use them in the United States Supreme Court.[110]

It is important to note that the threat to the basic interests of the average general practitioner is real. Many plans, such as the Kaiser Plan, involve contracts between unions and a group of plan doctors, in group practice with a prepaid, profit-sharing arrangement, with the degree of their profits dependent in part on reducing the amount of illness among the subscribers, who pay the same amount whether they are continually sick or completely well during a given time period. This threatens the business of general practitioners in two ways: it offers direct competition from a large organization and lower rates, on the average, than in the usual combination of general practitioner fees and hospital part-payment through the usual health insurance programs. The consumers are beginning to organize politically to demand this group form of service. As Garborino states,

> It is inevitable that the private practitioner of medicine should be disturbed by the prospect of the organized consumers and the organized suppliers joining forces, changing the market for his services, and forcing him to change his way of medical life.[111]

"Hospital power" is a phrase coined to represent the increasing desire on the part of all hospitals, especially the university medical centers, to become the *total* centers of medical care in the community, including the replacement of community-based solo practitioners by "satellite" centers of the hospital. In our comparative study, we have seen the great gulf that exists world-wide between the hospital and the community practitioners. By and large, the AMA and "organized medicine" are suspicious of such trends, while the university talks about "community medicine" and educates a new segment of the medical elite to push for greater medical school and hospital influence in the community. The poor, while using the hospitals as a general practitioner, are unsure about the motives of the hospitals in the community, as they have had bad experiences in the past with helpers and planners setting up shop in the community.

The strikes of hospital workers highlight another major issue. Neither the AMA-dominated nor the university elite hospitals have willingly raised wages significantly for those who work at the menial tasks that keep a hospital running. Thus organized labor entered the field and naturally has been organizing the hospital workers, with the support of the activist students in the field, who themselves have struck on occasion for higher wages and better working conditions. This issue is important, as it illustrates that the interests of a group sometimes take precedent over their ideology. University medical centers, which have staff that have worked with labor unions to plan health insurance legislation, are as great offenders in terms of low wages as the AMA-dominated smaller hospitals in the suburban and rural areas and the Middle West. Paying the workers more raises anyone's operating costs, but it is in the interest of the workers to strike.

Citizen participation in health services and delivery, and in the planning for this, is another important issue where there is near unanimity in underlying assumptions, despite a surface diversity in ideology, between organized medicine and the medical elite, ranged against the poor, the unions, the health radicals, and increasingly, the politicians, and the general public itself. It has become increasingly obvious to the citizen that the various conflict-of-interest battles which we have considered within the health field benefit him little, regardless of the outcome. The politicians have become increasingly aware that political solutions outside the profession and the health field may be more possible than solutions within it. The political conservatism of the AMA and the intellectual elitism (technocratic attitude) of the medical elite both mitigate against true citizen participation in health planning, and both the private health insurance agencies and the drug industry have come to see no good in agitation for government-based health insurance or a Nader-type consumer revolt against the drug industry and the health field. Nonetheless it is beginning, and the implications for the health field are of major consequence.

To sum up, all of these conflict issues illustrate a basic aspect of the professional mandate problem. For a profession to have the freedom to operate and plan its own destiny, it must possess both real skills and community acceptance of these skills. What has happened to the medical profession, the only truly independent occupation in the health field in the past, is that for reasons of its own self-interested actions, rising health costs, and internal warfare, it has lost some of its mandate with respect to the wider society. This fact, combined with the increasing awareness of the population that "health is everybody's business" has led to a greater desire to participate in a solution to the present chaos in the health field. Overall, the United States has fallen far behind Western Europe and the Soviet Union in the level of health care for the average citizen. The crisis is upon the health field, and the forces at work have been delineated. The future cannot be known at this time.

CHAPTER SIX

THE LEGAL PROFESSION

In complex societies of the past and present, the critical rules of social life are codified and their meaning enforced by more sanctions than simple disapproval. Wherever the division of labor has reached the point where such legal rules are necessary, a body of experts on their proper application and use arises. Since rules are critical to all societies, the occupation specializing in legal rules is a topic of central importance to the sociology of occupations.

THE HISTORICAL BACKGROUND

The role of the lawyer in history has been a subject of concern to classical sociologists such as Max Weber as well as to modern sociologists in the area of occupations and professions.[1] Although a specific beginning point is arbitrary we could initiate our historical review with the ancient Romans, where the jurisconsults, legal consultants to the Roman senate, advised on matters of legal procedure; they were the first major visible group of legal experts.[2] The history of law suggests that in non-Western societies the tribal judge or legal seer, dispensing what Weber called "cadi-justice," was another prototype of the legal profession. In societies organized on pre-industrial lines, the roles of custom in general and specific legal rules of procedure in particular overlapped. Therefore the customary judge in the society was able, from his broad knowledge of cultural rules, to dispense justice without any formal procedure or without appealing to a specific kind of procedure.[3]

CHURCH AND STATE: THE LEGAL ASPECTS

During the Middle Ages, as the Church gained in its political ascendancy and spiritual authority throughout the Western world, the law of importance and domain became, in place of Roman law, the law of the Church. Originally the law of the Church pertained strictly to spiritual matters, but as the Church itself grew as a bureaucracy and developed a hold over the secular state, canon law expanded to include many areas that would now be called both civil and criminal. As almost any kind of behavior can be interpreted in moral terms, the canon law became eventually a complete code of laws covering all conceivable aspects of human behavior, on each of which the Church had a moral stand. Those who would become experts in the canon law had to be members of the Church and the clergy. The training in scholastic orders prepared one for the special schools and training procedures which would eventually qualify one in the Middle Ages to practice as a canon lawyer. Although the highpoint of canon law practice was the Middle Ages, to this day there remain a group of legally trained priests within the Catholic Church who practice canon law with respect to the areas where the Church is still important to believers.[4]

As secular universities rose in the West, especially in Northern Italy and Central Europe in the thirteenth, fourteenth, and fifteenth centuries, with them arose independent or secular schools of law. In these schools the Roman law came back into importance, a law which could be conceived of as independent of the authority of the Church. Gradually, at the end of the Middle Ages and the onset of the Renaissance and Reformation, the role of Roman law increased, especially in commercial areas. The development of a secular legal profession began at this time.[5] Perhaps nowhere was this development so prevalent as in England, where the "Inns of Court" were developed. These were a set of four independent law schools, not connected with the ancient universities; in the Inns of Court, residence and a form of scholarly community provided socialization to the ethics and codes of lawyers and practice in the existing body of law.[6] It is important to note that in England a form of law called "The Common Law" developed. This originated at the local level and was the result of decisions made at this level. In contrast, on the Continent the combination of canon law and Roman law as practiced in the universities was exceedingly theoretical. Because lawyers who practiced this could only practice it at the courts at the centers of the kingdoms, on the Continent the law became a highly specialized profession and lawyers developed a legal language almost indecipherable to the average citizen. Thus by the time of the sixteenth and seventeenth centuries, two different legal traditions had developed — the Continental and the English. In the English, the legal practitioner was *not* essentially removed from the people. In local village courts, judges were in fact laymen and often the lords of the local manor. On the Continent the legal profession became elite, state-centered, and court-based, with a wide gap separating the profession from the public at large.[7]

THE AMERICAN EXPERIENCE

In colonial Massachusetts in the early years of the Puritan regime, we can see another example of the complex relationship between the legal profession, the law, and the wider society. From 1640 when the colony of Massachusetts Bay was founded until approximately 1660, lawyers were banned from practicing in the colony.[8] The rationale for this was essentially simple. The colony at this time was a form of theocratic church-state where laymen held the positions of governing authority in the colony but worked only in conjunction with ministers. Cases of legal nature were held in courts but the basic code of laws, which was developed by two ministers, could be interpreted only by ministers if cases occurred which were not understandable in terms of the existing rules. Thus the clergyman became the consultant to the court rather than the lawyer. The clergymen were important as accredited legal experts because:

> Englishmen of the sixteenth and seventeenth centuries were thoroughly conversant with the Bible and accustomed to looking upon it as authority. It is equally without question that the influence of the Bible upon conceptions of what the law ought to be was more pronounced and more inclined toward liberalism among the English Puritans than among their non-Puritan countrymen.[9]

But the pure Puritan church-state, or as John Winthrop called it, "The City Upon the Hill," was short-lived.[10] From about 1665 on, other Protestant churches were founded in the colony, over the protest of the Puritans. Perhaps more important, commercialization rose in the society. During the next two decades, businessmen increased their hold on the society at large, and trade with Europe and the West Indies increased rapidly. Soon the businessmen felt the need for legal expertise and the clergy was pressured to change the regulations dealing with the practice of law in Massachusetts. Finally the original statutes were rescinded and by the last decade of the seventeenth century, attorneys were formally admitted to practice in the courts of the colony. After the turn of the century and during the sixty years preceding the American Revolution, lawyers took an increasingly important role in the society. In the first few years they trained primarily in England but gradually an apprenticeship system was established under the few trained lawyers in the colony. The peak of political popularity by lawyers was perhaps reached by the group of lawyers under the leadership of John Adams and James Otis who tried a case in the courts of Massachusetts against the Crown. This case on the illegality of British taxation was one of the important turning points that led to the American Revolution itself.[11]

It should be noted that in America, as in most countries, lawyers have not primarily held revolutionary views, for functional reasons that we will go into later. It is important to note that a significant proportion, perhaps a third, of all the practicing lawyers in Massachusetts left the colony after the onset of the Revolutionary War, as their sentiments were Tory rather than Revolutionary.[12] Immediately after the American Revolution there was a sentiment against anything British including British law which, of course, was the foundation of the American legal system. This hostility to the trained profession of law reached its climax in the Jacksonian era when those states which did have laws requiring legal training rescinded these laws, and throughout the United States any layman was allowed to practice law. This deprofessionalizing of the American legal profession in the Jacksonian era — the middle third of the nineteenth century — was interpreted by Griswold as follows:

> Two prime factors underlie what has been called the de-professionalizing of the American Bar in the 1840s. First there was the phenomenon of the versatile and self-sufficient frontiersman. Frequently being in no position to call upon others for help, he learned to do everything for himself. Soon he came to regard himself as qualified to perform any service, and he assumed that other responsible citizens possessed the same comprehensive abilities. Secondly there was the great influence of the natural law concept. In its extreme form, this led beyond the view that every citizen was equal to every other and encompassed the idea that every citizen had a natural right to follow any business, profession, or calling.[13]

The modern foundation of the American legal profession can be considered to date from 1878, when the American Bar Association was founded in Saratoga Springs.[14] At the time it was founded it was deliberately intended as an elite organization of the leading and most powerful practitioners of the law in the major Eastern cities. These lawyers, who worked closely with the powerful businessmen and industrialists of the time used the Bar Association in its early years as a predominantly social gathering.[15] The professional functions of the association did not really get underway until the 1920s and the 1930s. The membership criteria became increasingly open; today a legal degree is the only requirement for membership, and approximately 50 per cent of all practicing lawyers belong.[16] A rather new movement, which we will consider below, is the rise among younger lawyers and others committed strongly to civil rights of the legal aid or legal activism movement, as a counterweight to the traditional close involvement between lawyers and business.[17]

TRAINING IN THE LEGAL FIELD

RECRUITMENT

The available evidence on a national study of "lawyers in the making" indicates a definite social stratification in the recruitment of new lawyers, although few if any law schools set up specific quotas in terms of particular ethnic, religious, or even racial criteria, except in the deep South.[18] The pattern of those entering the law is quite clear. More than twice as many of those entering law school as those not are from families whose household head is a professional. In fact prospective lawyers are extremely unlikely to come from families where the household head is in a manual occupation, except where the person attends an independent, non-university law school or a so-called night school. In terms of socio-economic status of the family, the evidence appears clear. A majority of lawyers come quite disproportionately from one specific group in the population — the college-educated upper middle class. For reasons which have to do with both culture and attempts to increase the mobility of their groups, Catholics and Jews are represented in a much greater proportion for their size in the population than are Protestants. The majority of law students are from the cities, but this is simply a consequence of the fact that the majority of people in the society at this time live in cities.[19]

A generalization can be made that lawyers do come from those who are high achievers in college. Considering graduating seniors in college, the ratio of those who go into law among the top 20 per cent of graduating seniors is approximately double the number going into law when all students in college are considered. The type of college is also a critical factor, as a much larger proportion of law students come from private colleges with relatively high tuitions than from state-supported schools.[20]

Sociologically one of the most important findings of this recent national study was the nature of the legal elite and the elite status of an extremely limited number of law schools. Fifty-eight per cent of students in the top rank of their universities entered eight particular law schools and these same schools took only 20 per cent of medium-ranked students and only 3 per cent of students with low academic standing. The next sixteen law schools in the ranking order took students in approximately equal proportion and the remaining one hundred law schools in the country took 28 per cent of the students in the top-ranking group, 41 per cent of those in the middle, and 73 per cent of the students from the lowest third. Here again there was a close correlation with the income of the family and the education of the father, with the high-status schools taking students of high-income fathers with high education, and the low-status schools taking the medium-achieving students of low-income and less educated fathers.[21]

There are obviously significant exceptions to each of these statements, but the fact of social stratification is clear. From the historical and anecdotal evidence available, this has been the pattern for perhaps the last fifty years. However one should note along with Griswold that this does not necessarily mean there is a specific legal academic conspiracy to remove the poor from law schools. Griswold notes with respect to these findings:

> The significance of these law school figures is far from clear. They do not necessarily show that there is any sort of discrimination in admission to law study except such as results from differences in ability, with family background recognized as at least strategically relevant in determining academic abilities. They do show, however, that relatively few law schools are entrusted with a high proportion of the nation's resources and ability. This puts on these schools a responsibility, shared, too, by all other schools to utilize their resources in the most effective manner.[22]

One factor not noted by Griswold is that scholarships for law school, as for medical school, are quite rare and the education is expensive. The consequence, therefore, is bias in favor of the upper and upper middle classes.

BECOMING A LAWYER

The socialization experience in law school itself appears to depend rather strongly on what type of law school the student is attending. The major contrasts appear between the university-based law schools on the one hand and the so-called independent law schools on the other. It should be noted that in the English tradition all law schools are independent, and only in the recent past have law schools affiliated themselves with universities. In America, however, the status difference is clear. The university law schools are those of high prestige which take the high-ranking students with the greatest demonstrated abilities, and the independent law schools tend to struggle along with small student bodies, less qualified faculty, and a kind of training program which is highly reminiscent of the old Class B and C medical schools, before the American Medical Association restricted the training of medicine to university-based and hospital-based medical programs. Lortie notes that the complex of student, faculty, and post-graduate training opportunities come together to make a rather different qualitative socialization and educational experience in these two kinds of settings. For example, in his description of socialization in the university law school setting, he notes:

> Movement from university to law firm appears to be continuous both in terms of role set and values. The student may relate to senior partners as to his professors, to other associates as to former colleagues and

> competitors, and may actually do the same library tasks he performed in law school. University men talk of law school as intellectually exciting (on occasion) and as raising their appreciation of law's importance — these themes are consistent with the law firm definition of success as within the core of law and based largely on professional competence.[23]

In contrast, given the lesser opportunities and the lesser amount of information as well as actual funds of most students attending the independent law schools, we would expect the rush toward success, or at least a living wage, to become more important to students in independent law schools. The practical nature of this education, ironically, is precisely what some of the students in university law schools wish they had received. But although they are in some cases rather surprised to find that practical legal experience is not the same as arguing a case in a moot court, their theoretical training and the prestige of their law school often do give them greater financial and career advantages in the long run. These advantages are not available by and large to students in independent law schools and since the students know this, there is a tremendous pressure to develop immediate practical ways of gaining a foothold in the legal profession. As to the atmosphere of this kind of legal educational experience, Lortie notes:

> The student leaving independent law schools, on the other hand, leaves teachers who are engaged in private practice and a peer culture which apparently stressed learning "the tricks of the trade" and the general usefulness of law in business and government. The consistency again appears in these themes, high valuation of monetary success is aligned with a recognition of the generality of legal training and a fluid approach to the pursuit of one's ambition for financial gain. We also find that the independent school graduates, generally deprived of the law firm man's apprenticeship, are most agreed on the need for more practical law school training. University men are more likely to defend a strictly theoretical curriculum, but this association is reversed when they enter private practice rather than firms.[24]

To amplify this contrast, the socialization experience after law school must be considered as much a part of legal training and socialization to the profession as training in the school itself. The apprenticeship in a legal firm serves a training function similar to that of internship in medicine. However, it should be noted that not all graduates of law schools receive this apprenticeship, whereas all medical interns do. Therefore the post-law school apprenticeship in a law firm becomes a major source of difference in further opportunity between the university graduate and the independent law school graduate. Of course other plans, such as combination of placement in a firm and legal education on the campus in a work-study arrangement, do exist in a few locations and such plans may provide a partial resolution to the conflicts arising from these two widely different styles in the education of law students.

When we consider the post-graduate experience of law students, the original pre-law school differences in social class and ethnic or racial group membership become evident. The stratification that exists in terms of who goes to what law school, and in terms of the kind of training that is given there, appears to persist in the post-graduate experience. Minority group members and those from low socioeconomic backgrounds take up the solo practice of law far more frequently than do those from the upper and upper middle classes with non-minority-group status. It appears that the primary alternatives for the socially marginal individual are either solo practice, an ethnic firm, or entrance into government or business, especially government where civil rights regulations tend to protect the minority-group lawyers.[25] Those who go through the high-status law schools may elect either a high-status law firm with a good apprenticeship system and excellent financial opportunities, or if they are idealistic, they may elect government or business as careers. However, in many cases the opportunities within government or business for this high-status law graduate may very well outrun those of his partner from an independent school when the decisions are made about promotions and prestigious career posts.

David Riesman has commented on another dimension of the socialization experience in law schools.[26] The legal profession is unique in the amount of independence it gives to elite students who are still in the educational process. The law reviews, which are the central professional journals of the legal profession, are in fact edited by students of the law schools rather than by the faculty. This kind of intensive experience provides the elite students in each law school with a professional responsibility that is essentially unmatched in the other central professions, or for that matter in business. By academic ranking the topmost students in each class automatically become members of the law review staff. Their job is to edit the law journal of their university, to accept, reject, and appraise articles submitted by faculty members of their school, by independent practitioners, or possibly by students. The competition is fierce, and the prestige of the law review member after graduation is high, allowing those of minority-group status a greater opportunity for post-graduate opportunities in a high-status law firm. However, Riesman notes that for many years there has still been a marked distinction between the nature of the status system within the law school and the opportunities after graduation. Riesman has noted for example that Jewish and other minority-group members tend very frequently to be the largest group on law review staffs, but this predominance is not seen in placement in the highest-status Wall Street law firms. Smigel's information on Wall Street lawyers would tend to indicate that in fact each law firm tries to take one or two minority-group members to show their lack of discrimination, thereby showing the reverse. However, it should be noted that this discrimination may be changing. In a recent issue of the Harvard Law Record, the undergraduate newspaper publication of Harvard law students, statements were made in terms indicating a growing student resistance to discrimination in hiring by the law firms, which may force them to discriminate less in actuality.[27]

To conclude, although recent evidence suggests that the socialization process in the law school is becoming less stratified, and although there are certain unique features of legal education which offer students a form of participation in their professional training that is unmatched in the other central professions, the profession of law in terms of its training situation, its present socialization process, is heavily oriented toward business and toward serving the interests of the upper and upper middle classes. We can inspect this further through an overall discussion of the division of legal work, or the division of labor in the legal area, with some modest cross-cultural comparisons to help illustrate features of the American case.

LEGAL WORK: THE DIVISION OF LABOR

THE ADVOCACY FUNCTION

To begin with it might be helpful to make a brief functional definition of the central contribution or occupational function of the lawyer. We may define this as *advocacy*, where the lawyer is involved in client relations either directly or indirectly in the defense of a client's interests. This defense may be direct through the lawyer's participation in all stages of the client's struggle, or indirect and involving a part of the preparation for his struggle. In theory the advocacy of the client's interest occurs only in a specified context, namely the courts and other legal organizations and institutions of the society, and the lawyer functions to gain for the client those redresses or privileges which are defined within the broader context of legal norms and statutes. We must note immediately here that it is impossible to discuss the role and functions of lawyers without making a statement about the role and function of law in the wider society. This leads us directly into complexities which, if we ignore them, will allow us to describe the overt behavior of lawyers in such things as court settings, but without gaining a deeper understanding of the functional contributions of lawyers and the conflicts which they create in the wider society.

The best way to begin the consideration of the function of lawyers might be to note that it is possible for a legal system, and indeed a legal system including a fully developed court system, to function without lawyers. The example which is best known here is again that of Puritan Massachusetts, where the laws were administered by lay justices of the peace in local courts.[28] These lay justices of the peace acted according to a legal code which had been established by a commission of the Puritans and written by two clergymen with legal training. The consultants to the judge were the ministers of the colony, and questions of law or interpretation of a specific case which arose would be settled by appealing to the consultative advice of the ministers. Another reason why lawyers were in fact banned from the colony was precisely this role of advocacy which we have defined as central to the role of a lawyer in a secular society. As the Puritan clergy noted with devastating logic, a lawyer prides himself on defending a client on either side of an issue. Since according to a theological understanding, there is both a moral and immoral side of any issue, one of the two lawyers in any proceeding must be at some point in his career defending actively the immoral side of the argument. This professional ethic of defending anyone, advocating any client in the court of law, was considered morally unacceptable to the Puritans and for this reason they banned lawyers from the colony. There were perhaps other reasons having to do with the role of lawyers in England and their defense of anti-Puritan interests in courts, but this is less central to the understanding of the role of lawyers in Puritan Massachusetts.

THE COURT SYSTEM

The court system provides the institutional framework for the application of the rules of the legal system through the power of the state. Thus the role of lawyers in the legal system must in most cases be understood in the specific legal setting of courts. Courts are institutional settings where the rules of the legal system on the one hand interact with the specific interest of clients or relationships between clients and the state on the other. Not all proceedings in court are adversary proceedings, as a vast majority of rules of law have to do with facilitating, regulating, or channeling activities in a given society. Civil law is full of examples of such rules which legitimate and legalize conduct, as in the case of wills and bequests. In all cases the role of the lawyer in court is to adjust the needs and requests and rights of his client in a situation where rights of others or rights of the state or requests of the state for behavior are presented by other parties in court. The court in most cases is headed by a judge or a judge figure of some sort; therefore the particular kinds of power relations which exist between the legal system on the one hand and the judge and the kind of power that he is given on the other hand tend to have very strong constraints or at least defining powers on the activities which lawyers in their role of advocate can carry out. These permissible and impermissible behaviors will vary by nation, by time period within a given nation, and especially by the political system within which the courts and the lawyers are placed. We can very briefly illustrate some differences by considering the division of labor in the legal profession and the primary function of the lawyer in three countries: England, the United States, and Soviet Russia.

A COMPARATIVE APPROACH

England: The Barrister-Solicitor Distinction. In the English system there is a primary division between two kinds of legal functionaries — the barrister and the solicitor.[29] The barrister is an individual who has been trained in the Inns of Court, the English elite residential training setting. The barristers for the last few centuries at least have primarily come from the English upper class with an Oxford or Cambridge education. The main function of the barrister in the English court is to argue the case in court at the bar, hence the term barrister. The solicitor, until quite recently distinctly of inferior status in the English profession, prepared the case for the barrister to argue. That is, the division of labor was between a small number admitted to practice in the courts and a considerably larger number who could prepare cases for the barristers; the latter group were not trained in the Inns of Court but rather by apprenticeship or other non-bar legal training. In the English system the courts, and the judges of the courts, occupy a more central role than in the American system. There are far fewer restrictions placed on what the judge may or may not say, on what he may or may not decide.

In the English system, solicitors do much of the work which in America is done by the poor solo attorney, such as bill collecting. There have been considerable conflicts between solicitors and barristers, caused especially by the solicitors' concern at being excluded from practice in the courts. But with more solicitors than barristers, there has been an attempt to sidestep the barrister by performing legal work outside the court situation. In the past decade, this has been increasingly successful and at present, the monetary rewards are nearly equal although the barrister, through class connections and tradition, maintains the higher prestige.

In the most recent years there has been some attempt to synthesize these two major subdivisions of the English profession. But even to this day they remain divided in England in a way that is unheard of in the United States. In the English system the barrister directly advocates the client in court; the solicitor advocates the client's interest by preparing information to defend him and thus is indirectly advocating the client's case, but is also forming a relationship with him. Referral networks between solicitors and barristers have been a source both of cooperation and conflict. To sum up the conflicts in the English division of labor in the legal profession, we can quote Abel-Smith and Stevens:

> In its cohesion the Bar [barristers] with its close association with the Judiciary, and its effective trade union (the Bar Council), has been a mighty force for resisting changes which would be damaging to its pecuniary interests. Over the years the junior branch of the profession has also obtained a cohesion and a powerful spokesman in the form of the Law Society, and the latter has pressed for many years for more powerful local courts.[30]

In the United States, as we noted before, the two functions of the English lawyer are combined in the role of the attorney. Another major difference in the division of labor has to do with the fact that American lawyers, although they can practice either singly or in groups, in most cases prefer to practice in groups, whereas in England the barrister may not by law practice as a member of a group. This means that a kind of organization security is possible for members of large law firms in America. Such things as mobility in and out of the legal profession, going for example from law firm to politics and back to the law firm, is not possible in England because the barrister has only his own individual clientele and no firm to keep a place open for him. Another major difference in the power structure, in the division of labor between England and America, has to do with the relative weakness of most lower court judges in the United States as contrasted with the much stronger role of the judge in the English courts and in the English legal system. In fact most judges in the American system until very recently were not necessarily even lawyers. In the Jacksonian era and afterward the position of judge in most lower courts became elective and thereby open to politics and to politicians who, in the United States, have usually not been distinguished for their academic or their professional training. In addition many restrictions have been laid down over the years as to what the judge may or may not do. In many cases he becomes almost a referee between two strong fighting lawyers and is limited to comments at the end of the argument, comments which are often strictly limited. Thus the judge in many lower courts is largely a figurehead, and it is only in the higher courts and the Supreme Court that judges in the American system have the power, the flexibility, and the authority that they possess much farther down the structure in the English legal system.

Legal Work in the Soviet Union. For purposes of contrast another important example which illustrates the division of labor and the function of lawyers in the system is the Soviet Union. Again we can only understand the function of lawyers by understanding the role of law itself in the society being considered and especially the power structure and general organizational principles of the society. On the role of law in Soviet society, Inkeles notes:

> In the case of Soviet society it is necessary to define law in a broader sense than it is commonly used in the West, since both in principle and in fact not only the decrees of the government but the decisions of the party have the force of law. In addition, law itself extends beyond statutes *per se* to phenomena such as requirements under the plan and centrally set work and fiscal norms.[31]

Thus the political and social directives of the totalitarian state, backed by force, are essentially "law."

The Soviet Union went through several phases. During the early revolutionary period, law and lawyers were essentially overthrown during the short and rather brief period of Utopian idealism which was succeeded by the onset of the Stalinist regime, with the reimposition of a rather strict set of legal codes backed by the power of the state; within this context over the last two decades at least the Soviet lawyer has had a specific and well-defined role. Taking the example of an ordinary case argued in a lower court, and assuming it is a minor criminal offense, we note that there is an attorney for the state and an attorney for the defendant, a judge and perhaps a three-man jury made up of a professional and two laymen — the so-called people's court. The important point here is that the function of the lawyers, both the lawyer for the defense and the lawyer for the prosecution, is defined theoretically as that of bringing about justice. In addition, as Berman points out, the judge and the court are viewed as "educators" of both the accused and of the two attorneys.[32]

In the words of one lawyer who formerly practiced behind the Iron Curtain, in theory the prosecuting attorney could ask for acquittal or the defense attorney could ask for punishment for his client, if they viewed the case in terms of the overall Soviet system and its concept of justice. In fact however what appears to occur in most cases is a collaborative arrangement between the judge, the prosecuting attorney, and the attorney for the defense; the rules of the state in the essentially bureaucratic and somewhat totalitarian system are decided upon ahead of time. The arguments of the prosecuting attorney and the defense attorney are adjusted ahead of time so that in fact the court case is not truly advocacy in the sense that it is in the English or the American system, but rather a formalistic ritual gone through to preserve the appearance of Western court cases, but not their reality.[33] The critical issue here is that the power of the state, transmitted down through the bureaucratic system, accrues to the judge, who in the realities of power if not in their overt forms is essentially the *boss* of both the prosecuting attorney and the defense attorney. Hence the judge, as the representative of the political system as well as the government bureaucracy, even in minor cases has powers far beyond that of the most powerful English judge. The role of lawyer in the Soviet system, although it allows for some ingenuity, is essentially that of trying to align the problems which a particular individual presents to the state with the state's request for organization, order, and control. In contrast to the American legal system, the rights of the state here are much more important than the rights of the individual. Within this philosophy the Soviet lawyer must operate. Again, as refugee lawyers who have practiced in Iron Curtain countries both before and after Soviet occupation note, even the semblance of jury trial and the possibility of preparing a case beforehand are waived in political trials. Here the lawyers are instructed by the state ahead of time as to precisely what they should plead and the manner in which they should plead it.

To conclude this brief discussion of the role of social structure and allocation of governmental power in the divisions of labor in the legal profession, we can see a continuum going from the United States to England to Soviet Russia in terms of the role of the judge and the extent to which the judicial system is integrated into the governmental framework. The independence of the attorney and the extent to which he can actually carry on the advocacy role in court appears to be related to certain other aspects of the position of the individual in these societies. It should be noted that the divisions of labor within the profession such as the English distinction between barrister and solicitor, the French distinction between avouer and avocat, are of importance for internal purposes. But the way the legal profession itself integrates with the state hinges on the role of the state and the way its power is expressed in the court system. It is impossible therefore to discuss the division of labor in legal work without understanding the particular society in which the legal work is being practiced.

Details of the American System. The division of labor in legal work within the United States can be considered in two major dimensions: the specific kind of legal work done and the particular setting of the practice. In both there is essentially a stratification based on the nature of the client served. For example, criminal law by and large deals with the poor, whereas most civil law has to deal with business matters. Thus the division of labor in terms of legal work is also a social stratification in terms of prestige and reward for members of the legal profession. The occasional flamboyant and well-known criminal lawyer is an exception; the lawyer tends to become identified with the kind of client he associates with. Division of labor by type of work setting — solo practice, group practice, law firm, governmental and house counsel work — tends in American society to involve a kind of stratification: the solo lawyer usually works with the poor; the Wall

Street lawyer and others in large and established law firms have the highest rewards in monetary terms. Certain top government lawyers and academic experts form another prestige group.

If we consider the kinds of practices which lawyers generally engage in, the list of major sections of the American Bar Association is illuminating. They primarily illustrate the business orientation of the American legal profession. Although certain of these sections deal with such matters as "labor," in most cases the important issues are the problems of businessmen in their dealings with labor unions. With some recent exceptions the best young talent usually elects to go into business-related legal instruction in law schools, then into prestigious firms where this talent is used in civil cases. In most cases this leads to a functional division of labor where the talent is on the private corporate business side of the fence. Llewellyn notes in the 1930s what is still essentially true today:

> The draining off of best brains into a single channel has meant that the fitting of law into new conditions has been concentrated on *only one phase* of new conditions: to wit the furtherance of the business and financing side, *from the angle of the enterpriser and the financier.*[34]

Criminal law is a growing branch of the legal profession, and the American Association of Criminal Lawyers has in recent years been given more funding and concern by government. Certain aspects of welfare state legislation (the Escobedo decision on every man's right to have a lawyer) also favor new positions and growth in this sector of the legal profession. The fact nevertheless remains that the majority of lawyers at present are going into civil law and into work which is concerned with furthering the interest of small and large business organizations. This is where the money is, and is the motivation behind entrance into law work by the majority of law students.

THE SETTING OF PRACTICE AS A BASIC PRINCIPLE

Recent research by Carlin, Ladinsky, and others indicates that most lawyers practicing alone are practicing in the lower middle class and poorer areas of communities. In Carlin's study in Chicago these lawyers appeared to be not as well educated, professionally skilled, or financially rewarded as the average lawyer in Chicago. Many of them have a law practice that often involves small-time corruption with respect to the agencies and officials of state and local government. "Many of them are of dubious ethical stature and embittered in their circumstances."[35] In terms of the socialization process, most solo lawyers received their training in the so-called independent schools. In many cases they have not had an apprenticeship in a large law firm, nor a chance for a secure career.

Working with the poor reduces their potential for collecting much in fees. They perform many of the tasks that in the English system are performed by non-legal functionaries.

By contrast the Wall Street lawyer is the epitome of the powerful corporate lawyer. His firm deals with clients of such stature and power in the society that decisions made by these lawyers may affect the course and future of the entire society. His concern is with legal issues which may be argued before the Supreme Court and which may affect not only national but international business and economic affairs. Smigel, in his study of the organizational setting of the practice, observed that although the firms are bureaucratic organizations, the amount of freedom and essential gentility of interpersonal relations seemed rather unusual for their size.[36] In addition, the politeness and restraint in their dealings with Smigel and his research were impressive to the sociologist on the setting. Smigel observed a sort of free conformity, a well-socialized and well-mannered bureaucracy of individualistic professionals, and observed that this kind of large organization behaved rather unlike most other large ones. In fact, the responsibility of Wall Street lawyers is tremendous, and the power they wield in society in terms of the consequences of their expertise and decisions are poles apart from the influence on society or professional contribution which a solo lawyer working in the slums could provide. Hazard comments:

> What the Wall Street lawyers do in their professional capacity is nothing less than to provide prudential and technical assistance in the management of the private sector of the world economy. It is this functional role of the Wall Street lawyers rather than the fact that like Carlin's Chicago lawyers they have an LLB, that explains why they don't wear flashy clothes, beards, or an open countenance.[37]

The governmental lawyer may in fact be in a position of high prestige, such as that of the Attorney General. In a lower position in the government bureaucracy, his prestige will probably be between the solo and the firm lawyer. The academic — the teacher of law in a law school — does not function as a lawyer in this country, although in Europe those in the professional ranks in the universities may occasionally argue a case in court.[38] However, the lawyer in a law school often functions as a consultant to both private industry and the government, such as advising the Attorney General in legal cases. This consultative role of the academic law professor is similar to the evolving consultative role of the academician in general. But we cannot consider this as a form of law practice in a limited sense, since these legal practitioners are rarely involved directly in the arguing of cases for clients in court.

Another important issue in the division of legal work is the relationship between legal training on the one hand and post-training work on the other. Students of the legal profession have noted that legal training is somewhat like engineering training. In both cases there is a specific training curriculum. But in both cases there is also a definite expectation that only a proportion of those trained in the techniques and skills of the profession will in fact ever practice the profession. Legal skills are sometimes skills which can have a payoff in the administrative rungs of the business world. Also, the kinds of skills which lawyers develop in law schools provide excellent background for the kinds of issues which arise in the making of law in the legislatures, an important part of the work of elected politicians.

Legal training can thus be viewed as a general training, a training in intellectual skills, in reasoning, and in the analysis of ad hoc situations useful to many careers. First, a student may go from legal education directly into a law firm or solo practice. Second, he may go directly to a career in government. Third, legal education can lead to a career of mixed practice and political action. Many lawyers have a distinct interest of an amateur sort in politics, an interest which can easily turn at the local level into professional campaigning or professional advice and involvement. This can lead to a full political career, or to an appointed rank in government. By another pathway, the legal education can lead to a career in the business world as house counsel, practicing as a lawyer in business, or it can lead directly from law school to what is in fact a business career and not a career of law in business.[39]

Finally, the division of labor in which law work, the legal profession, and the functional needs of the wider society are seen to be clearly integrated is the situation of circulating elites and circulatory career routes, whereby a person may go from a prestige law school to a high-status law firm, perhaps a Wall Street law firm, thence to an appointed job in government, and from there to a position of high executive rank in a large corporation. He may remain there or return to his high-prestige law firm. Indeed the circulation of individuals from Wall Street law firms on the one hand to high governmental and diplomatic posts on the other is matched only by their recirculation back to the firms, if there is a change in their interest or a change in the administration in Washington. The higher up the prestige ladder, and the closer to the functional centers of power in the society, the more the circulatory route of interlocking elites for those with legal training is likely to occur.[40] By contrast the solo lawyer tends to be stuck in his place, a poor neighborhood, and rather unable to get out by any route. Here again we note that the stratification in the socialization settings in the law schools leads to a greater or lesser degree of career flexibility in later life as a practicing legal professional.

A FUNCTIONAL INTERPRETATION

At the most general level, the functional approach to the legal profession must return to Durkheim's observation on the role of "contracts" in a social system of the modern type. The lawyer, possessing legal expertise, has a role at all only because of the existence of the body of used and obeyed laws which lie at an intermediate level between general social norms and values on the one hand and the individual on the other.[41] If the power distribution of the society takes individual rights out of the hands of individuals, as in Puritan Massachusetts or Soviet Russia, the lawyer's role (if any) must be that of state functionary, representing the state and its laws to the individual.

The manifest functions of the occupation's activity must be distinguished from its latent functions.[42] In a society where the individual has property rights and defined freedoms as well as obligations, such as England or the United States, the advocacy function becomes central to the profession. The question then becomes one of advocacy for whom. The latent function of the profession will be defending the status quo and its distribution of power, privilege, and wealth, to the degree that the elite but not the masses may profit from the profession's skills and services. Thus the advocacy function, existent because of the proliferation of specialized legal systems, must always be inspected in terms of the clientele defended, in the situations where the defense does or does not take place. It is to this task that we now turn.

LEGAL SERVICE FOR WHOM? A CONFLICT PERSPECTIVE

As in our inspection of the health field, we can consider the conflict perspective in its different meanings, meanings which may not necessarily point to the same phenomena at all. In some cases, they are the consequences of the present functional role of lawyers, and in others they are actual existing conflicts between different subgroups within the legal profession, or conflicts between the legal profession and the community, because of actions which it chooses to take with respect to this community. In broad terms we can consider first those conflict situations which occur because of changes in the overall society as these affect the occupational group in performing its function. Second, we can consider conflicts which are caused by competition and struggle over aspects of the division of labor in legal work. Third, we can look at the way legal services feed into presently existing conflicts of interest between haves and have-nots in the society. Finally we must consider the issue of lawyers as an occupational group acting for themselves, as an organized group advancing their interest at the expense of the wider community. Each of these areas involves the use of a conflict perspective, in which we will need to identify the central issues, the reaction of the legal profession to the issues, and the probable long-term consequences of the lawyers' and the society's actions.

SOCIAL CHANGE AND PROFESSIONAL CONFLICT

Broad-scale social processes such as bureaucratization, the population explosion, the technological revolution, and the onset of the welfare state in the West have each had major consequences for the performance of law work. First, bureaucratization would appear to have several consequences for the legal profession. It has been noted previously that there is a definite increase in the number of lawyers practicing within organized professional groups and those employed by large-scale organizations. This, combined with the downswing in the amount of reimbursement possible in working solo is pressuring individuals to either join the large-scale law firms, businesses, or governmental organizations, or perhaps follow some other career line after graduation from law school.[43]

The population explosion has led to an increase in the number of people who have legal problems, but according to Griswold, this has not been met over the last three decades by any significant increase in the number of trained young lawyers. Griswold notes that thirty years ago ten thousand young lawyers were graduated and that approximately the same number were recently graduated, although the population has expanded by 33 per cent.[44] In countries such as England, which have a somewhat different relation between legal system and state administration, the ratio of lawyers to population is even lower. This may be related to the increasing number of welfare state measures in Britain.

The technological revolution affects professions whose essential skills are based on science, such as the health field or engineering, but does not necessarily have a major immediate impact on professions such as the law, which has never been based on essentially scientific skills, but rather on talents relating to values and social rules. Of course, simple technological aids such as the computerizing of legal rules in data banks may aid the lawyer in his work, but will not essentially change his work.

Another major factor of governmental organization in the West — the growth of the welfare state political economy — is having distinct influences on the lawyer, even in the United States. In France and to a lesser degree in Britain a large number of functions relating to the lives of individuals, including many matters having to do with birth, inheritance, death, divorce, etc., are not necessarily carried out by lawyers. The state, through a series of regulations and administrative decisions, as well as administrative organizations, readily handles these simple functions in a way that minimizes or eliminates the need for lawyers at each step of the way. Thus the growth of the welfare state in a sense would mean the diminishing of a large amount of the business of lawyers. Most lawyers do not work with large-scale firms of the Wall Street variety. Most lawyers work in small firms with middle-class individuals and families on cases of interest to these persons and families and not organizations.[45] This is precisely the kind of legal work — accident work, wills, divorce cases, etc. — which a welfare state absorbs and defines as administrative routine rather than arbitrative or needing legal advocates, courts, or people functioning in any advocate capacity whatsoever. England, more advanced along this road than the United States, serves a much larger population proportion with their lawyers, as the state has taken much work out of the profession's hands.[46]

INTERNAL CONFLICT IN THE PROFESSION

In addition to broad-scale social changes potentially and actually influencing the practice of law, it is necessary to see that conflict itself is a part of the advocacy process. The lawyer mediates social conflict, Parsons notes, as a referee mediates a boxing match, with due concern for the rules of the contest.[47] That is, the formalized situation where lawyers confront each other in court is part of the definition of a part of law work. However, in contrast to the medical setting, where specific health groups are expected to cooperate both openly and subtly, the conflict in the court is defined as part of the central work task itself and so does not come under the kind of opprobrium which such conflict might come under in other professional areas.[48] However, the issue of competition between law firms or between individual and group practitioners is a major one in law, as those with the greatest number of wealthy clients prosper the most and almost all lawyers are in fact in business. Such practices as ambulance chasing are frowned upon by the bar committees of the legal professions and ethical codes oppose advertising the availability of legal services. These rules tend to benefit large firms with established contacts in the community and to penalize the young lawyer, the new lawyer, the lawyer working solo instead of in a large law firm. This type of conflict can be considered as part of the issue of competition within the profession.

OCCUPATIONAL CONSCIOUSNESS: "LAWYERS FOR THEMSELVES"

Class conflict in the more traditional Marxist sense is most clearly seen when we consider the kind of work which most lawyers do, and the talent of those who do the different kinds of work. As we have seen in our consideration of the socialization process and the division of labor, the poor are the recipients of essentially the least skilled work by the least skilled lawyers. In recent years there has been a definite attempt through the poverty program and other efforts by law professors primarily to get legal services for the poor or legal aid established as a general principle. Occupational altruism is on the rise. Idealistic young lawyers have been increasingly interested in doing work of this sort. The poor are often unaware of their legal rights, prosecuted unfairly by landlords and creditors, and victimized by illegal "contracts" to purchase or rent. The opportunities for social change, redress of grievances, and creation of conflict are unlimited. The monetary rewards are minimal for the lawyer in this field. However, the new laws allowing *groups* of citizens to sue for damages, as in a pollution case, can make it profitable for an activist lawyer to defend middle-class, or even poor, consumer interests, as he may get a small share of the damage award. But the main motivation of the altruist is not monetary.[49]

On the other hand, most of those who enter law schools enter with the same motivation as that of the young doctors discussed in the previous chapter — to succeed monetarily. Therefore it is no surprise that Dean Griswold, at the Centennial Anniversary of Harvard Law School, had to urge the legal profession to do more for the interests of the poor in the areas in which they badly need legal service, stressing the ominous consequences for the social order of a failure to do so. And, ironically, at this same centennial, the ABA president chose to speak yet once more on "unauthorized practice of law," i.e., the self-interest of lawyers as a primary professional principle.[50]

Professional ethics are considered one of the foundation stones of any definition of a professional group. The legal profession, like most major professions, has ethics committees and at the national level a committee on ethical conduct. It is noteworthy that many of the activities of ethics committees at the local, state, and national level have not been concerned with the ethics of lawyers with respect to their practices in dealing with the public, but rather with what they call "unauthorized practice of law." It appears that the ethics committees within the legal profession have what is predominantly a *guild* function in the historical meanings of that term. Bonomi notes that the committees do not concern themselves usually with unethical practice by *lawyers:*

> A lot of these committees spent almost all their time battling what the bar calls "unauthorized practice of law." You know, accountants, real estate brokers or estate planners who may or may not be doing legal work incidental to their regular job. Well, these committees may have been mislabeled a little — after all they were trying to *discipline* a bunch of others even if they weren't lawyers, but in a lot of places there was no pretence at all: the grievance committee was frankly a lawyer's protective

> guild, and the chairman had a private barony; he could protect his lawyer friends and harass his enemies if he wanted to, the first time they stepped out of line ethically.[51]

The issue of mandate, the willingness of the community to essentially agree that the profession has the right to define its working conditions and limit membership in its groups, is a ticklish one in the legal profession. There are many kinds of work, which lawyers in many states consider legal, which shade off into what is essentially the filling out of forms. The problem here is that they may charge extensive fees from $500 to $1,000 for the filling out of a few routine short forms, a job done by their secretaries in an hour or less.[52] Therefore the question of the regulation of the legal profession must be inspected within the wider context in which lawyers function. They function within the context of other lawyers, bar associations, the court system, and the legislature. However, courts are often headed either by fellow lawyers or political appointees who may in fact owe favors to the lawyers who helped get them elected, and the legislature is dominated in terms of occupational membership by those of the legal profession. As we will consider under the topic of the "occupational consciousness" of lawyers, or "lawyers for themselves," the self-interest of lawyers as an occupational group, as well as the specific kinds of social structural settings which allow essentially unchecked victimization of the public, are important in understanding recent trends in the mandate of lawyers to practice in the community.

Lawyers operating as an occupational group in their own interest can be considered both in terms of the normal practice of a professional and those practices which could be considered exploitative or at least to the distinct disadvantage of the groups whom in theory the professionals are serving. Well-documented cases illustrate the conflicts of interest that can occur when lawyers as a group confront the poor, the middle class, the incompetent wealthy, and the general public through legislative channels — especially those members of the general public whose work might prejudice the financial interest of lawyers should they lose their monopoly on such activity.

A report by Secretary of the Interior Udall in 1967 on a case of victimization of a small tribe of Indians who owned valuable property, by a set of lawyers appointed by the Court in their district to take care of this property for them, resulted in this statement by the Secretary:

> I am appalled by the state of affairs described in the report as not only existent under ostensible state and federal supervision; it has flourished. As a lawyer I find it particularly disturbing that much of the responsibility for the morally shabby state of affairs revealed must be laid at the door of some members of the local bar and court.[53]

He was speaking of the extraction of a half a million dollars worth of legal fees by a judge in Palm Springs and a lawyer. Both of them were practicing as conservator, and they had taken this half million in fees over the last seven years. As Bloom notes, as of July, 1968, none of the attorneys represented in this arrangement, which was terminated a few months before, had been disbarred, no judges disrobed, none of the excessive fees returned to the Indians.[54] This is simply one instance of a combination against the public which is a source of great concern to the academic segment of the legal profession and to those lawyers who are part of reform movements within the profession.

The evidence is extensive that disbarment — the loss of the right to practice law — is a rare procedure, and one done practically in secret with no names published. In fact in many states disbarment is not permanent; a candidate can reapply for practice in three to five years.

Minimum fees are often established by lawyers throughout the country on a scale that varies somewhat from state to state.[55] The ethics committee of bar associations have been known to prosecute individuals who charged less than the minimum fee, calling this "a violation of ethics." An imaginary parallel in medicine would be that of a local medical association suing a doctor for giving free medical care to a charity patient! Before such authors as Bloom enlightened the general public, many of the practices of lawyers were thought to be inevitable and unavoidable, but such practices are not found internationally.

In the United States, lawyers receive a percentage of the estate instead of working for a service fee. In probate work, that is in the majority of inheritance cases, this makes them partners of the inheritors and in some cases they receive a larger share of the estate than any small group of inheritors. Although changes are on the way, Freedman (a lawyer) is basically right in stating:

> Ugly catch words such as featherbedding, make work, closed shop, nepotism, and price fixing are never used to describe any facet of the law business. Not only have lawyers used their monopolistic position to impose whatever the market can bear, they have brainwashed their clients into thinking the system is inevitable and serves a necessary public function.[56]

Yet another example of lawyers organizing in their own interest is their resistance to plans of Professors Keaton and O'Connell to lower the cost of insurance fees, eliminating the need for lawyers in any cases under $10,000 in automobile, accident, and injury cases. This has met with widespread resistance by members of the bar and bar associations. Although this approach would be less expensive for the public, it would remove the adversary procedure in small accident cases. It would therefore remove a major source of income for many marginal and average income lawyers without influence. More than a billion dollars nationally in legal service money in 1968 came from such cases. The majority of these were in fact under the $10,000 range.[57]

We could go on and on with instances of this sort. The important point is not that there are deviate practitioners or crooked individuals. This is true of all professions, and the human species is indeed fragile morally. The important point is that the legal profession by and large, and the American Bar Association in particular, has agitated for neither major revision in the stance of lawyers toward the poor nor a major change in supervision of the legal profession to make its activities truly in the interest of the majority of people in the wider community. It is this, the occupation acting in its own interest against the interest of the wider community, that constitutes the main conflict issue of the legal profession at this time, and probably at most times in the historical past as well.

THE "LAWYER-JUDGE-LEGISLATURE" COMPLEX

In the American system of law, in contrast with the European and English systems, the judges in most lower courts as well as some of the superior courts are elected to office. As any politician in office, they must be responsible to the constituency which elected them, especially the constituency which contributed the greatest funds to their election. It is noteworthy that lawyers are a major source of campaign contributions to the elections of judges. This must be combined with the fact that some judges do have legal backgrounds, and that in those cities and states which do not elect judges, judges can be appointed without any specific set of criteria as to competence. This means that the combination of incompetent judges or politically indebted judges constitute a major problem for the community image and the mandate of the legal profession in the long run, although they present many short-run opportunities for profit on the part of dishonest lawyers and judges. As Bloom observed:

> In most cities I have visited, leading lawyers usually had a considerable consensus on which judges could be "talked to" or "reached." They were fairly matter of fact about it, and if you were representing a client before such a judge — and you suspected the other attorney of some kind of edge with the judge — you took steps.[58]

One of the reasons why judges are rarely disciplined, even if they are openly suspected of some sort of bribery or corruption, is that in most states the only way to remove a judge is by impeachment and then trial by the state legislature. In the past 180 years only eight federal judges have been impeached and only four were convicted. In California and a few other progressive states in very recent years a state-wide committee on judicial qualifications has been formed to recommend standards for the appointment or the election of judges or candidates for election for judges, and a special national organization of those interested in reforming the quality of judges has been constituted. The difficulties with any major reforms in the present system of appointing or electing judges is that the judge is in a position to offer many favors to the powerful lawyers or potential sources of opposition. They are also in a position to control rather drastically the career of a young lawyer who would wish to change the system by enlisting his energies in trying to reform it. For example because of the legality of probate work and the extensive amount of profit which can be made through the assigning of guardianships, the judges have a way of rewarding those who will support them and punishing those who will not in terms of private profit. Therefore attempts to reform the "judge-lawyer-legislature complex," as we might call it, must be made by those who have no interest in financial gain within the legal profession.[59] Furthermore, most state legislatures are composed primarily of lawyers, and thus the lawyers' solidarity is a further block to any legislative action against a particular judge, or against the profession itself.

THREE TRENDS IN THE LEGAL PROFESSION

The long-term developments of recent years portend for the legal profession a fate similar to that which is beginning to befall the American medical profession, and for essentially the same reason. These developments can be considered in terms of three kinds of issues: conflict between academies and practitioners, community sanctions, and the radicalization of young lawyers. First, a trend shows an increasing conflict between the academic professionals on the one hand and the community practitioners on the other. Law school professors are increasingly favoring the poor, working for greater restrictions for the practicing lawyer and higher qualifications for judges, and fighting the political conservatism and reactionary behavior of the American Bar Association. The legal profession practicing in the community is becoming increasingly opposed to these academic and liberal stands, partly as in medicine, because of the difference in basic values between the professor on the one hand and the practicing professional on the other. The practicing professional is interested primarily in profit; the academic in the overall standards of the profession; and the conflicts between the two certainly have a long history. However, recent scandals or issues which have been discovered are adding support to the stands of the academic professionals in this respect.

A second major theme is the increasing activism on the part of the community to resist the practices of lawyers which victimize community members. An important example of this occurred a few years ago in Arizona when a group of citizens drew up a referendum to protest the practices of the Arizona Bar Association.[60] In the middle sixties the bar association had decided that various kinds of para-legal activity could in the future be practiced only by lawyers, at rather great increases in expense and sometimes even paralysis of the activities of such groups as realtors and insurance men. The lawyers attacked the drawing of construction contracts by architects, estate planning by banks and trust companies, and they opposed claims adjusters, certified public accountants, life insurance brokers, and notary publics. Under the campaign slogan, "Stop The Lawyers," the referendum received 236,856 supporting votes with only 64,000 dissenting for a constitutional amendment to restrict lawyers from expanding their mandate into these other areas. It should be noted that the activism here worked through special political channels, outside the normal channels of the legislature where lawyers composed a significant proportion.

Other kinds of change directed by the community in progressive states are being brought about by newspapers, high-ranking state and federal judges, and by governors with a progressive policy toward aid for the poor as well as for control of the profit of the legal profession. They consist in passing legislation, establishing regulatory commissions, and forming investigatory bodies which inspect the handling of such things as probate court, divorce practice, and the ethics of the bar association itself. The combination of vigilance on the part of the community and pressure on the part of the academic establishment may be counteracting the excessive self-interest activities of a minority of the legal profession.

We have been investigating here the potential ways in which the legal profession has been acting as an occupation for itself in advancing its interests ahead of the community. On the other hand because it possesses a central function of importance to the society — advocacy and legal expertise — the community cannot afford to allow the profession to behave unchecked in the manner of a medieval guild. Thus as in the history of the medieval guilds, modern professions such as the legal profession are meeting with counter-pressure and counter-legislation on the part of community groups. This increased citizen participation in the process of professional definition, direction, and change may increase the value of the profession's work to the community, as well as decreasing the possibility of destructive class conflict and wholesale mistrust of the legal system itself. The consequences of the latter occurrence would be disastrous for the future of any society.

Thus, to conclude, the legal profession is under pressure to redefine its role with respect to the different social strata it serves, to democratize and liberalize its training procedures, and to place the advocacy of *all* the rights of *all* the population ahead of selfish interests as a professional group. The comparative perspective, however, shows us that even these goals of the lawyer, in ideal terms, are realizable to a far greater degree in some political systems than in others. Advocacy itself is relative to the world view of the lawyers, the system in which they practice, and the interest with which they identify themselves.

CHAPTER SEVEN

THE CLERGY

In all cultures, ancient and modern, primitive and technologically complex, there have been occupational specialists in the area of the society's values, its charters, myths, and explanations of existence. Durkheim gave religion a primary role as an integrating force, a representation on a higher plane of the rules and standards necessary for social order.[1] Yet the clergy have a history of radicalism almost as long as their history as representatives for, and preservers of, the status quo. Although we will be primarily concerned with the present crisis in the religious career, in its division of labor and open conflicts of interest, it will be helpful to know the ways in which present crises are as eternal as they are new in the experience of the clergy as an occupational group.

A HISTORICAL PERSPECTIVE

In Egypt, the priests constituted a major aspect of the power elite; Balk reminds us that one-third of the revenue collected by the state became the automatic property of the priests.[2] The only ruler of Egypt who ever tried to challenge the power and interests of the priestly caste was Ikhnaton, whose monotheistic theory was politically radical in a society where every god had its own group of priests. It was this challenge to the self-interest of the priests that led the group to join with the army and bring Ikhnaton's reign to a speedy conclusion.

The history of the relationship between church and state thus goes back to the earliest periods in the history of the West. In ancient Israel, a distinction could be made between what Weber called the traditional authority of the established clergy (the Kohaneen) and the prophets.[3] The Kohaneen were a family lineage, from which the professional clergymen ordinarily came; the prophets arose as charismatic individuals who were religious radicals and the first evangelists in the Judeo-Christian tradition. The prophets related to the people not through an established religion or organized churches, but by direct action in the streets. This contrast between the two forms of the professional religion, one essentially charismatic and unaffiliated and the other traditionally bureaucratic and related to the powerful interest groups of the time, is important because throughout the history of the clergy the main issues are relevant to this split.

Judy notes that in the first two centuries in the Christian world no major distinction was made between *clergy* and *laity*.[4] The first professional clergymen in the Christian church based their style as much on the prophetic tradition as on the bureaucratic, using an informal evangelical relationship to the group. The next major step in the foundation of the church organization was the establishment of Christianity as the official religion of the Roman empire. The Emperor Constantine, by making Christianity the state religion, gave secular power and what Weber called rational-legal authority to the clerical profession, defining their occupational role in terms of the Roman legal system and thus creating a *de facto* form of licensing.[5] At this point a pattern was established in terms of the clergy's relation to the state which would continue for centuries, to the time of the Reformation. From this time on, the amount of power they could at least indirectly wield was increased by the power of the army. Statements on religion were no longer a matter of personal taste, but had direct implications for citizenship and political freedom in the society.

In the Middle Ages the ultimate development of the theory of church and state was used to justify the status quo. The theolocial argument was roughly as follows. The authority of the Church was legitimated by God. The power of the Church, and the clerical profession, justified the power of the state and lay behind it, for the king ruled not in his own right but by the Grace of God. The Grace of God was superior to the right of the king and should it be necessary, the legitimacy of a given king's authority could be questioned by the Church, thus in effect depriving him of secular power and the right to rule.[6] As a consequence, the clergy was involved not simply in the intramural politics of the Church, but the politics of the Church and the politics of Empire were one and the same. The history of the Church as taught in theological schools has been the history of the written theories of the Church, its theological systems, and their development. But the actual history of the Church, and thus of the clerical profession, must be viewed as a form of political history, and viewed for that matter primarily in terms of power and conflicts of interest. For the Church was a large landowner and possessed armies of its own.[7] The present Vatican army consists of the Swiss guard, a small group of decorative foot-soldiers, but they are the remnants of what was once an army which guarded most of the land of central Italy.

The Reformation marked a turning-point between the clerical profession on the one hand and the Church on the other. Previous to this time, to be a clerical professional in the Christian tradition was to be a bureaucrat of sorts, going through bureaucratic channels. The stress which Luther placed on the scope of the minister as *minister* was rather different from his role within a formally organized setting. The Protestant pastor was in a *role* more than in an *office* or position. The role had to be carried out on a stage, and that stage was the pulpit of the Protestant church. One can gain an idea of the role of the pastor in Luther's time, and perspective on the issues which arise today in the same situation, by quoting Luther himself on preaching:

> First of all a good preacher must be able to teach correctly in an orderly manner. Second, he must have a good head. Third, he must be able to speak well. Fourth, he should have a good voice. And fifth, a good memory. Sixth, he must know when to stop. Seventh, he must know his stuff and keep at it. Eighth, he must be willing to risk body and soul, property and honor. Ninth, he must let everyone vex and ridicule him.[8]

Especially in those last two statements the Protestant clergyman can view himself in his profession as endangered by the community instead of in control of it. That the community must be won over or must be confronted in some way is alien to the institutional arrangements of the Catholic Church, integrated as it was with the power of the state and, in Luther's time, with private capital as well. The Reformation introduced the question of the mandate of the clergy with respect to the layman, through its affirmation that the layman had a valid role to play in the religious sphere. In other words, Luther created, for the Christian denominations, the idea of the clergy as an *occupational group* (with mandate problems) where before there had only been the idea of a set of positions within the bureaucratic hierarchy. In England, Henry the Eighth broke with the Pope and created the "Church of England" and a form of established Protestant religion which was under the *control* of the state; the "defender of the faith" became the controller of the clergy as well on political issues involving the interests of the crown. It was this attempt to subjugate the power of the Church to the power of the state that was the basic reason for Henry's excommunication.[9]

The clergy-layman conflict and the church-state issue were imported to the New World. The contrast between colonial Rhode Island and Puritan Massachusetts is instructive here. Roger Williams, the Quaker, settled Rhode Island and established the principle of religious freedom for all groups. By contrast, in the early years of the Puritan regime in Massachusetts, all religions except the Puritan were barred from the colonies.[10] Church support was mandatory through taxes, and each village had to have a community-supported minister, who would stay for life. This entire arrangement, especially the taxation and the official monopoly, was illegal by the English law of the time, which was supposedly in force in the English colony of Massachusetts.[11] In fact, as soon as the King of England found that the Puritans were barring other groups, he dispatched a legal document challenging the Puritan church and the secular authorities in Massachusetts to cease and desist. In the following year, 1655, they did so; henceforth in the United States as in England, despite some informal attempts to turn some colonies into church-states, the governing principle was voluntarism.[12]

In the Jacksonian era, as the country developed, the evangelical Protestant churches and the evangelical forms of religion grew to major proportions. By the middle 1800s, the majority of the population could be considered church-goers, but the evangelical denominations had greater numbers than the Congregational, the Presbyterian, or the Episcopal church. In a sense, the form of religion and the type of clergyman that took hold in America at this time matched the spirit of the time itself.[13] And at the same time that the more evangelistic groups increased in size, the older Protestant denominations lost their stability in terms of the relation between particular pastors and given congregations. In the old New England system, the church position was for life, and only grave misconduct on the part of the pastor or special permission by the leading figures in the denomination could cause a break in this bond. But Calhoun's research indicates that during the late 1700s and the early 1800s the tenure length shortened markedly. An over-supply of young ministers (trained in the new theology schools), an economic depression in the countryside, and increasingly organized and hostile congregations led to a rapid turnover in the parish ministry.[14] As in medicine and law, the Jacksonian era was a time of fluidity and turmoil for the clergy.

Along with the Industrial Revolution in the United States came the rise of bureaucratization in the American churches and thus in the setting of the clergy. Gradually the established churches, and especially with the wave of immigration from Europe, the Catholic Church, began to take over many of the powers and many of the congregations that in an earlier era had belonged to the evangelical churches. Gradually, therefore, organized religion grew to its present position of predominance in all denominations. The nature of the bureaucratization that occurred seemed to differ somewhat by denomination. For example, Protestants bickered among themselves, but all essentially developed a form of organization which involved super-parish, all-denominational "synods" or "conferences," with a separate staff at this level and a national headquarters. The Jewish congregations gave more power to the local group, but evolved national welfare organizations. The Catholic Church, with the centralized form of authority and a head in another country, constructed an American branch of their world-wide bureaucracy. As the Industrial Revolution and the bureaucratic revolution were completed, we find that these organized forms of religion have begun to lose effective force in the community. The onset of science and the increase in the level of education, especially among ethnic groups and in rural areas, have led to an increase of people who are critical of the interpretations of the major religions, and who have left the church. This in turn has helped to lead to a new crisis in the position of organized religion in the United States and most Western industrialized countries, but especially in the strongly organized and hierarchically dominated denominations such as the Catholic Church.

The onset of the crisis in human relations symbolized by such terms as civil rights, the war on poverty, and the war in Vietnam, has led to major splits within the clergy as well as between clergymen and their congregations. In all organized religions at present, there is a split between the activist clergy and the traditionalists. Both groups, but especially the activists, find allies across denominations and are disagreeing radically about the function of the clergyman in the changing scene. At present, knowing whether a clergyman is an activist or a conservative is sociologically more informative than knowing whether he is a minister, rabbi, or priest. Thus in most recent times, we have returned to the split in the clergy seen in ancient Israel, between the radical prophets and the organized, conservative clergy. One major difference, however, is that at present some of the most progressive clergymen are "congregationless" (members of national church organizations, or missions, or theological scholars, etc.) and are thus not tied to the conservative demands of a group of middle-class suburbanites, whereas the conservatives are not only in parishes but often see eye to eye with those in their flock. The split is thus similar to that seen in medicine, between the university elite and the practitioner mass.

ON BEING A MAN OF GOD

The term "vocation" in Latin means calling. Classically, the clergy is a primary example of a vocation. In considering the experiences of clergymen, several issues are basic: the consequences of receiving the call or the decision to join, the experience in training, the experience in the role, and, with a small but significant group, the decision to leave.

The consequences of acknowledging the call have been well described by a Catholic priest. Kavanaugh noted that he developed a desire to become a priest in parochial school, and then made a firm commitment. After this:

> I would never be the same again since I had decided to become a priest. I was never to date, to avoid women, etc. The pastor now invited me to his home, the sisters treated me with new respect, even my parents could not hide the special praise they saved for me within their hearts. I was a seminarian, a chosen man, the pride of the parish, the future elite of our church, and I was indescribably alone. I who had been the center of every group, a restless boy who could not wait for morning's light, was suddenly alone. I was in the world but not of it.[15]

The calling itself has major consequences for world view and self-perception. Obviously this is a rather extreme form of calling, to the Catholic priesthood, one which demands perhaps the greatest departure from everyday routines. But this type of experience is historically the most common to all religions, the experience of specialness. It is somewhat at odds with the experience now desired in the liberal theological seminaries, that of involvement. But the initial separation had a function of major importance. This was a training in tradition, a training in earlier and historical concepts used in viewing the world, and one of the most intensive socialization experiences of all. Again we are indebted to Kavanaugh for his insider's description of the socialization process in the traditional manner:

> It was an education without sympathy, a training without recourse. I heard what I was supposed to hear and said what the administration wanted me to say. Rebels were weeded out. Only the strong and legal minded or the naive and passive could last. Creativity was discouraged unless it pursued the accepted patterns which cautious minds approved. Heresy was a word which entered every argument and "the church teaches" was the narrow outline of every debate. I was not educated, I was formed. I was not encouraged to think but trained to defend. I was not asked to reflect but to memorize.[16]

This account reminds us that the socialization experience in a ministerial institution is simply one form of student experience. But here we are dealing with what could be called the *fundamentalist* socialization experience. It attempts to form, not to liberate, in line with the classical theological understanding of the role of the minister as the transmitter of religious tradition. Given such assumptions, this training is directly analogous to that used in India for Buddhist monks, trained for a traditional role in a traditional society.

However, the society is changing, and given this, we now have in some denominations a different kind of socialization experience. The conservative branches of the three major religions have the older form of orientation — the orthodox Jewish groups, the fundamentalist Protestants, and the more conservative Catholic seminaries. They also tend to recruit on conservative lines, from the families of the faithful.[17] On the other hand, the socialization experience and the recruitment pattern to the liberal branches are increasingly in contrast with this approach. The liberal groups tend to recruit from outside the faith and from those who have made mid-career decisions to a far greater degree. Also, Jencks and Riesman indicate that the more fundamentalist the doctrine, the less likely that college training will be required before entrance to theological school.[18] The idea of a liberally educated person is at variance with the fundamentalist idea of the role and function of a clergyman — to transmit a tradition and values intact and unquestioned to a new generation of parishioners. The more liberal the denomination, the more likely that the recruits will have not only a college background, but a liberal arts background. In fact, the elite divinity schools look with disfavor on most who have had a "denomination" education which combines ministerial training with liberal arts. Thus there is a spectrum in recruitment and background from the fundamentalist to the liberal which relates to the nature of the experience and the aims of the training to be had in the seminaries.[19]

Divinity school settings have been almost unstudied from the sociological point of view, although studies of the clerical profession are beginning to proliferate. Yet judging from autobiographies such as Kavanaugh's and discussions of the seminary experience by critical clergymen such as Wagoner, the intensive indoctrination experience of the clergy has at least as much impact as that of medical or law school.[20] In addition, there is a new dimension to the socialization experience in the elite schools in recent years — a form of socialization for activism. Harvey Cox refers to a new generation of ministers in all the denominations as "the new breed."[21] This group of people get their socialization experience as much from their fellow students as from the faculty, and tend to be at the less authoritarian seminaries which are in favor of college-directed education. They often goad each other into activist activities and into choosing an activist, non-parish form of post-seminary career. In many cases, however, they *entered* with this idea in mind and were simply confirmed in their conclusions. The students speak to each other over coffee, and the subject may be civil rights marches, radical activism and Father Groppi, or selling out to the suburban ministry. The kind of question being asked about the future and career in the elite divinity schools seems more of a continuation of the typical modern undergraduate questions than anything of a concretely professional nature.

There is a major conflict between the attitudes and aims of the elite clerical students and the job market in most of their denominations. There appears to be, at this point in time, far less job opportunity in the activist sphere than interest in it. Without having reliable research evidence on it at this time, it is still possible to hypothesize that the compromises the divinity students will be forced to make immediately after graduation, if they want a job in the religious order, cause crises and conflicts in the seminary. Since the institutions and the opportunities are changing much more slowly than the socialization experience, a conflict is created in the ministry similar to that seen between the medical students in most foreign countries and the research positions open in those countries; the majority do not want to serve out in the community, but the great bulk of the jobs are there, and there alone. There is the possibility of a radical clergy employing itself, of course, but this institutional arrangement would require major realignments between the clerical graduate seminaries and their own denominations, who view the seminary as a need-fulfilling and job-training setting for the community. Also, the communities being served in an activist way are almost always poor and often not able to support anyone who cannot provide his own salary. The goals of the socialization experience become more confused, as does the vocational future of the trainee, the more the seminary verges away from the traditional, fundamentalist model.

The experience of the clergyman on a day-to-day basis, the existential understanding of being-in-the-world as a pastor, is well stated by Kavanaugh:

> I am never Jim. I am the patriarch or Father, the man who seeth but half of life and seldom heareth the truth. People have been taught to fear me, to cater to me, to make few demands, to give me the benefit of a doubt. If I enter a roomful of strangers, I am the center of attraction without ever knowing the struggles of ordinary men. Sweet ladies hand me coffee and cookies, then laugh heartily at my slightest jokes. They clean up their stories, bore me with memories of priests they have formerly known, nod seriously when I smother them with clichés. . . .[22]

We need not take this narrowly as a statement of a Catholic priest, but simply note that the experience of the clergyman is qualitatively different from that of the layman. The definition of the clergyman as a mediator in *some* way between the congregation and God, or between the congregation and a higher morality, makes his experience different from other occupations. In the totality of the definition of his role it differs even from that of the physician. The social distance built into the role has been a puzzlement, a shock, and in the long run a disappointment for many gregarious young clergymen. The expectations of parishioners force an iron conformity upon the man that has something in common with the experience of the black man in racist circles. They do not *exist* as individuals, and thus are not taken seriously.

A recent comparative study of pastors and expastors by Jud, Mills, and

Burch delineates the way in which the experiences in the role may lead to a decision to leave the ministry.[23] First, they stress that only a small minority of ministers actually leave the church in a given year (approximately 1 per cent in the Protestant denominations they studied). But a profound morale and mobility crisis is in progress among many who have not left. The irrelevancy of the traditional church dogmas and activities to the problems of the day, the clash between the conservative congregations and the ministers, the choice of the pastor between moral capitulation and exodus, the liberalized theology of recent years which defines "ministry" broadly enough to include social welfare and social action work as ministerial activities, and the social and financial pressures on the wives and families of the clergyman — all these factors mount over long periods of time. In each given case no one factor or event is decisive, although "last straw" experiences lead to the ultimate decision. Within the parish, the negative factors mount, in a world where the education of the minister is useful for a variety of new and interesting jobs. Thus:

> Career-change decisions often have roots in years of deliberation but are precipitated by "tipping-point" experiences which coincide with the eroded occupational commitment. The combined effect of system conflict and accumulated dissatisfaction shift the hope-frustration balance and begin the search for other kinds of work.[24]

Finally, in the total experience of the Catholic clergy the official dogma on such issues as celibacy and birth control is leading to a rapid change in attitudes toward the ministry and an increasing desertion of the Church. Here, in addition to the stresses which the Catholic clergy face in the parish, there are the almost intolerable strains — to a liberal — between official theology and perceived moral needs in the society. This is especially true of the younger clergy, but not only of them.[25]

To sum up, the experience of the ministry in modern society is in most cases a trying one. Most clergymen who have developed ideals at variance with their congregations have the choice of capitulation to their wishes, entry into non-parish jobs within the denomination, or a "ministry" to the world outside the official role of clergyman. In the recent study by Jud, *et al.*, seven out of eight expastors still think of themselves as "ministering" to the needs of people.[26] This is a tribute both to the formative nature of the experience and to the realities of pastoral work, which make ministering more attractive outside the parish than within it.

THE DIVISION OF LABOR

Luther's clergyman is still at work today. He is the preacher, the shepherd who goes among his flock. He is the religious and moral instructor, and he tries to convey the religious tradition of the denomination and concern himself with the religious life of his congregation. But in the United States, the minister is usually recruited by the congregation, he serves at their pleasure, and the crisis in religious authority has led to his being expected to fill a wide range of social needs, only remotely related to religion in the narrow sense. If he does not fulfill expectations, he is likely to be discharged, or urged to leave. Those clergymen with a strong, central denominational organization feel more independent and seem to have a lower rate of turnover than those who work in settings where the lay church parishioners have total control over the conditions of their tenure.[27]

In order to fulfill the expectations of the congregations, the typical minister spends a large amount of time at public relations work, organizational work, social activities, and fund raising. Blizzard's research indicates that Protestant clergymen spend more time at administrative work than at any other activity, like it less than any other activity, and feel less competent at it than anything else that they do.[28] Yet in the "voluntary" American system, which in effect holds for all the major denominations, the clergy cannot initiate projects or preach doctrines unacceptable to the congregation and expect to endure. Luther's warning about "risking all" is touching but not relevant to the realities of the typical suburban congregation, with its subtle and not-so-subtle pressure on the pastor. Even in the Catholic or Episcopal church, the upper hierarchy sees no wisdom in forcing an "unacceptable" minister down a congregation's throat, and they too are dependent on lay support.

The division of labor in the American pastorate includes the work and functions of the minister's wife. Denton's study of this group isolated three styles of reaction to the pressures of the parish, a "participatory" style, a "withdrawal" style, and a "co-pastor" style.[29] In all cases the pressures of the parish role devolve upon the wife; the minister depends heavily on her for personal support in the group studied by Denton, and in the group covered by Jud. Statistics on marital problems in those who leave the ministry indicate that pressures on the family unit — often unrealistic and irrational — take their toll of marriages and force many decisions to leave.

The pressures to widen the definition of the pastoral role, combined with the pressures to maintain rapport with the congregation, have been leading to a movement which is popular with many suburban clergymen and their congregations — the activity known as "pastoral counseling." In spite of Parsons' warning that the minister cannot perform the value-free neutral role of the psychiatrist on moral issues, he can and does play the almost identical role of pastoral counselor to individuals, families, and groups.[30] In addition, as McCann found, the clergyman often is the first one consulted by those who are truly mentally ill, and some need for training is sensed by many clergymen.[31] Thus the minister becomes a source of referral to therapy, and a therapist himself. Given the pressures to "do something" and the stand of most congregations that this something be politically non-controversial, the past two decades have seen a major expansion in the use of "psychiatric" techniques, human relations group discussion formats, etc. This in turn requires training, and leads to the expansion of the role as subspecialty in large congregations.

A trend in the division of labor which has been causing severe conflicts for the clergy is the bureaucratization necessitated by the increase in the average size of some churches, especially in thickly settled suburban areas. Although the establishment of small churches in suburban areas has increased, so also has the trend to merge congregations into much larger working organizations. Judy suggests that an emerging solution to this problem may be a division of labor on "group practice" specialization lines, with the preaching, pastoral counseling, and educational roles taken by different ministers, and either a lay or ministerial administrator for coordination.[32] In addition, churches are increasingly servicing institutions such as mental hospitals, colleges, and the army; this has led to the development of chaplaincies or "in-house" clergy. Specialization has in some cases bordered on the ludicrous; Gustafson notes that one parish has a group ministerial arrangement which includes a Minister of World Peace.[33]

Increasingly within the larger denominations an executive world can be found, with the individuals at the peak performing in ways that are essentially more similar to their business counterparts than they are different. The national church executive, the corporation vice-president, and the labor leader are sociologically all executives first, and members of their base group second. As Gustafson notes,

> Denominational and interdenominational bureaucracies demonstrate the extension of specialized activities in the churches. Administration has become a skill in itself, the institutional life of churches, just as it has in science and in technology. Local councils of churches have executive officers who seek to engender cooperative planning and activity among the Protestant churches in a metropolitan area.[34]

In these larger bureaucracies, we may have ministers functioning essentially as members of other occupational groups, the clerical training being necessary to qualify them for the job in the particular bureaucracy but not necessary for the work. The parallel with the lawyer is instructive here, in that the legal degree is often a prelude to some other occupation, in which the skill is useful, but not required. Gustafson notes the rise of such experts within the clergy as racial relations professionals, social researchers, fund raisers, architects, and experts in public relations and mass media. These are to some degree an attempt, probably both conscious and unconscious, to extend the mandate of the clergy in secular areas, to make up for lost ground in the traditional and central function. The division of labor, under these conditions, becomes so complex and diffuse as to almost threaten the identity of the overall profession.

In considering the division of labor within any major occupational group, the issues of supply and demand, occupational prestige, and occupational mobility can add important information. The supply and demand situation in the American clergy must be discussed in the absence of any national studies. The primary problem in terms of studying the allocation of men to parishes lies in the complex set of sources for such manpower. The fundamentalist denominations and the Catholic Church, along with the orthodox Jewish group, tend to recruit through the parochial school systems; Fichter shows how the Church uses the setting as a screening device for this purpose. The liberal denominations recruit from graduate schools of theology.[35] This creates a pattern where the more conservative the denomination, the more plentiful the supply of candidates. Yet the most *demanding* congregations tend to be both suburban and literate, recruiting from the theological schools where the students are often anti-parish and somewhat radical, as are their teachers. The conflict which is created by the supply and demand pattern in the liberal faiths is thus most intense where the role diffusion is most severe. The widening split between the attitudes of the theologians and divinity students on the one hand and the local suburban congregations on the other is leading to a crisis in recruitment to the suburban parish ministry which is growing each year.

The rewards in terms of material wealth have never been high in the clerical profession, with some exceptions that we will consider in the final section of the chapter. But the prestige of the role is now falling as well. Because of the increasing amount of information now available in the mass media on the working conditions of the clergy, in a society which increasingly finds the traditional theology irrelevant and the church itself superfluous, the prestige of the profession is dwindling. To add to this, the suburbanite parishioners find the leaders of each denomination — the national office — essentially radical by many of their own personal political standards. The only group to whom the clergy seems to be increasing in prestige are those college students who see in non-parish, religious action work, and in radical theology, the chance for a prophetic vocation. It is in this awakening interest of the liberal and radical college youth that the church leaders see their hope for the future. But this is a hope that does not necessarily involve the ordinary institutions of the American suburban church, or the activities of its present suburban clergy.

A COMPARATIVE REVIEW

The power position of the clergy, and their role in the overall division of labor, varies in important ways internationally. We can inspect the role of the clergy briefly in totalitarian states such as the Soviet Union, nominally Catholic countries such as Italy and France, nations with established but somewhat powerless Protestant churches such as England, and nations with a complex ethnic and historical relationship between church and state such as Israel.

The role of the clergy in the Soviet Union is a saga in the ancient struggle between church and state.[36] In the early years of the Russian revolution, attempts were made to eliminate the Russian Orthodox Church, which was viewed as a sponsor of the Czarist regime, and which openly fought the revolution and the establishment of communism. Two decades of persecution followed. In the war, however, the Orthodox Church sided with the state and contributed heavily to the war effort against Germany. With the imposition of the Stalinist totalitarian regime, and especially after the war, the role of the clergy was gradually reassessed; they were then viewed as contributing to social stability and could thus be seen as playing a minor constructive role in limited areas.[37] As Inkeles points out, limited support of religion — a kind of controlled sponsorship of the clergy by the state — has functional consequences for the preservation of the present social order:

> First, continuation of a policy of open struggle with the church would have meant draining off energies greatly needed in the political and economic fields during the period of reconstruction.
>
> Second, such a policy would have meant the alienation — and in many cases, the active hostility — of large segments of the population, which might otherwise be expected to take a position of either active support, or — to use a phrase of Lenin's — of benevolent neutrality toward the regime.
>
> Finally, such a policy would have meant the loss of the services of the churches, in particular the Orthodox and Moslem, as effective instruments of Soviet foreign policy, a capacity in which they had already shown themselves to be of considerable value.[38]

Thus the Orthodox Church and the Moslem faith were preserved for reasons of state. On the other hand, in the case of the Jewish religious group and its clergy, the traditional anti-semitism of the Russian people became official state policy, alternating between periods of official persecution and periods of limited tolerance. As Lamm explains, since they are not useful *as a group* to the state (in contrast to their obvious contributions as individuals), they have been given far less freedom than the Christians and Moslems.[39]

It should be understood, however, that the Communist party remains anti-religious in basic attitude. All appointments to positions of importance in the Church, and all decisions with implications for parishioners, are now made in consultation with the local or national officials of the Communist party. Religious education has been banned, under the rather rational theory that the atheism of a new generation is of greater long-term importance to the state than the religiosity of the present one. The result is the atheist state, with religious functions of the clergy under the inspection of the central government's Council on Affairs of the Orthodox Church.

Although in the Soviet Union the clergy has been in recent years a conservative force in the control of the state, in some of the satellite countries, especially in the first few years but to some degree even today, the Catholic Church, with its international ties and sources of support, has been a major force in opposition. The rulers of the state must contend not only with these religious bodies, but with a population that maintains heavy allegiance to the church for political as well as spiritual reasons. For example, Cardinal Mindszenty of Hungary was only one of a long chain of religious leaders, going back to the origins of the Christian Church itself, who have resisted secular authority in the name of a higher goal. It is precisely because the rulers of a totalitarian state (or of any political power) fear a loyalty of the religious faithful higher than loyalty to the state, that the state feels obliged to control them in any way possible. But in the satellite nations, where the Communist leaders are not as securely in power as they are in the Soviet Union, the clergy still has some political power because of the unwillingness of the state to alienate the mass of the population by action against the clergy.

In nations with a nominally vast majority of its people in a denomination, such as France, Italy, and the South American countries, the nature of the church-state relationship is at once less intensely religious and more complex politically. Along with a legal system which follows Church dogma in many issues related to personal morality, the Catholic nations have both a lessened religious intensity (compared to American Catholics) and a heightened political participation of the clergy in the state government. For example, the Christian Democratic party in Italy, which was responsible for the defeat of the Communist party's attempts to gain control of the nation in 1948, is called the "party of the priests" and is heavily supported by the Vatican in a sub rosa fashion, with extensive campaigning by members of the clergy in their local parishes when an important election is in the offing.[40] In Italy, again, 30,000 priests are in the civil service, on the state payroll.[41] However, the relation between church and state in the Catholic countries is a perennial political issue between the population and the clergy, and each year sees a progressive reevaluation of this relationship which is diminishing some of the secular political power of the clergy. In addition, in the Latin American nations, the radical Jesuit priest who organizes the peasantry against both the church and the state is an increasingly important phenomenon.

In England, an established church gradually lost its power as other denominations rose in size. Today, the major function of the Episcopal Church is perhaps its role in leading the status hierarchy. The Royal Family and most elite families belong to the Episcopal Church, and their church has become a haven for the fashion-conscious, the status-seekers of the nation, and the same phenomenon has been noted in the United States. However, in spite of the elite membership of the typical congregation, this has not made this denomination necessarily the most conservative politically. Because the local minister does have backing from the regional religious administration and is hired by them, he has locally more independence from his parishioners than does the Congregational minister.

Finally, the case of Israel gives us important cross-cultural perspectives on the relation of church and state. Since the state of Israel is defined politically in terms of religious group membership, the clergy have a role of expert consultant to the state on issues involving citizenship. In a sense we have a parallel here to the role of the clergy in Puritan Massachusetts as consultants to the state on decisions involving the citizenry. As in nominally Catholic countries, legislation is constructed with the views of the clergy in mind, and changes in law on such issues as the Sabbath blue laws become major political issues in the society. Recent test cases on the citizenship of non-Jews have become political crises between different groups, for example the argument between the secular Supreme Court and the religion-influenced Parliament on the legality of some of the rules in force in the society.[42] The varying criteria for citizenship, such as ethnic group membership, residence, or religion highlight the complications which arise if one religion dominates the life of the citizenry, making this religion automatically a political issue whenever votes are cast on a problem relevant to religion.

In comparative perspective, therefore, there is a marked difference between the division of labor and the role of the clergy in totalitarian states, in states with an established church, and in states with an open or "voluntary" relation among congregations, clergy, and the state. The totalitarian state views the clergy as a rival for the allegiance of the people; the clergy in states where it is the established faith are often civil servants and politically influential in secular as well as religious terms. In the voluntary systems, the clergy must carve out its mandate in specific settings, where the clientele often have more control over the situation than the average clergyman. To return to Durkheim's problem, neither the clergy nor their religion seems to have the power to hold a modern society together, to integrate it. Their role is rather that of a follower or secondary supporter of a status quo established, maintained, and changed by others. In this sense, the majority of the clergy perform a *conservative* function for the society. Those who return to the original aims of the founders of the great religions are in every age the disturbers of this status quo and the critics of the functional role of the typical clergyman. They threaten the material interests of those clergymen who benefit by this state of affairs, as well as the justification for present arrangements which these clergymen provide. It is to this issue, the conflicts of interest inherent in the functional role of the clergy, that we must now turn.

CAESAR AND GOD: CONFLICTS OF INTEREST

As a student of the Industrial Revolution, Marx saw the clergy, and especially the clergy who dealt with the working class, as essentially conservative forces buttressing the new industrial status quo. In this context he made his famous statement, "Religion is the opium of the people." [43] The promised better life in the next world, he stated, was being used to quiet the dissatisfaction which the workers felt with life in this one. It paralyzed attempts to organize workers to better their life chances. Thus, religion was an ideology used by the clergy to defend the interests of the oppressing few.

Viewed in this way, the churches of the late nineteenth century were a partner of the capitalists in the emerging class conflict of early industrialization. John Wesley, preaching patience and diligence to the miners, could thus be seen as an example of a clerical, pro-capitalist ideologist. Although Wesley was a deviate in terms of his deliberate ministry to the poor, he was not an activist or a radical organizer of the poor but a preacher of moral uplift, whose unintended consequences were the political docility of the oppressed.[44]

The question is thus introduced: Whose side is the clergy on? The answer to the question is complex, and the subdivisions of the answer are the topic of this conflict-of-interest analysis. First, the majority of the pastoral clergy are effectively on the side of the haves, and the property ownership of the churches must be viewed as a form of material interest which is defended by both clergy and congregation. Second, a minority of the clergy are actively involved in "occupational altruism" on the side of the have-nots. Third, there are a series of issues which divide the formal leadership of the clergy — its occupational elite — from a majority of its practitioner mass. Finally, the clergy can be seen in these conflict-of-interest struggles as attempting to prolong their existence as an occupational group, and overall trends in the division of labor in Western society are threatening the existence of the group in its present form, although constructing potential opportunities for it in another form. Each of these issues will be considered in turn.

First, the majority of churches are owners of property, and in the West are beneficiaries of special laws which not only make them tax-free, but allow unrelated business investments and church-owned businesses to be tax-free as well. As Eugene Carson Blake states,

> When one remembers that churches pay no inheritance tax (churches do not die), that churches may own and operate business and be exempt from the 52 per cent corporate income tax, and that real property used for church purposes (which in some states are most generally construed) is tax exempt, it is not unreasonable to prophesy that with reasonably prudent management, the churches ought to be able to control the whole economy of the nation within the predictable future.[45]

The basic issue of the churches in business is highlighted by the relation between the church elders — the parish establishment — and the pastor. Invariably the powerful laymen in the churches are wealthy businessmen who view the church as a corporate business enterprise and view the pastor who threatens this enterprise, or its growth, as an unacceptable radical. Since business expertise is available and the favorable laws are in existence, the expansion of the churches into private enterprise has been escalating in recent years. As Larson notes, in *Church Wealth and Business Income,*

> A Presbyterian church in Ohio operates a cinder block business, the Seventh Day Adventists operate a multimillion-dollar vegetarian food industry, known as the Lomalinda Food Company of California, the Southern Baptist Board bought Burlington Mills of Cheraw, South Carolina, for $2.9 million and leased it back to the firm at rentals which will liquidate the debt in twenty years; the Baptist Foundation of Texas does a large business in lease-backs at a profit of at least 20 per cent on the investments, and an obscure sect known as the Self-Realization Fellowship is doing a very lucrative business with two restaurants in California.[46]

Internationally, the Catholic Church is perhaps the most skillful investor of funds. From near bankruptcy, they took the award of funds for church lands — the Lateran Treaty negotiated with Mussolini — and parlayed it into one of the world's most concentrated accumulations of wealth. LoBello comments:

> As one of the world's largest shareholders, the Vatican holds securities frequently quoted as being worth $5.6 billion. The sum is probably an understatement, for the Vatican has invested in exchanges throughout the world, and even a conservative estimate of its portfolio tends to show that the figure is in excess of $5.6 billion.[47]

The basic conflict of interest involved here is between the role of the capitalist and the so-called "business ethic" on the one hand and genuine morality on the other. All religious denominations are involved in a business world which acts to protect its interests, and the international corporations often favored for investment have been known to operate at the expense of the poor in the nations involved. South African mining stock and shares of corporations prominent in the military-industrial complex are present in the portfolios of many churches. The businessmen insist on these stocks being retained, for these are profitable stocks and they are in control of the business decisions made by their churches. It is often argued in defense of this type of policy that the churches are losing ground, and are losing money, which must be made up through investment and business expansion. Again, this is based on the informal image of the church as a business corporation, whereas at the same time the ideology of churches, directed at the community, stresses their sanctity, neutrality, and poverty. The majority of the parish clergy are not in a position to oppose this defense of wealth and profit, and thus help to support it.

On the other hand, in this age as in all others, some clergymen oppose the status quo and the business orientation of their own churches. At the turn of the century, at the time of the Social Gospel, Mann shows that the religiously based social reformer had a well-recognized position in such cities as Boston.[48] However, it must be recognized that the Social Gospellers, although extreme for their time, were reformers and not radicals. They were not, as are the group that Cox calls the new breed, determined anti-business radicals.[49] A typical situation involving the new breed is the rent strike,

> In the city's Negro ghetto, a protest organized and supported by a group of the town's white and Negro clergy. Despite the opposition of most of the white population, the clergy said they would continue to strike until repairs were made to the dilapidated tenements in question. If their stated reason for being involved in this action (the church must witness the poor, and this includes the Negro) persuaded only a minority of white churchmen to support the action, this minority is still a conscious and articulate one.[50]

The mandate of the clergy in the traditional social service areas has diminished with the years because of a major expansion of public and private welfare agencies outside the church. The new breed of church leaders are attempting to seize the initiative here, and to change the church's view of aid to the poor from the dispensing of social services to the political organization of the poor in their own behalf. Cox observes:

> In Buffalo, Philadelphia, Kansas City, Chicago, Oakland, and dozens of other cities, the new breed can be found organizing welfare unions, tenant's councils, rent strikes, and school boycotts. Wherever they

> have worked, they have evoked opposition both inside and outside the churches. The resulting tensions have made church politics livelier and more interesting than they have been for decades.[51]

The overall question, however, is the effect of the activists on the mandate and position of the clerical non-activists. Blue-collar working-class congregations and suburban congregations alike are still very much against this type of definition of the ministerial role. Although professional radicals work easily with the new breed, the majority of congregations force their pastor to state his position on these activities. He usually equivocates, and lets off steam at the national meetings of his denomination. In this sense, great segments of the clergy are forced to apologize for their prophets, and activism does not spread beyond the ghetto. Indeed, in recent years the white clerical activist is increasingly unwelcome in the black community. He is being told, "Go organize your own suburban parishes, or hold your peace."

Three issues which highlight the growing split between the clerical elite (the liberal university-national administration-theology student group) and the practitioner mass are the civil rights conflict, the issue of war, and the issues related to birth control and abortion. In the civil rights field, one of the first major milestones was covered by Campbell and Pettigrew.[52] They observed the role of ministers, especially Protestant ministers, in the Little Rock school integration crisis of 1958. They noted that only two white ministers out of the entire community marched in the protest procession, accompanying the children to school. One of these was the head of the local human relations organization and the other was the head of the interracial ministry in town. No person who was directly connected with a white congregation, as a pastor, accompanied children into the school. Immediately after the integration crisis, there was a city-wide prayer meeting where the clergymen all voiced hopes for law and order but did not overtly pray for integration. Campbell and Pettigrew asked the majority of the ministers why they had remained silent in the face of official statements by their national denominations in favor of integration. In all cases it was found that the congregations were essentially segregationist, but that in addition to this, the normal institutional role of the parish clergyman operated against activist integration activity. The factors in the situation which mitigated against activism were enumerated by these researchers:

> In the first place, the minister is required to be a cohesive force, to "maintain a fellowship in peace, harmony, and Christian love" rather than to promote dissension. Thus some ministers prayed during the Columbus Day services that members "carry no opinion to the point of disrupting Christian fellowship." Second, he is expected to show a progressive increase in the membership of his church. Pro-integration activity, lacking mass support, is likely to drive members to other churches.

> Finally, his task is to encourage maximum annual giving and to plan for the improvement and expansion of the plant. It's hardly surprising that several inactive integrationists who were engaged in vital fund-raising campaigns shrank from action that might endanger their success.[53]

In a later incident — the marches in Selma, Alabama — it was again the individuals at the higher levels in the church bureaucracies, not those directly responsible for parishes, who flew into Selma.[54] Ironically, therefore, the bureaucratization which is resulting in a division of labor between the parish and the larger church organization is freeing the high-ranking bureaucrats and technical experts for direct civil rights intervention work. Their administrative removal from the immediate checks and balances of the parish situation frees them for the ideological and moral work of a symbolic nature which each church theoretically engages in. On the other hand, the long-term consequences of this division of "moral labor" tends to perpetuate the status quo. Those not responsible to parishioners act morally; those responsible to them abstain. Each makes it easier for the other to continue as before.

On a second major issue, the war in Vietnam, the American clergy have been much more united than they have been on the racial issue. Partly this is because the issue is not as divisive, and partly because the direct interests of the parishioners are not as threatened by value statements in this area as they are in radical action against church holdings, or racial integration of the congregation and its neighborhood. Though the liberal clergy are almost united in this area, the fundamentalist Protestant and the conservative Catholic groups and their clergy have continued to support the war policies of a succession of American presidents, and they support the ancient cooperative relationship between the clergy and the military which is embodied in the form of chaplains on the front lines of the battlefield. In addition, some pro-administration clergymen make highly publicized trips to Vietnam and other places where American troops are concentrated, and by their public statements of "support for our boys" criticize by implication those members of their own profession who are not in favor of a war, implying that they are both unpatriotic and not in favor of the health and welfare of American servicemen.

A third major issue involves the self-interest of the poor as well as two major wings of the clergy: the religious and secular problems surrounding the control of reproduction, in particular birth control and abortion. This crisis involves as well the narrowing mandate of the clergy in scientifically relevant areas. Catholic laymen, scientists, and well-known theologians within the Catholic Church have ranged themselves on the side of birth control, because of their sympathy for the poor of the underdeveloped nations and their concern for the future of the entire world population. The conservative theological viewpoint, going back a thousand years, was espoused by Pope Paul in an encyclical in which he stated that he did not wish to deny anyone the right to sit down at "the banquet of life." [55] Given the starvation rates in underdeveloped countries, this one statement has done more than many previous ones to split the conservatives in the Catholic Church, and all fundamentalists who have values on this issue, from the liberals, the younger clergy, and the vast numbers of people who are presently not affiliated with any formal religious group. In a situation where the self-interest of the churches is defined in terms of preserving a rigid concept of rules and norms (whatever the human costs to the poor), the majority of poor and progressives inside and outside the Church have begun to speak of the moral bankruptcy of the traditional leadership. The scientific-religious value conflict is not the only factor relevant to the stand of fundamentalist and conservative groups. It has been observed that the more enlightened a peasantry is, the less likely it is to take on faith the political as well as the religious advice of the clergy. Thus the scientific-technological progressivism of the liberal clergy and the non-church groups is a direct menace to the conservative clergy in terms of their mandate with these groups, if the groups can be convinced the church's position is not in their best interests.

With each major professional group, we have considered the issue of the group acting in its own interests. Functional analysis has illustrated that each major profession possesses some particular skill, and plays, as a group, an important functional role in the ongoing social system. This skill-based leverage, combined with the internal ethics and external ideologies of the professions, puts the profession in a position to advance its interests as a group, at the expense of the wider community if necessary. However, when we consider the modern clergy, we are forced to ask, *what* leverage? We are forced to note that the central role of the clergy is either overdiffused or disappearing, if that role is defined as being the moral leader for the congregation. The leverage of the clergy in a voluntary system has never been great. In addition, in terms of the profession's attitude toward the uses of wealth and the need for social change, it is not possible to talk about one group at all. In terms of the expression, "a house divided cannot stand," the clergy cannot stand. Perhaps the Ecumenical movement is a beginning attempt to unite the clergy, but it is doubtful whether this will be allowed to progress to the point where material interests and church property are threatened. The clerical profession has not unionized, or even for that matter formed a national clergical professional association on the order of the medical or legal profession. "Occupational consciousness" is almost nonexistent, if this means any unity to oppose the aims of the laymen. Thus the majority of the clergy has neither sacred nor secular power, and is a profession of untenured servants.

In conclusion, the history of the clergy includes both prophets and clerical establishments, and in almost all ages the establishment has dominated; even when the charismatic leader comes to the fore, he soon leaves, and as Weber noted, a bureaucracy grows up where he once stood. The experience of training for positions in clerical work is now split as the pastoral role has always been split, with the university and theological schools of the liberal faiths becoming increasingly radical and anti-parish in vocational orientation, and the fundamentalist groups and the conservative branches of the faiths continuing to staff the suburban churches where the majority of the parishioners now live.

Recent years have seen a resurgence of the clerical profession in the public eye, because of the reversion to the ideals and actions of the early prophets by a vocal minority of the overall occupational group. The attractiveness of this profession to the idealistic youth of the present generation has been increased thereby. Since recruitment into any profession is one of the prime factors responsible for the perpetuation or end of its mandate, it is too soon to predict the disappearance of the group in the society's division of labor. The functional crisis that the society is headed for in many areas is in part unsolvable until values are altered — and this is a prime opportunity for prophets. On the other hand, the assembled material interests of organized religion will prevent a realization of this hoped-for renaissance until non-church public opinion acts to change the legislation so that it favors the prophets instead of the establishment. In a time when moral values are critical to the perpetuation as well as the solution of social problems, the clergy's mandate is related to the value needs of the society, as it always has been. If the people feel a need for change, this may give the prophets more of a mandate. But in all ages, and the present does not look like an exception, the primary mandate of the clergy, and the source of its security as a group, has been its function as a legitimator and supporter of the status quo.

CHAPTER EIGHT

THE MILITARY FIELD

It has been an ancient contention of the professional military man that there was no worry on his part about being unemployed, for human nature would always provide work for him. More recently, historians and economists have noted the role of economic interests in conflict, and the role of war in attempted solutions. Clausewitz stated that war was "the continuation of politics by other means." For an occupational group specializing in the use of violence, these are conditions that would seem ideal. And yet the military profession in modern America is in turmoil, in potential disarray, and threatened with both technological unemployment and broad-based citizen opposition. The reasons for this require a historical, biographical, functional, and interest-based analysis.

A HISTORICAL PERSPECTIVE

There is no known beginning to the role of the military man in history, but a reasonable place to enter is with the Greeks and Romans. Albion has concluded that both ancient Greece and Rome began with periods where citizen-soldiers were prominent and ended with regular armies and the use of mercenaries, that is, paid non-citizen soldiers.[1] In the earlier periods, in the Greek *polis*, the role of hero in battle was reserved for the free man. The economy was based on slavery; the leisure time given to all citizens was thus available for war and creative arts. Since slaves could be acquired only in war, the wars between the city-states had an economic as well as a value-based motivation.

But, as Albion argues:

> The system worked as long as wars were short and one could "commute" to the battlefield. Athens, however, developed wide-spread com-

merce and an empire. Citizen-soldiers could not very well be drafted for long garrison duty on distant islands. The state was prosperous, so it began to hire professionals who enjoyed soldiering. Other states soon took up this scheme. These "soldiers of fortune" even sold their services outside Greece.[2]

The pattern was repeated for Rome. The early Republic was small and had a citizen army. After the defeat of Hannibal, the Empire spread to Spain, Asia, and Africa. In 100 B.C., at the time of Caesar, the majority of legionnaires were professionals with years of experience in different areas. Some occupational mobility was possible from within the ranks, but the majority of officers were sons of the aristocracy. Gradually the use of foreign troops, non-Roman soldiers from the conquered regions, became common, and the patriotic citizen-army of the Roman republic gave way to a disorganized structure of mercenary soldiers with little central loyalty to Rome. The absence of strong patriotic motivation and political allegiance in the later armies was, according to Albion, an important factor in the fall of Rome itself.[3]

After the fall of the Roman Empire, at the time of Charlemagne, the alternation between citizen and specialist armies continued. In 800 A.D., in the Frankish kingdom, the army was essentially a militia. The type of service was based on income:

> Those who could afford to do so bought horses and became cavalry, just as in ancient times when the cavalry was the rich man's outfit. The "middle classes" fitted themselves out as infantry. The poor clubbed together. For instance, five men might purchase soldier's equipment for one of their number.[4]

The majority of the peasantry remained at home, to keep the fields in production.

During the major part of the medieval period, land tenure and military service were directly related. In return for the rights to land which the king or major lord granted to his lesser lords or vassals, they had to provide a number of armed men to fight in the service of the lord. The knight was in most cases a member of this lesser nobility, in the position of the officer, with a set of supporting and provisioning (but not fighting) men also recruited from the local area. As in the early Greek city-state, battle was the province of the elite. But in contrast to the situation in Greece, the opposing forces had a military code of honor, and the use of mercenaries was not required. The "contest" and the limited short-term engagement were characteristic of military actions in the medieval period. However, there were signs of change in the air. Military technology and strategy — in weaponry and siege techniques — were beginning to develop before the end of the Middle Ages.[5] The use of battalions of non-noblemen, as archers for example, meant that the knight-on-horseback strategy of early feudal times was weak when opposed by a feudal army composed of masses of peasants. As Vagts notes, foot soldiers from Swiss peasant communities defeated armored knights at Morgarten in 1315 and Sempach in 1386.[6]

Leonardo da Vinci, the model of the Renaissance man, epitomized an important aspect of the Renaissance era by his contributions to military technology. His genius was in part directed toward the construction of catapults, fortifications, and, in later years, the design of multiple-cannon rocketry.[7] The technological revolution in warfare was paralleled by the economic and social revolution of the Renaissance and the rise to power of the merchant capitalist groups. These preferred to pay mercenary armies to do their fighting for them. These armies had leaders, who would contract with a given city or state to undertake the defense of the region, for a price. From about 1300 to 1650, these *condottieri* and their armies fought as professionals but not as nationals or patriots. Thus,

> There was no particular advantage in killing or in being killed. It was more profitable to take prisoners who could be ransomed. As a result, casualty lists in important battles were often surprisingly low. The mercenaries, moreover, did not ordinarily favor decisive action. They were paid by the month, not the job. The longer they could make it last, the better for them. It was like a sort of international "soldiers' union" with mutual understandings on professional etiquette.[8]

The primary exploited groups here were the employer, and even more, the citizenry of the countryside, who were plundered and raped by these armies in times of war and times of peace alike. Having no local allegiances, the mercenaries had no compunctions.

THE ADVENT OF THE MASS ARMY

The Reformation brought about wars of religion and the creation of the ideological army, the army with its organization and goals based on a creed. For example, in the New Model Army of Oliver Cromwell's England, there was a strictly imposed discipline, promotion was by seniority and the recommendation of senior officers, the purchase of officer status was illegal, and politics within the army were limited. But Huntington does not think this was true professionalism, for the discipline came from devotion to an ideological cause, not organization and self-conscious occupational development with a body of military theory.[9] Walzer's study of the period, *The Revolution of the Saints*, considers the Puritans as the first radicals. This would make the highly disciplined New Model Army one of the first prototypes of Mao Tse-tung's revolutionary army in China; where the Communist armies have Marxian dogma, the New Model Army had Protestantism:

> The religious purposes that so often underlay the tactical innovations had to be made explicit. Fervor had to be encouraged even in common soldiers and war itself described as if it were a crusade. The saint and the citizen were more likely than the vassal, the mercenary, or the kidnapped vagrant to commit themselves to a long and difficult struggle on God's behalf.[10]

In the period 1650–1800 the national army came into being. As Huntington summarizes it, the military forces became owned by the king instead of by the condottieri. The officers were now the servants of the ruler instead of independent businessmen: "the military function was socialized; national control replaced private control." [11] This was the period when national monarchs were consolidating their power and in so doing they viewed a national, permanent standing army as important for both external protection and internal control. The head positions in the army and navy were deliberately given to the aristocracy, thus providing both insurance against revolutionary action by the armies and more thorough control over the aristocracy. This control lay in their employee status with respect to the crown, and the chain of command with the king at the head. The American and French revolutions modified policies of having wholly aristocratic army officer corps in these nations, but during this extensive period the military-political relationship was handled in most nations through a policy of keeping the elites in political and military areas related by blood. For those with wealth but not sufficient social background, prices were set on the officer positions, thereby guaranteeing that only the wealthy and the socially elite would command the military forces and thus safeguarding the establishment from military coups.

PROFESSIONALIZATION

It was Napoleon's citizen army, and the Prussian army's reaction to defeat at its hands, that is considered by Vagts and Huntington to be the foundation of the modern military profession.[12] Although citizen armies had been seen before in history, the vast size of Napoleon's national citizen army and its power in the face of the essentially amateur, aristocratically led armies of Europe, led to a reaction on the part of Prussia and the subsequent professional Prussian army was then imitated around the world. Aristocratic birth was no longer required for entry into the Prussian officer corps, educational prerequisites were set for positions, and specific academic training in military strategy was instituted. A body of military theory and strategy was written by the Prussian Baron von Clausewitz; the formal specialized knowledge of the military profession dates from this time.[13] The actual composition of the officer corps remained primarily aristocratic in most nations for some time after 1800, but the construction of professional standards and professional training which had begun about

1800 was about complete at the beginning of the twentieth century. Each nation had a standing army, a professional officer corps, and a professional training system by 1900. Membership and advancement were at least in part based on skill and merit, not birth.

In the United States, the development of the military profession began at the militia stage, during the Revolution, although in this early period the colonists used mercenaries (the Hessians especially) to augment the citizen militias. Hamilton's idea of a professional standing army was defeated in the post-Revolutionary period because the new nation feared that a military elite might take power in the formative stages of development.[14]

The Jacksonian era was critical for the American military profession, as it was for medical, legal, and clerical professions, and for essentially the same reason—the anti-elite sentiment of the time led to fear that a military elite would be a major danger to democracy. The period's impact on the military profession can be seen in two areas: the Jacksonian legislation which created the form of the profession, and the citizen pressures of the following years which forced the profession to organize itself tightly in defense, creating occupational consciousness and a sense of mission. The legislation of greatest importance was that requiring the recruits for West Point (established 1803) to be appointed by congressmen, who were *civilians* and not military, and that requiring West Point cadets to be recruited from all the states, in equal proportion, to avoid a concentration and a regional dominance of the military institution. The succeeding years, including the Civil War, saw a continuing suspicion of the military. These anti-elite attitudes led the military to turn to themselves and form a code of ethics, a set of standards, and a group solidarity. During this formative era major American military leaders toured Europe, studying especially the Prussian professional army.[15]

THE POLITICAL ROLE OF THE MODERN ARMY

During the period of the exploration of the West, the period of the American Industrial Revolution, and the growth of international expansionist and colonialist policies in the United States, the military became functionally used by the civil elite — especially by the capitalists in power — as a kind of domestic and foreign police force; they were used to make the Western expansion possible (Indian fighting), to aid the colonialist policies of American corporations, and protect foreign investments by the United States (the Monroe Doctrine, the Philippine War, the Spanish-American War). The *size* of the military was small at this time, and remained small except for a brief period in World War I.

The main professional-political turning point was World War II and its aftermath. Only in World War II was a citizen draft used in the United States, and for the first time a large standing army with a professional officer corps came into being. The atomic bomb and the onset of the Cold War created the conditions in which military leaders (and a significant number of civilian leaders) felt justified in maintaining a large military establishment in peacetime. The new cooperation between civil and military leaders which grew out of World War II politicized the military profession, and the post-war years have led to a series of political issues, such as the military-industrial complex and the role of the military in a nuclear age, which are with us at the present time.

Four major themes run through this brief review of the historical development of the military profession: the role of the leadership groups within the military, the relation of the military group to civilian power, the degree of professionalization of the military, and the impact of technology. Until the nineteenth century, the alternation of aristocratic, citizen, and mercenary armies could always be understood with respect to the desires of the civilian power structure to restrict the mandate and power of the group by "owning" its leading elite, either through blood relationship, citizen loyalty, or binding contract. The rise of nationalism led to national armies, to a national officer corps, and then to mass citizen wars. Once the citizens became a major part of the manpower pool, they began to press for mobility opportunities within the military profession. The role of the aristocratic and the wealthy has decreased in the profession steadily since the beginning of the nineteenth century.

Civilian-military power relations did not become a problem until the officer-corps became professionalized, having a life of its own not directly interlaced with the civilian society. In all times, the role of the military is stronger in war than in peace. In historical perspective, therefore, military professionalization was deliberately retarded for reasons of state until the time when the professionalized army was necessary for the survival of the state in wartime — when Prussia professionalized in order to resist the Napoleonic armies. Once the military was formed as a distinct profession, the existence of the group as a permanent entity necessitated the deliberate construction of laws on civil-military relations which acknowledged the separateness of the groups, and the subservient position of the military.

Finally, the role of technology is important in all eras, but until the present is somewhat overrated as a factor. Until the Renaissance at least, the major question concerned which groups fought, and the number of them, rather than the weapons used. Then, with the major advances in military technology, there was a decrease in citizen involvement; thus fewer people than might be expected were affected by the new technology. It is the combination of modern technology and mass citizen forces that has given war since Napoleon its total catastrophic effect. This combination of high technology and mass citizen involvement in fighting remains important until the advent of the atomic age, when the manpower variable becomes so overshadowed by the technological that the relevance of a large standing army is called into question; the technological progress tends toward technological unemployment of the military itself. In conclusion, the nature of elites in the military, conflicts of civil and military interest, professionalization as an internal and public activity, and the impact of technology are issues of concern to the military field, past, present, and future.

THE MILITARY EXPERIENCE

The point of view of the professional soldier has always been of concern to nations, for the understanding of any group's actions is increased by a knowledge of its motivations and its previous experience. Although the memoirs of generals have always constituted a rich source for historians, studies of the experience of *groups* within the military are a more recent phenomenon. We can approach an understanding of the military experience by inspecting the social origins of military personnel, the motivations for choosing a military career, the nature of the career pattern and its choice points, including leaving the field at different stages of the career, and the ultimate world views developed by different types of military men.

ORIGINS AND REASONS FOR ENTRY

The social origins of the non-officer groups in the armed forces of the United States have not basically differed from those in Europe since the time of Napoleon. The foot soldier has always been from the lower and lower middle classes. The major trends of interest, in terms of the nature of previous experience and viewpoints brought to training, have been those of the officer corps. Janowitz notes that the majority of those in the military elite — the group that became the generals up to the time of World War II — were white Anglo-Saxon Protestants with a rural, and often Southern, upper-class background.[16] He notes that the democratization of the officer corps has accelerated, for the last two decades show an increase in those from minority groups, from urban backgrounds, and from lower social classes.[17] Lovell shows the extent of this in data indicating that 33 per cent of the entering class of 1960 at West Point had fathers who were skilled or unskilled laborers. During the 1940s the professional and white-collar group constituted 60 per cent of West Point family backgrounds, but this had dropped to 45 per cent by 1960.[18] Considering the historical origins of the military elite in most periods, there appears to be no question that the policy of the nation has been to change the military elite from one of informal Southern social "aristocracy" to one broadly representative of the population at large. Whatever world view the officer corps develops, it cannot at present be considered to be based on the officers' pre-military social group membership. This is not to say that the elite groups are not represented at present, nor that their chances for attaining the very top ranks are still not higher, but these positions and careers are no longer reserved for them exclusively. Achieved status, performance before entry to the military academy and to officer training programs, is clearly more important than status ascribed by birth.

The specific reasons for the choice of a military career vary according to the level of career considered, except in the case of draftees, who have almost no choice at all initially. The primary concept of importance is the value-based nature of the choice of some officers, compared with the utility-based (what's-in-it-for-me) motivations of many other officers and most enlisted men. As Weber noted, a person can choose a career for general, value-based reasons — an abstract or emotional regard for an ideal which the vocation represents — or he may choose for more mundane reasons.[19] Both the ministry and the military field share this phenomenon: the sons of the socially elite choose these careers for value-based reasons, as they mean in most cases a step down in terms of material reward and comfort, whereas the sons of the poor choose these careers for mobility reasons, that is, they represent more raw power and prestige than other alternatives and better rewards in monetary terms. The reasoning here holds for the officer corps; in the ordinary ranks the motivations are primarily materialistic. The exception here is found in time of war, when patriotism is a reason for entrance into the military at all levels, but not necessarily a motivation for remaining after the crisis has passed.

For the elite of the military profession, the motivations for entry are seen to be as complex as for other levels. Probably at all levels motivations are mixed in terms of some value reasons and some material ones, even at the top. Janowitz summarizes:

> Four motive patterns, singly and in combination, were of consequence for those who rose to the level of general or admiral by 1950: tradition, or more precisely family and social inheritance; sheer desire for education and social advancement, with or without a career commitment to the military; experience in a military setting; and "boyhood" ambition. The potential officer's career choice was further influenced not only by his feeling that the armed forces had a vital function, but by the fact that the military had offered an adequate and respectable level of personal security in peacetime. Nor should one overlook the intermingling of these motives with a diffuse desire for an active, outdoor life.[20]

The "civil service" status of the military career and the governmentally enforced rules against discrimination (since Korea) are motivations for entry for racial minority group members, who enlist and become career enlisted men in greater proportions than the white group relative to the population, as opportunities are better here than in civilian life.

The draftee, even before the time of political protest against the institution of the draft, has usually had a negative motivation with respect to military service. The penalties for avoiding service outweighed the difficulties of serving, until the Vietnam War at least. At the time of the Korean

War, 83 per cent of college males at Cornell did not want to serve unless forced.[21] Two decades later a draft resistance movement is in progress, and basic questions are being raised as to the constitutionality of the draft in an undeclared war.[22] The objections to the draft, in addition to being political, are also understandable in terms of the relative deprivations which serving or not serving entails.[23] For example, as with entry at the other levels and by other pathways, it can be seen that motivations and satisfactions are relative to social position before entry. The poor have more to gain and less to lose by military service than the sons of the elite, regardless of the political implications of service in a particular war, such as Vietnam. Finally, a youth's family, friends, or parole officer may encourage a youth to enter the military as a form of rehabilitation: "The army will be good for you." In fact, preliminary information on experimental programs with felons and other groups indicates that for certain groups the military life does provide external controls.[24] But the military, basing their standpoint on years of follow-up research, and experience with training in several major wars, single this last group out for discouragement. Whatever else the military career is, it is neither undemanding nor unstressful, even in peacetime, and those whose personal motivations are based on personal psychological problems have been found to take more from the military group than they provide.

EARLY TRAINING

The first socialization experience of the new military man is deliberately constructed to have maximum impact, and involves the rite of passage characteristically found in job entry situations where high risks are involved. The aim is completeness of socialization. Janowitz and Little observed that the military establishment's emphasis on assimilation and socialization of the recruits involves not only the complex of technical skills but also "an elaborate code of professional behavior and etiquette, since membership in the military means participation in an organizational community which regulates behavior both on and off the job."[25]

There has been a marked evolution in the nature and functions of this initial experience. Classically, it was meant to be a "shock experience," to convey the authoritarian ideals and procedures of a rigid command structure. But in more recent years the emphasis on group adaptation as well as the research on battle behavior and adaptation to stress has led the military to deemphasize the "hazing" aspect of the transition and to emphasize the adaptive group social skills that are useful both in battlefield groups and in the most common military setting of all — the bureaucracy.[26] Thus the process is usually graduated in this fashion:

> Assimilation during initial training requires adapting the recruit to an all-male society and to a social organization committed to violence. The process begins with an effort to "strip" all of the novice's ties with

the civilian world which conflict with the requirements of the military and to substitute new bases for identification. At the most personal level the recruit faces a loss of privacy and exposure to a pervasive set of controls. The initial stage of training stresses combat roles; thereafter there is a progressive specialization which recognizes that most personnel will ultimately perform administrative and technical activities.[27]

The initial military training, in its modern form, thus consists as much of taking aptitude tests and experiencing group pressure as of strict battlefield training. Career experiences diverge early, even for the enlisted men and draftees. The more talented sheep are separated from the goats, who in time of war are sent directly to the battlefield; in recent conflicts, the latter have been black, poor, or both, in numbers quite disproportionate to their percentages in the overall manpower pool of the military. By type of setting, there is also an ideological element in the early socialization phase. In the elite settings — West Point, the Naval and Air academies — the traditions and history of the military are stressed to a group already interested in them. In the college-based ROTC and Officer's Candidate School — the latter for enlisted men who wish upward mobility — the advantages and opportunities of permanent military careers are stressed, for evidence indicates less long-term career commitment here than in the academy graduates, especially in the ROTC program group.[28] In the basic training for non-officers, a pragmatic "use the service for your own advancement" approach is basic to the sales message. Finally, there is an element of direct political ideology in recent military training. With the expansion of United States interest in fighting anti-revolutionary actions around the world, the indoctrination of recruits has been including counter-guerilla, anti-communist ideology as well as specific field training in the suppression of peasant revolts.[29] This kind of activity is reminiscent in many ways of the training and attitudes instilled in the recruit in an earlier era, as during the Philippine War. In general, in the initial phase of training, the drill and shock tactics of the earlier military initiation has been replaced by an emphasis on group manipulation, ideological and psychological indoctrination, and occupational salesmanship, with the military staff acting as career recruiters as well as basic trainers.

The initial training experience must be differentiated now from combat experience, which only a minority of men undergo, and which cannot be duplicated by the most carefully simulated conditions in the forests of a training camp. Grinker and Spiegel's study, as well as the series by Ginzberg and his co-workers, indicate that the well-integrated personality and the mentally and socially "endowed" individuals make better adjustments to combat than the less sturdy or the more rigid.[30] Studies by Stouffer, *et al.*, indicated the importance of the reference groups of the given men in understanding their satisfactions or feelings of relative deprivation in combat or on other settings.[31] In Korea and Vietnam a two-person buddy system appears to develop under combat stress, as a way of coping with the uncertainties of the military situation.[32] In all cases, there is little evidence to indicate that intellectual performance relates to combat performance, but good evidence that basic personality characteristics do make a difference, with the more flexible less likely to crack under the strain. Again, in spite of the great interest of social scientists and the military in this topic, it is important to note that even in wartime the combat socialization experience is a minority experience.

THE PATTERN OF MILITARY CAREERS

Career patterns within the military field share similarities and differences with the career patterns in the complex field of health occupations. As in the health field, the career patterns are stratified, with entry at certain levels resulting in a far wider range of opportunities than entry at other levels. Unlike the health field, however, upward occupational mobility from one career level to another is possible. In fact, a major source of officers at present is retrained career enlisted men. But the stratification still exists, and before comparing and contrasting the differing patterns it is necessary to review each level in general outline.

Entry into the officer corps at present is through three major kinds of experience: the military academy — the elite pathway, the college-based ROTC program, or the Officer Candidate School — the pathway for experienced enlisted men who are socially upwardly mobile. Only the first of these pathways guarantees opportunities at the very top of the military hierarchy; with the exception of the Air Force, academy graduates hold almost all of the top positions in the armed services.[33] The ROTC is a large source of new officers; combined with the OCS graduates, they make up more than 90 per cent of the entries into the officer ranks.

The pattern of the officer career can be looked at in two ways: in terms of content and in terms of structure. Increasingly, technical expertise is required in the many subfields where officers hold positions in the armed forces; with the increasing specialization, technical assignments outweigh administrative in the early years of the career. Unusual assignments, especially diplomatic posts, are also helpful for advancement. The farther the officer goes, and the higher the rank, the more the administrative skills become necessary. Thus at about the one-third point in the officer's career, after perhaps ten years of service, a sizable minority of each service's career officers enter a "staff" or administrative training school, and the top graduates of these schools are given the opportunity to progress further. The officer who is destined for a generalship or admiral's rank is offered, two-thirds of the way through his career, the chance to attend one of the service war colleges or instead the National War College. The latter attempts to provide inter-service higher military education; all are advanced management and military strategy schools that combine the "new theory" in military strategy with intensive training in management techniques and long-range planning. The further the officer progresses in this training sequence, the more contacts he develops with the high ranks of the corporate world who are invited to address the class, especially experts from the military-industrial complex and professors from the elite universities who are experts in military or game theory and international affairs. The policies of the war colleges are constructed to provide the future managers of the military system with the latest in strategic thinking and Harvard Business School-style management expertise. Only a small fraction of officers can be generals, of course, and so the war college experience is not at all typical, even for the higher officers.[34]

The enlisted man's career pattern is less well structured. The first major decision, after entry through the draft or volunteer pathway, is whether to reenlist. Regular status and high performance can lead to a chance to attend Officer's Candidate School, which will then put the man on the track toward a lower-level officer's career.[35] Careers within the enlisted ranks again can be categorized as essentially technical and specialist or essentially administrative, with the technical specialist groups now of such size and importance that the old rank systems of the service are becoming somewhat irrelevant. A structure is evolving in which few regulars are at the bottom and a dual mobility-career pattern exists: increasing technical expertise with increasing pay or increasing administrative responsibility with perhaps a chance at Officer's Candidate School.

The third type of career with respect to the military field is of growing importance in both a political and an economic sense — the careers of civilians within the military orbit. In a basic sense, the blue-collar maintenance workers, secretaries, military engineering specialists, and defense research scientists have military careers, or careers within the military field as defined in this book. In 1959, Lang indicates that 2.4 million civilians were on the payroll of the separate services and the Pentagon; for every two military men in uniform, there was at least one civilian employed in the military field.[36] Here the opportunities to rise to the top levels of the military hierarchy are nonexistent for the blue-collar or white-collar worker, for whom military employment is a form of public service work. But, for the highly skilled scientist or systems analyst, mobility into the top levels of the military hierarchy — the Pentagon planning and strategic elite — is now possible in a way that it may not be, ironically, for any but a small minority of officers who do well at the war colleges.

CAREER COMMITMENT AND OUTSIDE OPPORTUNITY

Commitment to these career patterns is related to a balancing of the outside civilian opportunities and the internal chances for advancement. Mandatory retirement age for military personnel has been far earlier than for civilian careers — many retire at age 45 — and thus after the initial socialization experience the calculation of relative advantages of staying or leaving begins.[37] There are several complexities and unknowns in the calculations, which make the choice to stay in or to leave difficult. But, nevertheless, certain groups of officers and enlisted men are now known to be more likely to stay and others more likely to leave, and the reasons for the existence of these groups explain something of the commitment dilemma. The long-stayers do so essentially because they believe military opportunities are better than civilian ones. At the high officer levels, staying involves a chance at the war colleges, top military positions, and then good placement in private industry. For the enlisted man who has entered and passed Officer's Candidate School, blue-collar background and enlisted status have eventuated in an officer position and midcareer upward mobility; officers who enter by this path are more likely to be long-term career officers than academy graduates or ROTC college graduates, as either of these groups is of higher socioeconomic status with more potential opportunities on the outside. As the academy graduate group comes to resemble the OCS group more closely in social background, rather than resembling the civilian college ROTC group, it may become more stable for the same reasons as the OCS group. At present, the length of stay in the military of OCS graduates is longer than that of any other group, including West Point graduates. In general, there is marked dissatisfaction, among military planners, with the very low level of long-term commitment of ROTC officers, who use the officer status as a short-term way of paying off military service obligations and then return to civilian life.[38]

In terms of skills, the services are in a major commitment-and-training dilemma. As the work of the military becomes increasingly specialized and technical, at both officer and enlisted ranks, there is an increasing need to give the occupational members the skills to carry out the job. To the degree that the career men gain the skills, they are often valuable in outside employment; this goes for management skills as well as technological ones. The poor learners are less likely to be attractive to outside employers and more likely to want to remain. Thus those least committed to the military career are precisely the ones most needed by the military sector to fill its functional roles, and the most committed often are the ones *least* wanted or needed. The exception here — the academy elite — has value-based and tradition-based reasons for commitment, but as the population of the academy becomes increasingly blue-collar, their reasons for staying or leaving may increasingly become the essentially materialistic ones of the other officers and the enlisted men. This issue of skill versus commitment is common in all public service occupations and it is of course a problem of the institution and the society, rather than of the individuals, who gain either way. But the dangers of the military career and the regimentation of the life experience (with frequent changes in residence), exert a strong push on the most skilled to leave the military for civilian employment. This has obvious functional consequences for the efficiency of the military sector. Given the initial reasons for entering the military, the differential socialization experiences, and the diverse patterns of military careers, it would be surprising to find one simple occupational perspective common to all military men. Lovell's evidence clearly shows, for West Point entering and graduating cadets, that a unitary military world view just does not exist with this group.[39] A variety of military outlooks characterizes the entering students, and they maintain them with little change. His research bears out the hypothesis of Janowitz, that there are different types of world outlook possessed by military men. Janowitz constructed an ideal type of two viewpoints — the "absolutist," or hawk, and the pragmatist, or moderate — and Lovell added a third, the "pacifist."[40] He also suggested that in reality there was probably a spectrum of attitudes on issues from the extremist hawk to the pacifist. The primary kinds of attitudes and positions investigated in Lovell's cadets and Janowitz's generals concerned the role of the military and the foreign policy of the United States with respect to the Communist bloc nations. Both of these authors suggested that the "absolutist" viewpoint is too extreme for the complexities of modern war and the modern managerial military establishment; managers have to be more pragmatic and adaptive in their attitude than do heroes in battle, where the decisions are more clear-cut.

Yet both the *absolutist* position (the United States political supremacy in the world seen as desirable, a felt need for massive defense and deterrent power, the Soviets viewed as potential world dominators, and all neutrals seen as potential enemies) and the *pragmatist* position (the United States seen as a competitor with the Soviets on a permanent basis, the need felt for graduated military deterrence, the Soviets viewed as expansionist) are justifications for the continuation of a strong military establishment. Both positions are examples of what Huntington called "conservative realism" or the military ethic:

> The military ethic emphasizes the permanence, irrationality, weakness, and evil in human nature. It stresses the supremacy of society over the individual and the importance of order, hierarchy, and division of function. It stresses the continuity and value of history. It accepts the nation-state as the highest form of political organization and recognizes the continuing likelihood of wars among nation-states. It emphasizes the importance of power in international relations and warns of the dangers to state security. It holds that the security of the state depends on the creation and maintenance of strong military forces.[41]

This much could be considered the hawk viewpoint. But Huntington adds that the military professional ethic, as a statement of public ideals,

> urges the limitation of state action to the direct interests of the state, the restriction of extensive commitments, and the undesirability of belli-

> cose or adventurous policies. It holds that war is the instrument of politics, that the military are the servant of the statesman, and that civilian control is essential to military professionalism. It exalts obedience as the highest virtue of military men.[42]

Military ethics, as any other form of professional ethics, must be understood as a form of public occupational ideology, used to convince others as well as the military themselves of the goals and standards of the group. And as with ethical statements and viewpoints of any occupational group, they are followed by, or even understood clearly by, some parts of the group more than others. In a sense, the issue of the "military mind" must be understood against the career experience of given subgroups in the military. With the exception of the academy graduates, who do have a sense of ancestry and group belonging and whose careers cross and recross to give them a chance to maintain their original world views and support one another as professionals, the majority of military personnel absorb aspects of the military ethic in bits and snatches, by osmosis or brief indoctrination. The justification of the meaningfulness of a military career, in the above general terms, makes far more sense to the elite than to the mass within the military. For them, the pragmatism of career choice and individual advancement appears to occupy their personal consciousness far more than ideas on the advancement of the profession as a whole through justifying the need for its existence or its professional neutrality in the political sphere. Just as career experiences are stratified, the breadth of viewpoint of the military subgroups is stratified as well. The experience of the civilian, the enlisted man, and the lower-rank and non-academy officer is often colored primarily by his dilemmas concerning career advancement within or outside the military field, although military occupational dilemmas are important to all in fact; the dilemma of the professional group as a whole is of conscious concern primarily only to the military elite, and to those segments of the civilian world who work with them for gain and profit.

In general, an inspection of career experience in the military field shows that an earlier and simpler model of indoctrination and career structure has been replaced by a more complex one. The motivations for entry to a military career have grown both more complex and more materialistic as the social origins of the officer group have been democratized. The experience itself has evolved from one of preparation to fight in a rigid command structure to preparation to serve in a complex, technically oriented bureaucracy which *sometimes* fights. As the field has expanded, it is possible to speak of civilian careers within the military, a notion alien to the smaller pre-World War II army. The world views and the overall stances of the military profession as a body vary accordingly; different elements favor different actions by the total group. The only common thread running through the ideologies is that the military are a needed group and that they ought to be "professional" and stay out of politics. But in spite of ideologies in this direction, the reality is another story. The real division of labor between the military and the civilian worlds — and their interpenetration — is our next subject.

THE MILITARY DIVISION OF LABOR: PAST AND PRESENT

In perhaps no other major occupational field has the technological revolution affected the meaning of the group's function as it has in the military. The technological advances in weaponry since the atomic bomb, especially the missile systems of the major powers, have redefined the nature and meaning of war, the role of civilian and military personnel within the military field, and the nature of the power relationships between them. Technological change can be seen as a major factor in influencing the three main principles upon which the division of labor is based in the military field: the distinction between military and civilian work, the hierarchical principle of classical military organizations, and the distinction between military functions in wartime and in time of peace. Each of these principles can be considered in turn, both in terms of overall changes from the pre-World War II era to the present, and in terms of the role of technology in particular in bringing about these changes.

THE CHANGING NATURE OF MILITARY WORK

The historical distinction between the civil order and the military group has been critical in understanding both the power relations between states and the power structure within states. Since in many previous eras a sharp distinction was not made between the civilian and the military, or as in Napoleon's time between the military man and the politician, the leader of military forces acted on the basis of general values and overall patriotism, rather than on a specific technical ethic or a professional set of standards. Thus the heroic model of the military leader is ancient. But modern armies and navies are dependent on technical weaponry and the complex integration of large numbers of men and material. As Janowitz indicates, there is a transition in military leadership and in opportunities for elite status from the hero, whose role is useful in battle but irrelevant elsewhere, to the managerial experts and the technical experts who now have the clearer track to the top positions.[43] But the technological change in the nature of warfare increasingly fits the technical expert who also has administrative skills for top positions, along with those who have been able to acquire political expertise in international assignments with diplomatic connections.

The change in division of labor is now relevant for enlisted men as well. Lang notes that the skill structure of the rank-and-file military personnel is not pyramidal but rather oval-shaped, with the greatest number of enlisted men neither experts nor unskilled, but in middle-level specialties in administrative or technical areas. Both for officers and enlisted men, therefore, there has been an evolution from the essentially "military" work of the battle soldier to the work of administrative and technical experts and technicians, roles which are frequently found in civilian life as well.[44] The following jobs are now found both inside and outside of the military field:

Highway traffic engineer	Yardmaster
Clinical psychologist	Labor relations officer
Machine records officer	Civil defense officer
Tissue pathologist	Real estate officer
Forestry officer	Radio broadcast officer
Postal officer	Laundry and fumigation officer [45]

In this sense the increasing bureaucratic complexity and technological sophistication of the armed forces have led to a division of labor which is, in the main, not strictly military, but rather a society-within-a-society, with both "military" and "non-military" roles required. The principle which distinguishes civil from military work in this division of labor is economic and political; the field is defined by participation in the Department of Defense's payroll and budget. Ironically, the most *military* jobs of all in the modern army are those of the front line soldiers, who are in large part essentially civilians who do not expect to have a career in the military. Thus, in general, in the modern army the need for administrative and technical skills puts a premium on these skills at the expense of the charismatic leaders and the fighters, lowering their prestige. Even more important, hero status in war is not seen any longer as a major qualification for administrative promotion after the war is over.

DIVISION OF LABOR: FOREIGN AND DOMESTIC POLITICS

A second major way in which the present civil-military relation differs from that of the past lies in the interpenetration of the civilian and military spheres in both domestic and foreign policy, symbolized especially by the role of the Pentagon. The Department of Defense is the largest single bureau in the United States government and has been responsible for the spending of about half of our federal budget for the last decade. The importance of the agency lies in its intermixing of civilian and military leadership in the elite positions in the national capital, and its role as a political action agency with respect to Congress, the President, and the general public. As the Cold War progressed, the Joint Chiefs of Staff in the Pentagon were given an increasing role in foreign policy planning. Masland and Radway summarize this role:

> The Joint Chiefs of Staff, as the principal military advisers to the President, the National Security Council, and the Secretary of Defense,

> are also heavily involved in international security affairs. In recent years they have addressed themselves to such matters as: the kind of military organization that should be established under NATO; the crossing of the 38th parallel in Korea; the selection of Latin American states to receive military aid and the amount of such aid; the rearmament of Western Germany, the wisdom of seeking air bases in the Mediterranean, of blocking Communist China, of suggesting revisions of the Italo-Yugoslav border, *and of relieving the French of part of their burden in Indo-China.*[46]

The Joint Chiefs often had their wishes granted, especially on the last point. We did "relieve the French of their burden" in Indo-China, or to use the other name for this region, in Vietnam.

Two other occupational groups indicate the nature of the relationship between the civilian government and the military: the military attachés routinely assigned to American embassies around the world, who are responsible to the Pentagon and not to the American ambassador, and the CIA, the secret para-military organization budgeted to the Department of Defense.[47] Vagts notes that the military attaché is a European invention; their overt role is the observation of the military actions of the host country, but their covert role is often being the recipient of military information gathered by espionage in the host country.[48] Here the foreign policy branch of the Executive (the State Department) supposedly works with the military (the Department of Defense), but the latter is often independent of the former. This is even more the case with the CIA, which as a secret intelligence-gathering agency is basic for the planning of military strategy and decisions and the stances which the military will take with respect to the President and the Congress on threats to national security. But as I. F. Stone and others have noted, the CIA acts not as an impartial information-gathering organization, but also as an invisible government decision-maker and action agency, supplying funds and information to the friends of the American military in foreign regimes, supporting coups to bring pro-United States leaders to power by deposing neutralists, and undercutting the enemies of regimes which the United States military and the government want to protect.[49] These interventions often backfire, but either in their success or their failure they enlarge the scope of military men not only in determining the foreign policy of the nation, but also in creating the very conditions to which the nation — and the military — must respond in the future.

On the domestic side, the boundaries between the civilian world and the military have become dissolved through the extensive military-corporate relationships built up by the defense contract arrangements necessary to produce the complex equipment of modern war. The military-industrial complex — the inter-institutional arrangement between the military, defense contracting corporations, and the politicians who control the defense budget — will be considered at length in the next section of the chapter. But the *existence* of the military-industrial complex is at least in part the consequence of the changing nature of war. Very few people got rich providing beans and bacon to a foot soldier army, but profits of a larger scale are possible on the expensive technological hardware of modern war, and major industries are needed to make them.

In addition to the close relations between the military and certain sectors of industry, the ties of the university to the military field have grown extensively as a result of the military's need for high-level expertise. Thus special Ph.D.-staffed research centers have been created such as the government-run think tanks (the RAND Corporation), or university-based research centers (MIT's Lincoln Lab), or centers for the study of military-political strategy (the Institutes for Defense Analysis).[50] As a consequence, an important segment of the academic elite has established ties with the Department of Defense, in scientific or political science areas. They also take an important role in the military war colleges, preparing the generals of the future. The needs for management skills have made the elite business schools an especially important source of consultant expertise for the military.

To sum up, the old line of delineation between the military profession and the civilian world has been replaced by *joint function arrangements* — the Pentagon, the military attaché, the defense production contract; by *"civilian" work by those in the military field* — the forestry officer and the traffic engineer in uniform; and *by actual civilian careers on the defense budget* — the army of maintenance workers and civilian scientists working in the military setting itself. In all ways, the changing nature of the military occupational field, combined with direct political action by the military in civil affairs both by invitation and design, has led to a breakdown in the older division of labor principle which made it possible to say where "military" work began and "civilian" work ended. This is one of the dimensions in Lasswell's original definition of the garrison state.

THE FATE OF THE HIERARCHIAL PRINCIPLE

A second major organizing principle for the division of labor in the military field is the principle of *hierarchy*, or chain of command. The military organization at one point in time, perhaps most extensively in Prussia, was a model of direct control from the top down. Max Weber probably had the Prussian officer corps in mind when he created his ideal type of bureaucracy as a perfectly functioning, rationalized human organizational machine.[51] But the dimensions which characterized the older-style military organization do not characterize the new; the clear division of responsibility by rank is being replaced by a dual, competitive system of authority by rank and by virtue of technical expertise. The technological developments of modern armed forces create functional power for the technical experts, who then possess a bargaining power concerning salary and working conditions (including independence) which the non-technical workers do not have. Although Janowitz and Little state that there are changes being made to reassert the dominance of ordinary rank officers over technical staff, the technical people in the service often have the ultimate weapon — they can get work, perhaps even better paying work, on the outside.[52]

The development of management training programs within the military has had several consequences for the hierarchial principle. First, the modern manager works by consensus and manipulation of motives, not by command.[53] Thus the very modernization of the training of officers and the training in the enlisted ranks tends to subvert the hierarchial principle. In addition, the increasing complexity of the military bureaucracy, its civilian links, and the special requirements of technical personnel, lead to dual or even triple chains of responsibility in some areas. Even the distinction between officer and non-officer is becoming blurred, as the military increasingly recruits its officers from the enlisted ranks. In 1970, a non-West Point graduate was installed as the new Commandant of West Point, and thus even in the relation of the military elite to the officer corps the hierarchial principle is on its way out.[54] Both weapons technology and management techniques are increasingly leading to a more complex structure of authority. This has limits, of course, and the battle situation is still an exception to this trend, though here too teamwork is replacing strict command.

WAR VERSUS PEACE: A DISAPPEARING DISTINCTION

A third major principle of the division of labor in the military field, which has also undergone revision, is that between the role of the military in peacetime and the role of the military in war. In times of peace or total war, a clear separation of power, or at least a deliberate cooperative arrangement between civil and military power, is possible. But it is Janowitz's conclusion, one which Huntington essentially agrees with, that the military during and after World War II were not allotted a clearly defined status, and the resultant lobbying for power and influence in the area of civil-military relations is a natural result.[55] Also, as Lasswell originally pointed out, the garrison state, in which a civil-military power elite controls the direction of foreign policy and domestic spending, depends on a continuing state of emergency, such as the Cold War.[56] It is also possible to extend or prolong the need for a garrison state by a series of military interventions and adventures such as Vietnam, where the threat of escalation of conflicts is used as a justification for maintaining force levels. Underlying all of these justifications, of course, is the role of the atomic missile technology. Once such a technology is developed, the threat of its use can supply the military with a major reason for the continuation of massive expenditures on weaponry and the continuation of a garrison state political relationship between civil and military authority.

To sum up, technological development, managerial revolutions, and the deliberate actions of the military as a lobby have created a situation in which a permanent standing army in a cold-war garrison state has replaced both the earlier roles of the military in a state of "peace" or a state of "war." The indeterminateness of the military's position in the present division of labor is a consequence of social change and international politics. In both areas the military have taken an active as well as a passive role.

THE MILITARY AS AN INTERNATIONAL GROUP

A comparative perspective, using the Soviet Union and the developing nations as examples, may highlight the universal and particular aspects of the American situation. In each case, the issues of importance to this nation are also of importance to the others, though the solutions and present policies definitely vary. Using political regime as a variable, in contrast to internal development of military technology and management skills, aspects of the military field which are universal as compared to those which are merely typical of Western capitalist nations are highlighted.

TOTALITARIAN REGIMES AND MILITARY POWER

In the Soviet Union, or in any totalitarian regime, the problem for the civilian power structure is similar to that in a democracy: whatever form a regime takes, it wants to pursue that form without danger of control from the military. In the totalitarian regime, under Stalin, the secret police and informers within the military kept the dictator informed of any attempts on the part of military factions to seize power.[57] On the other hand, even in a totalitarian state, internal and external enemies of the regime might require a strong army. Thus the general societal dilemma with respect to expert occupational groups and their functional power was found in the Soviet case: too much control and intervention in the military sphere could paralyze the effectiveness of the group and threaten the security of the regime against its enemies, whereas too little control could lead to an overly strong and independent military, as threatening to a totalitarian regime as to a democracy. Kolkowitz summarizes this issue historically:

> In the communist state, the military is in the ambiguous position of being at once the mainstay of the regime and its principal rival for power. Throughout the nearly five decades of Soviet history, therefore, the relations between the Party, which has a monopoly of power, and the military, the main instrument of that power, have been turbulent. The

> Party leaders who have had little difficulty in dealing with most other groups and institutions that have challenged or threatened their hegemony are faced with the dilemma of how to control, and at times coerce, the military without reducing its vigor and its morale.[58]

The rise and fall of Marshal Zhukov, the popular World War II general, adds a second dimension to the civil-military relations in totalitarian states. Alliances which he and other generals made with specific men in the Soviet elite led to their rise and fall from power along with their civilian sponsors. In addition, in Zhukov's case, his popularity with the people was too dangerous to the regime to tolerate without intervention.[59] More generally, as Garthoff and Kolkowitz both conclude, the periods when the Soviet regime is in transition from one leader to another is the time when the state is weakest, and it is in these periods that the military gain ground.[60] Furthermore, Kolkowitz notes that the secret police in the Soviet Union, since Khrushchev, have played a lesser role and overt terror has been minimized. These are typical totalitarian controls on the military as well as on civilians, and their removal or relaxation strengthens the power of the military group in the Soviet Union.[61]

The impact of technological development has changed the nature and role of the Soviet armed forces in ways directly analogous to ours. The technocrat in the Soviet army manifests his independence from *both* army and party by claiming "neutral technical expertise" and demanding to be relieved of attending the political indoctrination sessions, a Soviet requirement for all military men, which is considered a tedious bore. The refusal to attend is a sign of the group's independence, in this case from both the traditional military and the Communist state. In general, the upswing of technical workers in modern armies knows no political boundaries, and the internal hierarchy problems this causes in rank-command issues are similar to those of the United States. The missile technology gives the military leverage over Khrushchev's successors that the World War II army did not have over Stalin.[62]

The Cold War has affected the Soviet Union and the United States in parallel ways with respect to the role of the military in the overall society. In fact, it is possible to view the relations *within* each nation only in the context of the relations *between* them. To be specific, an increase in the amount of United States–Soviet cooperation reduces the bargaining power of each nation's military group, whereas an increase in tension adds to the bargaining power of each group. Thus it is in the interests of each nation's military to paint the international situation in the grimmest perspective, and if the internal power position of the military of one nation is internally threatened by political pressure, the quickest way it can gain leverage is to get the nation involved in a new military exploit. Thus the external international relations between great powers and the internal civil-military relationships are inversely and closely related to one another, as part of an international civil-military power bargaining system.

MILITARY POWER IN THE DEVELOPING NATIONS

In a recent study of the political role of the military in the developing nations, Janowitz concluded that the role of the military elite, though important, could not be understood without close consideration of the historical background and pre-independence status of the new nations, or the political-economic background of older, but newly modernizing nations. In general,

> Those organizational and professional qualities which make it possible for the military of a new nation to accumulate political power, and even to take over political power, are the same as those which limit its ability to rule effectively. Thus, once political power has been achieved, the military must develop mass political organizations of a civilian type, or it must work out viable relations with civilian political groups. In short, while it is relatively easy for the military to seize power in a new nation, it is much more difficult for it to govern.[63]

He notes a continuum of relationships as possible and observable in the newer nations, from essentially civilian domination to military oligarchy. Five main types can be distinguished: "authoritarian-personal control," where a personal autocrat such as Emperor Selassie of Ethiopia rules the nation, including the military; "authoritarian-mass party," where a civilian political group rules in an arrangement which provides secret police and informers to control the military (analogous to the Soviet situation); "democratic-competitive regimes," where civilian institutions control the military, though it does have a sphere of influence; "civil-military coalitions," where neither party rules alone; and "military oligarchy," often the end result of the civil-military coalition, which is considered a highly unstable form.[64]

The role of technological change is highlighted by the role of the military as the importer of modern weaponry and by the modern technical advisors; this often means that the first modern scientific equipment in a new or modernizing nation comes from the military. In effect, military training is viewed by the upwardly mobile in such countries as the quickest way to get an engineering education, and the military career as a short-cut to a position in the intellectual, technical elite.[65] The arms salesmen of the major powers attempt both to unload their slightly outdated technical equipment on the military of new nations and to gain a foothold in their internal military (and thus political) affairs through creating a kind of technical dependence on the selling nation.[66] In some cases, the expertise of the military can lead to a plan for the forced modernization of a nation, the primary example being the military dictatorship of Kemal Ataturk who forcibly modernized Turkey and then attempted to create a stable government to take over from him.[67] But the combination of technological expertise and the possession of force in unformed situations often makes it easy for the military to gain power.

One major complication to the role of the military in the underdeveloped countries lies in the nature of their position with respect to major powers. The United Nations does not have the power to protect new states; as Janowitz found, all of these nations respond to independence by creating a national army.[68] Being in a weak position, the state depends on the army for protection and for national identity, giving it precisely the political leverage required to gain complete control. Once in power by emergency request or coup, the military faces the problem of gaining citizen allegiance. The melancholy evidence exists that regimes formed on terror or a totalitarian basis and those with a strong ruling military elite are more stable, if less humane to live in, than the democratic form considered ideal by the United States.[69] In addition, the evidence indicates that by economically advancing, nations do not necessarily become either more democratic or less militaristic.[70] Furthermore, in all nations the role of the military in the overall division of labor is fluid at best, even in regimes such as the United States or the Soviet Union.

One could almost expect the military to have a major role in the early stages of a nation's development. The problem in many of these countries appears rather to be the relaxation of the early authoritarian regimes, which tend to suppress the poor, the intellectuals, and in general the freedom of the people. On the other hand, the major powers may prefer a more authoritarian regime to a more democratic one, and this creates another problem. As we noted above, certain United States governmental agencies such as the CIA and the Pentagon prefer a government they can work with to one that resists their ideas on internal and international policy. Intervention by the United States military, working in concert with the executive branch of the government, may be an important factor in the political development of new nations and in the role that the new nation's military plays in that development. This is not only an American procedure, of course, but one that is standard in international power politics.

In general, the political role of the military in new nations cannot be understood apart from the international relations of these nations with the major powers. Military power within developing nations, as in the United States and the Soviet Union, is related to the role of the nation in world power politics. In all nations, the technology of modern warfare and the military's function in possessing the organized means of violence make the group politically important. Thus the division of labor, in terms of civil-military relations, the hierarchy, or war and peace time distinctions, cannot be understood apart from the political implications of those divisions.

CONFLICTS OF INTEREST: THE MILITARY AND CIVILIAN SOCIETY

It has been impossible to present a historical, biographical, and division-of-labor analysis of the military field without getting deeply into conflict-of-interest issues within the military field, and between the field and segments of the wider society. Major social changes brought about by technology, bureaucratization, and democratization have had their effect on internal military conflicts of interest. The increasing interpenetration of the civil and military spheres has created yet another range of conflicts of interest. Only when we consider these issues can we arrive at the classical question asked of each occupational group: What degree of success has the military had in recent years in acting as an occupational group in its own interest?

INTERNAL CONFLICTS OF INTEREST

The three processes of technological change, bureaucratization, and democratization of the military field have had major effects on struggles for supremacy within the military elite, between the different service groups (Army, Navy, Air Force), and between the military elite and the mass military man in both the lower officer ranks and in the enlisted men's ranks.

In the elite, these broad changes have had their effect on the type of leadership style and experience which has been considered important and worthy of support by the elite and the civilian world, and the type of military-strategy philosophy which relates to that style. Following Janowitz, we can consider the three main leadership styles as heroic, managerial or "organization man," and technical, and the two main philosophies as absolutist and pragmatic.[71] With some exceptions, it is possible to identify the heroic leadership style with the absolutist philosophy; the technical and managerial styles both are usually found with a pragmatic military-strategy philosophy. The impact of technological change has led to the general weakening of the position of the absolutist hero and the strengthening of the position of the technical specialist and the military manager. But the increasing bureaucratization of the military field ultimately gives the managerial expert (or the technical expert with managerial skill) an edge over the purely technical expert. The democratization of the elite may be leading indirectly to a further weakening of the position of the absolutist hero type, as this type in the past has often had both a socially aristocratic background and an elitist social philosophy. Anyone, from any background, can develop the managerial and technical skills needed for success in the modern military. An example is the career of Admiral Rickover, whose Jewish background in an anti-Semitic Navy was counterbalanced by his expertise in atomic submarines, his managerial skill, and his political skill in relations with Congress. Between the services, a traditional rivalry and struggle over the resources available has been affected greatly by the process of technological change, bureaucratization, and democratization. The case of the Air Force is critical with respect to technological change, although the process has obviously affected the other services as well. In the pre-World War II period, there was little in the way of an Air Force. Technological change led to the concept of "air power" and, in the first postwar decade, a massive air defense system. Thus the change in technology led to an increase in the bargaining power of the Air Force. But this same technological change which worked in favor of the Air Force and at the expense of the Army and Navy in the 1940–1965 period threatens in the 1970s and thereafter to work in the opposite direction. The role of the automatic guided missile decreases the need for a massive Air Force. Technological progress eventually results in *nothing to fly*. Parenthetically, in Vietnam the helicopter aircraft are often piloted by Army or Navy men, and have a subsidiary role in support of ground forces, not an independent role. In addition, the "bombing" strategy of the Air Force has been questioned ever since World War II, but the Air Force has maintained this strategy at least in part because it is a justification for the use of planes, and thus their service, in a time when technological change is threatening this service with obsolescence.

Bureaucratization has moved against the interests of each of the three services and in the direction of civilian control under the Pentagon. Here, especially under McNamara and Kennedy, an encompassing of the interservice rivalries within the walls of a bureaucracy was finally made possible. This has not ended interservice rivalry, of course, but Masland and Radway's evidence indicates that the allegiance of high military staff is at least now *divided* between the interservice Pentagon elite and their separate services, thus making control of these rivalries more possible in bureaucratic ways.[72] Huntington suggested in 1957 that the comptroller in the Department of Defense was powerful because of his control of the budget; a decade later McNamara and civilian systems analysts and budget experts used this function to exert strict control over allocations to the different services, and thus put themselves in a position of political and economic control over them, in fact as well as theory.[73]

Democratization in the military field has had a more subtle effect on the interservice rivalries, but it may have led to an increasing popularity among recruits for the newer and less elitist Air Force over the more aristocratic Navy and the traditionalist West Point. In fact, as the data from Lang show, the actual recruitment in these services has been democratized to about the same extent.[74] The effects of democratization on interservice rivalries are thus not clear, except perhaps for the role of the Navy, whose bargaining power was always increased by the blood relationships between admirals and civic and political elite members in private life.

In a third area of internal conflict, the resentment of the enlisted men for the privileges and prerogatives of the officer corps and the conflict within the officer corps between the non-academy officer and the academy elite have been lessened by the onset of major technological change, bureaucratization, and democratization. The need for trained manpower in technical areas has put a premium on this skill which has deemphasized the importance of rank. In addition, the increasing centralization of control in the Pentagon under civilian managers has added a layer in the military field on top of the highest officers; in this way the bureaucratization of the service structure has dampened conflict. In democratizing recruitment into the elite academies and in recruiting a significant segment of officers from enlisted ranks, democratization has decreased the conflict between the mass and elite within the military field.

In sum, therefore, the broad-scale changes caused by technology, bureaucratization, and democratization have had selective effects; in general, the managerial and civilian-related skill groups, with a pragmatic philosophy, have asserted control within the field over the absolutists and hero types, the organization has become bureaucratized and centralized under the Department of Defense, and the distance between the elite and the mass soldier has narrowed. Broad-scale social changes thus do not seem to have intensified most of the traditional interservice conflicts, over resources and budgetary matters in most cases. But the fortunes of specific groups within the military — types of men, types of service, those with a type of philosophy — have been altered by these changes.

CONFLICTS RELATED TO CIVIL-MILITARY INTERPENETRATION

Huntington has observed that civil-military interpenetration is greatly fostered by the structural ambiguity in the United States Constitution, which gives the President the office of Commander-in-Chief, without spelling out the function of the role, and which gives Congress the power to declare war and vote on the military budget. The "separation of power" theory which lay behind this arrangement in 1789 causes trouble in modern America, as the division of responsibility is an open structural invitation, which the military have used, to play the Executive branch against the Congress. In addition, the laws deliberately blend civil and military power without drawing the lines where one ends and the other begins.[75]

As a consequence, the civil-military interpenetration causes conflicts of interest in many ways. The interests of the Executive branch of government, including the Department of Defense, have in recent years been enlarged and strengthened as the result of the Cold War, Korea, and Vietnam. Only in recent years is Congress beginning to reassert its interests in controlling the relation between the Executive branch of the government and the military profession. Secondly, the contractual civil-military interpenetration between the defense industry and the Pentagon by-passes the control of Congress, as it creates pressures on congressmen over employment of defense workers in their areas. Pilisuk and Hayden conclude:

> Is there, then, a military-industrial complex which prevents peace? The answer is inextricably imbedded into the mainstream of American institutions and mores. Our concept is not that American society contains a ruling military-industrial complex. Our concept is more nearly that American society *is* a military-industrial complex. It can accommodate a wide range of factional interests from those concerned with the production or utilization of a particular weapon to those enraptured with the mystique of optimal global strategies. It can accommodate those with rabid desires to advance toward the brink and into limitless intensification of the arms race. It can even accommodate those who wish either to prevent war or to limit the destructiveness of war through the gradual achievement of arms control and disarmament agreements. What it cannot accommodate is the type of radical departures needed to produce enduring peace.[76]

The conflict of interest between the military-industrial complex and the civilian world, therefore, depends on which civilians are being considered. Certainly we can expect the military to act as any other occupational group, seeking to widen its mandate and increase the resources and power at its command. But the critical issue is the help coming from other groups, who combine with the military for their own reasons. The poor do indeed lose out, if we make what may be an untenable assumption, that *they* would get the money if the military-industrial complex did not. But the interests of a considerable segment of the citizenry are on the side of military spending at present levels, and here, as Pilisuk and Hayden suggest, is the crux of the political problem.

Another aspect of conflict caused by civil-military interpenetration and the increasing similarity between these spheres lies in the new movement to unionize military workers, viewed now as workers rather than as soldiers. Since the labor force in the military field is primarily blue collar in background, and military organizational principles have evolved in the direction of private industrial management and away from the rigid command structure, the potential for unionization of the military mass has increased.[77] The issue of the illegality of striking in the military is a false one, as the striking public service workers in other areas have already shown, although military law may be stricter here than civilian. Again, the interpenetration of civilian and military spheres is leading to the creation of conflicts of interest within the military sphere that are part of overall societal conflicts. The conflicts of interest between executive and legislative branches, between the corporations and the workers, between the middle class and the poor invade the military field to the extent that the field merges with the wider society. In this sense, the military field is not unique, but simply in the forefront when compared with the legal or clerical profession, or with the health field, although the latter is rapidly approaching the military field as a sphere of conflict.

THE MILITARY FOR THEMSELVES: TO WHAT DEGREE?

As has become evident in the historical, biographical, and systems analyses of the military field, the field and the professional officer corps are far from identical, but it is not possible to understand the professional soldier's role without considering the structure and function of the military field as a whole. But, since the interpenetration of the civil and military sphere is so extensive at present, to what degree can we talk of "the military for themselves"? In answering this question, we are ultimately led back to the historical issue of the military profession, the eternal conflicts of interest between one segment of the society and another, and the usual role of the military in protecting the status quo of the governing elite, at the price of sharing in this elite's resources and power.

When Prussia created its professional army, it was as a response to an external threat which could only be met through a strong and highly organized military body working in defense of the state. Restrictions were placed on the degree to which the military could act independently of this civil authority. The chain of command from civilian to military was clear and unambiguous, and thus the Prussian army acted for all of Prussia, not for one branch of the government and one segment of its citizenry. In the United States, the years since the onset of World War II seem to indicate a progressive interdependence of military and selected civilian spheres, with a great degree of military independence during World War II and in the decades after it. The control over the military which was interrupted to some degree after the onset of the war in Vietnam was reasserted with vigor even in the process of the later stages of the war, as the growth of massive citizen opposition to the actions of both the military and the Executive branch (President and Pentagon) changed the political forces at work. In 1970, civilian pressure concerning military conduct in this war led to court-martial proceedings against generals as well as lower officers, including the Commandant of West Point, who had been in the war at the time of the military misconduct. These proceedings would be impossible to contemplate if the military had the power to run their own internal professional affairs; the equivalent would be the president of the American Medical Association publicly suing the dean of Harvard Medical School for malpractice. These latter gentlemen may have no love for each other, as the conflicts of interest in the health field indicate, but they are not forced to sue one another by a civilian group which commands them to do so. It appears that the public image of the military is in the process of being returned to its traditional American image as villain, because of its actions in an unpopular war.

There is no question that the military are fighting for more resources and an expanded budget, a wider mandate, and greater independence of action. Historically they have always done so, as has every other occupational group of any size. But the latest American war was declared by Executive order and commanded by a civilian-run Pentagon. The role of the military in the present era appears to be as the servant of those civilians who command them and those who may profit from them, i.e., the military-industrial complex and the workers in defense industries at all levels. The military man's public position as the perpetrator of the actual violence makes them the target, in a changed political climate, for the wrath of the population. They make a convenient scapegoat. The basic issue, however, is still the question of who is using the military for what ends, to advance *what interests,* rather than the actions of the military themselves.

CHAPTER NINE

BUSINESS AND INDUSTRY: OCCUPATIONAL ASPECTS

The production sector of every society is close to its functional center. Social analysts since Marx and Spenser have always singled out the production process, and the groups centrally involved in it, for special scrutiny. Because of this book's basic focus on *types* of occupational grouping and function, and because of the plan to include a wide range of groups which vary according to dimensions other than the purely quantitative, the major occupational and superoccupational groupings in private American business and industry are considered together in only one chapter. This is far less than is often allotted to the managerial–white-collar–blue-collar complex in books on occupational sociology. On the other hand, in other chapters we consider occupations in health, law, the clergy, and the military, as well as educational and public service occupations; this chapter will deal strictly with the central corporations in the industrial-business sector, and with the management-labor issue in particular. It is better for the type of analysis used here to consider the levels of management, professional, white-collar, and blue-collar occupations as parts of a functioning system called "the corporate world," rather than taking up "unions" in one chapter and management in another. It is possible to spend volumes on each area, of course, and other interpretations of the field such as industrial sociology or the sociology of labor-management relations do so, in far greater depth. But the main sociological issues in the field of occupational group behavior are more easily considered in an analysis which compares on-setting relations between groups with cross-setting group actions. Such an analysis requires a unified format, and that is the aim of this chapter, as seen from a historical, biographical, functional, and conflict-of-interest viewpoint.

A HISTORICAL REVIEW

In the introductory chapter on the historical approach to occupations, the main occupational groups involved in the production process were considered in a series of earlier historical periods: the slave economy of ancient Greece, the role of guilds and landowners in the Middle Ages, the merchant capitalists of the Renaissance and Reformation, and commerce in Puritan Massachusetts and Jacksonian America. To avoid covering this ground again, and in order to focus on the immediate history of the American managerial, white-collar, and blue-collar occupational groups in business and industry, we can begin the review of the major historical periods at the time of the Industrial Revolution in New England, from 1850 to 1880. Several natural eras follow this and can be considered in turn: the period from 1880 to 1900, the twenties and early thirties, the Depression, World War II, the Cold War era, and the immediate present.

Thernstrom's extensive analysis of social structure and occupational mobility in Newburyport, Massachusetts, during the period 1850–1880 gives valuable insight into the effects of the Industrial Revolution on the occupational structure. Thernstrom's study, using early census data, encompasses the early, middle, and later stages of Newburyport's industrial revolution, and adds a valuable perspective to the present situation in unskilled, industrial labor, craft, and white-collar occupations. In the Newburyport of 1850, the Horatio Alger ideology and the new ideology of "worker capitalism" were powerful forces, and the creation of a small savings account or the purchase of a small plot of land or of a house on mortgage were considered signs of "property mobility." Such workers, who had almost no chance of moving up the occupational ladder, were lauded as "capitalists" by the powers of the town. This had the effect of dampening any sense of working-class consciousness in a city that no longer had the unanimity of a Puritan community and was thus potentially more open to conflict.[1]

The onset of the Industrial Revolution did not result in a massive increase in occupational mobility opportunities, as the rate did not essentially change from 1850, near the beginning, to 1880, when it was well under way. In addition, Thernstrom's findings indicate a large pool of city-to-city migratory labor, unskilled and often Irish. The semi-skilled workmen were often more likely to stay in Newburyport than the unskilled. But among those who were unskilled and who remained, the chances were twice as great that they would still have an unskilled job after ten years as that they would be even one step up the ladder in factory work. Only one out of ten unskilled laborers worked their way into a skilled craft, a rung definitely above factory work in the society of the time. Almost no unskilled laborers became white-collar workers, as this required the schooling they could not get. Nor could these men afford public schooling for their children, who needed to work in order to keep the family alive, as there was no welfare system of any significance for the poor at this time. The white-collar ranks and the factory owners were primarily older settlers, but by no means were the majority of them "old Yankees" of the clipper ship era or before; the factory owners were the nouveau riche of the town.[2]

The ethnic progression in occupational areas which was to characterize the American urban society of a century later was already in force in Newburyport in 1850. At this time, the influx of Irish immigrants did not lead to their employment in the factories; jobs were reserved here and elsewhere for the poor Yankees first and the immigrants later. The sons of the Irish could and did get jobs as semi-skilled factory operatives. Then the sons of the industry-employed Yankees also moved up one more notch, to the skilled crafts. In an extensive historical and comparative analysis, Thernstrom was able to show that the Industrial Revolution in the East did not mean extensive mobility for the poor nor employment for the ethnic minorities, at least not until the 1880s, and that the "craft" world was neither dominant at the time industry came, nor was it destroyed by the onset of industrialization. Thus three prominent sociological myths were destroyed by the historical approach, through Thernstrom's careful research. Mobility at this time was similar to mobility now, as it was recently described by Blau and Duncan, with the Irish taking the place in 1850 which the blacks held at the time of the Blau-Duncan study. In general, Thernstrom concludes,

> that while these laborers and their sons experienced a good deal of occupational mobility, in only rare cases was it mobility very far up the social ladder. The occupational structure was fluid to some degree, but the barriers against moving more than one notch upward were fairly high.[3]

At the time of the Industrial Revolution, there were no unions in the modern form, although there were a series of utopian labor movements such as the Knights of Labor which aimed at distant goals and social fellowship without getting down to the essentials of increased power and wages for the workers. The period 1880–1900 saw both the rise of the first great powerful capitalists — the robber barons in railroads, steel, copper, and coal — and the rise of violent and repressive tactics toward the new unions in formation. This era is marked by the founding of the American Federation of Labor, in 1881, a union of craft workers, not industrial workers. Mann notes that they were definitely non-socialist and had a wage-directed program. These early years were years of tremendous struggle for the new labor organizations. Caplow conveys the feel of these times:

> These were the days of the Haymarket Riot, the Pullman massacre, the Pinkertons, and blanket injunctions. The strength of the unions was vastly unequal to the effort, the courts were uniformly unsympathetic, private armies were used to break strikes in Pennsylvania, and federal troops served the same purpose in Illinois. The industrial unions were decisively crushed.[4]

The era of the twenties and the early thirties saw the further growth and concentration of capital in large corporations on the production side, and a slower growth, far less significant, of the AFL and other craft unions. On the other hand, the potential for union growth increased. The growth of management, combined with its centralization, automatically began to concentrate workers in larger numbers, thus making their unionization far more possible, and increasing their leverage in a strike. As retail stores conglomerated into national chains, such organizations as the Atlantic and Pacific Tea Company (A&P) became the locus of unionization. Brody highlights the dynamics of this structural process in his study of the formation of the butcher's union:

> The chains were, for one thing, entering a new and difficult field. They had to recruit competent butchers, and these craftsmen were likely to be within the union in an organized town. Chain store employees, part of a large and impersonal concern as they were, had a kind of inclination to unionism that did not exist in the close, personal atmosphere of the independent butcher shop. Above all, the chain stores were susceptible to boycott tactics.[5]

In addition to the slow growth of unionization in the industrial and retail areas, the twenties saw more open violence between management and labor, the end of the short career of the radical International Workers of the World (IWW or Wobblies), and the use of criminal elements by both management and labor. As Adamic notes, the industrialists of the 1880–1900 era had hired gunmen and other criminals, but in general "criminals were drawn into the struggle between haves and have-nots." [6] The labor unions eventually responded with the use of the same techniques of industrial warfare:

> labor organizations, taking their cue from capital, began to hire professional strong-arm men to slug scabs, assassinate employers and foremen, and dynamite mills, mines, and uncompleted bridges and buildings.[7]

The problem of the unions here lay in the fact that they were organizationally weaker than the corporations and could not dismiss the racketeers and criminal elements once their job was done, as management could and did. The problem of corruption in unions dates from this time.

The Great Depression and the Roosevelt era saw the next major change in the two-party relationship between management and labor — the introduction of the federal government as a major third party. The National Recovery Act of 1935 and the Wagner Act which followed when the NRA act was declared unconstitutional gave labor the permanent right to collective bargaining with management and prohibited the joining of a company union as a condition of employment in business and industry. The growth of industry continued and led to the establishment of the first major national union for *industrial* workers, as against craftsmen — the Congress of Industrial Organizations or CIO.

World War II saw an even greater increase in the role of government as a third party between management and labor. The requirements of war production led to increasingly close relations between the major corporations and the government and between the unions and government, all on the War Labor Board. In fact, Brody suggests that the rivalry between the two giant unions, the AFL and the CIO, was modified by their need to present a common front against the government, which was limiting the wages of workers, and management, which was in control of many of *their* arrangements with government:

> Collective bargaining, as it developed during World War II, began to force the AFL and CIO rivals into an interdependent relationship. Their hostility persisted, but it could not prevent a common interest in negotiations. The erratic course of their relations reflected the conflicting pressures of rivalry and interdependence. Slowly, the latter became dominant.[8]

The era of the Cold War and in general the period of the fifties and sixties have seen a continuation of the structural forms which arose as a consequence of the social and technological changes brought about by World War II. Drucker notes that the corporate management level has followed the lead of General Motors and other corporations in decentralizing industrial production operations and centralizing planning and management policy-making.[9] Another related process is the changing scope of American corporations. The international growth of the giant American corporations is now so extensive that management itself is international, and both General Motors and General Electric, for example, now have a "domestic" division and an "international" division just under the top management level. As with the military profession, and perhaps to an even greater extent, the top managers of the major corporations are involved in the formation of American foreign policy and action, because of major American investments overseas.

A second major change in the occupational structure, under way during World War II but really coming to the fore in the past two decades, has been the relative increase in the professional-technical sector of business occupations, with a relative decrease in the proportion of jobs for blue-collar or "line" workers. Drucker describes the group and assesses their predominant loyalties.

> [They are] the large and growing group of employed professionals who work with their knowledge rather than with their hands — the engineers and accountants, scientists, salesmen, market researchers, and production schedulers. These people are employed. Yet they do not consider themselves "workers," nor are they considered as such by society. They are not "bosses." But they see themselves as "members of management" and are clearly seen as such by everybody else.[10]

This group — the technical and technologically related experts or the specialists in the planning of production, distribution, and marketing — should not be confused with another layer of white-collar, clerical, and secretarial occupations which have grown in the industrial sector as they have elsewhere.

A third major change has been the increasing convergence of the interests of "big management" and "big labor" in the major industries. Joint planning in wartime has led to joint arrangements such as that between the United Auto Workers and General Motors, which involves long-term contracts with agreements not to strike during the period of the contract, under the condition that the employer raises wages automatically in line with rises in the cost of living. Another management-labor arrangement involves welfare and pension plans under joint management and labor supervision but financed by the corporations.

In general, therefore, the increasing involvement of government in both management and labor decisions, the increasing growth of union size as a reaction to growth of industrial corporate size, and the increasing accommodation of big management and big labor to each other under government auspices and with government involvement, make it less and less possible with every passing year to speak of these subsystems in the industrial-corporate system as separate entities. This is not to say that there are not still inherent and basic conflicts of interest, but they exist within an industrial system that has its own form of organization. The experience within that system is our next concern.

THE EXPERIENCE: EXECUTIVE, WHITE-COLLAR, BLUE-COLLAR

Work experiences in the industrial and business world are the subject of countless novels, tracts, group-directed propaganda statements, and research projects by interest-based researchers such as psychologists and sociologists in the employ of management. On the other hand, the actual observational or case studies of specific situations are quite limited. Realizing that the literature is extensive in the first area, but that the few studies in the second area are far closer to our direct interest in conveying the *experience* from the participant's point of view, we will depend primarily on studies of the latter type. Exploring the issues which are important in this area, rather than giving a comprehensive review of industrial sociology and social psychology, is our aim. After considering the initial motivation and recruitment, and the nature of the different career patterns, we can consider experience and interaction in different relationships between groups on the industrial setting.

INITIAL MOTIVATION AND RECRUITMENT

In a recent book on the stresses of executive life, Levinson discusses the problem of the "bright young man" in business in the bureaucratic setting. He suggests that the senior man be nicer to the more nonconformist newcomer, as the problem of recruiting the really talented men into business is a perennial one. As Levinson observes, the attractiveness of the executive career is on the wane, especially to the idealistic generation of the present day:

> In short, most of these bright young people do not fit the corporate mold, they don't come with the kind of motivation which business ordinarily wants, they don't value the kinds of rewards business has to offer. . . . *Yet, the bright ones are increasingly necessary to business.* Survival depends on innovation and flexibility of adaptation. Both are hard to come by in large organizations. They are particularly difficult to achieve with people who become stereotyped in their jobs and views.[11]

The problem of motivation and recruitment at the executive level must be seen in terms of the social status of the universities and the university programs from which business recruits its executives. The elite training setting, such as Harvard Business School, expects to place graduates with an advanced degree in Business Administration into middle-level executive settings, and in effect recruits expertise for industry. The elite colleges, which in an earlier era were a source of many potential executives, are precisely the havens of idealism and professionalism which are strongest in anti-business ideologies. With each step down the prestige ladder in what Riesman calls "the academic procession," the number of business-minded, upwardly mobile students in undergraduate business programs increases.[12] But this is in inverse proportion to what the leading corporations want. The brightest youth (at least officially) are the hardest to recruit; the ones with the most pedestrian training, from less "impressive" social backgrounds or colleges are more recruitable (and more motivated) but less desirable to the corporations. On the other hand, in recent years the unpredictable or uncommitted career patterns of the elite students are leading some corporations to reconsider their prestige and class-based recruitment approach. Talent, commitment, and motivation are not predictable by the particular college attended, in the view of an increasing number of executive recruiters.

When the motivations and recruitment patterns for the technical-professional groups are considered with respect to entry into business and industry, a different issue arises. As Whyte observed, the role for the technical person in industry is more limited than the role for those with administrative talents.[13] Ferdinand, in inspecting the careers of engineers in industry, shows that technological progress results in the rapid obsolescence of those in applied science fields.[14] Thus the pure scientist or the research engineer may often choose the business world as only a second choice to that of the university, and once in it, view promotion into the administrative ranks as a definition of success in career terms. One typical example of career motivation here lies in the area of "programming," where the successful computer programmer graduates to management of a computer section, and then in rare cases moves elsewhere. But the intention of remaining an engineer, as against keeping an identity as a basic research scientist, may not be a main motivation even for entering such a career. In many universities at present, majors such as "industrial management" acknowledge this fact and anticipate the growing importance of technical expertise in business, by combining technical training and business management training, including "human relations" approaches.

The white-collar area comprises all those occupations which do not have requirements for special technical training or executive responsibility. Secretarial, clerical, and low-level office management jobs, as well as sales jobs numbering in the millions, are presently in the expansion phase. To some degree, the growth is an expression of Parkinson's law that the expansion of the size of bureaucratic work forces is a process independent of the need for such manpower. In part, however, the motivation to enter this kind of work (in situations where some skills are more in demand in terms of the economy) is due to the strong pressures placed on the children of blue-collar workers by their parents to choose a white-collar job — any technical, sales, or office work — over the factory conditions in which they have spent their own lives. This motivation on the part of the lower middle class to urge their children into white-collar work (even at a slight loss in pay) is found in all industrialized countries. For example, Crozier found in his study of the tobacco monopoly in France, that although 73 per cent of the blue-collar workers were basically satisfied with their job, only 28 per cent wanted their children to go into factory work.[15] Thus the pressure on the part of blue-collar parents to urge their children into white-collar work dovetails with the massive proportion of the American educational system that is devoted to high-school-level business training and clerical courses. In addition, Geer and others have shown that socialization-to-work, in its initial stages, when it is not done in the high school, is often accomplished by small, short-term "business training schools" which give crash courses in business techniques.[16] No information exists at this time as to whether either the high school programs in work-relevant areas or the new business-training schools are *necessary* in addition to on-the-job training in white-collar work, with the possible exception of clerical skill. Rather, their function, and the function of employment agencies of the nation, appears to be the intensification of motivations formed in the family setting, or the channeling of essentially "unmotivated" younger people into the most prevalent form of available work.

The motivations for entry into blue-collar work are systematically less well known than those for almost any other occupational sector. As research in an earlier chapter on the nature of the existential approach indicates, students are "cooled out" of white-collar and professional careers; this leaves blue-collar careers by default. In the United States, the quality of blue-collar training for industry in the public schools, with a few exceptions, is poor and irrelevant. (Electronics is not often a major subject, for example.) In addition, the size of the craft and industrial labor sector diminishes proportionally every year with respect to the white-collar sector in business and industry. It is viewed by the average high school student as less relevant, unless — and this appears to be a primary motivating factor — there is a direct occupational inheritance situation, that is, if the father is in a high-paying craft such as plumbing or is a skilled worker in a high-paying field such as aircraft assembly or missile plant work. On the other hand, the seniority system in unions and the known racial biases in many of them have lessened the motivations for going into blue-collar work.

At the bottom of the business-industry sector, the motivation for work is not career-related but rather subsistence-related. Work is viewed in a perspective that sees the advantages of not working as almost preferable to the type of work available. As Liebow notes, the resultant attitude toward entry into even temporary work is ambivalence.[17]

In general, the motivations for entering the occupational levels within the industrial sector vary according to the level of entry considered. The field is so unstructured that except at its extremes, motivations specific to technical, white-collar, or blue-collar occupational choices are hard to identify. At the executive level, the elite graduate training schools and the marginal college programs both produce highly motivated entrants. At the other extreme, the menial work available in business and industry for the poor makes their motivation to enter it, in any permanent way, very provisional.

THE PATTERN OF CAREERS

Initial motivations for entry into a career and the commitment to the career once entered have a close relationship to one another. In the hierarchy from executive to unskilled work, the concept of "career" in any sense except the accumulation of experience in one place loses its meaning as one goes downward in the occupational hierarchy. The idea of development, forward progress, is quite relevant to the executive's career and essentially meaningless with respect to unskilled work. The structure of career pattern and its subjective aspect — the experience of career continuity with its crises and choices — depends on one's position in the overall occupational subsystem. We can consider the initial and long-term aspects of executive, technical, white-collar, and blue-collar careers.

Executive Careers. Executive career patterns have been studied objectively and subjectively, with far greater attention to detail than is the case with white-collar and blue-collar patterns, although the situation at work has been considered as extensively for the latter groups as for the executive. In the elite executive echelon, one important entry point is the two-year Master in Business Administration program at Harvard Business School. The Harvard Business School catalogue describes the "case-analysis" teaching method used to train businessmen in decision-making skills in the face of uncertainty:

> Lectures are kept at a minimum, and if assignments of collateral reading are given, they are primarily for purposes of technical background. In the business world, where every decision must be appropriate to the situation and no two situations are identical, it is the ability to analyze, to judge trends, to weigh diverse influences, that leads to sound judgment; and that ability can be developed only through practice.[18]

The skeptic might ask why training in the "school of hard knocks" might not also be a good place to gain experiences of this sort. The obvious answer is the nature of recruitment to this elite business training school and its relationship with major corporations. Orth notes that the school:

> has established close ties with the business community, particularly those outstanding members of it whose performance marks them as examples of the end product the school hopes to graduate. Secondly, there has been, and increasingly so lately, an emphasis on the development of a body of knowledge about business — an extensive research program testifies to the School's leadership in this effort.[19]

The school also maintains its contacts with the business world by young executive and senior executive training programs, on the model of the military officer career pattern. The future leaders — or the ones the school hopes will be — return for a month or two of training at two similar points in their career development, under corporation sponsorship.

On the setting, the research team found a striking analogy to the medical student culture discovered by Becker, Geer, Hughes, and Strauss.[20] The same central phenomenon — the development of a student culture and norms on restriction of production to deal with "unrealistic" faculty demands in the face of uncertainty — were discovered in two section-groups in a first-year Harvard Business School class. Since these two 90-men sections went to all classes together, they soon constituted a cohort that began to develop a group culture; in one observed group this was "social" in orientation, in a second group it was "task-oriented." In general, however, both groups were characterized by strong group norms which appeared to punish the deviant, the original thinker, the individualist, and so on. It is striking that the manifest function of this experience — stress on pleasing cohorts, high pressure to produce rapidly under uncertainty — would seem to interfere with some of the *academic* goals of the business school, but its latent function is to prepare the executive for just such pressures in the business world, where pleasing associates, joint action, and the defense of risky decisions are critically important for career advancement.[21]

Other business schools at the graduate level — perhaps another five or six — could be considered to qualify as elite training centers for executive life. But all major corporations, and most small ones as well, now have an in-house executive training program as an important initial socialization experience. Whyte's observations of the General Electric program are essentially still relevant.[22] Company goals, operating procedure, and a short course in "human relations skills" are considered enough for a start.

The critical years of the executive's career, regardless of the mode of entry, are the first decade and a half, from about the age of twenty-five to forty. By this time, those very definitely on their way up have been clearly separated from those who have peaked. The stresses of executive life have become almost a part of American work folklore, as such movies as *Executive Suite* and such novels as *Cash McCall* attest. But in discussing the executive career pattern, a major distinction must be made, at the outset, between the *managerial* career pattern and the *entrepreneurial* pattern. The former is common and the subject of most research; it involves what is essentially a climb through a set of bureaucratic hierarchies under the sponsorship of those above in the organization. The entrepreneurial career, on which much less research has been done, consists in the high-risk creation of one's own opportunities through one's own business. In all areas, including electronics and computer technology, the failure rate of new businesses far exceeds the success rate. Thus entrepreneurial careers may revert back to managerial ones (the company may be bought by a larger one) but the managerial career pattern, once begun, is only rarely left for an entrepreneurial one.

The managerial pattern can be comprehended best by listing the relevant career contingencies. First, there are personal psychological traits, the extent to which the individual has an adaptive, coping personality structure that can handle forms of stress and uncertainty. Second, there is the degree to which the person possesses "interpersonal skills," a prized ability on which Dale Carnegie and the human relations trainers alike have grown wealthy and influential. But these interpersonal and psychological factors are real and they are also closely related. Hodgson, Levinson, and Zaleznik, in *The Executive Role Constellation,* show the complex interplay of internal psychological states and interpersonal behavior in a situation where both organizational "givens" and organizational uncertainties exist. The course of individual career development can only be understood in relation to the development of the executive group's career, as a functioning social organism.[23]

The extent to which the individual possesses the technical skills relevant to his chosen career — engineering background for the leadership of an electronics firm, economics and finance for the head of a brokerage firm — institutes a third set of career contingencies. But in addition to the qualities and skills which are brought to the setting by the individual, the chances and uncertainties of career development center primarily on the setting itself — the degree to which superiors are friendly, the degree of career sponsorship they offer, and the degree to which these superiors themselves are upwardly mobile and can take a protégé with them. A fourth set of contingencies depend on overall labor market factors from year to year in relation to the life span of the executive. For example, in periods of growth, the need for executives leads to high migration rates to other companies by younger executives, who can increase upward mobility rapidly by this pathway. But in a tight labor market, the company has more leverage than the executive, and the mobility-through-movement pathway is less profitable.

Finally, the meaning of a decision by an executive is always open to the working of brute chance. In spite of all attempts to gather information, a series of wrong decisions can compromise an executive's career even if mathematically none of them are his fault. Grayson carried out a study of decisions by oil and gas company managers on whether or not to drill a given well. Since drilling a well is expensive, and chancy at best, the author was interested in seeing how probabilities were calculated.[24] Two methods of coping with uncertainty were found, the informal and the formal:

> one, he looks at the venture as a whole, implicitly considers the many factors, and decides largely on the basis of judgment and experience, or two, he formalizes the facts and assumptions, explicitly relates them in an analytic form, and makes his decisions according to specified criteria (payout, discounted rate of return, profit risk ratio, etc.).[25]

Grayson goes on to suggest that mathematical decision models — or an artificial game which he suggests could be called "Gusher" — might help the manager make a wiser decision than he could through informal means. Although there are no guarantees for the new formalism now being seen in management areas (systems analysis, decision theory, probability modeling, etc.), it does appear to take the onus off the *individual,* since the equations and the information can be blamed or the probabilities quoted back at the critic. Perhaps because of the stress-relieving function of such technological development in management, it is becoming more popular in some areas in the corporate world. On the other hand, too great a preoccupation with models and too great an evasion of personal responsibility do not help an executive in his career advancement either, if Levinson's observations are accurate, and they jibe with those of other researchers in the area. As Hughes observed, executives are continually and inevitably "up against the wall of uncertainty," and the factors which are uncertain include the physical environment and the economy as well as social "others" or personal strengths and weaknesses.[26]

The later years of the executive career pattern present stresses only to the level that the person continues to hold onto upward mobility aspirations, as in most larger corporations the pension plans for executives and white-collar workers are reasonably well developed. But since in most larger corporations the city-to-city movement of executives is the choice of the corporation rather than of the executive, the problem of subjective interpretations of these moves is critical. Whyte calls this the "checkers" problem: Is the organization offering this move just to play checkers with me for the fun of it, or does it mean a promotion one step later if I take it? In many larger organizations, refusal to move is tantamount to an admission by the executive that he is forgoing any further upward mobility.[27] On the other hand, the expense of moving, the cost of housing, and a growing sense of group "occupational consciousness" by executives may be leading, at the present time, to an anti-corporate stance: "We will not be moved." It is too early to tell whether an *executive-group* occupational consciousness (as against an identity with the interests of the overall corporate owners) will develop as it did with blue-collar workers and is now doing with white-collar and technical people, but the deliberate conscious professionalization of management may be leading in this direction.

Scientific and Engineering Careers in Industry. We must contrast the meaning of an industrial career to a pure scientist and to an engineer with standard engineering training, before we make a brief comparison of the patterns involved with respect to their brethren in other occupational fields. The role of scientific skills in private industry is the same as that of any other skill. In a capitalist system (and more abstractly in a socialist system as well) the function of skills is to advance the interests of the employing system. As Allison observes,

> Certainly one very powerful motivation of the top manager, if not his prime motivation, is to make a profit. He is measured by his ability to do this and, indeed, he is rewarded accordingly. In turn — and perhaps instinctively — he measures the worth of the industrial scientist by the same rule: Is he profitable or not? The deadly thing about this question

> is not the threat it poses to the "not profitable" scientist. Rather, its deadliness is the fact that few scientists — however creative they may be, however "profitable" they may be — find sufficient satisfaction in their profitability.[28]

Engineers, in contrast to pure scientists, are interested by definition in the practical application and payoff of scientific knowledge. Thus the meaning of career experience to technical experts in industry relates to their inner values as much as to their outward work situation.

A stratification of career opportunity seems to exist at present, and it has a history which goes back to the foundation of the first major industrial lab by Whitney at General Electric in 1900.[29] The large corporations have the funds to endow major laboratory facilities, hire very competent scientists and allow them to enjoy the expensive freedom of constructing — within very broad limits — whatever they want. Thus at Bell Laboratories, where the transistor was developed, the organization has the facilities to subsidize nearly standard scientific careers. The smaller the organization, the less funds and freedom and the more closely the scientists and technical staff are pressured toward immediate profitability. Incidentally, the greatest payoffs in ultimate profitability appear to come from the freest research settings, but since only the large firms can afford this research atmosphere, they tend to get more of the good questions and the basic scientific breakthroughs. In other words, a graduate scientist who is considering a career might choose one in this order: within an elite university, an elite industrial lab, a small college, and last, a small business.

For both the scientist and the engineer, a career which involves promotions into management is possible and is viewed with far less ambivalence by the engineer than the scientist. On the other hand, if the organization is research-oriented (certainly if it is a government research institute such as that studied by Glaser), the setting is not antithetical to the pursuit of a scientific career without a major loss of identity.[30] One final note on the scientific career in industry is rather pathetic. In Allison's recent volume on the "research and development game," the point is often made by industrial researchers that industry offers more freedom to many scientists than their universities, where the Ph.D. thesis supervisor dictated the research of the student more than industry would ever be likely to do.[31] Again, however, this depends on the corporation. At Bell Labs, this might be possible; in smaller firms, the dictation of the thesis supervisor is replaced by the close control and direction of the company.

White-Collar and Blue-Collar Experience. Although much analysis of the structural role and existential stances of the white-collar worker has been done by investigators such as Mills, the career aspect has been less well covered. What appears to be missing are studies on the career *development* and career *structure* of white-collar workers, excluding the managerial and technical-scientific groups. Labor statistics on part-time employment and interrupted employment would indicate that a large segment of the clerical and office force is differentiated by sex; the male joining an office in business and industry has a chance for upward mobility, of at least a few levels, whereas the female often follows the pattern of post-high school office work, marriage and child-rearing, then return to the same job. The occasional single woman with upward mobility into management is an exception, and even rarer is the married woman with such mobility. The political implications of this occupational group — in terms of interest groups and struggles within business and industry — will be considered later in the chapter.

A recent participant observational study by Langner illustrates the experience common to many white-collar office jobs, in this case that of a customer service representative for the phone company, where the pressures for production had much in common with factory work:

> The situation produces desperation: How am I to get it done? How can I call back all these customers, finish all that mail, write all those complicated orders within forty minutes . . . ? My feeling that time was slipping away, that I would never be able to "complete my commitments" on time was intense and hateful. Of course it was worse for me than for the experienced women — but not much worse.[32]

The important point to be made here is that *production* in the office setting, in a situation where promotion more than one step up the ladder is rare, is becoming the same daily work experience of the mass of white-collar workers as it had always been for assembly-line workers. With the exception of promotion to lowest-level management positions, the clerical-office careeer and the blue-collar industrial plant career share more structural similarities than differences, and both can be marked off from the accumulation of skills that are still possible in the trade and craft occupations — electrician, plumber, building occupations, and so on. The *developmental* aspect of white-collar and blue-collar assembly-line "careers" seems missing, in contrast to the stages possible on the technical-scientific and the managerial levels. Perhaps the only recent major change that has occurred in the structure of both white-collar and blue-collar career patterns has been the increasing willingness of major employers to finance additional education for those at these levels in the work force. This policy may, or may not, pay off in future years for those presently in the blocked mobility areas of white-collar and blue-collar industrial and business occupations.

Another major aspect of the career experiences of the white-collar and blue-collar worker, which investigators such as Langner have commented on, lies in the stress on consumerism which pervades their interpretation of work.[33] Extra time spent on the job, for example, is not for the purpose of career mobility (which is not an expectable consequence) but rather for accumulation of funds to be spent on objects which are prestige and status symbols. Langner notes that the women of her office were extremely goods-oriented, and that work was for the purpose of consumption, which in turn led to a continuing need for further work, and so on. In effect, the career patterns of millions may not be measured subjectively by them in terms of their *work history* on the job, but in terms of their *purchasing career* based on accumulation from the meager revenues gained on the job. The "house-proud" syndrome in blue-collar working-class neighborhoods may be an example of this. The house is a symbol of an achievement point in an otherwise meaningless career.

In a study which in its detail and scope is still the exception rather than the rule, Form and Miller compared the structure of the career patterns of five different groups of individuals, over a span of their life from initial to eventual job. The picture they developed highlights one comparative fact of great importance to our understanding of career structure in business and industry — the higher the echelon entered after the first years on the job, the more steady the consequent career pattern becomes in terms of remaining at a given skill level. This can be summed up in a series of general statements. First, once one becomes an executive, or a professional, one almost always remains as such, although the career trajectory levels off in the middle years for most individuals. Secondly, once into the white-collar area, one usually remains there but with little chance of upward mobility. For blue-collar workers who enter at a skilled level, an alteration into and then out of white-collar work is possible for a minority, and a second sizable minority make it out of factory and craft work into the office. Those entering as unskilled may get into the skilled work ranks but seldom preserve this gain over a lifetime, and in most cases alternate periods of unskilled work, semi-skilled work, and unemployment.[34] In general, the national occupational mobility study of Blau and Duncan confirms for the entire nation what Form and Miller found almost two decades earlier.[35] The vicissitudes and contingencies of career development exist at all levels of the industrial sector; at the upper levels they may result in major opportunities, but at the lower levels the coping is for purposes of survival and not for potential or actual growth.

INTERACTION ON THE WORK SETTING

On the topic of interpersonal and intergroup relationships on the work setting, in contrast with the topic of career pattern and structure, there is an extensive literature. The highlights of this work are most clearly presented by subdividing the findings in terms of the types of relationship patterns and "pairs" found. At least the following have been the subject of extensive research: the effect of the setting on the worker, worker to worker relations, management-worker relations, management-to-management relations, community and other effects on the management-labor relationship. Each of these may be considered in turn for Western industrialized nations. A comparison with the major findings of a study of the industrial experience in developing nations will end this section, after we have presented the main outlines of the observational studies carried out in the United States and France.

The Effect of the Setting on the Worker. Two major constraints exist which workers at all levels must confront: the nature of the technology in use and the nature of the work setting, especially in power terms. To the extent that the worker is directly involved in the production process, to that extent will he be influenced by the way in which technology sets up his work. Hughes noted that when racial integration was attempted in a plant he was studying, it did not work until it was done on a three-person work-group basis, with all three of the group black. Apparently, in the late 1940s, in the industry he studied, the technology of the particular operation demanded three-person groups, and social bonds at work were formed on this three-person basis.[36] Gouldner, in his study of a gypsum plant, contrasted the informal social organization in the mine pits, influenced by the conditions of work in this setting, with the formal organization of work in the above-ground plant and industrial offices.[37] Meissner's review of this literature clearly shows that stability or change in technology will bring change both in the organization of work groups and the meaning of this experience.[38]

The nature of the deliberate chain of command and the management-directed forms of social organization are a second major principle or constraint. Friedmann's study of the experience in industrial assembly work suggests that the meaningfulness of even routine assembly work can be increased if a group of operations are done in sequence, giving the workers the sense of "accomplishment" that presumably they do not get in routine work.[39] In fact, both the literature on the alienation of workers from work, since Marx, and the industrial psychological literature assume that the technological constraints in the situation are a constant and that the social relationships (of worker to management, of workers to each other, of workers to the work) are the field for alteration. In all of the research on actual industrial settings, however, it is a third set of variables interacting with the technological and power-command constraints that result in the observed social process. These are the evolving social relationships which arise on the setting and the various interaction pairs that are its constituents. These need to be considered in turn.

Worker-to-Worker Relationships. In what has become a classic statement in the evolution of an occupational culture on the setting, Roethlisberger and Dickson compare the social popularity of workers in a worker group to their productivity, within the overall worker's norm on restriction of production:

> Thus the productivity of individual workers in this group was closely related to the membership positions they held. Their productivity was more affected by the rewards they received from the group in terms of acceptance than by the rewards they received from management in terms of pay and job status. These rewards from the group were highly prized by the workers. But these rewards did not maximize productivity; they tended to keep it to the minimum that management expected.[40]

The norm of production-restriction must be understood as part of a defensive counter-culture which workers evolve in any setting where they are under pressures they view as intolerable or unreasonable. Roy's study found that a technique often used in assembly work was the overproduction of items to gain a "backlog" at one point in time so that spare time could be taken later.[41] Again, this is a defensive move to increase the free time of the production worker. Zaleznik's study confirmed the observation of Roethlisberger and Dickson, as did Homan's observations on the functioning of group norms in industry.[42] In general, the worker-to-worker relations are in part a function of social compatibility, in part a function of the technological constraints and power relations on the setting, but in the industrial area the relations and the culture formed are basically in defense against what is perceived as an oppressive reality constructed by management. The human friendships which grow up on the setting eventually develop a meaning to some individuals in their own right, of course, but their protective and reactive quality is undeniable.

Management-Worker Relationships. A good place to inspect the difference between management ideologies and the reality of worker-management relations is in the role of the foreman in industry. In theory, the foreman is a "marginal man" in Park's sense, standing between management and workers.[43] In fact, he is a worker, and has no chance in modern industry to advance into management. Crozier's observational study in France and Zaleznik's in the United States agree that the foreman is under a conflicting series of stresses. As Crozier points out, to the extent that the foreman can identify with workers and act as one, to that extent is he happy with his job.[44] On the other hand, as Zaleznik points out, a foreman may have to relate to, and please, a series of "bosses" and he may both be torn apart by their conflicting demands and rejected by these bosses to the extent that he sides with the workers.[45] But the critical issue here is his lack of upward mobility potential. Foremen do not become managers. Given this fact, and given the increasing unionization of industrial workers, all major crises between management and workers are handled by the union steward and the plant's management labor negotiator, quite independently of the foreman. In fully unionized industries — that includes all large ones in the United States — the entire grievance machinery has come to replace the foreman with formalized, and often professional, labor-management negotiating teams. Crozier suggests that the bureaucratic situation borders on an "estate" model; it is replacing attempts to construct a given person or role as an on the setting go-between in the labor-management relationship.[46] The increasing agreements readied between big labor and big management are made at the national and contractual level, not at the level of the foreman.

The wildcat strike, such as the one studied by Gouldner, is an excellent place to observe another aspect of the dynamics of labor-management relations. In Gouldner's case, as in many others, a crisis of legitimacy of worker representation occurred because the formal union leaders in the shop were *too cooperative* with management. As the plant went through a reorganization and tightened up controls, the workers increasingly felt that their formal leaders were siding with management and against their interests; this then led to their selection of new informal leaders who gave them encouragement and leadership in the calling of the informal, non-union-sponsored or "wildcat" strike. The opposition of worker and management interests, though it can be mitigated by manipulation and "human relations," is built into the capitalist system of production and ownership and thus cannot be engineered out of existence by changes in technology or constraints in the social organization of the work setting.[47]

Management-Management Relationships. Within the broad orbit known as "management" a series of sub-set relationships have been the focus of recent case analyses. These include the relationships between top-level executives and the second in command, executive-technical staff relations, and relations between the executive ranks and the white-collar groups. In each of these cases, however, the social distance observed in the relations between management and blue-collar groups is not found, although conflicts of interest are observable to both participants and researchers.

Crozier noted, in his French factory, exactly what has been noted for the American executive ranks by Levinson — that "generational" problems exist quite naturally between senior executives and young men on their way up. The hortatory literature on management relations and the observational evidence coincide, however, on the usual resolution of this problem — a move on the part of the younger man or the creation of a senior-junior sponsorship relationship. The lack of forced commitment to the setting, on the part of the younger man, modifies the seriousness of this choice to some degree.[48]

The relations between the executive and the technical-scientific staffs have been the foundation of two depth studies in the United States and that of Crozier's in France. Barnes, in his study of two companies, one with a restrictive command structure and one with a more open and participatory relationship between management and technical-scientific staff, found the level of both productivity and creativity higher in the latter setting.[49] Walton, in his study of unionization of technical-professional staffs, found a difference between the managerial-to-technical staff relations and the managerial-to-blue-collar relations in the same settings, when both groups were unionized. Although unionization appeared to give the technical-engineering staffs more power vis-a-vis management, their "professional" orientation did not lead to changes in the direction of restriction of production but rather demands for *greater* responsibility and work task involvement.[50] In France, Crozier noted that the functional power of the technical chief engineer in the factory related to his ability to handle the critical production problems caused by the breakdown of the machinery, and that this important functional role, when recognized by management, led to the kind of power-standoff and mutual respect that Walton found on both the open and unionized setting, with regard to relations of technical and managerial personnel. Strict command relationships between upper management and technical staff, with or without unions, appear to be gained only at the expense of destroying the productivity of the group, thus undermining the achievement of the goals of the organization.[51]

Both Mills and Langner agree that the typical relationship between higher-level management, lower-level office management, and the white-collar work force, is dramatized by a careful graduation of responsibility and an ideology of the potential for upward mobility with every secretary identified by management as a part of itself.[52] This deliberate management policy aims at the satisfaction of status and dependency needs by lower-level clerical personnel and the avoidance of a militant class consciousness by the white-collar work force. Relations between management and white-collar groups are probably, in most settings, characterized by more care and politeness than in any other intra-management relationship pattern. Given the *size* of the white-collar work force in modern corporations, the political motivation behind this politeness and care should be obvious. But in the experience and outlook of the white-collar workers themselves, the approach seems to work far more frequently than it fails. The white-collar worker experiences his or her career as a "management" career and prefers glory by remote association to group solidarity and a working-class identity.

The External-Internal Relationships Issue. The relationships between the external setting — the community in which the business is located — and the internal relationships within the industrial-business system are of major importance in understanding the experience on the setting. The management-labor relation in a one-industry town differs radically from those in a major industrial, metropolitan area. For the United States, Turner and Lawrence have shown that the ethnic, city-based working groups express less concern with the details of assembly-line work and a higher level of satisfaction with it than do the workers in a predominantly "Yankee" region, in a smaller town.[53] The investigators suggest that the external relations make up for a lack of on-setting satisfactions, and make the work itself less critical. In the one-industry "company town," on the other hand, the power structure of the community, and its authority system, are the same as the one in the plant, so accommodations must be made in both settings or in neither. In many ways, therefore, the external community relations affect the internal, and vice versa, with these effects increasing in approximate relation to the isolation of plant and community.

In France, the work of Crozier suggests that French cultural norms on the importance of both rigid structure and open bargaining in social relations influence the way that relationships are created and perpetuated on the work setting.[54] In another hypothesis in this area, Eisenstadt distinguishes between what he calls the *participation* of an ethnic group in the industrial setting and the *commitment* of workers in a given group to such settings.[55] We will review the cross-cultural evidence for developing nations in the next section, but the general impression exists on the basis of preliminary research findings in the United States and elsewhere that the community environment is a complex influence on management-labor relations and cannot be reduced to a simple set of formulae.

The Eventual World View of System Members. Little attention has been paid to date to the resultant world view of executive, technical, white collar, and blue-collar workers in the corporate system after years of experience in it. One major theme in the research on management group experience lies in the progressively negative evaluation of human nature and the potential of *any* form of social arrangement in the industrial work setting for providing an ultimate solution to the problems of human relations. Crozier sums up the progressive process of disillusionment on the part of younger executives, as they grow older:

> his view of human relations has now become rather skeptical and conservative, and will become increasingly so as the possibilities of his own achievement narrow down. Things do not change easily, he feels, and perhaps they ought not to change easily. Human problems are the key to everything, but a key for locking rather than for unlocking. Humanism in this context will mean recognition of the other fellow's right to oppose change, i.e., acceptance of the status quo.[56]

For the white-collar and blue-collar ranks, the aspirations have never been as high as those implied here for young managers, so the disillusionment ratio is in most cases lower at the end of the career. The idea of an occupation-based world view, in groups so broad as those we have been considering here, is rather difficult to isolate or to describe. The interests of these groups can be understood clearly enough, but their world view is somewhat difficult to summarize.

On the other hand, as a result of the common experiences of workers in the industrial settings in all societies, an overall attitude toward one's place in the industrial order may eventually result, after the early years of socialization by foremen, co-workers on the setting, the distant imperatives of management, and the constraints of the actual technology on the setting. Inkeles suggests that

> These forces conspire to impress upon the worker a particular view of himself and his relation to the world of work and beyond. His image of the world is, as a result, likely to be that of a place of great complexity, whose workings are not too easily comprehended by the common man. He has rights, but he needs friends who are more powerful or knowledgeable, who can explain things, tell him where to go, or help him by putting in a good word in the right place, like a key in a special lock which opens closed doors. For his own part, he feels he should stick to his job, not ask too many questions, and stay out of trouble.[57]

The fact that in present American society the "powerful friends" are more likely to be union representatives or national professional labor lawyers than paternal managers or foremen does not change the basic issue; the overwhelming pressures and impacts of industrial work, although coped with in the form of an on-setting occupational culture, must nevertheless be *coped* with and not operated upon.

THE INDUSTRIAL EXPERIENCE: A CROSS-CULTURAL APPROACH

To the degree that the industrial setting, and the bureaucratic order within which it is set, is becoming internationally the way in which a major sector of all nations' work is carried out, we could expect that the constraints of technology and the bureaucratic model of power relations would form a common experience for men around the world. This was the thesis of Inkeles in "Industrial Man" when he noted on the basis of studies done by others that place in the industrial-corporate hierarchy — manager, technical-professional, white-collar, blue-collar, unskilled labor — would have a cross-cultural similarity in relations between the groups within each nation. That is, the findings on such variables as satisfaction with work, general optimism, and the degree of overall life satisfaction would be highest in the upper occupational ranks of each nation and lowest at the bottom. With minor exceptions for the aristocracies of the world, who are really out of the system at the top, this pattern was found, differing in details but clear in the case of major industrial nations, such as the Soviet Union, the United States, and the nations of Western Europe:

> We see striking confirmation of the differential effect of the job situation on the perception of one's experience in it. The evidence is powerful and unmistakable that satisfaction with one's job is differentially experienced by those in several standard occupational positions. From

> country to country, we observe a clear positive correlation between the overall status of occupations and the experience of satisfaction in them.[58]

Over the past decade, Inkeles and his co-workers have been carrying out a study of the impact of the industrial order on the peasantry of developing nations. This gives us another chance to see the effect of industry on the experience of those in the worker role. In an early description of this study, which aims at comparing the peasants of these nations who remain in agriculture with those of long and short-term experience in industry, the aim is again to see whether the resultant experience in the factory setting changes the world view and the values or attitudes of those exposed to the system:

> In more than a metaphorical sense, the factory may function like a school, teaching both explicit and implicit lessons with regard to time, authority, calculability of others, distributive justice, technical competence, cooperation, and numerous other issues.[59]

This research has been taking into account the very factors we have just reviewed for experience in the American and Western European settings. That is, workers don't live only in factories. The world outside interacts with the world inside, in the effect of the outside setting on the workplace and in the fact that the workers live in two worlds, the plant and the community:

> It is clear that the impact of the industrial experience will be affected by a number of factors other than the qualities of industrial management. These influences include the personal qualities and culture of the men who came to the factories, the nature of their ties to the traditional community, the length of their stay, the condition of the local community in which they live, and the state of political stability and social cohesiveness of the larger society.[60]

The findings of this study basically continue the pattern seen in the fully industrialized nations. In general, the factory experience is essentially a constant, with an overwhelming similarity in all nations, but one which is *stronger* in effect than external family, political, and cultural factors in some nations and regions and *weaker* in effect than these same factors in other nations or regions. That is, the resulting experience will, in the setting, be almost the same everywhere, but whether this experience plays a *dominant* or simply a contributing role in the world view of a worker depends on the nation, the setting, and the social networks of the workers involved.[61] Three findings, out of many, will help to illustrate the complexities here. Oloko found in Nigeria that the regime which a management set up in a factory — its degree of liberality or strictness — rather than the nationality of its factory managers — Nigerian or European — made the major difference to worker satisfaction. He also found that the more Westernized tribal groups experienced the factory setting with greater satisfaction than the more rural tribal workers.[62] Ireland found that the factory experience was a strong tipping-point factor for the worker, having more of an impact on worker experience and outlook in areas that were neither totally industrialized, in which case the experience would not be a new one, nor rural peasant areas, where the ties in the rural area to family and community "undid" the effect of the work setting.[63] In Mexico, in a study independent of the Inkeles group, Nash found the same thing in a Mayan area — until the overall area is partially industrialized, the people can isolate the experience from the rest of life, because in effect they can remain 9-to-5 moderns and evening and weekend traditionalists.[64] In general, therefore, the studies of the industrial experience in fully industrialized nations and in developing nations show variability of many kinds, but there *is* something we can call industrial experience.

In this section, on the experience of workers at different levels in the industrial hierarchy, we have considered the initial motivational and recruitment patterns for the major subgroups, the nature of the career pattern with the key experience at different stages, the set of interaction relationships on the setting, and finally, the nature of the industrial experience as reflected in attitudes and world view. As with the major occupational fields we have already considered, the *scope* of career opportunities and the possibilities for fulfillment are related to the hierarchy of occupational groups. With every step up the social structural ladder, increasing career complexity and stress is made up for by increasing opportunity and material reward. The society-wide patterns of the industrial-corporate division of labor, and the interest-group structure which is a consequence of this pattern, is no more unique to this nation than is the experience within the system. It is to this overall pattern that we now turn, in a combined division-of-labor and conflict-of-interest analysis of the role of the different groups in the overall social system and the power they have by virtue of their role.

THE INDUSTRIAL PATTERN: COMPARATIVE ASPECTS OF THE POWER RELATIONSHIPS

Raymond Aron has written that:

> Europe and Asia are not composed of two fundamentally different worlds, the Soviet world and the Western world — they are made out of one single reality, industrial civilization. Soviet societies and capitalist societies are two species of the same genus or two modalities of the same social type, the progressive industrial society.[65]

And Wassily Leontief, in doing a major analysis of the patterns of economic exchange between the different sectors of European society on the one hand and the equivalent internal patterns of exchange in American society on the other, has noticed a striking similarity both in quantitative and in relative or proportional terms between the European and the American pattern.[66] In another place, Aron notes that, "The relation between the directors of the means of production and the holders of state power are not the same in the Soviet Union and the United States."[67] And Leontief would agree here as well. In general, the industrial division of labor, as a concrete pattern, is as similar from nation to nation across the society as is the pattern for division of labor on the work setting itself. The interesting problem becomes the role of each of the four major groups we have considered — the managers, the scientific-technical people, the white-collar workers, and industrial labor — in different types of *political* regimes with essentially the same degree of industrialization. We can briefly inspect this problem — the functional role of management and labor within a wider socio-political system — by comparing management and labor in four different kinds of nations: the United States, France, the Soviet Union, and Japan. The aim here is not a complete comparative analysis, but an introduction to the idea of political power as it relates to an occupational group's function within a given regime.

MANAGEMENT IN COMPARATIVE PERSPECTIVE

In the area of management, the recent and increasing role of the United States government and the evolution of a "professional" management do not mean, at least in comparative perspective, that the American manager is either ordered around by government or independent of the owners and stockholders of his corporation. Certainly there is government intervention in decision-making and pressure on owners, as Borchardt's study of management problems in the communications industry indicates.[68] The *image* of the professionalized manager is sought, especially by the postgraduate business schools. However, the reality is still that executives who advance the interests of the corporation are retained by the owners, and those who act too independently of it or threaten its basic interests are fired. Thus in large corporations in America, management operates in most cases rather independently of government, with minor restraints in the form of legal regulations, but not at all independently of the corporation's owners, especially the large owners who hold a major share of the stock.

In France, as both Cohen and McArthur and Scott have recently shown, the centralized planning of the French economy is a complex process to be understood only in terms of the overall French social structure.[69] In the first few years after World War II, the French industrial planning process was powerful, simple, and centralized; gradually it has become more complex and less relevant to an understanding of the direction of French industry. In all periods since the war, however, the French industrial managers have been part of a social-technical elite, in which there has been major circulation between the central government planning bureaucracies and private industry. This has not only been considered acceptable, but in some cases has been officially encouraged. In understanding the role of management in the French system, Cohen stresses that the large corporations — the French giant combines — work with the government planners (their colleagues and former classmates) to ensure that what is planned for France will be of benefit to them. The smaller corporations, and industrial labor, are invited to "participate" in this planning, but are not given a central role in decision-making. This social phenomenon is typical of the government-management relationship:

> The business executives and government officials are of similar social backgrounds. They share the same attitudes, the same values, the same modes of expression. They have a common intellectual formation and orientation. They have a way of defining a "pattern" and they think about those problems in the same manner. Often, they know one another. They attended the same schools, they frequent the same social circles, and they marry each other's sisters.[70]

In microcosm, this reproduces what Mills stated, with less evidence and in a more complex social situation, for the American "power elite." The major difference is that in France the collusion is deliberate, conscious, open, and *legal*, and the training in the French university is deliberately directed to bring this centralization about. If the American manager can be seen as the servant of corporate ownership, the French manager functions as a go-between for large corporations and the central government, with the large corporations preserving their power and independence through their ability to manipulate the government's plan and place "their" men in central planning posts.

In the Soviet Union the state and, in particular, the Communist party preserve political and administrative control over managers; at the same time they have decentralized the specific direction of the day-to-day plant activities. As Granick notes, the bargaining and haggling with the state and the stresses of the Soviet executive share many similarities with the experience and problems of the Western manager.[71] But their importance to the Soviet system does not give them functional power to the degree that they can choose independently of close state control. Hough's study indicates the special and specific local role of Communist party representatives in observing managers in action and their role as a type of troubleshooter and bargainer in local management-labor disputes. This preserves political control of management and ensures their pursuit of centrally decided goals.[72] In another recent study, Azrael summarizes the role of managerial power in Soviet politics:

> At almost every step, the technicians have bowed to the dictates of the ruling elite, and in those cases where they have proved somewhat re-

> calcitrant, their resistance has ultimately been futile. What political influence they have had has been primarily a function of their unquestioning acceptance of an instrumental and dependent role, and the only periods during which they have acquired a certain independence have been those in which the central leadership has been internally split.[73]

Thus, the centralized power system of the Soviet Union affects the independence of all occupational groups. Occupational consciousness and group occupational self-interest action are almost impossible except during periods of turmoil at the center. As we recall, the clergy gained some strength during World War II when they were needed in the crisis, and the military gain in times of political infighting within the Kremlin.

The Japanese system of industrial organization has been called "industrial feudalism" by several of its observers, in reference to the corporate "world-within-a-world" arrangements which the major Japanese corporations make for their management and labor force, with company living quarters and company hospitals as standard arrangements. In addition, the major industrial combines, or *Zaibatsu*, control not only the management policies of a major sector of the economy, but also the regulations of the government with respect to industry. A second aspect of the Japanese situation is similar to the French, but to a greater degree — about 40 per cent — of Japan's corporations are owned and run by the government, on the approximate model of the TVA in the United States. This interlocking of major capitalist groups and government planning provides the manager in the *major* corporations with functional power, but this is power inherent in the role, not in himself as a person, unless the manager is also an owner, a blood relative of the major Zaibatsu families.[74]

TECHNICAL AND WHITE-COLLAR GROUPS: ON WHOSE SIDE?

The role of technical and white-collar workers is complex in comparative perspective, and is an area less well researched than either management or industrial labor. Technical, professional, and white-collar workers are "management" in the United States and "labor" in most Japanese industries, through participation in labor unions which are national in scope. In the United States, the deliberate approach of business management across the nation is to stress to all white-collar workers that they are indeed *management;* the occupational hierarchy is structured in small steps upward, with a minute graduation of responsibility, so that only new recruits are "privates" and all others can manage at least one small group of people, giving them a taste of the "management experience" and identifying them with company goals. In Japan, by contrast, the social class system does not allow such identification with upper management, for the mobility into this level is still mostly by birth or marriage.

In the French system, only the elite become managers, and the second-run schools produce both the technical and the white-collar workers who have little chance for upward mobility in the rigidly bureaucratized French system. In the Soviet Union, an ideology of mobility and the extensive series of self-improvement programs and adult education make some upward mobility possible. But the unique aspect of Soviet "labor" unions is that they include, on a plant-by-plant basis, *all* technical and white-collar people as well as blue-collar workers, excepting only top management. Much further research needs to be done on the rather blurred occupational categories of "technical," "professional," and "white collar" as these apply comparatively to the industrial situation.

THE ROLE OF LABOR GROUPS

The role of the labor (blue-collar industrial) groups in these four regimes is instructive especially with respect to the role of management groups in the same system. For example, in the United States the early history of labor militancy in industry has been replaced by increasing cooperation between "big" management and "big" unions in the major manufacturing industries. Although times of inflation or depression change the degree of cooperation, in large part the labor unions accept the legitimacy of the capitalist system; in fact a number of major industrial unions have pension funds whose income comes from investment in the stock market and thus in the very corporations with which they deal as a theoretical "opponent." With the exception of the broad areas of service work, transportation, and public employment, where militancy is now increasing, the groups of organized labor are participating in the industrial system far more than opposing it; their actions are for a greater share of profits within the present political-economic system.

In France and Japan, this is not the case. Here, in both nations, the workers constitute a group that wishes an alternate political system — socialism in most cases — and their political activity is directed to this end. Cohen writes of the French planning system that

> The trade unionist delegated to the plan is not only an outsider in respect to access to critical information about business decisions and practices, he is also socially isolated from the businessmen and civil servants.[75]

The ideological struggles of the past, and the aristocratic and feudal heritage of both France and Japan, leave their echoes in the present day. That is, the entire history of these nations is refuted by working-class movements in a way that is not found in the statements of American workers. As Cohen summarizes for France:

> The trade unions see themselves as an arm of the working class engaged in a struggle with the ruling bourgeoisie, and not as a pressure group, accepting the fundamental structures of bourgeois society, and fighting for

> a larger chunk of the pie. Their function is to contest the basic legitimacy of the capitalist order. Their goal is to replace capitalism — whether it be "neo" or traditional capitalism — with a fundamentally different socialist society.[76]

In the Soviet Union, where in theory the workers — and everyone else — owns the state, the situation is ironically more like the United States than it is like either France or Japan. On the topic of ideology, Ossowski notes that the "mobility" or "Horatio Alger" ideology of the United States and the "classless society" ideology of the Soviet Union serve the same function for the working class, especially the industrial workers. They make it possible to accept a reward in line with their place in the occupational hierarchy, and help to lessen the possibility of a class-based political movement.[77] In the Soviet Union, the government is a major — let us say the only — arbitrator between "labor" and "management" in a given plant. Brown, in her history of the role of labor unions in Soviet society, notes that under Stalin the national and local labor unions were strictly propaganda and terroristic organs of the central government to which all workers had to belong. Under Khrushchev and thereafter, the Soviet labor unions were still centrally administered by the government and still not allowed to discuss the economic (wage) issues central to the West. But they do now apparently perform a function as a check on mismanagement at the local level. That is, in grievances on safety and other working conditions, the locally elected labor representatives and the local management must work out their disputes, without if possible but with, if necessary, local Communist party representatives.[78] One notes, therefore, that for different reasons — part ownership in the case of American workers and central government power over all economic issues such as wages in the Soviet — the everyday activities of the labor unions in these two industrial nations share much in terms of their task-directed, as opposed to political-party-directed, activities. Yet the political power of the Soviet labor unions nowhere approaches, in ultimate terms, the potential power of a combined labor movement in Japan or France, or, if it were desired and under different ideological conditions, in the United States as well.

To sum up, in this chapter, historically, interactionally, and in systems-conflict terms we have seen that the roles of management and labor as major occupational super-groups share both major similarities and major differences, within the overall industrial pattern common to them all. We have given only the barest outlines of these differences here, but certain conclusions are possible. First, historically, the rise of industrialization led to the organization of the industrialists and the owners years before the organization of the workers, and once government entered as a third party, it did so more on the side of management than on the side of labor, in the Soviet system as well as in the West and Far East. Once the industrial pattern was established, career sequences and career experience possibilities were generated in the new hierarchy from unskilled labor to top management. The division of labor on the work setting and the consequent experience and norms in such settings show striking similarities around the world. The differences lie in the power relations between management and labor. These can never be understood by themselves, but only in the context of who owns the industry which is being managed and worked in, and what relationship these owners have to the political power centers of the society. The course of the conflicts of interest between the groups found on the industrial setting can be understood only in terms of what goes on in this setting in social interactional terms. This is the lesson which Marx and C. Wright Mills have for Roethlisberger and Dixon and other students of the settings where work is performed. We are, however, no less indebted to the latter than to the former, for the industrial experience is a complex, near universal reality with both deep existential and broad political implications. Indeed, the two are ultimately aspects of a single, greater reality.

CHAPTER TEN

SCIENCE AND THE ARTS

The creative occupations, those based directly on man's ability to discover new combinations of experience and new methods of solving old problems, constitute a special problem in the sociology of occupations. This problem has several facets. The relationship between individual creativity — especially in the case of the genius — and the function of larger numbers of individuals in the occupational group is an important issue. Another issue lies in the distinction between the "pure" scientist or artist — defined as one who pursues the creative activity "for its own sake" — and the applied practitioner, who works toward other ends besides the creation of new forms. This chapter will compare the scientist and the artist because the advantages gained thereby are not realizable in treating each group alone. At a deeper level of analysis, the creative functions of the basic scientist and the dedicated artist are very similar, if not identical, in terms of their role in changing the ideas, and eventually the process, in a given society.

A HISTORICAL COMPARISON: THE POSITIONS OF ARTIST AND SCIENTIST

In ancient Egypt, although there was a developed technology which had its origins in unrecorded antiquity, there were no individuals or groups consciously identified either as scientific theorists or as experimenters. By contrast, the artist had a role, within a collective group of workers in an art workshop whose duties involved the construction of public monuments and religious edifices. As Hauser notes, this did not leave room for creativity in the sense in which it is presently understood:

> With increasing demands the custom grew of working according to sketches, models, and uniform patterns, and an almost mechanically stereotyped technique of production was developed which enabled the different objects simply to be constructed from separate uniform components. . . . And as originality of subject-matter was never very much appreciated in Egypt, in fact was generally tabooed, the whole ambition of the artist was concentrated on thoroughness and precision of execution, which is so conspicuous even in the less important works and which compensates for the lack of interest and piquancy in the invention.[1]

Although there were periods in Egyptian art, such as the earliest eras and the reign of Amenhotep IV (Ikhnaton), when more freedom existed, in most of the classical age the artist was a functionary of the state and the priesthood, a hired craftsman.

In the Greece of the "golden age," there were several differences of importance within the arts and in the relation between "science" and art. First, the mathematical theories of such giants as Pythagoras and those in the Alexandrian school can be considered as the basis for much further theory in science, and the rudiments of experimentation were also present, for example in the work of Archimedes. In a sense, this form of "science" was considered a branch of philosophy and thus acceptable as work for those who were either in the elite or who were at least freemen. By contrast, much of the craftwork and even the sculpture of the classical period was the work of those low on the social scale. The verbal arts, poetry and drama in particular, had a higher social status ranking, and here the realm of "science" and art came together, in terms of the products of the workers and in terms of the worker himself. The audience for both natural philosophy and the drama was the nobility. As Hauser notes, the poets and philosophers were either aristocrats themselves, or like Sophocles and Plato, they identified themselves with the nobility, from their position in the upper middle class. There were exceptions, of course, such as Euripides and the Sophists, but the Greece of the fifth and fourth centuries B.C. was a time when the aristocratic mathematical and humanistic philosophers were a privileged elite, the architectural and sculptural craftsmen and the engineering experts part of the working mass.[2] Perhaps from ancient Greece we can date the division of labor in the creative occupations between the "pure" or theoretical elite and the applied practitioner mass.

Rome was a place of great creativity in the forms of government and the application of existing (especially Greek) knowledge to a larger scale of problems, but most scholars do not view it as a time of great originality in either science or art. Still, in the *applied* sciences (Roman engineering in particular) and in the employment of applied craftsmen, the period of the Empire must be considered an important era. Concurrent with the later stages of empire and the early years of the Holy Roman Empire, the Arabic renaissance brought to birth many modern mathematical concepts. The invention of the zero and of algebra were major contributions which Arabic science made to the era of the Middle Ages in Europe. (Art, with each passing century, became more abstract and "theological" and less representational in form.)

By the time of the twelfth and thirteenth centuries, a new regime had arisen in Europe and with it, a new set of rulers for both the "scientist" and the artist. In the Middle Ages, the artist did not have individuality as the maker of a particular work of art; group forms of work which had characterized the earlier Egyptian and Greek eras also characterized this one. After the period of Charlemagne, when artistic production was centered in the royal court, the monarchy and the Church became the sponsor, haven, locus, and reason-for-existence of the artist. Art and sacred art in the early Middle Ages are nearly synonymous, though with every passing decade and century, especially with the growth of towns in the later Middle Ages, a change comes about.[3] Whereas the crafts as well as the verbal arts were Church-based in the early Middle Ages, the later period sees a split between the Church-run, university-located philosophers and theorists (in both art and science) and the secular, guild-based craftsmen (artistic and engineering). In the theoretical realm, the "natural philosopher" was neither the modern "scientist" nor the modern humanist philosopher. In the thirteenth century, philosophers were more akin to the ancients than to Renaissance men; although they had begun to talk of experimentation, it was not linked to theory directly. As Crombie states:

> The natural philosopher of the thirteenth century regarded the investigation of the physical world as part of a single philosophical activity concerned with the search for reality and truth. The purpose of his inquiry was to discover the enduring and intelligible reality behind the changes undergone by the world perceived through the senses.[4]

Although in its early form this was an Aristotelian, and essentially unexperimental, mode of activity, with each succeeding century the idea of *testing* the theories became more common.

The Renaissance was the first major period when both the artist and the scientist emerged from the group or corporate occupational group as individuals. As Hauser notes, this was the first time for centuries that the concept of creative genius as a quality of an individual was found relevant to human lives.[5] Ullmann marks the Renaissance as the time when the concept of the public man as "subject" was replaced by the concept of man as "citizen"; it was a time when the individuality of art work itself — the products — began to develop along with the individual identification of the makers of the art. From this time it becomes possible to identify both the individual geniuses in science and art and the groups which still existed and performed much of the journeyman craft and engineering.[6]

After the onset of the Renaissance, the history of science and art is the history of individual genius as well as that of occupational groups; only in the present can we find the data that once again make it possible to study the groups as groups, and genius against the background of the typical occupational group member. The groups were always there, of course, and the history of both art and science are continuous; each man "stands on the shoulders of giants." Vasari's *Lives of the Artists* made it clear that apprenticeship to a master was part of the experience of all the painters of the time.[7]

Barber characterizes the sixteenth and seventeenth centuries, in science, as the time of "takeoff," or the birth of science as it is understood in the modern sense of the term, the time when rational theory and deliberate experimentation in terms of the theory were brought together. But he also acknowledges a slow growth of the use of experimentation.[8] Crombie agrees:

> So far as scientific method is concerned, the whole period from the thirteenth to the seventeenth century can be seen as one in which the functions both of the experimental principles of verification and falsification and correlation, and of mathematical techniques, were understood and applied with increasing effect to reduce philosophies of nature to exact science.[9]

In addition to the internal development of scientific thought, it is possible that certain religious ideas were more compatible with scientific thought than others were. For example, Puritanism, in dissenting both from Catholicism and older forms of Protestantism, put a high emphasis on rationality and direct observation of nature. Merton, in a study of scientists in seventeenth-century England, found that Puritans were disproportionately represented in the Royal Society, the scientific society of the day.[10] He concludes that "the combination of rationalism and empiricism which is so pronounced in the Puritan ethic forms the essence of the spirit of modern science." [11]

From the Renaissance through the Reformation and late into the Enlightenment, the "public" for both creative art and scientific thinking was primarily restricted to those few who were educated — the nobility and the mercantile elite. Thus the social position of the artist remained dependent on patronage, even if he had an individual identity lacking in earlier eras. The concept of pure art, divorced from use or developed apart from the commission process, was not common. Comparing this situation with that of the maker of science, we find that the scientist of the seventeenth and eighteenth centuries was far more likely to be a gentleman of leisure than a working man, for basic science had no more payoff in the political economy than did art. Science was a "gentleman's plaything." It was not until the time of the Industrial Revolution that the practicality and profitability of basic scientific research began to be seen by the powerful of the time.

In the American case, in the Puritan and colonial era, the first artists were the *limners*, essentially craftsmen with pictorial skills who painted, among other things, portraits. As Larkin explains,

> In England also labored a host of inconspicuous craftsmen who could produce a florid coat of arms for a rich man's coach or a signboard for a tavern, and for whom the making of a likeness was but one variation of their craft. It was those all-but-nameless limners, both English and Continental, who either came to the new country or who were bred here and whom one calls America's first painters.[12]

The later colonial period and the pre- and post-revolutionary years were also the peak of the "classic" or Georgian style in American architecture, which gave to cities such as Boston, Philadelphia, and Charleston, South Carolina, the "colonial" look that is still widely imitated. Science was taught early in the Puritan-run Harvard, though as much for its philosophical as its experimental value. In the American Revolution itself, artists and especially writers from Paine to Adams played a major part.

The Jacksonian era and the following decades were a time of major expansion and social change, a time of ferment in both American science and art. This was the time of Emerson and Thoreau, of the New York School of landscape artists, of the plantation architecture of the South. In applied science, it was the time of the development of the cotton gin and the steam-driven mills for the processing of raw cotton into cloth. The technology originating in the Jacksonian era was to blossom eventually into the American Industrial Revolution from about 1850 to 1880. Once the Industrial Revolution got under way, we see the beginning of the modern divergence between the central, sponsored, and powerful institutional position of the scientific group and the marginal, unsponsored, and powerless position of the pure creative artist that characterizes the modern era.

In the most recent period, we may be seeing the reconvergence of the activity (and some of the role) of the artist and the scientist, as art begins to approach technology and spreads into the use of technological media such as film and television. However, in the modern era as in any other period, the *content* of art and science — the production of the artist and scientist — must be separated from the social status and role of the scientist and artist in ongoing social processes. If art is approaching science in form and content, the present social position of the artist, with a few exceptions, is far beneath that of the scientist in terms of power, prestige, and reward. Although the two may be equally creative, in the abstract sense of adding new ideas to the present society, the use of scientific ideas by a more powerful and resourceful group than that using those of the artist means that the average scientist is rewarded far more than the average artist. But this is characteristic of one time period, not a universal pattern for all times and places.

To sum up, the role of the creative individual in the creative occupation must be understood in a double perspective — both in terms of the product of the worker and of the position of the creator as an individual or the position of the creator's occupational group. In almost all eras, the product has been of value to the elites, who have been in a position to reward the creator or the creator group as they saw fit. Only extreme genius brought even partial independence. In earlier eras, it was the artist who was more useful. In more recent eras, the skill of the average as well as the excellent scientist has met a market that has given him, and his group, functional power and thus some independence. The role of the modern artist, by contrast, has remained marginal to this system, unless some groups within the system find a way to exploit the talent to their own ends. The rumored onset of "mass culture," presumably the beginning of a larger market for the basic creative artists, is not indicated in the recent study of Baumol and Bowen, except for limited areas such as the East and West coasts.[13] In conclusion, the development of the creative worker cannot be understood without knowing where the occupational group stands with respect to the technology and social structure of the day, to the political economy of a given nation at a given point in history. Thus our comparison of the experience of the present-day artist and scientist must be understood in part as consequences of a unique set of forces in the present socio-political order.

THE CREATIVE CAREER: SOME COMPARISONS

The most striking comparison that can be made between the career of the creative scientist and that of the creative artist lies in the fully institutionalized nature of the former and the almost completely open and chance-controlled quality of the latter. There are career alternatives within science for those of high, medium, and low creativity, whereas there are few career opportunities in the arts for any but the most talented. If we can consider the forms of creativity as closely related, if not two species of one human gift, then the career contingencies of the scientist need to be compared with those of the artist in order to understand their similarities and differences as forms of occupational experience. We may do this by comparing the scientific career with different forms of artistic career on the following topics: initial ability and motivation, early development of identity as a creator, basic training period and commitment point, the contingencies in the adult career, and resultant occupational world views.

INITIAL ABILITY AND MOTIVATION

Psychoanalysts such as Kubie and White have pondered the internal personality factors that differentiate the creative individual from the noncreative or less creative one.[14] In addition, studies of scientists and artists by Roe and Eiduson have attempted to isolate the "special" personality characteristics that seem to characterize the creative person.[15] This literature is extremely indecisive, for several reasons. First, most of the studies are retrospective, in that they identify characteristics of those who have "arrived" as scientists or artists. But if any characteristics are identified (and they usually are not, or else they are restatements in functional terms of creativity itself, such as "lack of rigidity," "flexibility," "innovativeness"), it is not known whether these also characterize the ones who did not arrive, or the average citizen for that matter. In general, the literature on *blocks* to creativity, from early childhood on, is more suggestive. Since the observations of Kozol and Holt on the American public school system, especially in the ghetto, we know how the natural creativity of children can be stifled.[16] In line with this, the scientific career presupposes the achievement motivation and social backing through college and graduate school which is out of the reach of poor children. Similarly, most of the careers in the creative arts require either sophisticated education (writing and poetry), early commitment with parental backing (music and dance), or special courses in public or museum settings (painting). In each case, the social class of the young creative child will predetermine a set of factors in his or her environment which will nurture the talent of the middle-class and upper-class individual and obliterate the potential of many of the poor. That an occasional poor child makes it into the ranks of top creative workers is a tribute to human ability in adverse circumstances. But as Wilson's review for arts and Klaw's for science makes clear, the early socialization and environment of the poor is not conducive to the development of even the first stages of a creative career, in almost all cases.[17]

EARLY SCHOOLING AND THE "CREATOR" IDENTITY

In our society, on the basis of preliminary research, it appears that the artist is identified earlier in the life cycle than the scientist, in terms of creative ability. Because of the difference in the amount and quality of training required to show creativity in science as compared to art, it is possible to tell as early as elementary school who has talent in painting, music, and the other arts, whereas talent in both the verbal arts and talent in science must wait until high school for its first recognition. The prodigy syndrome, found in both artistic and scientific-mathematical careers, is an exception to this rule, but the identifiability of talent has an immediate effect when noticed on the individual's formation of his own identity as a creator. With an elementary school or high school "artist," the identification by others — and the self-identification — is a two-edged sword. Early commitment to any career line by definition is non-commitment to others, but early commitment to an artistic career which does not pay off has far greater consequences for the young proto-artist than for the young potential scientist. As Griff explains,

> by placing demands on the individual's time and artistic ability, the teacher enters and commits himself to an obligatory relationship. This requires him to be lenient toward the academic faults of these students in comparison to others in the classroom. Combined with the student's loss of time from his studies, this leniency is responsible for lowering the academic grades of the student.[18]

This increases the risk of the early commitment:

> Entrance into art school, however, is based not on formal course grades, but on proclivity and potentiality for painting. This means that the possession of talent may seal off other careers from the time the student is awarded a scholarship, even though the scholarship may be won as early as grammar school years.[19]

And there is no known proof that the graduates of formal art schools are more successful than the self-taught or those who took on some form of apprenticeship to a well-known artist. By contrast, since a scientific career requires academic high school and college training as a prerequisite for graduate school (where scientific creativity is first usually seen) a switching out of such a career line holds no penalties at all, as the general training is useful both for applied scientific careers or for any other type of occupation demanding college training.

Because the "creative" ideal is valued in the American middle class, but the realities of artistic career futures are known to most parents, the child with talents is encouraged to express them until the idea of career commitment arises. Then, if a career in the arts is desired by the youth, a rapid reversal of attitude occurs in the case of the average parents. Even if the parents are themselves in the arts, there may be opposition, if the parents feel they are a good enough judge of the child's talent or if they have had a difficult time in their own career. By contrast, increasing support is given the child whose talents lie in scientific lines. However, this picture is complicated by social class. For different reasons, the poor and the upper middle class parents, according to both Griff and Rosenberg and Fliegel, seem less opposed to an artistic career than those in the lower middle class.[20] For the poor parent, talent and the outside expert (art teacher, musician) hold greater prestige than they and their opinion do; many upper middle class parents know it is "low status" to make too much of an open fuss about a child's decision on an artistic career, as much as they may have misgivings about it. The greatest opposition (and ironically, the source of the greatest number of recruits to the arts in America) is found in the lower middle class. Here an art career is most socially embarrassing and most counter to the mobility striving and *ressentiment*-laden attitudes of the parents. And yet, although parental opposition for irrational or realistic reasons is strong in the background of many artists, it is not thought by Rosenberg and Fliegel to be destructive of career possibilities. Rather, and in almost a proof of Erikson's idea that adult identity must be forged in conflict with real and loved parents, the artist who has succeeded as such uses parental opposition as a hurdle and a challenge to confront and make firm his own commitment to this career. The authors believe that the "pseudoartist" — the non-political rebel youth with a sketch pad — is the one who is still bound up with parental conflicts and essentially uncreative in most cases. By contrast, those artists who did have parental opposition in their earlier stages of development seemed able to handle it because of an earlier and deeper commitment of these parents to these children as *individuals*, giving them the confidence to withstand the parents' later disapproval and confidence in the wisdom of their own decisions.[21] On the other hand, the basic question of the expression of talent is as much one of social structural as it is internal; for the highly talented artist who is identified early, the consequences in terms of life risk are infinitely higher than they are for the early-identified scientist. These risk-pressures, together with the ordinary turmoil of growing up in our society, are likely to produce a greater proportion of unhappy and conflict-laden artists than scientists.

THE BASIC TRAINING PERIOD

Creative occupations vary in many ways, but one of the most striking variations concerns the time of onset of the basic training period. If we can make an approximate continuum from creative occupations which are overwhelmingly intellectual, without a physical performance component, to occupations where physical ability and dexterity is a primary component, we may find that this continuum is related to the age of onset of what we call the "basic training" period. For example, in the physical sciences and in prose and poetry writing, the length of preparation is on the order of high school and college training before the question of creativity or true talent can reasonably be raised. In the graphic arts, such as painting, high school training (in a specialized art school or in museum classes) may be followed by post-secondary art school training, or by apprenticeship in small classes run by some expert painters, but there is an even mixture here of intellectual-expressive and manual skills to match the earlier age of onset of basic training. In the fields of music and dance, the age of training is yet earlier, for the discipline of the body and basic skills must accompany and not follow the actual biological development of the individual. Here elementary school age music and dance training (especially for classical music and ballet) is viewed as a necessity, forming the opposite pole in quality of creativity, in its strong physical component, from the totally intellectual work of the physicist, the poet, and the novelist.

The age at which the person "outgrows" the career is another way of looking at this complex dimension. For example, although a novelist can "burn out" early, no restraint inherent to the production of the creative work holds him to a time span; the physicist and novelist may be creative in later years. By comparison, the painter may, in some cases, be stopped more easily by physical disability, but this is not a major factor in this group. The performing artist — the operatic singer and dancer — has the greatest "burn-out" rate because of this dimension. The modern forms of performing artists — jazz and modern dance — allow a kind of direct life-cycle career extension that was not possible in classical music or especially in the dance. We do not know, however, the extent to which, especially in the performing arts, it is public stereotypes concerning the "proper" age of rock singers or ballet stars that adds a social factor to the biological dimension.

The issue of commitment to the creative career is complex because of the risks involved, and the commitment dilemma is intensified for those creative occupations where the reward is extremely low. For example, commitment to a career as a nuclear physicist or mathematician places one immediately into stiff competition with known others in a highly structured academic and professional evaluation, but the penalties for not being overly creative have to do with fame and prestige, not with sheer survival. For example, the pressure on many graduate scientists is to "produce," which does not give them time to try more creative approaches. On the other hand, the young scientist is not about to starve. He may in fact have more time for a limited amount of creative work than he would in a second-run university, or a small college, where he will be burdened by large classes and administrative work. Training in the sciences guarantees survival of occupational identity for almost all who enter the gate of graduate school.

By contrast, the commitment problem in an artistic career is complicated by the variables of the early stage of the life cycle at which the careers begin and the risks of failure involved in almost all of them. In general, with the more intellectual arts such as writing and painting, the career commitment dilemma is modified by the kind of commercial career alternative that exists for the less creative scientist. Where the non-star young scientist goes into industry, the unsuccessful novelist can go into advertising and the journeyman artist into commercial art. In the sciences and the non-performing arts, high and *recognized* talent results in a "pure" career and the life-cycle time of entry makes an individual choice possible. By contrast, in the case of careers such as concert musicians, opera, and dance, the parents of the child must commit the child to the career as much as the child himself, since if a person wishes to commit himself to such a career after puberty he is already in most instances too late. Both the risk failure and the need for early commitment increase as we go from the intellectually creative occupations toward the pole of the physically relevant performing arts. The intensity of conflict over career commitment found especially in the creative occupations is a product of past commitment by self and others, as viewed against the certainties and unknowns of the occupation's role in the social structure of the given society at a given point in history.

The peer groups of the scientist and artist perform functions for the group in the commitment period that can be found in other occupational career patterns. The society of scientific graduate students has been well described by Klaw, and the wider academic community by Caplow and McGee; it is both a mutual support society, a mutual education-and-criticism society, and a place for the perpetuation of occupational myths and valuable occupational information on career possibilities.[22] Artistic careers have been less well studied from this viewpoint, but it is hinted by Ryser's study of dancers and Rosenberg and Fliegel's study of artists that the greater social *anomie* in artistic occupations is also found in peer relations.[23] The role of the sponsor, if one exists, is critical if in either science or art he begins to relate to the student as a peer. This can lead to a reciprocal desire to prove the worth implied in the compliment, as when Hans Hoffmann, a well-known artist, began to talk with a small group of young artists in his school, using the words "we artists."

CONTINGENCIES IN THE CREATIVE CAREER

At least four major kinds of externally relevant social contingencies affect the development of creative careers: personal characteristics relevant to those who have power over career development, the settings on which the career is experienced, the sponsorship or economic relationship between creator and consumer of that which has been created, and the critics of the created work — those who have a legitimate position to evaluate, in the eyes of both creators and eventual consumers.

The personal characteristics of the creative person are the same characteristics that produce major career contingencies elsewhere. The female sex has been discriminated against in both science and in art. In science, one of the major team members in the discovery of DNA was Rosalind Franklin. Watson, another co-discoverer, apologizes to her in his book for not taking her contribution seriously enough, because she was a woman. This was in the late 1950s.[24] In art, in addition to the bias of some male artists, there have been until recently biases on the part of art dealers and museums to showing the work of females. In the performing arts, where there has not been overt bias, there has often been sexual stereotyping (e.g., the female harpist and the feminine stereotype of dancers of either sex). Racially, in addition to the almost automatic difference in the quality of schooling and availability of support, the biases in universities, the art world, and the performing arts have been well known. Though the genius of the "wrong" sex or race has been able to succeed in science and art, there has until recently been little chance for the moderately creative person with marginal social characteristics. This is ironic, given the supposedly "cosmopolitan" ideology of science and art, but it can be understood if not condoned in terms of the social affiliations of university elites in America and the prejudices of the art public. In most recent years, and in reaction to this, "black militant art" is on the rise. Whether art can be both directly creative and propagandistic is a critical and unsolved problem in the field of art criticism. But it is an unavoidable fact that personal characteristics have been a strong set of contingencies contributing to the degree of success or failure in creative work.

The second set of contingencies — the setting of the career — is clearly relevant to both science and the arts. For science and the verbal arts, the university has become a primary haven for the creators. There is a critical distinction between an elite university position, with time off to write equations or verse, and the typical position, with teaching and administrative commitments of an extensive nature and a salary low enough to make summer work a necessity. The status of the university setting where the individual works, as Caplow and McGee demonstrate, is often a product of where he trained, with the elite route (Harvard to Berkeley, Michigan to M.I.T.) taken by one group, whereas others find far less time to create.[25] For the artist — with the exception of an occasional artist in residence and the development of visual arts programs in some universities — the setting of the work is usually solitary, excepting also the occasional artists' coop. But the region of the city where the artistic group lives is often localized to form some kind of social contact. The performing artist has his setting defined by others, and practice is either solitary, or, if the medium demands it, in the least expensive settings available.

A third kind of contingency — the economics of the sponsorship relationship — creates a series of major conflicts for individuals in creative careers. For example, the stress of the United States government on applications of scientific research has meant far less money available for basic, or truly creative, research, than for applied research. In a direct parallel, the art world of dealer and museum is an economic *market* world. The dealers (including the museums) want art that will sell, i.e., that is popular, that will be bought by those with money to spend or that will draw a paying crowd to a museum. In each case, the role of the intermediary — the sponsor or patron — in the present is more restrictive than was, apparently, that of the patrons of the past. Physicists look on the federal government and artists on the art dealers and nouveau riche collectors as necessary evils. But in being necessary they are definite career contingencies which affect not only the success or failure of the creator's career but the degree of freedom within which he may practice his creativity.

Finally, and perhaps the most important career contingency of all, there are the officially and legitimately acceptable *critics* of the work of the creator. The leading scientists in the area of the new ideas will judge their colleagues' work, deciding if it deserves research support (federal funds in most cases), and the media critics will perform this function for the artist. In each case, the ambivalence is intense. Any creator — scientist or artist — must have faith in the value of his idea and of its importance. He can neither accept the judgment of a critic who disagrees with him nor do without the need to have this official, "objective" validation of the worth of his creations. What Rosenberg and Fliegel say for artists applies to any creative worker in art or science, in relation to the career contingency of the evaluations made by the critic:

> The final sober consensus is that critics are a weighty factor in the art world, that their responses are more influential in determining art futures than those of all other groups combined. This is an agreed upon fact of artistic life, no matter how the individual artist delineates it.[26]

In general, the scientific career is a "professional" career in that the career contingencies of given individuals are more internal to the occupational group than external to it; even in the case of government grants the critics within the field make the decisions on allocation as consultants to government. On the other hand, for the arts the contingencies are external to the occupational group far more than internal — the public, the agent-dealer-impresario middlemen, the owners of performance settings, and the critics themselves. This has both a manifest and a latent effect on the potential for creativity. In the obvious case, creativity is less open to misunderstanding in the scientific colleague group than in the more anomic and less "ingroup" world of the various art publics. On the other hand, a *radically* different approach — extreme creativity — will for just this reason be more difficult to carry out in science than in the arts. For no scientist can end-run the scientific critics; he must fight them (and often lose, even if later proven correct), whereas in the art world, one may, as the Beatles or the Pop artists did, end-run the critics and the agents to create a demand to which these arbiters must respond, one which may force them to reinterpret their original perception and evaluations. In other words, moderate or minor creativity is possible in both scientific and artistic careers, without too many contingencies entering in. But radical creativity, radical change in approach, may be far more possible in the arts than in science, although it may be no less necessary for the latter than for the former.

THE CREATORS AND THE SQUARES: AN OCCUPATIONAL WORLD VIEW

Individual creators vary on an infinite number of dimensions, and the inherent loneliness of creative work does not make it easy to speak of an occupational world view. On the other hand, the experience of creative work in what is in many ways a conformist and materialistic society forces most creative individuals to take a stance toward the enemies of their creative freedom. One of these enemies is tradition: — the rigidity of previous approaches to a problem. Thus Watson suggests that because some of his research team were amateurs and not professionals in biophysical research their discovery of the shape of the double helix DNA molecule was not impeded by "knowing it was impossible" to do their kind of investigation with their lack of knowledge of the standard approaches to the problem.[27]

Another common aspect of the creative outlook is the stress on creation for its own sake. Painters warn each other that the minute they start worrying about what a work will bring, they are creatively dead, as their innovation becomes other-directed and market-oriented rather than intrinsic and expressive. Another general attitude is the desire for space; "don't fence me in" is a creator's cry and it is for him a functional one, as industrial research studies have indicated. The statements of creative workers in totalitarian states have the same theme. More specifically, although the creative individual is not usually a joiner, he or she is capable of evolving a generalized attitude toward the "square" or outsider who is the ultimate consumer of art, or toward the engineer who uses atomic physical insights to build a bomb. These publics are often not well liked. Becker's jazz musicians could hardly conceal their contempt of many of their audiences, and Rosenberg and Fliegel's artists respond the same way:

> I publicly avow that the public is stupid, I make no bones about it.
>
> The modern art audience is really a spineless and recumbent mass of people.
>
> Most people don't understand what they're looking at, they don't understand what they're talking about, and they don't understand what they think they're interested in.[28]

The eternal war between the creators and the "squares" has, at least in historical perspective, been due to the double dependency situation: the public and the society need creativity and the creators need to be needed. Yet societies seldom offer creators the situation they need, and creators turn upon their fellow men. The division of labor in creative work cannot thus be understood without considering the social context. Early training, career commitment, contingencies of development, and resulting outlook all originate in specific societies in specific political regimes. From the point of view of careers these are contingencies for individuals, but we may now also inspect them as a problem of the overall social division of labor.

CREATION WITHIN A SOCIAL SYSTEM

As our historical and existential approaches have made clear, creative work is not carried out in a vacuum but in a social context. The division of labor as an overall societal pattern is of special importance to us in the study of creative occupations. Numerically a very small segment of all occupations, these occupations have an importance far out of proportion to their numbers. Basic questions which we need to consider in understanding the division of labor in creative work — and between creative occupations and the rest of the social system — include the social system relevant to the created *product* (as against that relevant to the producer), the contrast between the creator considered as an individual and the far more amorphous concept of a creative occupational *group*, the manifest and latent functions of creative work, general dimensions of the division of labor in creative areas, and the comparative viewpoint on creators in different types of political regimes. On each issue we can compare the scientific and the artistic types of occupation.

THE RELEVANT SOCIAL SYSTEM: CREATION VERSUS CREATOR

In any social system or subsystem which can be defined, a set of norms or values can be seen as governing the way the system is set up. In the scientific world, Merton identifies these values: universalism, organized skepticism, communality, and disinterestedness.[29] By contrast, the artist's subjective engagement in his work is considered a necessity; thus we can contrast the qualities and talk about uniqueness, emotional commitment and partisanship, individuality, and "interestedness" as basic guiding values in the arts.

In general, the social system relevant to scientists is the same system relevant to their created products; they are the primary consumers of their own creativity, in the direct sense. In contrast to the relatively closed social system of science, where the groups relevant to creators and creation are the same, in the art world the creators may be isolated individuals or from loosely affiliated groups, but the different publics — the dealers, impresarios, museums, and critics — are outside the creator group yet very much a part of the social system in which the creator's products — the art work, the concert, etc. — are involved. In the arts, ultimate recognition lies in the creation's social network; in the sciences, in the group of creators themselves.

INDIVIDUAL CREATIVITY AND THE CONCEPT OF OCCUPATIONAL GROUP

In the overall analysis of the division of labor, we have always made it clear that "occupational group" was an abstraction, but that the real grouping of people within the concept would have some reality. Thus, for example, the "health field" and "doctors" are categories with group reality. So too are the categories "scientists" and "artists." Yet by talking about the creative occupations and placing science and arts in a central position, we do not mean to imply either that creative work is not possible in other occupational fields, nor that every scientist or artist is creative. This is far from the truth, but what is inescapably the case is that creation is the central reason and task for scientists and artists, not a positive bonus in addition to the ordinary requirements of the work. The non-creative scientist or artist is not a scientist or artist at all if the more stringent creativity definition of the field is applied. In reality the decision as to who is creative and who is not involves the relevant social systems of creator and created product, and the usual sociological procedure is to allow almost all non-applied scientists and artists into the category. But this creates an unavoidable confusion between the somewhat rare creative individual in science and art — the real innovator — and the journeymen who make mild and slight changes in their repertoire of combinations. Can we talk about a creative group, then, of scientists and artists? The answer depends on how stringent our definition of creativity is.

THE SOCIAL FUNCTIONS OF CREATIVITY

The act of creation is by definition the addition of something new to an ongoing social system. This addition may make the perpetuation of the system more possible for those in positions of power, or the new production may threaten existing interests and ways of thinking. Since social systems have a degree of inertia and momentum, a truly original creation in either science or art is likely to threaten existing ways of thinking and experiencing. Poggioli notes that in the modern era, beginning perhaps with the France of the late 1870s, the concept of the "avant-garde" has had at least two basic meanings. The first is the essentially neutral one of the "very new" as an element in creative evolution. But he notes that the second meaning of the term is the political one — the avant-garde as an organized radical movement of creators who confront the status quo as well as creating new productions for it.[30] In this sense, artists can be distinguished from scientists by the relation of the overall value system to the mode of creating. The scientist's values of detachment and objectivity force him to let the product speak for itself; partisanship for a new theory in biochemistry is considered outside the pale, since the idea, no matter how radical and opposed at first, will win if it is proven right through the experiments of those who did *not* proclaim it originally. By contrast, the natural engagement in and partisanship for one's creations which is found in the arts lends itself far more easily to avant-garde action, by an organized group of proponents. We are not talking here about the political role of creators as *political* partisans, but rather about the inherently conflict-producing functions of both scientific and artistic creativity. However, the former exists within a colleague system that can assimilate the challenge, though at times (as with Galileo) the wider social system will intervene. By contrast, the artist creates forms and experiences which may threaten or challenge people's deeply held values and ways of thinking about themselves in the world. Here the committed and emotional partisanship of the artist to his creation — in political as well as artistic terms — may be necessary to prevent the obliteration of the creation or the stifling of the creative worker because of the committed and emotional opposition of the different publics to his work. Thus the manifest relation of artist and scientist to their work seem opposed, yet on a more basic level *partisanship* for the artist concerning the value of his work may serve the same latent function that *objectivity* serves for the scientist vis-a-vis his work — to protect the creation and to accord it a serious consideration by its intended publics.

THE DIVISION OF CREATIVE LABOR

"We can't all be Picassos," the art teacher consoles the struggling young student. And in science, most graduate students soon begin to understand that they will *not* be the Einsteins of their generation. What then are the principles for the division of labor within the creative occupations? The major ones appear to be: "pure" versus applied work, individual versus group production, and generalist versus specialist approaches, or interdisciplinary versus one-area expertise.

The pure versus applied distinction in creative work relates directly to the opposition of creator to social system that was just considered. The opposition means that applied science or applied (commercial) art are more readily supported by governments, corporations, or the public precisely because their function is to add to existing processes rather than challenge them. The period when basic research was extensively sponsored by the United States government — the fifties and sixties — was an era when the eventual practicality of basic research was believed in, as Storer points out.[31] In art, artistic talent is used to sell products to consumers and is a major source of employment for those trained in the creative fields. The extremely creative scientist and artist may find far less support, not accidentally, but rather because the radically new is of less use to the ongoing social system than the mildly different and unchallenging.

The historical position of the scientist and artist with respect to the issue of solo versus group work collaboration shows an interesting inversion. In art, from Egypt to Greece, throughout the Middle Ages, and to some extent in the Renaissance, art was carried out in workshops, and in many cases the verbal arts — myths, ballads — were works in collective, oral folk tradition that were not identified as that of an individual. Now, except for those arts where in performance a group is required (symphony orchestra, dance), the artist works alone. By contrast, in the seventeenth and eighteenth centuries, science was the plaything of individualistic gentlemen, and even into the early years of the twentieth century the work was considered an individual's pastime. With the dual growth of technology and the university graduate programs, the idea of working in groups, or of having a director and a group of assistants, made the physical sciences laboratory the apprenticeship workshop of the present. The cyclotron lab operates in ways similar to the artists' workshops of the Middle Ages and the Renaissance from the viewpoint of the sociology of occupations. In both cases, economic factors — the cost of equipment in science, the lack of profitability in art — are related to a historical point in time. In an earlier era, the research of the scientist did not demand a great investment of manpower and dollars, beyond that needed for free time. By contrast, the style of group work in art seemed necessary at those times for both economic and cultural reasons. In the most recent periods, we may be beginning to see both a reversion to individual (or small group) styles in science and a recurrence of collective styles in art. Again, the reasons for change in production arrangement are a mixture of cultural and economic factors.

A final major principle in understanding the division of labor in creative occupations is that between the specialist and the generalist, either within science and art or between the two creative fields. For example, Alberti and Da Vinci were, in pre-Renaissance and Renaissance times, creative geniuses in both what we now label as science and what we now call art. Contrast this with C. P. Snow's two cultures of the present, whose members presumably cannot understand each other.[32] What appears to be happening, perhaps increasingly at the present time, is a cross-fertilization within the sciences and within the arts, and in some cases a re-fusion of science and art itself. Again, since creativity involves combinations which are new, it is only reasonable that once potential combinations within a creative field are exhausted, the next step is combination across boundaries. For example, there is now a field of bio-physical chemistry (the Watson-Crick group were pioneers in it), in addition to the older fields of biology, physics, and chemistry, which still exist as separate cultures. So too in art — plastic art, three-dimensional painting, light shows — the mixing of all media is a present trend. In occupational terms, the important point is that each cross-boundary invention within science or art — or even cross-"cultural" inventions such as computer art and cinematic technology — means a change in the division of labor. In the creative occupations, the neat categories of the past are under deliberate and conscious attack by the creators themselves.

COMPARATIVE ISSUES: POLITICAL REGIME AND THE CREATOR

In technological societies such as those of the United States and the Soviet Union, the pure and the applied sciences have a major and powerful contributing role, especially, alas, in the science and technology of war. In the Soviet Union, in contrast to the United States, basic scientists have comparatively more prestige and reward than in the United States, but operate under the same conditions of political control that characterize the relations of the Soviet regime with the other occupational and professional groups. Only an outstanding and irreplaceable scientist, such as Sukharov, may speak out against this condition.[33] By contrast, although the leaders of American science do not suffer in terms of prestige or reward, their position relative to, for example, industrialists or medical specialists, is lower, but their freedom to innovate is considerably broader than that of their Soviet counterparts.

If the nature of the political regime affects the freedom of the scientist in totalitarian states (the Stalinist genetics of Lysenko being a classic example), it by definition should affect even more the freedom of the creative artist who works with values and who must take a partisan view toward his work and his society. Thus in the Soviet Union the poet may speak but must be circumspect in his criticism. He becomes very popular in a political as well as an esthetic way by simply speaking about life at all. The novelist may *write*, in the more recent years, but if his works do not follow the Party line, he may not publish. As a defense, the public and the authors in such regimes turn to the organization of clandestine presses, or chain-letter copying by hand of manuscripts. In the Soviet Union, the name for this institution is *Samizdat*, or self-publishing manuscript. On the other hand, and ironically because no profits for criticizing the state are possible, the true creative artist looks at the commercialism of Western writers and cannot understand their orientation toward money or fame.[34] Thus art for art's sake is possible even in a totalitarian state, though it must be barred from the public along with any other form of alternative world view. Most Soviet artists, given a choice between unsupported freedom to starve and state-sponsored and controlled art, would choose the former. On the other hand, the equivalent of the Western artist's selling out to commercialism is the Soviet artist's selling out to the ideology of the party in power. In both countries, the artist who holds to his own convictions is rare, but in the Soviet Union or in any totalitarian state, the risks of so doing are infinitely greater than in other forms of society. Art is as powerful a political force as science, perhaps even more so, especially in those states which limit the exploration of human possibilities.

To sum up, the systems approach to the creative occupations reveals differences between science and the arts in terms of guiding values and colleague-public relations, but underlying the more superficial differences there is a level at which the social functions of creative occupations call forth reactions in the society related to the interests of the society. The protective stances of creative individuals and creative groups aim at a maintenance of the freedom to create. Even restrictive regimes seem unable to either do without or repress man's creativity. But in looking at the functions of creative occupations and the principles which are relevant to the division of labor within the fields, the issue of conflicts of interest inevitably arises, and we must turn to it again at this point.

CONFLICTS OF INTEREST: CREATORS AND THE GENERAL PUBLIC

Since the work of creators is so intimately involved with challenges to the existing status quo, the major conflict-of-interest issues have been raised in the historical, experiential, and functional approaches. If we consider them further at this point, it is to restate them explicitly in a form that will highlight their importance. The critical issues with respect to conflict of interests here are the same as those raised elsewhere: the occupational consciousness of creator groups, the rôle of creator groups with respect to haves and have-nots, and the role of the group as causes of or objects of social change in the broad scale.

OCCUPATIONAL CONSCIOUSNESS AND THE CREATOR GROUP

Poggioli notes that even the most inventive avant-garde member must sometimes compromise or collaborate with at least part of the public and restrict some of the creative directions that might be traveled. The role of fashion is critical here:

> The chief characteristic of fashion is to impose and suddenly to accept as a new rule or norm what was, until a minute before, an exception or whim, then to abandon it again after it has become a commonplace, everybody's "thing." Fashion's task, in brief, is to maintain a continual process of standardization: putting a rarity or novelty into general and universal use, then passing on to another rarity or novelty when the first has ceased to be such.[35]

Occupational consciousness for the creator can thus be understood in opposition to this dictatorial pressure: freedom to create independently of fashion and freedom to have at least control over the work setting. Both of these factors relate to the degree of organization of the creator group. For example, the colleague group in science is organized and powerful enough both to impose fashion upon the potential creators and to exert control over the work settings of a professional, self-regulating sort. To the extent that the scientific group is not within a community setting (with the exception of a few major industrial laboratories and often not even there), the community does not have control over fashion or product. An important issue is raised by this, however. Even in the scientific area, are the fashionable ideas necessarily the lastingly important ones? In fact, they are not, but rather the earliest new idea which proves durable even though at its time of first presentation it was most unfashionable indeed. Merton's study of "priority" in scientific invention proves that scientists do know the value of truly innovative ideas, and wish to be identified with them, but they also acknowledge that most creativity will be along already established lines.[36] In the arts, his lesser control over the direction of fashion-setting places the creator in a much less enviable position. He may either have no control over his workplace (the performing arts) or he may be forced by the art of intermediaries to produce fashionable work or starve. The organization of artists into interest goups with a conscious self-protective function is still in its early stages at present, when contrasted with the rather tightly organized interest groups in pure science. The consumers of the artist's work — the dealers, collectors, and museums — do not wish to see organization of creative artists any more than the nightclub owner or the symphony orchestra board of directors enjoys dealing with the popular or classical music branches of the national musician's union. The exploitation of the unorganized artist is commonplace in our present society, but recent years are seeing the organization of the artists vis-a-vis their publics in their own interest. In this author's opinion, this will be in the ultimate interest of the public as well.

HAVES, HAVE-NOTS, AND CREATORS

It would make a neat contrast to say that all scientists are on the side of the powerful elites in American society and all the artists, being poor and pure of heart, are on the side of the poor. Not only do they convey stereotypes, but these statements confuse two dimensions that must not be confused: who the group is working for, and who they *could* be working for. If a creative group can only be seen as meaningful in relation to a certain public or source of support, this distinction would disappear. But in neither science nor art is this the case.

In the field of science, the relations between the leaders in scientific areas and the governmental officials in a position to use their abilities has grown close in the last two decades. As Price describes it, the phrase "scientific estate" is far more accurate than the phrase "scientific group" to the understanding of the role of leading members of the different professions with respect to government. Until perhaps very recently, when the level of spending on research began to level off, they formed an increasingly privileged elite. One aspect of this relationship between scientists and politicians is suggested by an ideal typology that Price calls the continuum from truth to power. At one end, the scientist who pursues truth cannot serve in a power position and "by definition" remain a scientist, since this activity demands the pursuit of truth disinterestedly, whereas a power position means defending policies regardless of their truth value. He suggests a continuum from the administrator and politician to the professional to the pure scientist.[37] Two implications are suggested by this continuum. First, one cannot move up the ladder of power without losing one's inherent identity as a scientist. There is some truth to this. But second, it is implied that scientists who are not within the governmental structure are essentially rather neutral politically and without extensive influence on the political process, or that those in administrative positions do not lobby for their fellow scientists on the outside. Personal lobbying for group interests is a commonplace with scientists no matter where they fit on the "continuum from truth to power."

In contrast to the politically powerful and elite role of the sciences, the arts are peripheral to the world of power and even elementary governmental support. Now the issue of artistic integrity versus government control of creativity — especially modern anti-establishment art — is always raised when government support is considered. Most American artists do not trust the government to be neutral. Many of the more intelligent and politically sophisticated artists fear the future selling-out of artists to the fashionable governmental request, as they now see the prostitution of talent in the case of commercial artists and artists on top by chic galleries. On the other hand, as Baumol and Dickson made clear, most of the performing arts are gravely threatened by lack of support in an era of rising production costs. If government subsidy is not given, many existing dance troupes and repertory theatres, as well as many symphony orchestras, will go under.[38] Thus what is a necessity for "big science" may also be a necessity for the arts. Yet the very act of subsidy by the powerful in the society means that an anti-elite or truly revolutionary art is impossible, given the present power structure which aims to use the society's resources in war and economic expansion at the expense of others at home and abroad.

In spite of the "bought" nature of much of the scientific elite and the commercial orientation of many artists, the creative occupations are an altruistic as well as a materialistic force, in the person of anti-elite activists such as the physicists who formed the *Bulletin of the Atomic Scientists* in realization of the uses to be made of science that they felt were against the best interests of humanity. The engineers at many universities have formed an "Engineers Against War" group and have been joined by some of their compatriots in industry. The graphic symbol of the red fist was first inked onto a white t-shirt at the Harvard School of Design by students there in celebration of the occupation of University Hall. It became a symbol for student protest against the role of the military in government in the United States, and a symbol of the struggle against political repression at home. Art in Cuba is an integral part of revolutionary activity, although the political uses of art can be as much conservative (for example Soviet Socialist Realism) as radical. In general, therefore, artists and scientists vary in their political sentiments, and it is not possible to stereotype scientists as "conservatives" and artists as "radicals." Instead, as in other dimensions of their behavior creators can have conservative or radical political views. The nature of the work may influence the stance they take toward the work, but does not determine the political stance they may take toward society.

Finally, social change has been both a cause of scientific and artistic creativity and a consequence of such creativity. What is seen as a creation inimical to the interests of a society at one time may lead to a situation where the very creation brings about the changes in social conditions which lead people to retrospectively appreciate the role of this creator. Perhaps it is the role of the creator — the engine of social change energized by the changes of the past — that has placed those in creative occupations in such an exposed position with respect to the power of the public and the governing elite of a society. Historically, in terms of career experience and division of labor, as well as in terms of who benefits by their work, the creative worker and the creations of that worker are both deeply political. They introduce changes into an ongoing social process which make it impossible for that process to be the same as it was before their creations entered the world.

CHAPTER ELEVEN

ILLEGAL OCCUPATIONS

As long as men have worked, some occupations have been defined by the majority as "beyond the pale." And yet, historically, these occupations have persisted; prostitution is called, only semihumorously, the oldest profession. In general, we will make a distinction between occupations which primarily provide a *service* to a clientele, such as that of the prostitute, the abortionist, and the bookmaker, and those occupations which are predatory upon the public, such as the thief and extortionist. In general, both types of occupation have existed throughout history, and it is historically also important to notice that occupations which were illegal in the past are not to be confused with those presently so. We can inspect the two major types of illegal occupations and the growth of organized crime historically, in terms of experience, functionally, and as a problem of conflicts of interest.

A HISTORICAL PERSPECTIVE

In ancient Egypt the prostitute was a commonly accepted service worker, with a hierarchy from the common worker to the temple elite. The predatory occupations, beginning at least here and continuing throughout history, have always been illegal by the standards of the time, although the organized predatory systems of modern times are a new development. In ancient Greece, the contrast is again illuminating. There were four classes of prostitute, for example: the hetairae (or courtesans), the auletrides (or dancing girls), the dicteriades (or streetwalkers), and the slaves, who were located in many cases in households and became, in effect, the concubine wife of the head of the household. By contrast, depending on the definition of "predatory" and of "illegal," the entire Athenian economy was based on slave labor captured in war. This was legal by their standards, however, no matter how predatory it was in a more abstract sense. In effect, predation outside the city-state was legal and acceptable, but predation within the state was illegal, unless it was by the ruling group concerning an internal subject population. This remains one of the common dimensions in modern states' definitions of illegality of occupational frameworks.[1]

In Rome the role of both service and predatory occupations changed drastically from the small tribal groups in the early era to the complex era of the later Empire. The increasing turmoil on the roads of the later Empire — internal and inter-Empire escalation in corruption and predatory crime — is considered by historians as an important index of the degree of overall *anomie* as the Empire came apart.

Throughout the Middle Ages, as Ullmann pointed out, there was a distinction between the *theory* of the medieval state and the actual feudal local government which grew up. In this local system, the service occupations had an accepted role, and in the courts the royal courtesans also had their place. As the Renaissance developed out of the later Middle Ages, the service occupations rose in status to positions of importance to (and in consort with) both kings and popes:

> The wealthiest and most powerful nobles of the period did not hesitate to marry courtesans; and, of course, there are the famous anecdotes about Pope Alexander VI, who repeatedly entertained prostitutes in the Vatican palace, where they staged erotic exhibitions for his pleasure, and that of his children and friends. Other popes of the period also associated freely with prostitutes and courtesans — and profitably taxed their incomes, a papal practice brought to Rome from Avignon.[2]

In the Reformation, the rise of the much more moralistic Protestantism occurred at the time of the first great European epidemics of venereal disease. As a consequence, for the first time laws were passed to regulate or suppress prostitution. Service occupations which did not accord well with the ideas of the time were always disapproved, but the combination of disease and disrepute led to the first major restrictive actions.[3] For a while, even money-lending — under the concept of usury — became suspect as a service occupation in a way that it had been in the Middle Ages, when it was relegated to the Jews.[4] But the attempts at suppression of the service occupations failed, for the reason they must *always* fail — these occupations have a mandate, for they serve deep community and human needs, and the customers create the demand.

In colonial America, the rapid transformation of Massachusetts from the "City Upon a Hill" to a commercial sea-trade colony brought with it the creation of the typical range of service occupations for seamen and cosmopolites. The witch was not, in this society at least, an occupational worker, although those who were accused of practicing witchcraft and hanged for it were most definitely pawns in a struggle between church and state. One of the three peaks on the main mountain of Boston (the Trimount) was called "whoredom hill"; as Whitehill observes, this area, later leveled as fill land, is now the elite section known as the Front Side of Beacon Hill.[5] In the area of predatory occupations, the early seaside cafes were of course a haven for thieves, pickpockets, etc., whether imported or homegrown. In addition, the major swings in the economy caused much unemployment. In periods such as this, no welfare existed; thus the poor man who helped himself by stealing was likely to survive, and he who remained honest would be likely to starve.

The folklore of the Frontier gives the American past a rich range of illegal occupations, which must be understood against a background of migratory populations, lack of women, unstable town governments, and an adventurous and excitement-oriented spirit. Thus we have the first great American centers of service: the Barbary coast and New Orleans, where concubinage as well as the more usual forms of prostitution abounded. In the West, the folklore of predation — Jesse James, the Daltons — was based on fact. The entire predatory economy of the South was increasingly viewed as illegal by the standards of the North, although at the time of the middle third of the century the North began its form of exploitation in the form of factory labor. Again, however, to use Sutherland's term, although both the slaveowners of the South and the factory owners of the North were a form of "white-collar criminal," in neither case would they be prosecuted for their "crime," as businessmen in a later era would on rare occasions be so punished.[6]

The time from the late 1880s to the onset of World War II constitutes a time of major inversion in the United States, in terms of the relation between service and predatory occupations. In this era we see the development of two processes that are presaged in earlier eras such as the Reformation. Increasingly, the service occupations became suppressed and illegal, in our modern sense, in the wave of Victorian and post-Victorian moral enthusiasm. Once they were suppressed, organization on occupational lines in self-defense became necessary; at the same time this was occurring, and partly because of it, the predatory occupations became organized and bureaucratized. In addition, by this time the immigrant population had flooded the urban centers, and ethnically based organizations such as the Sicilian Black Hand or Mafia, now called the Cosa Nostra, began to grow and form as a partial consequence of the suppression. Predation became secondary and organized as well as primary. In addition to the eternally present group of minor predators — pickpockets and con men — we see the development of organized crime as a predator upon the direct service and predation relationships. The "cut" is a cut of proceeds from now illegal transactions in prostitution, betting, and at one time, alcohol consumption. Thus we arrive at our present condition: direct service and predatory occupations, essentially unorganized, and a secondary predatory complex, or organized crime, which involves the legal institutions and preys primarily upon the relations which the public has with the direct service occupations, or the relations which predators have with each other and with "fences" and similar representatives of the straight world. In effect, therefore, a new level of illegal occupation has grown up to profit from both the service and predatory occupations of earlier historical periods. The basic issue here, and we will return to it, lies in the interpenetration between this secondary, organized predatory structure and the still essentially predatory legal social system within which it operates with impunity, with some sympathy on the part of those in power within this larger system.

THE EXPERIENCE OF ILLEGAL WORKERS

The field of criminology has not been principally concerned with the criminal career experience per se, although criminologists and other applied social scientists have attempted to "predict" what turns and twists a man and his fate would take with respect to the law. Our interest here is somewhat different; in line with the approach taken to other occupational fields, we will examine the structural and experiential elements of criminal careers the patterns of motivation and recruitment to the occupations, the period of early socialization and career commitment, the career pattern as a shape, the major career contingencies, and the overall forms of world view.

MOTIVATION AND RECRUITMENT

Psychological, economic, familial, and broader environmental factors have all been singled out by various theorists as predisposing one to a "life of crime." Yet the evidence to date on the strength of these factors is unimpressive; complexes of factors and the role of conscious, individual choice seem to be the only answer to why a given individual chooses a given illegal career (or any career, for that matter). The psychological factor has been of particular interest to the students of prostitution. Benjamin and Masters' review of this literature suggests that sexual motivations are relevant to only about 1 per cent, but that traits such as "laziness" could be applicable.[7] Little evidence exists on the psychological attitudes of either small-time predators or members of organized crime.

The economic factor is clearer. By virtue of the demand for illegal services and the lesser amount of talent that is required of any but service elites (i.e., call girls), the illegal occupations provide rewards not otherwise attainable for those with the given level of training. Merton and Cloward's concept of the illegitimate opportunity structure is relevant here — in certain areas such as the ghetto, the only ways to get off welfare are through one illegal occupation or another.[8] According to Sutherland, the minor predatory occupations are not terribly lucrative, especially those which require teamwork.[9] But it is questionable whether most of the practitioners could make even these incomes legitimately, and the work would certainly be less interesting. The strongest motivation of an economic sort appears to be in those who become interested in a career in organized crime; only here is the hope of steady reward at such a level that economics alone can be seen as a primary motivating factor. However, the elites within the service occupations, such as call girls in prostitution and the physician-abortionist, also receive heavy monetary reward, a point relevant to their entry in the first place under conditions where it really was not in most cases necessary for them to do so vocationally. Schoolteachers with expensive tastes, general practitioners with a specialist's spending habits — these are the ones who will choose prostitution and abortion as careers. But in general, the lack of economic opportunity for women and the dull exploitative jobs in factories and offices available to them, at present as well as in the past, have been a powerful factor predisposing them toward prostitution and related occupations.

Familial influences are, in the mythology of social work and psychiatry, powerful factors predisposing individuals toward a criminal career. But the evidence is clear that millions of poor individuals from "broken homes" have joined the legitimate occupations of the lower middle class. The work of the Gluecks on the influence of the family is open to major question here, as has been stated elsewhere by the author, and their own research in a twenty-five-year cohort study indicates that progressively fewer of the delinquent group engage in illegal acts every year.[10] Very few in fact ever could be called members of illegal occupations.

For predatory occupations, no reliable information exists on the career experience. The only thing that is probably true, and it was first observed by August Aichhorn in Vienna, is that children raised in the families of thieves or prostitutes may get an occupationally relevant training and set of experiences that lend familiarity and legitimacy in terms of their own developing values and lead to the choosing of such a career for themselves with parental approval.[11] In this sense, the family of the thief breeds thieves for the same reason that a family of musicians breeds musicians; value-laden psychiatric jargon and namecalling is not necessary for an understanding of the relevant sociological dynamics.

The wider community environment — the social ecology within which the illegal occupations are practiced — is classically considered a major predisposing factor for illegal occupations. Again, this makes sense for both service and predatory occupations, and it makes the most sense of all in lower-class ethnic communities, where blocked upward mobility in the legal system is a major problem. The early analysis of Whyte of the role of the rackets in Boston's North End is still one of the best analyses of this situation. In 1938 in the Italian area of Boston the opportunities inside the community — college removed people from the area — were limited to the rackets and the Organization. This was a major factor in career decisions for many of Whyte's subjects.[12]

EARLY TRAINING AND CAREER COMMITMENT

Again it must be stressed that the great majority of those with illegal occupations do not seem to have been juvenile "gang" members, although they may have begun early to compile a record in their later chosen field of activity. Nor do the majority of delinquent gang members become lifetime members of illegal occupations. The primary process of early socialization in both service and predatory occupations appears to be a combination of trial-and-error adventure and what could be called peripheral, informal apprenticeship. For the service occupations, such as prostitution, Benjamin and Masters suggest that in most cases the individual "tries it out" to see how it feels.[13] If it feels acceptable, it is tried again. For the predatory occupations, Sutherland suggests that a typical initiation procedure is in effect which rather closely resembles the way the aspiring actor or actress breaks into summer stock. "Hanging around" the place where the thieves congregate, the aspirant may be invited to come along and do an almost meaningless unskilled task. Successful completion can lead to apprenticeship and on-the-job training in the form of work practiced by the group.[14] In the case of the major groups in organized crime, either close family connections lead to a *legitimate* career as a background for an assured career in the role, or the minor predatory occupational training process is used as a screening device for those to be selected for a career at a higher level.

Becker and Geer's concepts of commitment are especially relevant to the illegal occupational fields. In perhaps no other area are their paradigms so closely followed; at the time when the individual finds that the alternatives are unattractive and he has already built up a network of contacts and an investment in either tools or contact networks, he discovers that he is *de facto* committed to a career in these occupations.[15] This is probably more true for the service and the minor predatory occupations than for organized crime, however. Whyte makes it quite clear that the choice to run bets for the organization is made deliberately and knowingly, and indeed hopefully by the young aspirant. Here, within the Italian community, as Whyte observed, the knowledge of the true role of organized crime is not a secret from the young apprentices. They have made their peace with it, and with their relatives in and out of the Organization, before they take the first deliberate step to join.[16]

One other major factor in constructing or bringing about commitment to illegal occupational careers lies in the foreclosure of other careers implied in imprisonment, combined with the socialization received during incarceration. Neither the prejudices of employers against ex-cons, nor the anticipatory warning and illegal-type occupational training received in the prison is sufficient alone for commitment to an illegal occupational career in most cases. But in most cases they go together, and compounded with the low formal skill level found in most of those convicted and imprisoned for the first time, we can thus find the prison acting not only as a confirming socializing agent but also as a basic graduate seminar training center for careers in service or predatory occupations.

THE OVERALL CAREER PATTERN: SHAPES AND CONTINGENCIES

At least three main elements contribute to the overall structure of illegal occupational careers: the degree of physical as opposed to mental endowment necessary, the degree of specialization inherent in the career plan, and the role of prison interruptions in the development of the career. The degree of physical endowment seems highest in the female service occupations; the girl who rises to become an expensive call girl has just so many years at the top before nature begins to affect earning capacity. Here the comparison with the career of a ballet dancer is striking indeed. The minor predatory occupations, with the exception of the "confidence man" swindle, seem to take a mixture of physical dexterity and some planning ability as well. But an aging pickpocket or a slowing-down bank robber are human testimony to the importance of physical abilities; they are critical in many service occupations and in most predatory occupations as well, with all this implies for career structure and longevity. In the world of organized crime, however, violence and the need for physical skills such as those involved in burglary are almost irrelevant. The work here is essentially as unphysical as that of legitimate business. Brains, organizational ability, and political skill in conflict situations — the same skills that are useful to any business executive — are the primary traits determining the shape (and length) of a career in organized crime.

In terms of the degree of specialization, the choices are inherently limited by the operating conditions under which illegal occupations exist and the market conditions for their services. For example, although there may be some prostitutes who specialize in sex deviancy of some sort, and some abortionists who prefer one technique, in general the demand for service is unspecific and the possibilities for specialization are limited. This is less true with minor predatory occupations, where apprenticeship training is required for most, and where skills are not transferable. In some specialties, e.g., safecracking, the formal expertise that develops is nearly professional, but this is rare. Sutherland's informant suggests rather a seeking out of the specialty which is congruent with personality and skills; the smooth talker winds up as a con man, the introvert as a second-story man.[17] The longest career patterns of all, and the most complex, are probably those in organized crime. Through a combination of energy, good apprentice work, and contacts through family and ethnic group ties, individuals can advance through the structure of the Cosa Nostra to leadership positions. In recent years, as organized criminal groups have become increasingly involved both in the legal world of courts and police and in corporate business enterprise, the career pattern increasingly involves, for the heirs of the future, college training plus graduate work in business administration or law, leading to placement in either an administrative job in the gambling network or a position in one of organized crime's legitimate businesses.[18]

The third major determinant of career pattern — the degree of time spent in prison — is in fact a consequence of other factors besides whether or not the individual was caught. The degree of influence and extent of social contacts within and outside of the law and the degree of backing which the individual has make as much difference to the role of prison in the career as the nature of the crime committed. For example, both prostitution and abortion are illegal, but the physician and the prostitute usually exist in different relationships to the power structure. So too in the world of predatory occupations. The jail terms of pickpockets, although not as frequent as those of unprotected prostitutes, are far more frequent than those of the members of organized crime groups. With every degree upward on either the scale of social class of practitioner and clientele, or the scale of degree of closeness to the power centers of organized crime, the jail term becomes an increasingly less important aspect of the illegal career pattern.

CAREER CONTINGENCIES

A series of contingencies modify the three main career determinants of degree of physical versus mental ability, the issue of specialization versus generalism, and the role of jail in the career pattern. These include social characteristics (age, sex, race, and ethnic group membership), talent, the role of police and the legal system, size and cohesiveness of organization of the occupational group, relations of individuals and groups to secondary predators, and the role of overall social change. In terms of the social characteristics, the world of illegal occupations is not exempt from the prejudices which affect careers in the legitimate occupational world. In general, increasing age (except in the high levels of organized crime) is an increasing career handicap, and there are no pension plans or Social Security checks in the world of illegal occupations. Sex is clearly a stereotyping factor, even more than in the case of legal occupations, and the female's position in prostitution is that she is prone, not just physically but economically as well, exploited in most cases by customers, pimps, and organized crime. In terms of race, it was not until recently that organized crime allowed black criminals to operate in the gambling area even in Harlem, but in contrast to the lily-white nature of organized crime, the racial factors relevant to blocked mobility mean that an increasing number of service workers and minor predators will be black. One consequence of this is their inability to make the arrangements with the police of the nonghetto areas that white workers could; thus they concentrate in the ghetto and exploit and prey off each other to an extent not seen before in the American experience.

The role of skill is unquestionably a career contingency in the world of illegal occupations. The professional's contempt for the amateur is at least in part because he has made a business — and an art — of his work. But in many areas, for example, an organized pickpocket ring, the talent includes the ability to work as a team, i.e., to have good skills in what executives call "personal relations":

> A mob must be a unit and work as a unit. These rules and understandings have developed primarily for the purpose of preserving the unity of the mob. In spite of the rules and understandings, there are some persons who are hard to get along with and who tend by their actions to disrupt any mob. In such cases, the procedure is to have nothing to do with them, especially if the difficulty concerns business rather than social relations.[19]

The role of the police and the legal system is a major career contingency in illegal occupations, as well as constituting a major factor in the division of labor in illegal work itself. Illegal service occupations, predatory occupations, and especially organized crime cannot carry out routine operation without the cooperation of the police and dishonest judges. The honest policeman becomes a disastrous career contingency, but his interference in the criminal career is more of an exception than a rule, at least in the areas of prostitution, professional theft, and gambling.

Even more relevant as a career contingency than the degree of corruption or honesty of the police is the degree to which the particular occupation is organized internally. For example, in the era when prostitution was practiced organizationally in brothels, the house could protect the individual, whereas in modern America the anomic situation of this group leads to a high degree of risk and an irregular career pattern. By contrast, the small rings of minor predators, such as bank robbing groups and pickpocket rings, provide some protection for the professional. But neither group can compete with the organized predation on their activities. For example, the degree of selfishness or generosity of a pimp or the local branch of the Cosa Nostra may determine the degree of profit a prostitute may keep or the amount of protection she may need to pay. The degree of control which organized criminal groups at the state and national levels have over operations such as betting will determine the degree of upward mobility possible for the average bookie.

Social change is a subtle but very real career contingency. For example, changes in overall sexual morality may affect the business of those who deal professionally in sex. As many prostitutes are complaining, amateurs are ruining the business. In another example in the area of morality, where legislation changes with broader social processes, the abortionist as *abortionist* may in the American scene be disappearing. The mandate of any service occupation, after all, is based on the conflict between the need served by the occupation and the laws which make the occupation illegal. With the legalizing of a previously illegal occupation, many changes can occur: the practitioners can become regulated but protected by law, as prostitution is in some European nations, or the practice can be restricted to only a segment of those previously able to profit, as with abortionists, while opening the practice to others who would not carry out the work under conditions of illegality, as in the case of the average gynecologist or obstetrician.[20]

In contrast to the major effects which changes in moral legislation have for careers in service occupations, societal changes do not have such a marked effect on the predatory occupations. Sutherland's thief is clear in his statements on the subject of human weakness and venality; the confidence game and most kinds of petty thievery are not affected by social changes, but have been with us in all eras. However, it is possible that because of the increase in communications technology and the trend toward larger organizational forms for occupational tasks, the large network of organized crime may have flourished under changes that have not necessarily been helpful to either service or predatory groups of the older variety.

THE WORLD VIEW OF OCCUPATIONAL MEMBERS

Sutherland's thief was explicit on the point that he saw illegal work not as thrilling but as routine. In addition, there appears to be among minor predators an operational code of ethics, especially on the issue of "squealing" and invasion of one another's territory. One is reminded, concerning this routine approach and the essentially typical self-protective occupational cultural rules, of Hughes' characterization of professionals as those to whom others' crises are their routine. The main difference here seems to be that the predator *produces* the crisis of the victim instead of treating it. Here, of course, we are talking only about the predatory, not the service case. But in the instance of both occupations, the risks of illegality make an emphasis on "keeping cool" the mark of the professional.[21]

Other ideologies are found among those who are members of illegal occupations, but in many cases these ideologies are really more common to the amateurs than to the professionals. For example, P. T. Barnum's phrase, "There's a sucker born every minute," is essentially an anti-square and hostile ideology. But the prostitute and the thief wish their clientele well; if the customers become too poor, business becomes bad for them.

In the case of the professional practitioner, the act which is the basis of the occupational skill is not confused with personal emotional expressions toward the victim — the clear mark of the amateur. The only exceptions here seem to be the victimization of one who has gone to unusual lengths to make the practice difficult, such as hostile and punitive policemen or exploiting fences. Finally, a common ideology among amateurs, but not professionals, is a racial-political one — the black "get whitey" attitude and white exploitation of unorganized blacks by amateur thieves and legitimate businessmen. In each case, the victim-oriented ideology of the amateur should be contrasted with the occupation-oriented ideology of the professional.

To sum up, the motivations for entry into illegal occupations are complex in a situation where little reliable information is available; the early training and commitment phase is gradual, and deliberate choice to join a given occupation is not the typical pattern, but rather gradual assimilation to a deviant occupational subculture and later *de facto* commitment in Becker's sense. The major career pattern issues relate to physical skill, degree of inherent specialization in the field, and the role of jail in the career. Contingencies such as basic social characteristics, degree of talent, the role of the police and the legal system, the size and cohesiveness of the occupational group, the relation of groups to secondary predators (organized crime) and political-legislative changes all have their effect on individual futures. Yet in spite of these complexities, there is a suggestion that the professional in illegal occupations has a different outlook on his work from that of the amateur. Our evidence is fragmentary, but it indicates that the occupational experience within illegal occupations is more like the experience in other fields than it is different, with similar patterns of contingency in effect. The closest parallel seems to be in the career experience of the performing artist, and coincidentally or not, many small-time predators view themselves almost completely in this way.

THE DIVISION OF LABOR: WHERE CAN THE LINE BE DRAWN?

The relativity of the term "illegal occupation" is immediately apparent if we compare a series of occupations labeled in the United States with their corresponding social position and function in other nations. There is always a difference between the real and the ideal or theoretical occupational structure of any society. All societies have "illegal work." The question is: Who does it, and with whose cooperation or opposition? After we consider the manifest and latent societal functions of the three main types of illegal occupations in the American case, we can widen the analysis to a comparative inspection.

ILLEGAL OCCUPATIONS: MANIFEST AND LATENT FUNCTIONS

In the service occupations, the manifest function of the work within the society is clearly to provide a service which, although legislated as illegal, is desired by a clientele sufficient in size and permanence to guarantee the continuity of the occupation over time. In Hughes' terms illegal service occupations perform a function in doing some of the society's "dirty work"; because of the illegality the work is "dirty" by definition and in most cases the original legislation is perpetuated because of moral values concerning the work involved.[22] The *latent* function of most illegal occupations lies in their ability to handle the unsolved problems (premarital pregnancy, sexual frustration in marriage) which may burden individuals within the existing social system. In this way, service occupations, through their "safety valve" function, aid in the preservation of a given social status quo; they are deviant in obvious terms, but have the long-term function of supporting conformity.

The predatory occupations have, as an obvious function, predation. But the poor suffer more from this predation than the middle class, the middle class less than the rich. However, as the number of predatory acts rises in a society, the political justification for repressive action to eliminate civil rights for the accused also seems to escalate. As a consequence, an escalation in predatory crime, for different reasons, leads to a perpetuation of the status quo as does the operation of service occupations. Organized crime's manifest function appears to be predation on both the service occupations and predation on the front-line predatory occupations — it takes a cut of profits from both types of illegal occupations. But a long-term, unanticipated consequence of the functioning of organized crime is far more serious in terms of its application to the social system. Prolonged operations in the area of organized crime can and do lead to the perversion and capture of local government and the legal system itself. In general, Durkheim suggested that the role of "crime" is positively functional for the social system. The society, in gathering together to punish the criminal, supposedly unites and reaffirms its charters. Thus, Durkheim suggested, we *need* some crime; its function is ultimately conservative.[23] We agree with Durkheim's observation on the conservative function of illegal occupations, but disagree with his explanation and his recommendation. Our typology suggests this conservative function is not due to mass psychological reaction but rather to the different systems functions of the occupational groups in upholding the status quo.

A COMPARATIVE VIEWPOINT

When the laws of other nations are considered, two facts become evident. First, few nations are as restrictive on the range of occupations we are considering as the United States is, especially in the area of service occupations. Second, the range of rulings on the legality or illegality of a given occupation is understandable within the double framework of culture and political regime.

For our first example, let us take the Soviet Union, and a series of occupations or "complexes" which we will reconsider for other nations. The abortionist in the Soviet Union has either been an underground practitioner or a physician in a community health clinic, depending on which historical period one was considering. Immediately after the Revolution very progressive ideas on abortion were held and the job was a function of the physician. But in the pre-war, wartime, and post-war Stalinist eras, population growth was a primary goal and the abortion practice was severely repressed.[24] Prostitution has always been both taboo and practiced in the somewhat puritanical Soviet regime, where political ideologies on the exploitation of women are also in force. In addition, since women have many more mobility opportunities in the professions and management than in the West, the pressure toward this occupation for monetary reasons is not as great as in non-Soviet societies. The professional bookmaker or bettor is illegal and not common, although thievery and the black market have always existed in the Soviet Union and there is an extensive body of criminal law to deal with the predatory occupations. On the other hand, the national power and scope of the Communist party and its grass-roots organization are too much of a force to allow the growth of organized crime on the scale we find in the United States.

In Great Britain, the abortion laws and the laws relating to deviant practices in general (such as homosexuality) have been liberalized in recent years; thus the choice of a medical or lay abortionist is primarily a financial decision. Prostitution, though illegal, is only mildly suppressed. Betting is culturally and socially acceptable and off-track betting through bookmakers is legal; the local bookmaker is a well-known and accepted figure in the community. On the other hand, the predatory occupations are no more accepted in England than in the United States. Organized crime has not been considered a primary problem in Britain.

If the Soviet Union presents an example of sociopolitical contrast, Japan presents an example of a cultural one. The service occupations do not seem "immoral" in terms of Eastern value systems; thus prostitution, abortion, and professional bookmaking *serve* the population within the bounds of legality. Again, however, and indicating a cultural universal, the predatory occupations are illegal and under surveillance and repression in Japan as everywhere else. As the nation becomes more Westernized and industrialized, we may see the growth of an organized crime sector, but given the lack of repression of service occupations found there, there is less fertile ground for secondary predation on illegal activities than in the West. The activities are open and not in need of anyone's protection.

Thus we find a situation where the Soviet Union and the United States may be more similar in their treatment of illegal occupations than either is similar to Britain or Japan in the service area. These latter countries share a more open policy toward service occupations; by not pushing them underground they create fewer of the conditions predisposing a nation toward organized crime. In the Soviet Union, the political regime restricts the growth of organized crime, whereas in the United States the power structure and the organized criminal world appear to be intertwined in some localities. In summary, the United States appears to have neither a reasonable attitude toward service occupations nor a governmental ability to handle organized crime; it appears to neither successfully handle the issue of the needs for service occupations nor control the predations of organized crime as do Britain, Japan, and the Soviet Union. Defining a wide category of occupations as "illegal" without the ability to control them makes the role of such occupations in the American division of labor seem greater than it is for most complex modern societies.

CONFLICTS OF INTEREST: WHO BENEFITS?

In our review of what is an almost unresearched field — the sociology of illegal occupations — certain contrasts have been suggested between the legality and illegality of an occupational group and the degree to which it serves a social function. The evidence reviewed suggests that the most predatory group of all — organized criminal "mobs" such as the Cosa Nostra — is the least touched of all by the working of the police-court system, whereas the groups who do at least provide a service desired by their clientele are most frequently affected by arrest and prosecution. The question this raises is basic to the overall understanding of the role of illegal occupations. With each group or subtype, who benefits and who does not? The question is best approached through considering occupational ideologies, inter-occupational conflict, and the role of the poor and the power structure vis-a-vis illegal occupations.

OCCUPATIONAL IDEOLOGY: A SPECIAL CASE

In most of the fields considered previously, the occupational groups could be seen to possess an ideology which they were consciously using to convince the community of the legitimacy and desirability of their occupational function. If an occupation is illegal, can it still be socially legitimate in the eyes of a clientele, and can the group use ideologies to fix or develop this idea of legitimacy further? The answer to this question is complex. In the simple sense, prostitutes probably cannot openly campaign for the legitimacy of their activity, nor can abortionists or off-track bookies. On the other hand, the kernel of service is there, as is a real human need. Thus with the service occupations, either pro-service groups are formed by the clientele to advance the interests of the occupation ("legalize abortion") or the occupation's members themselves, in their citizen role and not defined as members of the occupation, can campaign in the open community forum. But it should be noted that they are only campaigning for legitimacy, not for an increased share of the profits.

In contrast to the potential (and sometimes successful) campaigns by members of illegal *service* occupations, no pickpocket or thief or confidence man is likely to organize for public political action, the arena within which ideologies are relevant. Rather, the minor predatory occupations and organized interstate crime operate by sub-rosa complexing with the legal system and even, in some cases, complaining victims. Potential objectors are bought off or physically threatened, and judges, juries, newspapers, and the police force itself are bribed into a conspiracy of silence. The use of power and money in these selective areas works, whereas a public, ideological attempt to convince people that organized crime is good for them is not attempted, except, one might say, by novelists such as Mario Puzo, who write adulatory biographies of Mafia heroes, or journalists such as Jimmy Breslin, who in finding the Cosa Nostra "harmless" and a subject for humor may in fact be inuring the public to their continued exploitation by these groups.[25]

INTER-OCCUPATIONAL CONFLICT

As we have noted, there is inter-occupational predatory behavior in the illegal field. In this game, the strong exploit the weak, but the weak cannot organize because in most cases to resist would take so much of their time and resources that they would have little time for their work. As a consequence, the usual procedure is an arrangement between a front-line occupational group (service or predatory) and a group or "family" within the syndicate or organized criminal network. This arrangement usually involves a given share of the profits in return for two types of protection: against the patron organization itself and against other "families." As a consequence, conflict between lower-level occupational groups and organized crime is seldom seen, as the arrangement is beneficial to both partners, though of course more so to the "bosses" than to the "workers." But between-family conflicts, or racket wars, are a nearly pure case of anomie. The police stand aside, as do the citizenry, as two families fight for supremacy and control over a given area. However, the open war between Cosa Nostra families is the exception, not the rule. Instead, there seems to be a hierarchy of mobs with territorial rights clearly understood and the "great families" acting as an informal court of appeals in inter-group squabbles. As Cressey describes this arrangement,

> The authority structure of Cosa Nostra "families" and of the relationship among Commission, councils, and bosses is the structure of a government as well as a business. Even the title used by the participants

> for two principal positions in Cosa Nostra's division of labor — lieutenant (captain) and soldier — are governmental titles rather than business titles.[26]

As Cressey goes on to note, there is a formalized code of conduct; the penalty for major violation is death. In the government-gathered information on a middle-rank Cosa Nostra member in New Jersey, one of the major occupational requirements of the group appears to be taking care of relatives and constructing a social security system in terms of guaranteed work for older soldiers. But the small problems of the everyday operator should not mislead the reader into underestimating the scope on which operations are regularly carried out. In general, their extent and complexity require the talents of diplomacy and the leaders of the operation greatly prefer such skills to the use of violence. It should be clearly understood that the relationships within the different subfields are based on the threat of the use of violence, and the police either stand aside, or as has been seen repeatedly in the investigation of organized crime, they are themselves an active participant on the side of the large mobs and against the interests of the front-line worker.

HAVES, HAVE-NOTS, AND ILLEGAL OCCUPATIONS

There is a hierarchy of power and profit within the field of illegal occupations. Perhaps the most important question is: Who benefits from this field at present, and who suffers the most? It would appear that have-not groups in our present society are both more preyed upon by the predatory occupations and less able to afford needed illegal services than are the middle class, who have more police protection and can afford whatever illegal services they desire. Therefore we would have reason to suspect that the poor have more to gain from the removal of illegal occupations than do the middle class; it is no accident that revolutionary governments are more "puritanical" than elite-run governments, for in repressing predatory and service occupations they are at least equaling the balance to some degree. Of course laws can change, so that most service occupations can be returned to their historically legitimate roles.

But the position of the organized crime confederation, or families, on a national scale, presents a problem of a different sort. Here all segments of the society, with the exception of those in collusion, can be seen to lose in either a direct or an indirect way. Entire cities, such as Newark or New Orleans, may have a government and a business world so interpenetrated with the members of an organized crime "family" that the citizens may pay higher taxes and have no legitimate protection because of police, judicial, and governmental involvement in crime. Cressey traces some of the interpenetrations:

> The members of this organization control all but a tiny part of the illegal gambling in the United States. They are the principal loan sharks. They are the principal importers and wholesalers of narcotics. They have infiltrated certain labor unions, where they extort money from employers and, at the same time, cheat the members of the union. The members have a virtual monopoly on some legitimate enterprises, such as cigarette vending machines and juke boxes, and they own a wide variety of retail firms, restaurants and bars, hotels, trucking companies, food companies, linen-supply houses, garbage collection routes, and factories.[27]

The overall problem of the role of illegal occupations is shown by this set of arrangements. Services which people want — gambling, prostitution — are used to strengthen a system which is predatory on a wider system and so governs the power of communities that other occupations in the field can practice overt predation — which people do not want. The collaboration between illegal and legal occupations with common interests results in group profit at the expense of the public. But there is no place, analytically, to draw the line finally between organized crime and organized legitimate business. The Cosa Nostra itself, legitimate businesses owned by the Cosa Nostra, and legitimate businesses owned by "straight" stockholders all victimize the public and subvert the legal process to avoid prosecution. It was Sutherland, years ago, who called the greed and the operations of major corporations a form of "white-collar crime." What seems certain is that without unified citizen action, the future of predatory occupations seems assured.

CHAPTER TWELVE

THE FIELD OF EDUCATION

The transmission of a society's knowledge, and its guiding values, has been the province of the educator since at least the time of ancient Greece. As a group specializing in such work, educators have been crucial for any society depending on knowledge and social commitment more than brute force. In general, the more complex and technical the society, the more probable that it will have a specialized educator group. And yet at all levels the field of education is a battleground, precisely because of its intellectual and emotional importance to a society, to the parents of the children and youth, and to the generation in contact with the educators themselves.

HISTORICAL PERSPECTIVE: FROM SOCRATES TO TEACHER'S UNION

Perhaps no era has awarded the educator the prestige of the present era, in all probability because of the need which society has for the skills which he may impart. But in almost all eras, including the present, we must make the critical distinction between the educator in "primary" and "secondary" areas and the educator of advanced students, who have been located in universities since the Middle Ages.

In the classic age in Athens, the division of labor in primary and secondary areas was between the *pedagogos,* or slave-servant-companion and moral instructor of each middle- and upper-class youth, on the one hand, and the teacher himself, on the other. Both positions were of low status in the society of the time. Castle comments on the teacher:

> In the first place, he was not in immediate contact with the home, whose master delegated authority to the paidagogos; in the second place

> his was a paid and badly paid profession, and therefore rated very low in the Greek scale of social values. And, even more important, he had no special qualifications for the job. Throughout the whole history of the antique world the schoolmaster's was a humble trade, plied by those who had seen better days or had no other skill to offer the community.[1]

In Athens, as in many nations in centuries to come, education at all levels was private. From seven to fourteen, primary education by schoolmasters was given in the palaestra and the music school, and an elite had a secondary education in rhetoric and philosophy. Military-athletic training was the final step at this level. The second stage was the battleground of the different philosophical schools — Plato's school and the far more popular Sophist schools, which taught a more applied or "how to succeed" form of skill for aspiring politicians and sons of the elite of Athens.[2]

Hellenic education became Hellenistic in settings such as Alexandria, and the Greek format, far more organized, eventually became the basis for Roman education. In Rome, a more standardized three-step model for education — and thus a hierarchy in the education field — was constructed after the Greek model. The "three R's" were taught in elementary school, by the *ludi magister* or *litterator*. Secondary schools, after the third century B.C. were led by the *grammaticus*. A third step was necessary for those aiming at a public career in the school of the *rhetor*, or teacher of rhetoric. Castle believes that Roman secondary education was superior to Greek because, although more restricted in conception, it "performed thoroughly what it set out to do." [3]

Both in Greece and Rome, therefore, although there was a small elite group in secondary education, there were no schools that could be considered universities. These grew up after the fall of Rome and as an outgrowth of monastery-based education. As the so-called Dark Ages passed into medieval times, the system of education became coterminous with the bureaucracy of the Church. Although primary education could be acquired at home or in village schools, advanced education was a form of religious education. As Carr-Saunders and Wilson point out, the undergraduate faculty and the three professions of theology, medicine, and law were all ecclesiastical in approach, and those teaching in the university were by definition members of the clergy and in holy orders.[4] On the other hand, the major professions and the university developed the guild-structure common to the craftsmen of the time. Thus they had both the official protection of the Church and the informal organized strength of the craft guilds.

The Renaissance saw a great outburst of talent and creativity in science and the arts, and the first possibility of a secular professoriate. Instruction in science and art, as we noted in an earlier chapter, was often by the apprentice method, which had been the method of training for the crafts since the Middle Ages. The universities did become centers of scientific activity, in the advanced faculties of major centers such as Bologna and Florence, but in general one cannot equate the creativity of the Renaissance with a group of men narrowly called "educators" or "academics" in the modern sense of this term. The Reformation, although leading to the construction of alternate Protestant and Catholic-run primary and secondary school systems and universities, did not have much of a basic impact on the role of the lower-level teacher, though great controversies raged in the universities.

In Puritan Massachusetts, Harvard was founded in 1640 as a general college, with a *de facto* function of training ministers.[5] Some towns had schoolmasters because of Harvard College's habit of producing more ministers each year than the colony could use. Although it was not typical for the colonies in general, in Massachusetts, at least, educated men could be found in the schools. The schoolmaster's job became a common stopover point before going on to a pulpit or into another less related line of work. But as the Puritan utopia evolved into a Yankee state, there were major changes which affected the role of the schoolmaster, though leaving the university-tutor-instructor in essentially the same position. Massachusetts in early Puritan times was also the birthplace of free public education for all children. Smith summarizes the changes which were observable as the utopian Puritan colony developed into a commercial trading state:

> The schoolhouse was replacing the family home as the place of formal elementary instruction; women teachers were replacing men in the lower schools; private schools in technical and vocational subjects, whose masters were usually not college men, were serving large numbers of students in the commercial centers; schools were being created for a secular commonwealth.[6]

The nineteenth century had its first major turning point in education at about the time of the presidency of Andrew Jackson, when the expansion of the population westward, including families with children, created an instantaneous demand for schooling. Tyack uses early Oregon as a case study to show how the Protestant clergy were an important force in campaigning for public education in the new frontier towns. They were also active in setting up denominational elementary and secondary schools themselves, if they could not persuade the community to do so.[7] Hofstadter reminds us that they were "trying to bring the ordinary restraints and intuitions of a civilized society into an area which had hardly any culture at all." [8]

If the mid-1800s was an era of expansion westward and foundation of public primary and secondary schools, it was also a time of great factionalism within societal subgroups, a situation which led to the founding of a wide range of special-interest colleges. According to Jencks and Riesman:

> By 1900, there were special colleges for Baptists and Catholics, for men and women, for whites and blacks, for rich and not-so-rich, for North and South, for small town and big city, for adolescents and adults, for engineers and teachers.[9]

It is further noted by these authors that the special-interest college could serve several subgroups simultaneously, such as the college that might appeal to "Methodists who were also Texas chauvinists." [10]

The turn of the century was a critical period in the education field, with the solidification of the elementary and secondary public school systems on a local and state-wide basis, the development of land-grant colleges into major centers for higher education, and the development of the first major graduate programs in medicine, law, and arts and sciences, at places such as Johns Hopkins, Harvard, and Columbia. The departmental system of universities was devised at this time, and the elective system for course credits. At the same time that graduate programs in arts and sciences were constructed, thus beginning the modern "academic" profession, there began the undergraduate and graduate programs for the training of teachers in elementary and secondary education. From the turn of the century, therefore, we can observe the formalization in occupational training programs of the division which had existed informally for centuries — that between the schoolmaster and the professor, now to be trained in different settings entirely.[11]

In the course of this century the field of education has gradually grown as an occupational sector to match both the increasing number of students in the system and the increasing importance of skills to a complex Western society. In this century, as in most others, the vast bulk of the education and the vast bulk of the educators have been concerned with applied matters, with what is essentially socialization and training for the status quo of the time. However, since the post–World War II period two separate yet interrelated trends have increasingly marked the field of education at all levels: the first is the increasing organization of the consumers, the other is the organization of educators in associations such as the National Education Association, the American Federation of Teachers (AFL-CIO), and the American Association of University Professors. Gradually the field of American education has become politicalized and activist in its own interests and some segments of it have also become altruistically active on behalf of causes of a general political nature, such as anti-war activity, or the ultimate aims of education. In historical terms, the increasing militancy and activism of the educator is of very recent origins, contrasting with a long past in the service of the powerful at the expense of occupational and individual self-interest and, in many cases, at the expense of the pursuit of truth as well.

THE CAREER EXPERIENCE: SIMILARITIES AND DIFFERENCES

The career patterns and experiences of the elementary and secondary teachers are seldom compared in parallel fashion to those of college professors, yet sociologically the field of education includes both groups, as part of an overall occupational and motivational system. We can compare these two occupational subgroups on the issues of motivation and career choice, early socialization, the function of gatekeepers in the career path, the overall pathway itself, career contingencies, and the consequent occupational world views.

MOTIVATION, CAREER CHOICE, AND EARLY SOCIALIZATION

The literature on motivation for choice of the teaching career is inconclusive, because of the various levels of motivation involved in any career choice and points in time at which a choice may be made. However, there are obvious historical trends in this area. In the pre-World War II era, elementary and secondary teaching was a female profession, college teaching was for males, and thus sex limited the choice initially. In addition, at this time the primary pattern for training was in a teacher's college for women and a university or liberal arts college for men. The latter were to populate the world of the professions, business, and colleges. For both groups, the middle class was the sole source of recruits. In the past decade, however, the working-class male has begun to enter elementary and secondary teaching, and a later, post-college career choice has become possible for both male and females, through the growth of one-year Master of Arts in Teaching programs. In fact, Conant points out that even in 1963, only 20 per cent of the elementary and secondary teachers came from teacher's colleges.[12] Programs in universities, and post-college training, accounted for a greater number of teachers. This makes possible a later decision based on a broader experience in the world and various forms of post-college idealism (as well as strict opportunism), instead of the early vocational commitment to teaching which used to be required of the high school student thinking of college.

The early years of socialization in the education field are now almost overwhelmingly carried out in university and college settings, with some applied experience built into the elementary and secondary track; for university jobs, teaching experience is a very common consequence of doctoral study toward a Ph.D. degree. Conant, in his famous report, *The Education of American Teachers*, criticized sharply the quality of both theory and practical exposure in the non-college programs.[13] The experience of "practice teaching" is often more of an unrealistically structured exposure than a true apprenticeship. As Brenton observes,

> Typically, the school he is assigned to for practice teaching is in a good part of town. It has plenty of facilities. It services a middle-class group of children. His cooperating teacher is one of the best in that school. He is given a limited amount of work to do and learns something about planning lessons and relating to children.[14]

The graduate student in the arts and sciences experiences a socialization far different in quality from that of the typical "ed major." For one thing, the majority of education students are *undergraduates*, whereas the majority of arts and sciences students are graduate students, oriented toward a Ph.D. Second, an attempt is made, sometimes successfully, to have the academic graduate students socialize and educate each other, whereas the education programs have a rather mechanistic quality about them. Hence Kohl's advice to college graduates in liberal arts thinking of a graduate certificate in education, which they need in order to teach:

> Schools of education that consider themselves little more than "credential factories" are more likely to let one through than schools with a "philosophy." This may seem an excessively cynical view, yet it has been my experience that little of interest is happening in *any* school of education, and therefore if one wants credentials one might as well get them in the easiest and least painful way.[15]

In contrast to this, there seems to be no way to "routinely" go through the training and socialization process of graduate academic education. Precisely the same set of uncertainties in the sponsored relationship exist here as do in the relationship between a young executive and those in positions of responsibility over him. In addition, with the exception of the natural sciences, the material to be "learned" is far more amorphous in graduate academic training than in either undergraduate or graduate educational training. This adds to the need for constructing a student culture to exchange information on professors — what "they like" and what "they want."

The first experience in the teaching role is critical for both the school and the college teacher, and in both cases, it occurs not under ideal but under the most difficult of conditions. For the inexperienced schoolteacher, the first assignment is likely to be the lowest status job around, a job in a ghetto school. This leads to reactions of despair and a high early dropout rate. For the graduate student in academic areas, the first exposure is often as a "teaching assistant" with grading and group-discussion responsibilities in a large introductory course, and at lower prestige universities or at large, well-known but factory-like ones, the *teaching* of such a course. The lack of experience in both cases is extreme, but the consequences differ, for the graduate student is dealing with college students who are to some degree motivated to learn, whereas the first experience of the schoolteacher is usually with the "disciplinary groups." Some idea of the difference in status here can be gained by noting that at some large universities, graduate students in sociology will teach graduate students in a "Foundations of Education" course in the university's school of education; the reverse would never happen. In addition, although the amount of drudgery is high in both cases, for the high school teacher the first course is essentially solo work, whereas the university teaching system is more classically an apprenticeship system, with the graduate students somewhat exploited, as all apprentices are, but still apprentices with a chance to gain experience at less risk than that provided the high school teacher in the first job. In general, therefore, the pre-professional students make their decisions later on the basis of more information, have a more complex and less routinized experience in the early years of training, and face their first job under more constructive conditions than do the school-teachers just out of a school of education or a short Master of Arts in Teaching program.

THE CAREER PATTERN: STRUCTURE AND CONTINGENCIES

Gatekeepers function in an extremely important way in educational careers, at the start and at key points along the way. Perhaps the most striking contrast between school and university career patterns lies in the degree of importance of non-occupational gatekeepers in the school career. For example, the boards of certification giving temporary or permanent certification to teach in the public schools are composed of state bureaucrats. In addition, community members may in local cases as members of school boards approve or disapprove the hiring or firing of a teacher, in the first job or at other points in the career, and in most cases the boards are composed of laymen or non-educational professionals. The criteria for hiring and firing are external to the ability to teach, in many cases, and such factors as age, sex, race, and religion have weighed heavily in the past. The school of education where the teacher was trained is often a factor in this gatekeeping situation, as these organizations work with the state departments of education politically in joint lobbying activities and exchange information and advice on certification requirements. But the degree of non-educator involvement in the gatekeeping functions is in marked contrast to that of the academic profession, where only one's colleagues may grant the Ph.D., and the degree alone fully qualifies one for a top-rank career.

Four major patterns appear to exist at present in terms of the structure of school careers in education. The first could be called the "standard" pathway: from undergraduate school of education to ghetto school and then by seniority out of this setting and into a more "prestigious" and possibly less stressful environment. This pattern was noted by Becker in 1952, and is still relevant to most school systems today.[16] The second pattern can be termed the "elite" pattern: beginning with liberal arts training, then on to a prestigious (Harvard, Columbia) graduate school of education, and then directly to a top-rank suburban school. The third pattern can be called the "deliberate altruist" career approach: from community work (sometimes from a minority background as well), the candidate elects to go directly to the ghetto school in order to change it, and indeed does deliberately stay there. These patterns are all ideal types, of course, for many a deliberate altruist pattern turns into a standard pattern when the realities of the ghetto school are experienced over a period of time.

Finally, there is the common pattern of in-and-out again, at different stages of the career. The most frequent point of leaving is at the very beginning; major dropout rates occur in the first year, diminishing gradually after this time. Because of the low wages that are standard in the career and the prevalence of younger women, careers are ended by marriage or childbirth, and men leave the ranks of teaching gladly for a promotion into administrative work, or, failing to get this, drop out of the profession whenever the financial burden becomes too great. In general, the career pattern of the schoolteacher appears *reactive* rather than planned, except for those who deliberately choose a ghetto setting and wish to remain there. The primary course is to go from unbearable to bearable settings in terms of working conditions, but the career pattern does not seem to be related to performance as an educator, in the class room, in the great majority of cases.

Caplow and McGee's study of the college academic career pattern remains the major work on this issue and offers a contrast to the structural patterns seen above. First, and following Riesman, the career patterns cannot be understood locally or even regionally, but only within a prestige structure of national scope. Where the individual's graduate training was received — the place of the initiation into what Riesman calls "the academic procession" — will usually determine the level at which the first job is held, that is, the prestige of the first job situation. Also, the higher the level of the setting where training is received, the greater the probability that the first job will be in another institution at essentially the same level. For example, further research recently showed that the "top" five or six departments in the field of sociology, ranked according to a set of criteria used by the elites in the field, exchanged their people almost incestuously both as to first jobs and later career patterns. Those not in such a club at the start had a far more difficult time entering it, unless world fame made a late entry possible.[17]

The teaching ability of a person is shown by Caplow and McGee to be no more relevant to career progress at the university level than it is at the school level. For the university, the basic rule remains "publish or perish," and teaching skill is a pleasant extra but by no means a necessity.

A common pathway for advancement is through research. Here the amassing of grants and the "research-professor" appointment allows a flexibility of time and a freedom from routine which makes publication more possible and rapid advancement more certain.[18] On the other hand, the grant-getting ability of any researcher is directly related to what the government is interested in funding at any given time and can lead to opportunism and sometimes to intellectual sterility, of a man or of an entire field.

With each promotion in rank the bargaining power of the academic increases until the point where his work begins to peak, by which time in most cases he has received tenure at some setting. In the university situation, the career pattern issue relates to the inter-setting bargaining situation, or, to use Caplow and McGee's term, the academic marketplace. In times of high need for skills — as in the business-executive labor market — younger men can move ahead more rapidly in ordinary times by moving geographically; in times when jobs are tight, the degree of setting-to-setting mobility and the bargaining power of each individual with respect to his present setting diminish rapidly.[19]

The classical career contingencies relevant to every other occupational field apply to the educational occupations, and with minor differences they apply in the same way to school as to university careers. For example, the age factor is relevant, in terms of seniority and retirement regulations, to both the school and university faculty, although most universities tend to have more flexible rules in this area. In terms of sex, although the school segment of the educational field is still more female than male, the upward mobility to department chairmanships and into administration is possible primarily only for males; the academic profession has been almost adamantly anti-female in hiring and promotion policy until very recently. Racial prejudice has blighted the pretensions to objectivity and truth-seeking of the entire educational field, at all levels, in the North as well as the South. Finally, religion and ethnic group has been a powerful factor in hiring and career development in primary and secondary education and, before World War II, in graduate education as well. At the school level, the primary factor seems to be the degree of racial, religious, and ethnic "fit" between the teacher and the immediate local community. Those who do fit add to the public relations image of the school program and are likely to find themselves more rapidly promoted and better paid than those who do not. Although religion and ethnic group have become less critical in the past few decades, it is still instructive to note that many of the successful "Ivy League" minority group professors soon develop a WASP style of speaking and manners, perhaps in order to become cosmetically more in tune with their surroundings. The young radicals in the elite schools can be exempted from this trend, however, as their entire aim in many cases is precisely to proletarianize the elite school itself, and its students.

What about teaching skill as a career contingency for members of the teaching profession, at any level? It would seem reasonably relevant as a criterion, but the evidence indicates otherwise. Teaching ability is not systematically rewarded by career advancement at either the school or college level. In the school area, seniority, personality, and compatibility with school administration count for more; at the college level, the scholarly productivity of the man counts for more. As a consequence, we have a strange conflict between the overt function of a field and the actual determinants of career patterns within it.

RESULTING OCCUPATIONAL WORLD VIEWS

The education field is now so extensive and so heterogenous that an overall generalization or ideal type of "the educator's world view" is impossible. But it is possible to note how the experience can lead to a set of contrasting attitudes toward the work. At least three major ones can be identified at both levels, which can be called (the first two after Gouldner) the "local," the "cosmopolitan," and the "activist." [20]

The "local" attitude toward occupational activity and loyalties arises as a consequence of adjustment to the realities of the settings on which the teacher decides to remain. This is not primarily an occupation-oriented world view, but rather a locally oriented one. The important aspects of the work become the relations with colleagues and administrators on the setting and relations with the community. The aim is not either professional advancement or activism, as these are either unpalatable or judged to be unrealistic. The majority of teachers at all levels in the education field are probably "locals" in orientation, although almost all will prefer to label themselves as "cosmopolitans" for ego-building purposes.

The true "cosmopolitan" is oriented to his occupation on a national (or international) basis, far more than he is to the members of it on the setting where he happens to be at the moment. The key words are "at the moment." Cosmopolitans may not necessarily move so much more frequently than locals, but their orientations and loyalties are not local but occupation-wide. The mailbox is the most important article in the department office of a cosmopolitan, not the person whose office is across the hall. In general, the cosmopolitans are the inveterate convention-goers and the occupational politicians, the paper-givers and journal-article writers. Eventually their careers culminate in positions in the national professional organizations. The scarcity of true talent in the education field, and the extra energy needed for this life style, combined with the strains, conflicts, and jealousies between the cosmopolitans and the locals in the work setting, make this a more stressful (but far more exciting) world view for those who hold it. The successful NEA officer and the committeeman in a national academic association are examples of the cosmopolitan, as are the consultant-grantsmen in social science with friends in every foundation.

The third major orientation toward the teaching field, newer than the almost ancient cosmopolitan and local orientations, is that of the "activist." Having experienced the grave discrepancies between the theoretical aims of his field — the advancement of knowledge — and the reality — the socialization of individuals to preserve the status quo — he determines that he will devote his occupational energies to changing the function of the occupation itself. This means different things at different levels, however. Since at the school level the teachers are nearly powerless in a situation where administration and community school board (and thus the laymen) have control of what is taught and in what way, occupational organization is seen as the pathway. Since, further, the cosmopolitan orientation until very recently has been tied up with the national professional associations which were essentially conservative, the pathway the activists have been taking is through unionization, especially the American Federation of Teachers of the AFL-CIO. Here the union organization serves several functions. First, it can raise the salaries of teachers dramatically, and second, it can increase control over the classroom situation by including it as part of negotiations on "working conditions." Recently the National Education Association (the "cosmopolitan" or profession-oriented organization in the school field) and the AFT may be reaching some degree of rapprochement, as in occupational unity there is strength. However, it is only fair to note that it is primarily the young, and those from a working class (and union) background, that are in the forefront here. On the university level, the activist shares similarities and differences. Because the academy group has been more organized and has more of a mandate and freedom since its union (the AAUP) has been pro-independence, the activist has been playing more of an altruistic and less of a self-interest role than in the school sector. Activism in academia is primarily directed at the occupation, not only to change its working conditions but even more its value bases and its role in supporting the power structure in its present form. The activist orientation here does come close to altruism, as the very structure of the university makes it profitable for the university professor to continue as before in most cases. It is quite against his material interests, in the short run, to engage in this kind of action. Yet, as the history of the 1960s has shown, this has not prevented the growth of a definite activist orientation in the universities.

To sum up, the local, the cosmopolitan, and the activist orientation all are reactions to the career experience of teaching, the patterns structured by the society, and the contingencies inherent in these patterns. And world views are not permanent; yesterday's local can become tomorrow's activist, given sufficient provocation. What is absolutely clear, however, is that the function of education itself in the social system is now in question, by its practitioners and by the community. To understand the past, present, and potential future role of the teacher it is thus necessary to turn to the functional, interest-based approaches.

EDUCATORS AND THE SOCIAL SYSTEM: FUNCTIONS AND CONFLICTS OF INTEREST

Parsons made a perceptive observation of the typical elementary school classroom when he concluded that both intellectual and value data were being transmitted to the child, and that learning the latter was as important if not more important than learning the formal lesson.[21] There is a difference between *socialization* — the transmission of socially desired attitudes and values and standards of behavior — and *education* — the "leading out" of individuals of their greatest potential to think for themselves, to question the world that is, to create, to realize their innate capacities. The manifest function of the educator's role is that of education, but the latent function in all but a minority of cases is socialization — socialization for the existing status quo. In this sense, the history of the educational field and the career experience of educators become reasonable: no community or nation really wants, nor can it afford to have its educators really *educate*, for this could be subversive of the status quo; it wants its youth socialized. As Parsons and White note, the most valuable product, as far as the society goes, is the "properly socialized" individual himself.[22] With this basic function in mind we can understand the hostility of school boards and principals to innovative schoolteachers, the enmity of the governmental power structure and the corporation to the radically oriented profession in leading universities. "Education" is a political activity by definition. The ability and desire to criticize the status quo is either transmitted or it is not. In either case, there are major political consequences for any society.

The division of labor in the educator's occupational field can only be understood against this background of the manifest versus the latent functions of the educator's role. Other groups in the school field, for example the guidance counselors studied by Cicourel and Kitsuse, make the latent function manifest; their job appears to be the deliberate channeling of students by social class and by values based on middle-class prejudices into the different tracks of a high school program. Here the aim is to reproduce the previous class structure; in some cases the counselors are aware of this to a degree that most teachers are not.[23] In addition to the overall function, there are the usual problems related to the division of labor in this occupational field, problems such as the supply and demand of teaching personnel, the prestige structure within the field, the lines between auxiliary, teacher, and administrative roles, the functional relationships between the teaching world and external institutions, and the issue of "complexing" between educators and other occupational groups and institutions in the wider society.

SUPPLY AND DEMAND: THE NEEDS OF A GIVEN STRUCTURE

A given structure has given needs for manpower; if one changes the structure, the manpower needs may disappear. If, for example, the certification laws were repealed, anyone with a college degree and expertise in his field could teach in the school systems and the "manpower problem" defined in the old terms would become irrelevant. Given the present structure of the educational field, what is the manpower situation at each level and in what ways is it appearing to change?

The first evident pattern is that there is neither a massive over-supply of teachers nor a massive under-supply, but this condition is recent and was not the case during the peak period when the "war babies" of World War II were in the school system and university. As a reaction to this boom, the schools of education and the universities accelerated their production of degree holders in education and Ph.D.'s in the arts and sciences. But to talk about numbers is to miss one of the most basic points. Since the Conant report there has been little in the way of basic change in the *quality* of the manpower in schools, in contrast to the universities. Conant's scathing indictment of the standards in schools of education was written in 1963. Yet as Brenton notes,

> In 1965, a U.S. Office of Education study of graduate students' undergraduate achievement showed that only business and commerce majors did worse, that is, got a lower percentage of A's and A—'s and a higher percentage of C's and C—'s, than education majors. In 1952 education majors ranked lowest of sixteen professional categories on the Graduate Record Examinations. In 1963–1964 they ranked lowest again. In 1968 they ranked lowest once more.[24]

These findings simply confirm what has been assumed for years. The more talented have chosen other areas because of the low prestige and rewards of school teaching in our present society. The present maintains its continuity with the past.

In the late 1960s and early 1970s, a problem of *oversupply* may be hitting the university sector. The massive expansion of the number of Ph.D.-granting departments and the upswing in the number of degrees granted at each one, compared to the much lower expansion rate of job offerings, is making the competition tougher and changing the pattern, removing the bias which led to an oversupply at the elementary ranks, a slight undersupply at the secondary ranks, and a major shortage in the universities. The "war babies" got to graduate school and are now getting their Ph.D.'s, with obvious consequences for the labor market. The major issue here, from a more philosophical perspective, is that governments and sociologists see fit to discuss the labor market for educators in essentially the same way they do the labor market for steelworkers. "Bodies" and routine service are almost implied by this type of analysis, but this is what the system wants and these are the terms in which it thinks about the supply and demand for educational manpower.

PRESTIGE STRUCTURE AND THE DIVISION OF LABOR

The nature of academic prestige structures has been essentially constant since the early years of the present century, although the actions of the training settings and the educational professionals in recent years has been modifying the concept of what an "elite" job ought to be. Throughout most of the present century, the status setting has been the private elite university, where the top-value Ph.D.'s and graduate degrees in education were earned. These in turn led to placement in other top-ranking universities or in the elite school systems of the wealthy suburbs. At least two major demands have been influencing the nature of prestige structures in recent years — alone and in combination with each other: the increasing role of the federal government in education and the increasing political activism of segments of the occupation at all levels.

Federal involvement in the financing of university programs and especially in the grant programs for support of organizations (the usual way for schools) or individuals (college and university faculty) has led to a situation where training institutions do not overwhelmingly determine the status of an individual or a setting if the government can be mobilized to support it. That is, the active slum school whch gets grants from the Office of Economic Opportunity can boost its prestige and that of its staff independently of the run-down nature of the rest of the school system. At the college or university level, a man may choose to remain the sole grantsman and baron of a small department to being a fish in a larger or more prestigious academic pond elsewhere.

Activism is having its subtle and not-so-subtle effects on the academic procession. For example, many elite students now consider it a "copout" to teach in a suburban school rather than in the ghetto, and the VISTA programs, though hardly making a dent in the manpower needs of poor schools and underdeveloped regions, have intensified the prestige of reverse placement. In this sense, non-material motivations are increasing in prestige, but they are occurring at an unusual moment in history — when the schoolteachers are organizing in their own self-interest in unions and militant professional organizations. Although altruism may be more general, it seems that we may be dealing with two somewhat differentiated populations. For the first — the lower middle class who are now going into teaching in increasing numbers — increased status and prestige is defined materially in the older sense, whereas for the sons and daughters of the elite and the upper middle class, prestige (and action concerning desired career placement) is measured in a contrasting way. But the fate of idealism in the long run is still unknown. What the VISTA volunteers do after they leave the program (whether they return to the ghetto school permanently, for example) may be of more importance to a change in the overall prestige structure of the field than what they do in their youth. Likewise, the elite college radical graduate student who goes to work in this elite college orbit after his degree, in spite of his protestations about the elite university "corruption," belies a *real* change in the university's prestige structure and thus in the overall prestige structure of the occupational field.[25]

In general, the division of labor in terms of the continuum from custodial to auxiliary teaching to administrative staff shows important similarities and differences between the school and university sectors of the occupational field. In both, there is no question that the "auxiliary" is expected to be subservient to the goals of the instructor. Yet Paul Goodman's suggestion about universities — that administrators be no more important and have no more power than custodians — shows in its utopianism the present division of labor and power relations between the teaching and the administrative staff in educational settings at all levels.[26] Both the schools and the college educational settings are bureaucracies, and cannot be run without some central organizational role. Given this fact, and the fact that administrators are often paid better than the teachers within their settings, there is still a difference between the schoolteacher attitude toward administrators and the attitude toward such men by the faculty of colleges and universities. In general, until the most recent years, upward mobility for schoolteachers was defined as for engineers — promotion out of the ranks into administration. For the university professor, however, the faculty career offers a flexibility, and the chance for extra earnings as a consultant, that the administrative role does not provide. Furthermore, creative work in a field — scholarship — is not required in the school career but is a major index of success in the college one. Since creative scholarly work is almost incompatible with the demands of administrative work, going into administrative work is viewed by the cosmopolitans in the academic sector as an admission of intellectual sterility. In both cases, the "radical" is least likely to go into administration, the "cosmopolitan" occasionally, and the "local" most readily, given their respective orientations toward bureaucracy and the profession on a national basis. Administrative work within the *profession* is common for cosmopolitans of course, but this is not to be confused with a job administering an educational setting.

CONFLICTS OF INTEREST: COMPLEXING IN THE EDUCATION FIELD

Perhaps the major difference between the pattern of the division of labor in schools and in universities, and the resulting conflicts of interest, lies in the nature of complexing relationships with wider societal groups and institutions. In the elementary and secondary education field, the primary relationships which have "power" are between the schools that train the teachers, the state bureaucracies that license them, and the national teacher's associations such as the NEA. The advantages to be gained by these relationships deal with the advancement of interests of the teachers as a group, perhaps at times against the interests of the community or the nation.

For example, the militancy of teachers in their own interest represents an effort at present to gain power and independence from community political intimidation (as Ziegler described it) and to gain a living wage and basic occupational self-respect.[27] The functional power of the schoolteacher, once a sense of occupational consciousness develops, is real, and thus his bargaining power is real also. As Rosenthal puts it:

> One thing has become crystal-clear. Public school teachers, once the docile handmaidens of public education, are no longer quiescent. Spearheaded by resolute state and local organizations and stimulated by the competition between the National Education Association (NEA) and the American Federation of Teachers (AFT), the "teachers' movement" is gaining strength nationwide, and particularly in large cities. The former widespread, if passive, consensus on the operating rules of the educational game has undergone erosion.[28]

Rosenthal's study of the political role of teacher groups in school politics shows that cities vary in terms of militancy and degree of opposition by the bureaucracies and state law.[29] Schrag's study of the Boston educational bureaucracy, Rogers' of the one in New York, and Resnik's of the one in Philadelphia, all testify to the entrenched power of school boards and bureaucracies in opposing both self-interest activism and reformist activism to change the function of education itself.[30] But the complex in the school field, between the community and the board, is now in the process of dissolution, especially in the ghetto areas, as a consequence of direct citizen activism. The role of the teacher is problematic in all this; teachers appreciate opposition to the board, but not the desire of the local community to dictate what goes on in the classroom, an old desire on the part of the local community.

In spite of the vehemence of the rhetoric and the importance of the struggle to its participants, the conflicts of interest in the school field are minor compared to those in modern American universities. The relations between the groups in the school field do not deal with the centers of power and profit in our society in the direct way that the universities do for a dual reason — the product controlled and the skills of the occupation itself. School pupils and the schoolteachers are not of as much value to the powerful groups in the society as are the skills of university professors and the trained college and graduate student, especially those in the natural and social sciences. In other words, the division of labor within the field of education leads to an internal complexing situation at the non-college level; by contrast there is a national or power-involved complexing at the university level, directly involving professors in the labor of the overall society, as members of consulting firms or as consultants to government and the major corporations. Ridgeway concludes, for example, that

> The idea that the university is a community of scholars is a myth. The professors are less interested in teaching students than in yanking the levers of their new combines so that these machines will grow bigger and go faster. The university has in large part been reduced to serving as banker-broker for the professor's outside interests.[31]

Although this is an overstatement, the deemphasis on teaching is understandably relevant to a significant sector of the academic world, as the student revolt of the 1960s indicates. The military research done on campuses by professors with contracts with the Department of Defense still runs into billions of dollars, with the university taking its cuts in the form of "overhead" charges.

From a systems and conflict-of-interest viewpoint, therefore, the division of labor and the accompanying differences in status and prestige are not accidental as one goes from the one-room schoolhouse to the professorial elite at major universities. Those individuals and educational groups that function more clearly and closely to advance the interests of the society itself (in its presently constituted form) receive a higher share of the rewards and perquisites than those individuals and groups within the field that are less useful to the corporations, the Department of Defense, and the federal government.

COMPARISONS: THE SOVIET UNION AND DEVELOPING NATIONS

The selective importance of one segment of the educational field to the overall society is hardly unique to the United States. Neither the intrinsically political meaning of education nor the understanding of the educator as a national resource has ever been ignored in Europe. In the Soviet Union these "systems" issues have been raised to national programs of top priority and backing. From the start, as Grant makes clear in his review of the Soviet educational system, education is understood as a form of political socialization into the Marxist-Leninist world view, and more generally and especially in the primary school, socialization into loyalty to the state.[32] Using essentially a structured European pattern of education, with close centralization and central control, the Soviet Union has managed to deliberately improve the level of education to the point where the "Sputnik" crisis surprised the American educational field by revealing the seriousness and efficiency of the Soviet educational effort. Education became a top-priority resource, although the salaries of most teachers remained at a low level. There are obviously positive and negative aspects of this kind of mobilization; its efficiency is bought at the expense of creativity and freedom. But to the Soviet Union or to any other nation far behind in the race for expertise, it appears to be one of the few realistic approaches presently available.

The primary difference between this type of education-government relationship and that seen in our country lies in the lack of maneuverability of the elite academic. As with the factory, the Communist party of the Soviet Union is closely involved with educator's activities at all stages. They run the national youth organizations, the Pioneers and the Komosol, the latter for late adolescents and young adults. Advancement within the academic ranks is easier for Party members than for others, and whatever "outside" arrangements which consulting professors are allowed to make are also under the scrutiny of the Communist party. In general, therefore, although the Soviet educational field may be more efficient and better organized than that of the United States, it is not an even partly independent occupational group in the Western sense, because of the relation between the state and the occupational group. Functionally, the critical role of the educator and the advanced students is understood in the United States, as it is in the Soviet Union. The difference, of course, is that the Soviet Union can control the way this skill is used, within rather broad limits, and if necessary against the will of the educator himself.[33]

The developing nations have problems in setting up educational systems which highlight the critical functional role of educators and education itself in Western industrial society. The problem of many developing countries lies in the large gap between the totally illiterate mass and the educated elite, in the absence of major programs of public schooling. The educators who do exist in such countries may construct their educational settings for prestige rather than functional reasons, as they have had to get their advanced education in other nations and are sometimes impressed by them. For many of these nations, therefore, the training of primary and secondary teachers is really a more important priority than the training of advanced technical scientists and engineers. Yet prestige striving has led to an overemphasis in many such countries on educational opportunities for the elite and the neglect of public educational systems. In this respect, the Soviet Union and Cuba, as well as Communist China, have been more explicit about the need for good primary public education than many of the Western-oriented developing nations. The elitism often natural to these countries is thus not countered by an explicit political ideology on the subject of education for the workers, which *is* characteristic of the Communist bloc nations. The result of this is the politicizing of education in these developing countries, as part of a struggle between East and West, with the views of the university students and faculty explicitly blunt on the functional role of education in the present and in the revolutionary social-system-to-be. Since industrial societies of whatever political form depend on skill, and since the role of the educator is to provide that skill, the decision as to who is to receive the training is a basically political decision. All regimes understand that he who controls the educational system controls the future of the nation.

THE EDUCATORS' MANDATE: THE FUTURE OF A BATTLEGROUND

In presenting the different perspectives on the field of education, one theme inevitably arises. Conflicts of interest occur within the educational occupational field, and between it and the wider society. At both the university and school level, these are a set of cross-combinations which essentially pit one segment of the field, with its outside allies, against another segment of the field, with *its* allies. The involved groups are, at a minimum, those educators who presently benefit from the system (or who aspire to), those who wish to radically change it toward other ends, the corporations, the local community, the students, and the national government. In other nations and in our own, the relation of the regime to the educational occupations determines much of the present and potential future mandate of the group. It is the conclusion of this inspection that the temporary or permanent resolutions of these conflicts of interest, among the parties just listed, will determine the educator's mandate in the future, as it has in the past.

Within the educational field itself, at both the school and the college level, the radical reformers are still most definitely a minority. First, all those who are unionizing must not be classed with the reformers or revolutionaries; their goal is avowedly a bigger slice of rewards, or greater control over the present system. Kozol has suggested that a non-certification educational system be set up outside the present public and private school systems, but the subsistence of teachers or the vocational future of students in such a system is still an unsolved problem, one which demands the revision of the old boundary between school as training and work as post-school experience.[34] In any case, the radical reformers could conceivably conflict quite strongly with the self-interest groups, were certain issues raised about the future role of the "professional" education field. Goodman, for example, suggests school in the streets, with the firemen and executives as the teachers. Where does this leave the graduate from the teacher's college? [35]

At the college level, reports of reforms such as the Muscatine Report on educational innovations needed at Berkeley suggest a series of revisions at the collegel level, but few reforms go as far as to change the occupational role of the professor, his privileged position in the academic hierarchy.[36] Indeed, the struggle between the progressives and conservatives in education seems the same as ever, except for the added element of *political* radicalism. The fact that education and educational settings are inherently political in function has now been deliberately singled out by reformers, and the "value-free" nature of education itself is increasingly less accepted as a truth by the layman or the student. Thus, in the future, the concept of "expertise" may change, especially in the social sciences and the humanities. This will make the definition of a given educator's mandate, or a school's, one that is more in the hands of its clientele or consumers and less of a professional prerogative. In other words, the increased understanding of the political role of education — by teachers and community at all levels — is leading to a "politicized" occupation in the overt instead of the covert sense of the term, and politics here means not simply internal occupational politics but the politics of the community and nation. Political events in the wider society will then have a greater effect on the role of American education than ever before.

The corporations have been attempting to complex with the schools. Textbook publishers have always done this but the new electronic gimmickry is being pushed at school systems everywhere. However, Oettinger and Marks show that equipment doesn't pay off on the setting in any way related to its cost; fund-pressed systems are becoming aware of this.[37] Although the corporations view the schools as a market to sell in, they still need the colleges as a market to recruit in and as talent to be exploited toward their ends. Here, the changing political attitudes of professors and students toward the corporations, and the labor-market leverage which they could have if organized, may preserve some of the freedom in the future which the colleges have allowed to be threatened in recent years. But the military-industrial complex is still quite strong on campus. The conflict in the education field comes between two sets of forces: conservative professors and administrators and Department-of-Defense-related corporations on the one hand; radical students and professors, along with moderate anti-war groups, on the other. The national student strike of May, 1970, illustrated the extent of political action which can be expected under some circumstances from one segment of the field in the future.

The redefinition of the relations between the education field and the corporate world is under way. It will have major implications for the role of education, and thus of educators, in any future society.

Finally, the government has viewed educators and students as manpower resources about which "policy" decisions could be made. But in the last several decades, it has become increasingly clear that the conflicts of interest are major, between a government protecting a given status quo and the interests of the new educators in turning out critics of the system and builders of a new one. No longer can education be considered a "policy" question to be decided by those who are neither teachers nor students, any more than it can be decided alone by the community and the non-education world. One thing, in conclusion, is certain. The mandate of the educator has always been a political issue. In the past, it was a subtle and somewhat unnoticed problem; at the present, it has become an open issue involving the whole society.

CHAPTER THIRTEEN

PUBLIC SERVICE OCCUPATIONS

No society known to man has ever managed to survive without some contribution on the part of most of its adults to the common good. On the other hand, the idea of "public" as against "private" employment is a product of a later era in history, and it is only in the modern period that we see public service workers as a sizable enough segment of the population to merit separate treatment. With the advent of the welfare state, and the complex service-based society, the functional power of such workers increases yearly. The sudden and deliberate interruption of mail delivery, police protection, and garbage collection have in recent years brought great metropolitan regions, if not the nation as a whole, to a grinding halt. Such an occupational sector grew slowly, and has only recently been developing new ideologies, new functions, and a new concept of its own interests.

A HISTORICAL REVIEW

Egyptian society can be taken as an example of the role of "public service" occupations in a large, complex, and yet still essentially traditional society. The functions which were considered both *elevated* and *public* were the province of the priests, who in another context could be called religious professionals. On the other hand, the great "public works" of the time, the pyramids, were built by slave labor. There was a middle range of public occupation as well as the ones characterizing the elite and the lowest echelons of the society. Such occupations as surveyors and measurers of grain were performing work in the public service, if by public we mean service to the king. In Egypt, therefore, as in all periods to come, there was a stratification from high-status public occupations, involving power and influence in the society (or those in control of it), to low-status work, done at little or no personal reward to the workers.[1]

A similar stratification system can be seen in Periclean Athens. The elite only had citizen status, and they alone could act in the political forum. The major service workers of the city, such as policemen, often came from the slave class. The *type* of public service work — the degree to which such work could be considered "clean" (debating in the public forum) or "dirty" (refuse collection and constabulary work) — seemed to determine as early as classic Greece *who* would do *what* in the ranks of public service.[2] In Rome, the greater and more rationalized social organization of the Empire, and the complex governmental forms which grew up, allowed a far wider range of citizens, as opposed to slaves, to participate in public service work. The administrators of the Roman Empire were the ancestors of our present federal bureaucrats, located as they are both in Washington and in regional headquarters throughout the nation.

In medieval times the theory of public service work and the actual existence of public-serving occupational groups appeared to diverge. In theory, the feudal system was so arranged that every worker — from peasant to manorial lord to noble — worked some percentage of his time in support of the king, the taxes gained in this way being used to sustain the kingdom in difficult times and to bring arms and armies needed to protect the land. Also in theory, there was no such thing as a citizen; all were *subjects* of the king and, as such, theoretically in his employ to the degree God (and the king) willed it and the nation needed it.[3] But in practice, as Homans showed in his study of English villagers in the thirteenth century, the villages were self-governing, elected their own sheriffs and bailiffs, their own constables and watchmen, and paid them for their work (usually part-time) out of a local village treasury.[4] With the growth of cities in the later Middle Ages, the craft guilds grew strong, and the mayors of cities such as Paris had to contract with them for the construction of roads or municipal buildings. All the modern conflicts between strong unions and the upper echelons of a social system were anticipated by such actions as the mason's strike against the Mayor of Paris in 1490 over the question of payment and hours worked in the building of the city's brick streets.[5]

The Renaissance, a time of major civic growth and expansion, saw the beginning of the subversion of public service work toward the ends of private capitalists and entrepreneurs. The intrigue that characterized the Italian states was nowhere so evident as in the governmental realm. Machiavelli, it must be remembered, was a somewhat disgruntled civil servant and minor aristocrat who retired to write *The Prince*. The turning of public works to private ends — and thus the manipulation of the public service occupations — became more possible than in the Middle Ages because of the early actions of the merchant princes in smashing the power of the guilds.[6]

In the succeeding centuries, in the seventeenth and eighteenth in particular, the foundations for the European civil service were laid down in each major nation, reaching perhaps the peak of efficiency in Prussia and the peak of inefficiency in Czarist Russia and the eastern Europe described by Franz Kafka. In England, a tradition of public service by the social elite grew up which is present even to this day, although Young states that the high bureaucracy is increasingly becoming a "meritocracy" rather than a preserve of Old Etonians.[7]

In the American case, there has been a slow progression from the essentially feudal concept of public service found in Puritan Massachusetts to the present wide and complex sector of public service occupations. In Puritan Massachusetts, the community policed itself and governed itself at the village level, very much on the model of the English village of the thirteenth century.[8] Thus most public servants were part-time, except for the schoolteacher. This innovation, in the area of public education, has been discussed in the last chapter. It is one of the first recognitions of the need for a "professional" type of public servant.

The Jacksonian era is known as the era of the spoils system, when supposedly the appointments made by Jackson, even at high governmental levels, contrasted heavily with those made by John Adams and Thomas Jefferson, who deliberately only appointed the social elite to federal positions. In fact, as Aronson's study indicates, nepotism and elitism characterized the federal appointments of Jackson almost as much as they did those of Jefferson and Adams. There were both functional and ideological reasons for the change in image, however. Jackson had been elected on an anti-elitist platform, yet he knew that only educated men could be trusted with high governmental office and the only educated men were members of the elite. So he compromised, by slightly increasing the proportion of self-made elite members in his cabinet and in high federal positions. But the majority were still, inevitably, the descendants and relatives of the earlier American aristocracy of birth and wealth.[9] In the South, the planter aristocracy either directly monopolized the public offices or saw to it that "their" men held them. Only at the lower ranks did the mob enter and overthrow the political adherents of the previous inhabitants, at the local and state levels and the lower rungs of the federal bureaucracy. It was the turmoil at these lower ranks that eventually led to the establishment of the civil service system as a protection, as a form of job security and insulation from direct political qualifications for government employment.

Although the rise of public employment following the Industrial Revolution was closely related to the rise in number of schoolteachers and the growth in population size and its concentration in cities, it was not until the reaction to the Depression of the 1930s that a new quality entered the public occupational sector — its massive increase in size, functional importance, and thus, ultimately, its power in the overall society. Much of the Roosevelt legislation created new public service jobs, or so expanded the welfare system of the nation that its administration began to demand an increasing number of employees at all ranks, from the professionals to the Civil Conservation Corps members. Following close upon the Depression came World War II, and the barriers between public and private sectors dissolved, in effect permanently. Today we have millions in public service and millions more employed in corporations that do 80 per cent or more of their business with the government. May we call the engineer in the Bureau of Sanitation a public employee and the engineer in a defense plant working for the Department of Defense, under contract through his employer, a civilian employee? Technically, yes, but sociologically, at a deeper level, the issue is clear. The trend toward the present complex society has led to an increasing need for coordination of activities which is being filled by government bureaucrats, private monopolies of public service functions (the Bell System), or corporations under government contract. The segment of the society in public employment is now large enough that an analysis of the public service must specify the subgroup of the public sector being considered. In fact, at the present time, the biggest problem is to distinguish an experiential, functional, and conflict-of-interest analysis of the public service sector from an analysis of the whole society.

THE EXPERIENCE OF PUBLIC SERVICE

The sector of public employment is now so broad as to make even the complex world-within-a-world found in the military and the educational fields nothing but subgroups of this sector. Keeping in mind that most educators and all military men are public employees, and that we have already considered the experience and world view of these occupational groups, why should we treat the "public service" experience as an entity? The answer to this question is partially related to the aims of the book; covering the same ground more than once is not unacceptable if each new approach *adds* something. In this case, what is of interest is the distinctively *public* nature of public service occupations, in terms of the contingencies which this public status has for experience in the occupational groups.

For an understanding of the experience of public service work, the social stratification of the field is of critical importance. Under the common umbrella of public employment lie such jobs as President and diplomat on the one hand, and garbage collector on the other. Thus in considering the usual experience-related issues — motivation for choice of job, career pattern, career contingencies, occupational culture, and overall occupational world view — we will need to make our comparisons between high-status, medium-status, and low-status occupations in the public service sector.

MOTIVATION AND THE CHOICE OF PUBLIC SERVICE

The stereotype of the typical public employee is that he "fell into" his job, or that "no one else but the city would hire him." In fact, as the complexity of the field indicates, it depends on which jobs are being considered. Some public service occupations, especially those near the top of the power and prestige ladder, demand major sacrifice, and many at the bottom are not sinecures but rather grueling, unpleasant, poorly paid work.

By level of entry, those at the top levels, especially in the federal system and at the peak of the bureaucracies in major cities, have a level of altruism, or at least non-material interest, in the choice of a public career. On the other hand, the opportunities for experience in this complex and conflict-ridden atmosphere may outweigh the lower salaries which the individuals with college and post-graduate experience could almost always make on the outside. In addition, as Neustadt and other students of presidential and high governmental power indicate, the experience of being powerful enough to work one's will on the system is a strong pull for some into public service. Whether they will succeed in this effort is not the issue. The belief that they may be powerful, in those who desire power, is a classically strong attraction to the upper ranks in the public sector.

The middle ranks in the public orbit are best subdivided in terms of "upper middle" and "lower middle" occupations. The professionals in service — the social workers, engineers, psychiatrists, and sociologists — enter public service out of a mix of materialistic interests (especially in federal employment), interest in being where the decisions are made (a form of power-seeking), and some genuine altruism. There is in most cases some sacrifice involved, though not as great as for those appointed to the top ranks. The "dedication" syndrome of the technocrat in government is a reality, especially at the federal level, though it is mediated by a keen interest in most cases in the outside professional consequences of working permanently in the public service.[10] For the "lower middle" public occupations, the classical reasons for entry are probably most appropriate: friends in clerical work in the bureaucracies, a family whose elders were also in the civil service, the certainty that at least overt racial and religious discrimination will not affect salary level. Specific regional factors are also relevant to entry in given communities, as with the Irish ethnic group and the education field in Boston.[11] The group who, as a matter of course, would enter such employment at this level, by and large come from the lower middle class, where such work can reasonably be viewed as steadier if not more lucrative than non-public employment at about the same skill level.

The poor have until quite recently been excluded from public employment through the education requirements for temporary or permanent public employment. With the exception of the least desirable jobs, such as garbage collection or road work, the poor do not have the qualities required. Also, even in one of these examples (road work), nepotism and political pull often operate to provide summer work for the college student or sons of politicians rather than for the fathers of poor children.

THE CAREER PATTERN: STRUCTURE AND CONTINGENCIES

In general, the career patterns of those who are in public service at any given time can best be understood in long-term or developmental perspective by contrasting what the government needs from the individual with what the individual needs from the government job. Those who are in demand have the leverage to construct any number of a set of alternative career patterns, and they do so; those who need the government must conform to its rather structured and limited definitions of "acceptable" career pattern. In almost all cases this latter pattern is the classical bureaucratic step-by-step progression noticed by Weber in Prussia and idealized into his model of the bureaucratic career.[12]

Individuals who enter public service in or near the top — by appointment or professional qualification — have at any time the option of leaving this service for better paying jobs on the outside, unless for example there is a major recession, in which case the government regains its leverage even on its most skilled members. But in general, because of the demand for skill and the capacity of private industry to pay, as well as a desire to have ex-government men "parachuting" into their plants for contract and grant purposes, the skilled top men in the federal and state bureaucracies and those in top positions in major cities can structure their careers in a continuum of arrangements between being totally "in" the government and being totally "out." A minimum of possible arrangements include the following: the "in-and-out" pattern (Daniel P. Moynihan in the Kennedy and Nixon administrations), the consultant–inside job–consultant pattern (Kissinger in the Kennedy, Johnson, and Nixon administrations), the long-term consultant pattern, the *ad hoc* special commission pattern, and the in-with-a-simultaneous-university-teaching-job-out pattern, a new arrangement which some government employees in the professions prefer and have been able to get their agency heads to accept.

As we noted above, the career pattern of those in the lower middle ranks and below is along the lines of *de facto* commitment over a period of years which may in many cases be officially recognized as "civil service status." Here the pattern is determined by the complex of higher administrators in the given bureaucracy, the individual's ability to change jobs from one bureaucracy to another (very difficult to do except in Washington, D.C.), the budget levels available to create new bureaucratic positions, and thus create more opportunities for rapid internal mobility, and finally, the policy of the bureaucracy on internal promotion versus the reservation of upper middle and upper jobs for the various forms of in-and-outers. As with private business and industry, the lower on the occupational ladder one goes, the less the concept of career as phased development and increase in responsibility is relevant and the more the idea of "years of service in the same job" becomes the concept of "career" used both by the employee and the bureaucracy itself.

Contingencies for career advancement within bureaucratic channels show a posture of official ideological difference as compared to some prominent career contingencies outside the system and a set of marked actual similarities to such outside contingencies, in spite of the ideology. For example, discrimination according to sex is theoretically prohibited in government service, but the same male-female ratios in the clerical as compared to the administrative jobs are found in most public employment areas as they are in private. In federal employment, the racial discrimination in recent years has diminished somewhat, but the barriers to administrative advancement outside the federal area are still clear. Until the advent of black central cities, this racial barrier in public employment will probably still hold for the major industrial areas. In addition, the ethnic variable is relevant in those areas where an ethnic group is a major constituent of the electorate. In general, the lower the status of the job, the more the social characteristics of the individual become the major career contingencies, whereas the higher the status of the work, the more basic skills and outside social contacts become the relevant variables.

THE EVOLUTION OF OPERATING STYLES

The experience of public service work is distinctive primarily because of the public-representative nature of the job definition. Even at menial levels, the person represents "his government" to the community. But communities differ, and the evolution of personal and group styles depends to some degree on the nature of the community with which the occupational group is in continuous contact. What may happen in individual interaction can also, given a reasonable time period, become the operating style of a group. Wilson's study on the operating styles of policemen in different types of communities, for example, isolated at least three major styles for acting out this particular public service role: the "watchman" style, the "legalistic" style, and the "service" style.[13] In general, the watchman style entailed observation and non-punitive intervention, whereas individuals and police departments with a legalistic style tended to "enforce the law," with more parking tickets and higher arrest rates, for example. The service orientation — the policeman as courteous helper to the community — seemed far more possible in the homogenous upper-middle-class suburb than anywhere else. The important point to be made here, and it is emphasized by Wilson for the police but may very probably be generalized to many other public service occupations, is that the style of operation of the public servant group can be specific to a locale. It evolves out of the personalities of the administrators, the activities of the group of service workers, and the types of stresses or supports from the public which the group is "serving." The angry, frustrated white policemen in the black ghetto will evolve an operating style relevant to his setting, as will the teacher in an upper-class suburban high school. The experience of the public servant inevitably involves the public in a direct way, as the consumer of services. The public encountered will make a difference to the operating styles.

FOUR OCCUPATIONAL WORLD VIEWS

The experience of dealing with the public under the conflict-laden, confusing working conditions of public occupations necessarily results in a set of divergent world views as well as operating styles. In the case of the elite in high government positions, the occupational world view can shade off into a form of occupational disease — one might call it "bureaucratic messianism":

> The functionary's characteristic version of the public interest reflects both a pious, self-effacing, "good soldier" ethic and a monumental arrogance fit for a Florentine nobleman. The arrogance grows out of the piety: "I am in the service of a Cause; everything I do is for It, nothing is for Me." [14]

In general, the "credibility" gap that often develops between the public and those who are presumably serving them in high places originates in part in the powerful bureaucrat's view that "we know the best for them." The technocratic attitude — that the experts in government should plan for the people and not be restrained by their "uninformed" wishes — can easily be combined with autocratic political form, although at present it is found in all types of industrialized societies.[15]

A common occupational outlook found in the upper-middle ranks of the power hierarchy in public service is the "cosmopolitan" orientation, using this term both in its sense of orientation toward a professional group rather than a locale, and toward the national scene in governmental affairs. The participation of "cosmopolitan" bureaucrats both in national governmental associations and national meetings of their original disciplines is quite common. For example, a cosmopolitan mayor will belong to the national association of mayors and the police chief with this orientation may be a member of the international association of police chiefs. In addition, the workers with this orientation are more likely to be academically inclined and are more likely to use consultant expertise than are the "locals." As in education, in public service at large the vast majority of public service workers are probably local in orientation, and the residence rules in many cities (as a condition of civil service status) do nothing to counter this trend. This complicates the function of the worker in the community, however, especially in regulatory agency work. Loyalty to one's ethnic group or neighborhood, or to the local politicians whose influence got one the job, often supersedes loyalty to the bureaucracy where one works or to the citizenry which is employing one. In many major cities there is a marked increase in absenteeism during the times of local elections, when the "informal" patronage system is revealed through the extensive campaign work done by cadres of local civil service workers.[16]

Activists are beginning to enter the public service occupations. Their perspective tends to bring about a contrast with the views of the citizenry who disagree with their politics, the powerful groups in the community, and also with many powerful people within the bureaucracies where they work. Perhaps the classical case here was described by Moynihan when he showed the way the phrase "maximum feasible participation" was interpreted by different groups of young workers in the Community Action Program of the Office of Economic Opportunity. The idea was to have community representation (but not real community power) in the action programs. But what happened in a segment of the communities was a concerted effort by OEO-paid activists to organize the community to take over the Community Action Program's staff functions and to fight both city hall and the federal government.[17] In most cases this led to the eventual firing of the activists. This was not surprising; as Coser remarked, governments do not finance their opposition.[18] However, this last issue brings us to a problem which we can consider more thoroughly in a functional manner — the degree to which *changing* any social system is possible by those who work within the system in those positions which exemplify its structure and which by definition are constructed to serve all of it.

DIVISION OF LABOR IN THE PUBLIC SERVICE

TYPES OF BUREAUCRACY

In carrying out the public mandate, public service occupations can be seen as performing different sets of overt and covert functions for groups in the wider society. Following Howton, it is possible to note at least four major functional types of public service occupations.[19] The first two are the *core* occupations, dealing with the central problems of the maintenance of order and public safety — the courts, the police, and the fire department — and the *regulative* agencies — the Federal Communications Commission, the Security and Exchange Commission, and the Atomic Energy Commission. On the differences of these two kinds of functions, Howton notes that the former are definitely basic and require the application of laws without too much flexibility, whereas occupational tasks in the second group are interpretive by definition, and afford far more scope for creativity and ingenuity in government service.[20]

The third type of role, that of the health and welfare functionary, deals with the adjudication of rights to public service required by the people, in contrast to the rights and responsibilities in the economic sphere which are the area for the regulatory agencies. Finally, there are "action bureaucracies" such as the Office of Economic Opportunity and the urban renewal agencies, whose functional role is to change the nature of the existent status quo (or so they present themselves, at any rate).[21]

To the society's elite, its middle class, and its poor, the latent functions of these four types of bureaucratic functions differ, depending on which level of the society is being encountered by the bureaucratic groups. For example, the "core functions" of police and fire work and garbage collection, routinely protect and serve the elite and the middle class, but police brutality and lack of adequate public service are characteristic of the ghetto areas of communities. For the "regulative" occupations, the problems are usually at the level where the elite and the middle class have relevant activities, and relations tend to be cordial. It is here that the exchange in job career pattern between the government and the private occupational world is especially high.

For the service occupations, the clientele is usually defined as the poor, and there are often divergencies between the theoretical aims of such programs and the actual services provided. Most societies do not have an overwhelming commitment to their poor, even with the existence of welfare programs. Thus either the rules for public support of the poor are gradually amended to benefit the middle class at the expense of the poor, as Titmuss has observed for England and as the author has recently observed for the United States,[22] or a major structured strain is built into the role itself, as the author showed with the role of the rehabilitation counselor in a state agency.[23] In this case — one of many such in public service — caseload size, lack of funds, and time pressures force the counselors to serve the least handicapped first, for they can be served most quickly at the least expense. The more marginal, the poorer, the racial minority group member all are avoided in terms of first preference for service. The pressures on the front-line bureaucrat are in part ultimately political pressures on the high bureaucracy to limit the amount of money spent on such people. Thus studies in the public health and welfare field indicate that mental and physical disease rates increase, and rates of service for those in need *decrease*, with every step down the social class structure of the society.

The fourth type of bureaucratic group, the action bureaucracy, has the manifest function of changing the society in a "positive" direction, i.e., of improving it in some way. Yet the OEO was directed primarily at the middle-class voter, in terms of the political usefulness which the action had as a token that "we are doing something," e.g., fighting a War on Poverty. But it is documented that when a group of such bureaucrats become action-oriented on the side of the poor, as did the Child Development Group of Mississippi, the powerful federal bureaucracies and politicians (e.g., Senator Stennis of Mississippi, the Chairman at the time of the House Armed Services Committee) act immediately to stop the expenditure of public funds for such projects. By contrast, Anderson documents the way the federal urban renewal program was used by private developers as a way of getting their friends in mayors' offices to confiscate land from one private party to sell to them at cost. The "federal bulldozer," to use Anderson's term, always managed to tear down slums and relocate blacks, diminish the available pool of housing, and remain unresponsive to the wishes of the poor and the black.[24] In general, therefore, though the manifest function of core, regulative, service, and action bureaucracies is to provide for public needs, they do so most thoroughly for the elite and the middle class, and in many cases to an insignificant extent for the poor. "Them that has, gets" is a fair observation of the latent function of public service bureaucracies in the American society of the present time.

COMPARATIVE ASPECTS: THE SYSTEMS ROLE OF PUBLIC SERVICE GROUPS

The division of social labor in terms of the distinction between "public" and "private" is obviously relevant only to capitalist countries. In socialist and communist countries all are, at least in theory, working for the state. Thus we must ask a set of questions on the role of "public service" occupations in different types of regimes. First, are there inherently "public" occupations, even if the entire population is publicly employed? Second, how does the public occupational sector relate to the process of industrialization? Third, what is the relationship between the exercise of broadly *political* power and the political-social role of bureaucratically based occupational groups? These three questions can be briefly considered for the Soviet Union, the developing areas of Africa, and South American nations such as Argentina, Brazil, Venezuela, Peru, and Chile, all of whom share a contrast between a Western or Ladino urban population and a rural Indian peasantry. We cannot analyze the role of public service occupations in any sort of definitive manner here, but the comparison should allow us to raise a series of questions for further research.

In the Soviet Union, although there is an economic system whereby everyone works for the state as a "public employee," it is as possible as it is in the West to differentiate between a government bureaucrat and a worker who is not a member of the government. The critical issue is rather a functional one — to what degree is the worker in the primary industrial sector, in secondary production, or in the area of *services*. All Communist party officials and members of the government bureaucracy, as well as those in bureaucratic managerial roles, can be considered as government officials, along with the Presidium and Politburo of the Soviet Union and those responsible for internal and external surveillance. Beyond this it is a matter of definition. Since the health service system and the educational system are centrally administered and are service-providing, it is possible to see the existence of a Soviet service sector parallel to that in the United States; we have considered both health and education areas previously for the Soviet Union. So too with the basic order-preserving and defense services. The regulatory "agencies," although they exist functionally in the Soviet Union, do not exist in the American sense, as all agencies are regulated through the central and regional planning arms of the economic ministry and the Party. "Activist" bureaucracies in the sense of the OEO are not considered necessary by the Soviet Union, but the propaganda-based mobilization of the population to meet norms of production is a constant activity of the central government. Formal opposition to the regime as part of the regime is officially prohibited and administratively unheard of, but of course this does not prevent internal warfare between informal groups in the government. These battles, however, tend to be ideological in nature, except for the long-term conflict between the military and the civilian sectors of the government, which we considered in an earlier chapter.

Industrialization in the Soviet Union may have led to an increase in the size of production organizations, and thus in the broad sense of the term to an increase in the number of "bureaucrats." But the Czarist civil service was extensive in size. The question of political power versus bureaucratic power, a third area for inspection in a systems approach, would seem to support the idea that in the Soviet Union the Communist party holds the major decision-making power for the overall system, and that conflicts within this structure lead to temporarily greater independence for subsectors such as the military or factory managers. In general, although the Soviet Union is not a totally monolithic state, it is definitely a heavily centralized socialist state with a single bureaucratic chain of command. The role of the public servant cannot be understood as clearly in occupational terms as it can in bureaucratic positional terms or in political terms of membership or non-membership in the Communist party elite at a given time.

In the developing African nations, a different set of problems revolves about the role of public service workers in the social system. As Bottomore notes, they are the educated elite in nations that are in large part illiterate. Having as students a European experience as well, they are often somewhat sympathetic to the European powers or the American corporate power in their nations, but are capable of being radicalized more rapidly than any other segment, should they change their viewpoint.[25] The elite bureaucratic corps in these countries are in a cross-pressured situation. For a minority, the educational experience and the role in the developing country lead to a change toward radical (and in earlier years) anti-colonialist activism; in the more conservatively oriented, it may lead to a political stance which supports either traditional tribal elites, foreign corporations, or a combination of power blocs. The questions we are asking relate to this dilemma. In the rapidly industrializing state, whom does the native bureaucrat *serve?* The traditional elements in the society may oppose him, whereas the colonial or external powers support him. Second, industrialization may lead to the increasing complexity of his society and the breakdown of traditional "social service" relationships, so that a new mandate is created for public service workers such as himself. Finally, although the bureaucratic elite in developing nations may be an elite, it is often in second position compared to major tribal leaders, new politicians, and the owners and managers of the foreign-owned and domestic corporations. In general, the bureaucrats serve as go-betweens. They mediate the conflict between traditional leaders and the international corporations, and the conflict between the rural and the urban regions. As such, they are often under strong pressure, even more than is the case with these groups in the Soviet Union or the United States.

The case of the South American nations illustrates a variation of the African case, but here there is a racial and regional split between the "Ladino" city-dwellers and the rural, primarily Indian and mestizo peasantry. The traditional rural dislike of the bureaucrat, or the Federale, is based on a combination of the gap between city and countryside and the historical record of exploitation of the rural Indian poor by the elite of a different racial and cultural background, who used federal and local government agents to act out their wishes.[26] Thus the onset of industrialization in such countries had complex effects, and since only a few regions in a few South American countries are presently heavily industrialized, the traditional patterns of relationship between urban Ladino bureaucrats and rural peasants are still more often in force than not. In defining whom the bureaucrat serves in this system, therefore, we are required to answer geographically and racially. "Public service" in the Latin American regions has historically meant service to the elite or in the interests of the elite. Industrialization has not essentially changed the direction of the service, as those in power have not, except in certain periods in certain countries, aided the poor through any major increase in the public health and social welfare programs. As to political power, the pattern of the Latin American countries is more similar to the Soviet case than to the African case in terms of the lack of independence of the bureaucratic group, even as a secondary force. They are used in the majority of these countries by the elite to serve its interests. The Cuban experiment is perhaps the only major deviation from the typical Latin American pattern. Here the participation of the citizens in government, and the special form of socialist state which is under construction, finds few parallels in either East or West, with the possible exception of some similarities it shares with Yugoslavia and other modified socialist regimes. A more socially representative and responsible bureaucracy appears to be found here than in the more usual form of Latin American oligarchy.[27]

CONFLICTS OF INTEREST: PUBLIC OCCUPATIONS AND THE PUBLIC

PRESTIGE VERSUS FUNCTIONAL POWER

In addition to understanding bureaucratic roles in terms of the relationship between the group and the community — as order-maintaining, regulatory, service-providing, or action-oriented — it is possible to look at the groups from the point of view of the prestige they have in the wider society as contrasted with the latent power they have to paralyze the society if they act differently from their usual mode of operations. From this viewpoint, the progression above is from the general to the special, for all the community needs the fire and police, whereas special segments deal with regulatory, service, and action agencies. On the other hand, the scale of prestige and reward does not follow this pattern, and groups needed by all are not always rewarded as if they were. The scale of functional power — degree of importance to the system — is discrepant in some major areas from the scale of prestige and material reward. This is an inherent and potential source of conflict which is becoming more of an overt one with each increase in the unionization of public employees and their willingness to strike. Four kinds of combinations (actually each variable is continuous) are basically important: occupations which are high in functional power and also high in prestige and reward, those which are low in functional power but high in prestige and reward, those high in functional power but low in prestige and reward, and those low in both power and the prestige-reward dimension.

The high power-high reward group are the classical bureaucratic elites of Europe, the cabinet officials and top-level American federal bureaucrats in the federal government, and high ranking state employees and the managers of large cities. These groups are, as we noted before, often recruited from outside elites or upper socioeconomic strata and consider government service a form of patriotic sacrifice. The power they have is not used to mobilize higher prestige or reward, for they already have a fair amount of personal prestige, and extra rewards are possible at any time by leaving public service. Therefore in this group one does not normally find occupational combination against the system of an occupation-based self-interest motivation, although of course corruption in high places can be found anywhere in the government, at any level.

Those with low functional power but with reasonably high prestige, often with a professional skill, do not often consider striking in their own interest for essentially practical reasons. There are many cases when those with professional skills may be nearly powerless within the government but in good position to operate occupationally with freedom outside the government. The conflict for individuals of this type — the heads of regional offices in the federal bureaucracy are a good example — is that the positions are much less powerful than either they or most others assume. But as W. I. Thomas stated, "Social facts which are perceived as real are real in their consequences." Many medium and lower-level bureaucrats will tell their friends and colleagues that they "control" several million dollars in grant funds, whereas the reality of decision-making and power tells us that they are a minor cog in a big wheel. Still, the lack of consciousness of occupational self-interest makes this group as politically system-loyal as those with high power and prestige.

One of the two critical subgroups, and the main cross-pressured group in systems terms, are those occupations such as police, firemen, postal workers, and garbage workers, which are high in functional power but low in prestige. In these cases the leverage is extensive — think of the Montreal police strikes or a refusal of firemen to work, the New York City garbage workers strike of 1969, or the national postal workers strike of 1970. This leverage — the ability to rapidly paralyze a complex social system because of the critical nature of the service provided to all in the system — is becoming the basis for bargaining power. The *potential* for pressure on the system to raise the reward, if not the prestige, has always been there. But the lack of occupational consciousness — and the unwillingness to break anti-strike laws — withheld this group until, in their eyes, the rewards fell too far behind their inherent functional power to get more in the way of rewards.

The fourth major group, those medium or low in functional power and also low in reward, presents a different problem. One example of this is the mental hospital aide. The mental hospital aides, as most workers in low-paying and non-critical jobs, know that few people care enough about mental patients to cause a major crisis in a few days if they should strike. Thus what they need and see ahead is a form of strong unionization *across* bureaucracies and occupational lines — such as the American Federation of City and State Municipal Employees — to collectively bargain across all state settings, under the threat of a *general* strike of state employees. In numbers and cross-setting unity there is strength, for these state employees who are low in reward and low in functional power. This parallels the difference between political activism and power of the professional organizations, such as the AMA, who have functional power on occupational lines, and the CIO, whose power is national and cross-setting in industry, rather than occupation-based.

PUBLIC INTEREST VERSUS OCCUPATIONAL INTEREST: EMERGING ISSUES

Because of the increasingly important role of public service occupations, the issues within these occupational groups become basically important issues to the wider society. With the onset of the welfare-state form of bureaucratized societal organization, Thoenes suggests that the "bureaucratic elite" has begun to develop a potentially totalitarian leverage over the average citizen. He suggests that if a bureaucracy gains enough power it may then be able to use the withholding of its services — medical care in a socialized system, for example — as a threat for those who are not compliant.[28] It is not necessary to go as far as Thoenes in his suspicions of the political attitudes of bureaucrats to see that a highly centralized system, regardless of its general ideological rationale, can have an influence on people to the extent that they depend on it. This leads us to ask the basic question which is raised in different ways by a historical, existential, and comparative functional approach: how much may a public service occupation act in its own interest if this may compromise the public interest?

To begin with, it should be understood that there is no scientific answer to this question, which is essentially a value problem. Restated, it becomes, how much *should* public servants have in terms of power and reward, and how much power *should* the citizens have over what the public service occupations have in these areas? This immediately brings the problem down to the level of competing values, such as freedom versus efficiency. The Soviet educational system is extremely efficient, for example, and Mussolini got the trains in Italy to run on time. The level of independence or dependence on public intervention which a nation allows its public bureaucracies is essentially a political issue and one which will change from year to year.

Another aspect of the problem lies in the area of relative reward for service rendered. In a totally "public" system, such as a socialist state, the conflict between "public" and private wage scales does not exist in theory. But in practice the rewards to members of the Communist party and those loyal to its aims are higher than to the ordinary citizen-worker-employee. In systems with competing public and private occupational spheres, the issue is complicated by questions of proportion of groups within or outside the public sector, as this relates to their capacity to organize and increase the resources at their command. For example, in the American system, most physicians are in private practice and most teachers are public employees. Organization on occupational lines by physicians becomes a professional interest-group form of politics, but when teachers organize — regardless of whether they do so through the NEA or the teacher's unions — they are organizing as a group in public service with a vastly different set of political consequences. The newer legislation passed under the Kennedy administration for federal employees, and some state legislation for state and city employees, legalizes "collective bargaining," but in most cases does not legalize their right to strike.[29] Yet strikes are an increasingly common phenomenon. The public reacts strongly against such actions, for the public is the eventual consumer of public services and the eventual source of the public servant's pay as well. As the salaries of public service workers climb to competitive levels, the public is certain to be even more politically involved in attempts to determine the mandate, role, and powers of public servants as organized groups as well as individuals. Suburban communities have voted their schools out of existence in a few cases, and local ghetto communities insist on a greater role in the service staffing as well as the determination of service goals.

The ultimate issue in this increasing politicizing of the public service occupations lies in the exchange which is presumably at the base of all occupational relations. Historically the public has exploited the middle and lower rank public servant in the sense of paying these individuals far less than their functional contribution to the maintenance of the society would merit on some more impartial or abstract scale of reward for contributions made. Given this set of conditions, a vicious circle was created in which the less talented went into public work, ultimately justifying the low rewards in the eyes of the public, who could point to the inefficiency and incompetence of those in the jobs. The new militancy may lead to increased conflict, but also to a future situation where the more talented and efficient will choose to go into public service work, as it is attractive materially as well as in value terms. So a clear distinction needs to be made between the values governing the way the occupational field is presently set up for recruitment and reward, and the needs of any complex society for a skilled public service group that is working in their interest. If a society desires, and votes to perpetuate, an unskilled and powerless civil service, refuses to reform it in constructive ways, and refuses to reward the workers for services rendered, then any such society will sow what it reaps.

CHAPTER FOURTEEN

THE CAREER ACTIVIST

In each occupational field thus far considered, the overall functions of the occupational group contributed to the preservation of the existing exchange system, and thus to the overall social system. In a few fields, the activities of the members have sometimes had an unnoticed role in changing the system, such as the role of the truly creative scientist or artist. In addition, altruistic activists in many occupational fields are becoming more common. These individuals work to transform the goals of their particular field from service to the haves to an increased pattern of service to the have-nots. The distinction between these occupation-related forms of creative social change and the persons to be called "career activists" is subtle but important. The career activist is a full-time lifetime worker whose skills are those of the organization and leadership of men to bring about social change. Social change itself is their profession. Because of the extreme sacrifices which this type of career involves, a high measure of value commitment of an altruistic sort is usually necessary, and the number of individuals in any given society who maintain this commitment, and this role, over a lifetime is rather small. But their sociological importance is far out of proportion to their numbers.

HISTORICAL DIMENSIONS OF ACTIVISM

Michael Walzer suggests that the Puritans in England were the first true political radicals and career activists, because of their program producing a new type of modern, value-committed man (the "saint"), a new form of social organization (the congregation), a new and consciously constructed form of social contract (the covenant among the brethren) and a new kind of society (the holy commonwealth).[1] He comments on the radicalizing effect of Puritanism, and the Puritan divines, in the political arena, and suggests that biographical study of the new leaders will show that

> in the sixteenth and seventeenth centuries radical innovation in politics (especially when this involved the cooperation of numbers of men) was inconceivable without the moral support of religion — and that religion probably provided the major incentive for innovation.[2]

When the Puritans came to the New World, they created in Massachusetts a form of "holy commonwealth" that very soon began to punish dissenters, such as Anne Hutchinson, driving them both from the community and the Puritan church.[3] Although the Puritans were activists in England, in the New World they became conservative defenders of their newly created status quo. This first historical example illustrates an important point — that the career activist maintains his function and does not necessarily stop with his first success in order to defend that achievement — a point ignored by amateur activists without a sense of history.

The American Revolution provided two forms of career activist with an opportunity: the social reformer from the elite and the pamphleteer. In the latter group, men such as Thomas Paine were truly far more radical in their long-range aims than men such as John Adams. Thus with the winning of the war against England and completion of the Constitutional Convention, the elite leaders made an abrupt turn toward the conservative side, and the more radical activists found themselves suddenly far more isolated.

The historian Turner believed that with the expansion of the frontier to the West a natural, frontier-based radicalism grew up out of the wide-open conditions of the West, one which "bred" decades of American radicals from the 1830s to the 1880s.[4] Yet a more careful inspection of this period, and of the period of the Civil War in North-South relations, suggests rather the urban origins of many of the career activists in the areas of abolitionism and anti-monopoly activism. For example, Destler shows that the theorists and activists of Populism were based in the East and big cities of the Middle West, such as Chicago, and their aims were to unite the farmers and urban labor as two groups exploited by the robber barons and the corrupt government of the time.[5] The career abolitionists — Channing, Phillips Brooks, William Lloyd Garrison — were essentially urban intellectuals whose career activism took them into rural as well as urban areas.

In the later years of the nineteenth century, a new type of activist grew up on the American scene. These individuals were in many ways pragmatic in their aims and specific in their target groups, for example, Samuel Gompers and the ladies' garment workers of New York City.[6] Interest-based activist organization for short-term gain became the goal of these men, in contrast to the broad idealism of the Populist agitators or the moral fervor of the abolitionists. In their narrow orbit, they were successful, and their success led to the formation of the first durable working-class interest groups. However, the question of the scope and long-range aims of activist orientation was raised by this development more clearly than before. Although activists had always been aware that only some segments of the population would respond, the career activists who set out to organize the labor unions deliberated and then narrowed their focus at the outset to the organizable craft groups.

We cannot go into the political history of the period from the turn of the century to World War II. But the contrast between broad idealistic movements with diffuse aims (the International Workers of the World) and the development of new organizations for new specific groups of workers (the CIO) demanded the different career activists we have discussed for earlier eras. The fifties and sixties, however, have introduced two new types of activism and activist career patterns to the more traditional species. The first could be called the "own-group" activist and the second the youth-focused activist. In the fifties, the first major expression of indigenous activists on a large scale was found in the civil rights movement. It must be noted here how many of the well-known activists in history — Kropotkin, Lenin, Phillips, George — were members either of the elite of their society or its middle class.[7] In the civil rights movement, increasingly, the idea grew that the career activists should primarily come from within the ranks of the group itself. The impetus to organize might come from outside, but the recruitment patterns increasingly involve those activists who come from the group itself. Thus Alinsky sought out Mexican-Americans such as Chavez, because he knew they would be more effective than he, Alinsky, would be in working with the people.[8] The black power concept, when it was first presented, spelled an end to white career activist action "on behalf of" the black community.[9]

Finally, a new activist career pattern appears to be developing which will probably be around for quite a while — the career activist who chooses youth for its constituency, because of their critical and strategic role vis-a-vis the rest of the social system. This involves those of middle age, such as Dellinger and the activist lawyer Kunstler; those no longer of college age who were founders of student movements, such as Tom Hayden, one of the organizers of SDS and now a general anti-establishment activist; and the youth of college and high school age themselves.

A newer development in the young activist ranks is traceable to elements of revolutionary ideology of a non-Western variety — "every man his own leader." The ideal here is essentially antithetical to the actions of the professional career activist. In a sense, a segment of the anti-war and anti-establishment movement at the present time believe that the professional career organizer can be coopted, or at least identified, isolated, neutralized, and perhaps imprisoned, by a repressive regime. To this way of thinking, specialization by given individuals in social change will not lead to social change itself, which cannot occur unless all are transformed in value terms to work together, toward new goals.

Whether it is functionally possible to have a movement with organizational direction and without leaders, thereby disproving Michel's "iron law" of the inevitable oligarchical development of political movements, is not possible to say at this moment.[10] There are problems involved, in all eras, in carrying out the work of an activist. But it is possible to say that the variety of career activists presently observable on the modern American scene — diffusely moral, specifically interest-based, race and issue-based — testifies to the flux of the present social process. It also signifies that a repressive regime is not yet upon us — for nothing signifies one more quickly than the absence of this occupational group.

THE ACTIVIST EXPERIENCE

Erik Erikson has written at length on the complex of psychodynamic, social, and historical factors that go to produce the careers of such men as Luther and Gandhi.[11] Once the simple perspective of one intellectual discipline is breached, it becomes obvious that no one can completely explain why one career activist becomes world famous, or even simply succeeds, when another one fails to make a mark at all on the world. Yet there are some patterns that seem common to most activist careers, in terms of initial motivation and career entry, the confirming experience, typical career patterns, career contingencies, and types of activist world view.

ENTRY INTO ACTIVISM

Although many individuals at some point in their lives burn with a sense of injustice and wish to dedicate themselves to changing the existing status quo, only a small proportion ever make the step to a career. For some, such as Alinsky, the choice to become an activist comes when a career (in his case in criminology and prison work) becomes secondary to avocational interests. In his words:

> So I started doing my job as a sort of sinecure. I quit right when quitting time came and I got involved in raising money for the International Brigade, for the sharecroppers down South, helping stop the evictions of city people who couldn't pay rent, fighting for public housing. Wherever you turned you saw injustice. The issues stuck out as clearly as they did in a prison. You knew what was good and what was evil. Life was very exciting.[12]

Others, such as Chavez, the leader of the California grape workers, were recruited after outstanding performance in "amateur" activity; in Chavez's case, Alinsky recruited him for a special activist training institute that he was setting up.[13] In most cases, the initial entry into activist work is a combination of part time work, almost always without pay, and recognition by those further into a social movement that the potential recruit would make a good full-time worker. One possible exception — the government-paid "activist" in a government action agency — may have more luxurious initial entry conditions. Whether the "professional reformer" who is a government employee, as in the Poverty program, can be qualified as a genuine activist is a serious question, and one which we considered in the previous chapter.

THE CAREER PATTERN: CONFIRMATION, ALTERNATIVES, CONTINGENCIES

In each activist career, there appears to be a point beyond which continuance of activist work is considered to be, by the individual himself, a point of no return. To the black youth who staged the first sit-in demonstration, this came at a meeting in their college dormitory the previous night when they were challenging each other as to their sincerity. In general, the first jail experience is said to be a very important period in the career commitment — often the time of the activist's first book. Martin Luther King believed that his first jail term served this purpose, as did Ghandi. Saul Alinsky commented that the time was so constructive for him that he *almost* did not want to leave.[14] In general, the *commitment* exists in large part before the first major opposition to the activity of the activist; the *confirmation of the commitment* comes when the individual realizes that no external pressure is going to divert him from his path.

Although activist careers begin with determination and persistence, it is the rare activist who ends his career in the way he began it. The patterns which deviate from this "straight-line" one do so because of a mixture of internal and external forces. For example, one possible end to an activist career has always been a brutal death. Malcolm X, Martin Luther King, Robert Kennedy, Che Guevara are only a few in a long line, and no realistic activist — of whatever political persuasion — counts on a safe career. More commonly a choice by the individual to leave activism can be made because he either rejects the group that he previously identified with, or finds the pull of outside offers too strong to resist. In recent years, the forces of the status quo have increasingly used the cooptation procedure as the most effective way of removing opposition. Thus Alinsky is bombarded with lucrative offers from status quo organizations, and Cesar Chavez — quite early in his career in the California grape strike fight — was offered a salary of $21,000 to work in the Peace Corps.[15] The reverse form of leaving is more final than a choice by the individual. A man may either fall too far behind his constituents, or, like Malcolm X, develop too far ahead of them too fast, and be rejected for this reason.

The contingencies of the more standard occupational fields might be thought to be less relevant to the career patterns and experiences of activists. In general, however, the sex of activists — with the exception of sex-related groups such as the WCTU in the past or Women's Liberation in the present — has been male. Still, the radical organizers are very recently becoming more aware of these biases. In general also, the majority of *career* activists are not young, by definition. It is the one who remains an activist after he has reached adulthood that is a career activist by our definition. Once into the field, however, the age factor does enter into the decision to leave. The need for security which seems so irrelevant at twenty or thirty is viewed differently at forty or fifty. In racial and ethnic group terms, the professional activist is increasingly matching his constituency, but techniques for crossing over the boundaries, plus the reputation of some professional activists which crosses racial lines and inspires trust, can lead to modification here. In socioeconomic status terms, the primary difference observable between the past and the present is the greater number of career activists at the present time who come from the oppressed groups themselves; the altruistic medical and law students are not categorized here as career activists. In general, the degree of communication between an activist and his group — his ability to mobilize them — and the ability of the state and private interest groups to interfere with him make up the most powerful career contingencies of all to those in activist careers.

ACTIVIST PHILOSOPHIES: MORALISTS AND PRAGMATISTS

There appears to be a surface contrast between the outlook of moral reformers such as Martin Luther King and pragmatic organizers such as Saul Alinsky. For example, Alinsky's viewpoint on the civil rights movement was that it was long on values and short on grass-roots organization. In fact, however, the career activist who is primarily single-cause in orientation cannot even maintain the momentum of his group without some practical organizing skills. Nor can a pragmatic organizer endure his many defeats and setbacks or engineer the arrangements between groups which are necessary for progress, without some type of moral commitment to his general cause. In fact, it would seem possible to make a contrast only between the *committed* activist and the essentially inauthentic or self-serving mover of men, who, like Huey Long, provided benefits to the people as a technique for increasing his own political power.[16] Here we may note that in recent years individuals have become public figures who clearly enjoy the adulation of some of the young, but who have no program to espouse and no basic concern for the interests of their constituents. Such exponents of indulgence as Jerry Rubin ("do it") ask little of their constituents except followership and praise, and reap the benefits of national media coverage in their book sales.[17] The mass media have made it easier for such "instant heroes" to gain an audience. But in the long run, the dedicated activist is recognized by his persistence and his willingness to put the *cause* ahead of himself and personal interests. As has been said of Chavez, one doesn't necessarily notice the skilled activist organizer at work, nor does he stand out personally. It's just that when he leaves, things start to happen in a place where he has been, and they don't stop happening until the people get what they want.

The continual concern about cooptation of movements with which the career activist preoccupies himself is an agonizing problem in strategy but not a personal problem if he is truly committed. The powerful helpers of a movement who wish to adopt and run a movement are legion, and even Alinsky accepts money from national foundations to carry out his work. But as long as personal aims do not tend in the direction of power for its own sake or personal gain through national notoriety, the leadership of a movement may remain reasonably on its track. The non-distractibility and cool of the professional activist in the midst of chaos is perhaps his most characteristic feature, one which results from his world view and the deep conviction that the changes being wrought are for the best, regardless of the short-term interpretation which may be placed on them.

DIVISION OF LABOR: TYPES OF ACTIVISTS

In any consideration of an occupational field, a division of labor by function is helpful in grasping the way the group relates to the wider social system. Activists are no exception here, with one important qualification. We may discuss different types of activists as members of an occupational field, but subjectively the different types may not recognize themselves as being that much akin to one another. In other words, sociologically we may talk of politicians, reformers, and revolutionists as types of activist, and in terms of their announced aims to "change things" they may all fit under such a broad occupational category. Yet functionally they may serve quite different purposes in a given social system, and thus from their point of view they may be right, after all, in refusing too much in the way of kinship.

THE POLITICIAN: ACTION WITHIN THE SYSTEM

Max Weber wrote that politics could be both a vocation and a job.[18] The degree to which a given politician is motivated toward change is extremely difficult to ascertain, and yet critical from a sociological point of view if one is to classify some politicians as activists. Perhaps what distinguishes the "activist" politician from the more status-quo oriented is his desire to *mobilize* the system toward achieving its theoretical or ideological goals. To "really make the system work," McCarthy campaigned against Johnson in the New Hampshire primary of 1967, and Robert Kennedy began to seek out a constituency among the poor.

In functional terms, the activist politician may therefore be working toward the preservation of a given political system in its given terms. The ideologies used by politician-activists tend to be the national political myths of the moderate left, the right, or the center, with the implication that the constituency should "live up to the ideals" by following his lead. The target groups for his ideologies are broader than for either of the other two types of activist, for he is appealing for support in terms of the system itself. However — and this is the cross which non-reformist politicians have to bear — he usually lays himself open to charges of false promises by those who are being oppressed by the present system and who believe that unless it is changed, they will continue to be oppressed. In any social system where a minority are in the oppressed condition and the majority are fairly well off, the politician-activist is certainly the type of activist who will gain widest support. However, precisely because this support comes in part from those who are powerful in and benefit by the present system, the changes he is likely to espouse are minor. Still, again because the threat to the position of the majority is not major, the politician-activist is likely to get the broadest support for the minor changes he espouses and has the highest probability of success in achieving them.

THE REFORMER

In contrast to the functional role of the politician-activist as a member of the government when elected and thus part of the central power system itself, the reformer is not usually campaigning for a formal office. He is not, however, advocating the overthrow of the given political-economic system but rather its *reform* — constructive changes in it. Inherent in the assumption which a reformer makes about a given socio-political order is that it can function better, that it does not have inherent or built-in contradictions which will lead to its downfall. In this sense, for example, Saul Alinsky is a reformer and not a revolutionary radical, for his efforts to organize a Chicago slum neighborhood into TWO (The Woodlawn Organization) represent an attempt to "make the system better" by adding organized citizen groups as an element to compete with the formal governmental-political system in a city; his efforts to gain more stockholders more power in the running of the major American corporations assume that the corporations are capable of acting in the interests of the majority of the people, if only they can be influenced to do so.[19]

Since most reformers do not work through the usual political channels of elected office, although in some cases politicians run on a "reform" ticket, it is important to inspect the borderline between the politician and the voluntary-organization activist on the issue of reform. We are not saying that politician-activists may not espouse programs and statements which are reform-directed, but simply noting that once in office a politician has the constraints of the bureaucracy and the entire citizen constituency, which he did not have when running for that office. In contrast, the reformer can build an organization which can act as its own constituency and as a force against the system, bringing about change in this way. Although Banfield and Wilson observe that the governing of cities is done by exchanges of favors and supports, they are always done with an idea of the long-term functioning of the system within which all have to work. Thus the degree of opposition which a reformist politician in office can afford to arouse is limited.[20] By contrast, the role of the reformer, in his outside position, allows him to proceed, with the encouragement of ad hoc coalitions, independently of a permanent structure to fuse interest groups into a power bloc. Alinsky describes this process after the organizer has helped to set it going. The groups began to say to each other such things as:

> "Well, I need your help to desegregate the schools, and you need my help to get rid of the dope pushers, and to make urban renewal a decent program for the poor as well as the others. So let's make a deal. I'll support each one of you, and you support me." This is the stuff of which organization is made.[21]

Carmichael and Hamilton, in *Black Power*, agree that useful coalitions with whites, based on common interests, are possible, but not "we love you" type of arrangements, which fall apart at the first sign of trouble.[22]

Ironically, a successful reform or change of system will go further in many cases to preserve the system than a mild or near-meaningless change by a politician-activist elected to office on a change-directed platform. If a given socio-political order is actually building in internal pressures to the point where significant changes in the redistribution of power are necessary, then the conflict provoked by the reformer and the changes brought about by him will lead to an *evolution* rather than a revolution. In general terms, Coser points out that moderate conflict has a safety-valve function for social systems; the polarization of a series of groups on either side of an unsolvable issue is the first step toward the creation of a basic revolutionary condition.[23]

THE REVOLUTIONARY ACTIVIST

Lenin once remarked about the Russian Revolution that "Power was lying around in the streets. We just picked it up." Although he was obviously understating the case, and denying the number of his own and his opponents who died picking up the power, he nevertheless had a point. No revolutionary can act successfully in a society which is not ripe for revolution, as Che Guevara found out in the jungles of Bolivia. In general, the actions of politicians and reformers must have failed to change a system over a period of years, and the people's hopes have been greatly raised, while an oppressive socio-political order continues to operate, before the revolutionary can get his audience. The revolutionary activist, in contrast to the politician-activist and the reformer, wishes to supplant the old system with a new one. Although full-scale successful revolutions are rare in world history (until recently), it is nevertheless true, as Pareto notes, that "history is the graveyard of aristocracies." The circulation of elites is at least in part caused by the degeneracy of those at the top, and the strength of those groups that supplant them from below. But the circulation of elites within a system that remains is not the same as the replacement of one system by another, an occurrence that requires far more drastic social conditions than mere corruption. Also, a palace revolution — the replacement of one dictator by another — is not the work of activists, who need a broad support from the people and are working in their interest. Activists are present in most societies, but only in some conditions do they choose revolution as a technique. The conditions and the times pick the man and his approach as much as the reverse.

In general, the politician-activist has the greatest probability of success with the least opposition, the revolutionary activist the least probability of success with the greatest probability of "backlash" or counterrevolution which places a social order further behind after the attempt than before. And yet the politician-activist and the revolutionary have certain beliefs in common. Perhaps the greatest is the legitimacy of *some* given system; in the case of the politician, the system that exists, in the revolutionist's case, the system presently existing only as a dream. But the irreverence which the reformer has to any given system is another thing, qualitatively.

The lack of a revolution or a change (the usual politician's result) or a failed revolution (the usual consequence of most revolutionists' actions) have more in common with each other than with the real and moderate changes which are the consequence of a skilled reformer's actions. On the other hand, as we noted before, the successful *reformers'* actions usually lead to an evolutionary change in a social system rather than a drastic amendment of it. In general, therefore, it is the revolutionary activist that brings about major social changes, or who speeds them on their way. If revolutionary activists were fully rational, they would never act, for the changes and forces against them are always overwhelming, even when conditions appear favorable for their work. Of course, there would have been less of a chance for the development of Protestantism, the United States, the independence of India, or black power.

ACTIVISTS AND INTEREST GROUPS: WHO FIGHTS FOR WHOM?

It would seem obvious that the role of activists would be to fight for their constituents. Yet the picture is complicated by a series of factors that modify the effect of activists in carrying out their work in this ideal fashion: broad social changes, cooptation as it affects the diligence and persistence of activists, conflicts between politician-activists, reformers, and revolutionaries, and questions on the extent to which activists are acting in their own interest, as against the interests of their constituents. Each of these questions has a common base in the problem of conflicts of interest.

It is only in the democratic or parliamentary systems which have developed rather recently in world history that the idea of a "politician-reformer" seems at all possible as an occupational role. In fact, only the onset of the welfare-state ideology has made such a role respectable with even a minority of the electorate. But social change is a broad concept, and it includes the growth of such phenomena as bureaucracies and the industrialization of nations. In this perspective, the area of operations and the potential public for reformers and radicals have increased as the area of turmoil and disorganization has increased, and a consequence of industrialization, bureaucratization, and, in the United States, the growth in power and influence of the military-industrial complex. Perhaps the large number of activists which are presently on the scene in the United States and in other nations simply is an index of anomie, defined as the number of people who no longer believe that the old rules and restraints have legitimacy any more.

COOPTATION

In an earlier era, the primary response of groups in power to the actions of an activist was reasonably simple — they murdered him if they could, or exiled him if this was a wiser step, if he had too many allies to make murder a wise course. In more recent times, the procedure for reformers and even for radicals, on the part of those in the centers of wealth and power, has been to enlist the services of the activist in a course only slightly less radical than his aims and hold out the promise of major subsidy for the amended course of action.

The process of cooptation should not be immediately or simple-mindedly equated with the acceptance of funds. For example, Alinsky got his start as a reformer through a grant which founded the Industrial Areas Foundation, and this grant came from Marshall Field, the Chicago businessman, out of the encouragement which *he* received from the Archbishop of Chicago. In later years Alinsky continues to claim, now with Rockefeller Foundation support, that the dollars do not dictate the program.[24] We must agree that indeed, in his mind, that is the way he sees it. On the other hand, we must always ask this kind of question — why does the Rockefeller Foundation want to give him money? And we must also ask — if an activist receives support from any quarter, regardless of the quarter — then will he be willing to oppose the source of support in future actions, if his fund source should be found to be in partnership with known opponents of the activist? In general, therefore, the cooptation of a group or of an individual leader is both a matter of the subjective intent of the activist and the objective reality of the lack of future opposition. Most coopting bodies do not care about the subjective state of mind of the activist. What they are buying is insurance against future opposition.

ARGUMENTS WITHIN THE FAMILY: SOME CONCLUDING COMMENTS

Within social action movements in recent years, there have been few sights that have been more common than arguments over the proper strategy to use in a conflict situation. The politician-activist feels that the reformer has no faith in established reform processes, and both the politician-activist and the reformer dislike the radical revolutionist, for fear he will bring a repressive reaction down upon them all and will make any form of organized and citizen-based social change almost impossible. In general the degree to which it is possible to speak about "the" career activist as an occupational field is brought into relief by these disagreements. It is possible to see that activists at the same level of change desired (a conservative and a liberal politician, a conservative and a liberal reformer, an organizer for the Birch society and for SDS) can see kinship with one another in terms of operating procedures and assumptions about the desirability of their particular form of activism. It is the quarrel between different *types* of activist that is the strongest source of disunity in the activist field.

The role of the public in according mandates to these three types of activist is important in preventing a unity between the different types of practitioners. A majority will support the politician-activist, but only in unusual circumstances will a revolutionist have a major bloc of support. In this situation it is in the specific self-interest of the politician to deny the revolutionary and his approach and to qualify his support of reformers who may be working in the same direction. For the mandate of the people is the only thing which an activist is basically concerned with — their support for his program, in return for his promises, is what he exchanges with them. He cannot demand too much from too many under this rather imbalanced exchange situation, and must always work with the pressures that circumstances beyond his control place on his clientele. Here again, however, he is not in control of their reaction to these circumstances, any more than he can really know how they will react to his direct work as an activist. In such a tricky line of work, therefore, severe arguments over tactics and aims would seem to be quite understandable.

The question of the self-interested nature of some activists' careers — the extent to which they use movements for their own ends — will always be debated. The proportion of each subgroup of activists who are, as individuals or as a power-hungry clique, essentially using their actions selfishly, is almost impossible to ascertain. For it is precisely here that the interests of people are so closely related to their perceptions; they often attribute nothing but the basest motivations to those who threaten their position. Nor do most activists or their adherents always have a clear understanding of their own position. The increase in the use of cooptation techniques, or of choices out of the activist field, are in part related to these conflicts. Also, what to a radical is cooptation is, to a reformer, a pragmatic coalition with those in a position to help. Thus when an individual switches from one approach to another — as sometimes happens — he may be accused of selling out to advance his own interests when he has simply decided to change his tactics to benefit his group.

In general, the field of activist work is not populated by greedy individuals. There are a lot of better ways to get rich and most people know it. The career contingencies are brutal and the chances of success inversely proportional to the significance of the work attempted. As a field, activism is so fluid that it almost defies sociological analysis in the usual categorical terms. It is by actions that one knows an activist. But as a sector in the world of work their importance to social change and thus to the sociology of occupations is unquestionable.

PART THREE

FUTURE RESEARCH

CHAPTER FIFTEEN

THE POLITICS OF SKILL

Occupations are living social groups as well as abstract conceptual categories; this book has been concerned with the latter only as they relate to the former. As groups, occupations mediate between the individual and society, and as the historical record indicates, there are few changes at the level of the overall society, and few movements initiated by leaders of change-directed groups, which do not have repercussions on the functions of an occupational group within that society. In addition, the actions of organized occupational groups are political in their own right, and may alter not only the role of the occupation in the society, but the overall quality of relations between individuals and their society quite outside the given occupational group. This study of occupations and professions in the social process raises a series of questions which cannot be answered with any certainty at present, but which will need to be the subject of much further research. At least three main areas bear discussion from this point of view: the politics of skill, the role of youth, and the future of work itself.

THE POLITICS OF SKILL

Lasswell defined politics as the process by which it is determined *who* gets *what, when, where,* and *how.*[1] This book considered these issues in detail for occupational groups. A series of questions have been raised which will need further inspection. These include: occupational boundaries, or what properly constitutes an occupation, an occupational field, or a complex of occupational groups; the effects of broad-scale social change on the functions and power of occupational groups; the obvious, short-term, and manifest function of an occupational group compared to its unnoticed, long-term latent function; occupational ideology in action, occupational consciousness, and occupational altruism; and the overall concept of the politics of skill itself.

THE DEFINITION OF OCCUPATIONAL FIELDS

The question of boundaries has confronted us in many ways. Far from being simply a choice of conceptual frameworks, the structure of an occupational field is of major consequence to the participants themselves. The degree of *cohesiveness* or lack of integration within an occupational field is a central problem in understanding the actions of subgroups with the field. To some degree, the inherent nature of the work itself imposes a form upon the occupational field, in what can be called organization through the division of labor. To some degree, an outside analysis can discern a similar set of functions which an otherwise dissimilar set of groups perform, such as the fields known as "communications" or the category which economists call "the service occupations." And to some degree groups see enough common occupational functions to view themselves as "factory workers"; a doctor and nurse both consider themselves health professionals. But the critical boundary questions concern the relationships between these different ways of viewing occupational structure and group organization. When is an occupational concept — as compared to a class or life style concept — used by a group to identify itself? Is this strictly a matter of the high prestige occupations identifying themselves in occupational terms and the lower prestige groups using less specific terms, e.g., "working class," because of the lesser interest in identifying themselves with work they consider menial? And what about the width of the identification by the group, as against the width of their *action* in occupational interest terms? For example, physicians both *view* themselves as an occupational group and *act* as such, whereas a turret lathe operator or a garbage collector may view himself as a member of a given occupational group, but would not dream of acting *only* in terms of that group. What factors determine the breadth of the occupational boundary which is relevant for an understanding of social dynamics from an objective standpoint, and what factors determine the difference between such objective analytical understandings and the persistent desires of groups to form their own definitions of boundaries?

THE CONCEPT OF FUNCTIONAL POWER

The functional power of an occupational group was a factor that arose repeatedly in our consideration of occupational fields. In general, we used an operational definition — functional power is the potential of an occupational group to coerce a society through the withholding of its occupational services. This raises a whole series of questions. What constitutes the nature of this "system power"? Is it truly the case that some occupations are more important to the social system than others? The reasoning of functional theorists is based on a set of "thought experiments" and, in recent years, on observations of the consequences of collective actions along occupational group lines. This is creating a series of real experiments on the functional power of occupational sectors. But the elements of the situation are only vaguely understood at present. How or in what way does the power of the state and the power elite of the society intertwine with or differ from the power of organized occupational groups? How can we compare and understand these two kinds of power with respect to each other?

Our brief inspection of the comparative aspects of this problem would indicate a rough inverse relationship between state power and occupational group power. But the issue is not simply a two-factor one. Each "power" type is in fact a composite of types of relationship. For example, in theory the Soviet Union is a powerfully centralized state, and thus in theory it should not be possible for occupational groups to either organize as pressure groups or exert their will against the interests of the state. Yet the *functional* power or leverage of the Soviet military — its use in protecting the state against attack and its inherent power in military terms — make it a force in its own right in "state" terms. In other words, "functional" occupational group power and "state" power may be ideal types rather than actually different, and we may need to look at the picture in terms of the "occupational quality" or the "governmental quality" of a type of power. In general, far more research needs to be done on the definition and specification of power as it relates to the functions of occupational groups in the social system.

SOCIAL SYSTEM CHANGE: THE CONSEQUENCES FOR OCCUPATIONS

The role of system change was highlighted by the historical and conflict-of-interest perspectives on occupations. In each era, the production groups — those engaged in the management and ownership of the primary production sectors — played an important role in the political life of the period. But as the modern period approaches, technological changes and the ascendance of the bureaucratic form of work organization made an understanding of the political-social role of occupational groups less possible in terms of the group alone. The *context* of the group begins to have increasing importance on such dimensions as manpower demands of new technologies as these affect the future of old occupational groups. The value changes of a technological and scientific era, and their consequences for value-based professions such as the clergy and the law, are another set of overall changes with occupational consequences, as are the redefinitions of man made possible by the new devices, and their consequences for groups such as physicians and systems engineers. The rise of the welfare state, with the consequent growth of the public sector and public occupational counterparts in many occupational fields, is another pattern imposed on the previous pattern of occupational fields. In each case, societal changes on the broad-scale level have led to changes in the very meaning of "functional power" to an occupational group. But in this book we have simply raised the issue, and indicated a broad series of patterns. The details must be filled in, and the dynamics of the process considered much more thoroughly.

Time is the dimension upon which all analysis of social change must be built. Merton's distinction between the manifest and latent functions of a social process is essentially a time-related distinction.[2] The short-run, obvious function of an occupational group's contribution to a social process may differ from its long-run, i.e., later-in-time and cumulative contribution. For example, it has been seen with group after group of occupational reformers within different occupational fields that the majority of such reformist groups manage to preserve rather than change the essential functional role of the occupational group.

In the understanding of the differences between long-run and short-run consequences of occupational activity, a distinction must be made between the central role of a group in its ordinary operating style and the functions which are peripheral to this style. For example, it is important to know what tasks are *truly*, as against ideologically, central to an occupational group, in order to know how the long-term role may change with respect to this. The preaching role of the minister, for example, is a peripheral one in time spent and functional importance, when compared to his central role in administration of the parish. Given this fact, the long-term consequences of an activist preacher, and an activist ministry, with a moral crusading stance, may lead to the destruction of the property and clientele base of organized religion. To understand the long-term effects of a change, one must know how the system was *originally* operating as well as where it is going.

OCCUPATIONAL CONSCIOUSNESS AND ALTRUISM: SIMILARITIES AND CONTRASTS

It has become obvious that the degree to which an occupational group is organized in its own interest, consciously using its occupational role as a framework for activity, is the degree to which it has the potential for political action. The concept of occupational consciousness was introduced in connection with self-interest action, but we know that the *altruist* activist groups in occupational fields also have a concept of themselves as a cohort group with a mission. Therefore we need to know more about the conditions under which a group or subgroup in an occupational field develops a pro-change ideology and the conditions under which groups choose the path of advancement of self-interests. It is clear that it is not simply a matter of the social class membership of the groups involved, nor of the status of the occupational group in a national prestige structure, for the conservative action groups now include the upper-middle-class American Medical Association and many labor unions; the radical groups include the middle-class sons of the AMA members in their radical medical student action organizations, and such organizations as the League for Industrial Democracy and Chavez's grape workers; the latter are certainly not much above the poverty level. It is important that future studies indicate when and how occupational activist groups develop, and why they choose self-interest or altruist goals, as well as how these aims, goals, and activities are modified over time.

In general, the findings of our analysis indicate the need for a combination of the field of the sociology of occupations and such fields as political sociology and the sociology of knowledge. A political sociology which does not treat the political action of occupational groups is risking irrelevance, whereas an apolitical sociology of occupations and professions misses what has *always* been a major dimension of these groups' actions. We need to develop research in what Lasswell called "the politics of skill." [3]

YOUTH AND THE CAREER EXPERIENCE

The stress on career experience which characterized our approach to occupations has raised some basic questions on the meaning of work to all those either entering or working in an occupation and the factors influencing changes in the nature of this experience over time. At least the following areas will need more research in the future: the anti-establishment activism of young people in relation to existing occupational forms, the degree to which social factors continue to exert force on limiting possibilities in career structure and career opportunity, and the role of broad-scale social changes in affecting the subjective meaning of the career experience.

First, it is clear that the present occupational structure in America is neither radical nor altruist in its goals and orientations, nor in its functioning. The youth who have these values thus feel that the joining of an occupational group is very much like making a lifetime commitment to the preservation of the status quo. Only in the professions and in the arts does one find altruistic activism on a scale that merits consideration as a force strong enough to change patterns. The crux of the problem lies in the need to eat and the lack of alternative existence-maintaining settings where a non-career or a flexible and atypical career is possible. A pathetic aspect of this was seen in a conference of radical students held recently in an Eastern city, where the topic was "jobs suitable for young radicals," jobs which they could hold and still maintain their integrity as change agents. Not surprisingly, this conference wasn't too successful, as there just weren't any jobs in the system for those who wanted to be paid for opposing it.

We must therefore ask a set of questions about what could be called the inherent political conservatism of any occupational structure. Is it possible to construct an economic exchange system which does not develop vested interests in its maintenance? We might compare the occupational groups in various forms of utopian societies with the aims and programs of change-directed occupational groups in American society. In general, the long-term consequences of altruistic activism on occupational lines are still relatively unknown. We have suggested that such action is obviously change-directed but has long-term conservative functions. But much more research needs to be done in this area.

In a second research area, it has been clear that the effects of sex, age, and race still play an overwhelming role in career contingencies in all occupational fields. Recent years have seen activist campaigns by women, by the elderly, and by members of racial minority groups to change, mitigate, and ideally to eliminate the effects of these factors. But early in this book, when we reviewed the literature on the relation between school settings and work preparation, it became obvious that these factors determine the basic socialization experience in general in our society; thus we have every reason to think that the effects of sex, race, and ethnic group membership on basic socialization experiences should be compared with their effect on career experience.[4] In addition, the cross-occupational patterns we have seen in the dynamics of *inadvertent* and *deliberate* commitment should be studied more systematically under more carefully controlled circumstances. The effects that the basic "demographic" variables have on the dynamics of commitment should be the subject of much further research.

Thirdly, broad-scale social changes do affect the meaning of career experience. The statistics indicate that a smaller proportion of the students in elite colleges have an interest in business careers and military work than they did a decade ago. But it is also true, as a *Fortune* study recently showed, that the majority of college students are not in liberal arts programs — and the other programs tend to be almost completely vocationally oriented.[5] Thus it may be quite possible that an appearance of "revolution against standard careers" on the part of a minority of youth tends to obscure the continuing interest of most in obtaining places in the present occupational structure.

But what we do not know are the facts relating to the history of attitudes toward careers. One observation has been made in several chapters — that the early altruism of young activist professionals may not be a lasting thing. This is a critical life-cycle study, which has not been done for any occupational group, but it must be done for many before we can assume that youth have the capacity to change these occupations.

In general, we must ask some difficult-to-answer questions which will require a combination of historical and observational research. There is a need to do comparative biographical studies of men in the same occupation during different historical periods, in order to ascertain the effects of social change on career experience. We need more quantitative and controlled studies on the relationships between a *set* of individual career patterns and a given social milieu, in order to ascertain the proportion of careers and career opportunities that have been really changed by a broad trend in societal evolution. The major problem in career experience research on topics such as youth activism, social factors in career opportunity, and the broad-scale effects of social change, is that the information is still too sketchy to allow much beyond impressions. Future research here should have a high priority.

THE FUTURE OF WORK

One of the most popular pastimes among those who engage in the sociology of technology is the prediction of levels of unemployment resulting from changes in production techniques. When the problem is seen as the "impact of automation," various assumptions on rates of technological development lead to various conclusions on the rate of unemployment.[6] Yet if this book has indicated anything about the dynamics of stability and change in occupational fields, it is that trends are to some degree determined by the political action of groups, actions which are only partly predictable with any rational approach. The prediction of the future of work, or of the possibility of a "leisure society" cannot be made outside an analysis of the power politics of a given country at a given time and the probabilities of its alignments staying the same or changing.

The work of DeGrazia is sensitive in its understanding of the inability of many people to use their leisure time and adds a further insight about the nature of predictions in this area, one which will need further research.[7] Desires for constructive achievement are said to be either inborn or socialized into the personality at an early age. Yet the observations of DeGrazia and the comments of such cultural critics as Riesman are that many people do not desire a creative career if it is too risky (they do not have what Riesman calls "the nerve of failure") or that they prefer to work as a means to gather money for consumption and passive entertainment.[8] These observations raise an important question which is related to, but not the same as, the political questions. To what degree does the average individual *care* about the lack of spontaneity or creativity in his work, and to what degree is he willing to act to change anything in this area, assuming it were possible to do so at some cost in other areas?

This in turn raises a question which also cannot be answered here, but it is an important one for a meaningful and human sociology of occupations. To what extent is it possible for most men and women to have a creative experience in the world of work? The vast majority of present jobs are enmeshed in a bureaucratic system and are part of a production-and-consumption oriented society. The future of this society rests on the maintenance of its present production system and present levels of consumption. A mass desire for creative work within such a system would be unmeetable, but it is very probably not an accident that this has not happened. The educational system has been directed at the production of unquestioning individuals who have not had their creative capacities developed to the point where they will be made into misfits for the industrial-bureaucratic society. Education can be a subversive activity if it is truly liberating, for it can create dissatisfaction with the social order and the occupational world, which may lead to pressures for change. Those who are recognized as creative, or who manage to survive this system of socialization for conformity, are at present under constant pressure to join the powerful. Cooptation is the most modern form of opposition to change.

Thus both change-directed political action by groups and the attitudes and values formed in people by the existing system are important keys to understanding the developments that may occur in the field of occupations and professions. The history of work grouping tends to suggest that the broader evolutionary paths of a society and the direction of occupational development will bear some relationship. In the industrializing nations of the present time, some of the history of the West is inevitably going to be repeated; changes in the role of occupational groups and wider cross-occupational complexes will approximate some of those found in the English and American Industrial Revolutions. The differences between modern occupational revolutions and historical ones are an important area for future research. Each historical situation is unique, but it is certain that in all eras, individuals and groups act as members of occupational groups in playing a role in the observed changes. In the future, as in the past and present, men and women will play some role in the creation of their work. How much of a role is the critical question.

NOTES

INTRODUCTION

[1] Vilfredo Pareto, *The Mind and Society*, Vol. III (A. Bongiorno and A. Livingston, trans.). New York: Harcourt, 1935, p. 1430.

[2] John Langdon Sibley, *Biographical Sketches of Graduates of Harvard University in Cambridge, Massachusetts*, Vols. 1–3. Cambridge: C. W. Sever, 1873.

[3] See Sigmund Freud, *Civilization and Its Discontents* (Joan Riviere, trans.). New York: Cape and Smith, 1930.

[4] Everett C. Hughes, *Men and their Work*. New York: Free Press, 1958.

[5] Émile Durkheim, *Suicide* (J. A. Spaulding and G. Simpson, trans.). New York: Free Press, 1951. See Chapter Four of this book for a further discussion of Durkheim's idea.

[6] The Editors of *Fortune*, "American Youth: Its Outlook Is Changing the World," *Fortune* 79 (January, 1969), entire issue.

[7] Rue Bucher and Anselm Strauss, "Professions in Process," *American Journal of Sociology* 66 (January, 1961), pp. 325–334.

CHAPTER ONE, A HISTORICAL PERSPECTIVE

[1] Gerhard E. Lenski, *Power and Privilege*. New York: McGraw-Hill, 1966, pp. 94–116.

[2] Ibid., p. 109.

[3] Ibid., pp. 117–141.

[4] Alvin W. Gouldner, *The Hellenic World: A Sociological Analysis*. New York: Harper Torchbooks, 1969, p. 31.

[5] Ibid., p. 145.

[6] Ibid., p. 32.

[7] Ibid., p. 145.

[8] Walter Ullmann, *Individual and Society in the Middle Ages*. Baltimore: Johns Hopkins Press, 1966.

[9] Ibid., p. 42.

[10] Marc Bloch, *Feudal Society*, Vol. II (L. A. Manyon, trans.). Chicago: University of Chicago Press, 1961, p. 443.

[11] Alexander M. Carr-Saunders and P. M. Wilson, *The Professions*. Oxford: Clarendon Press, 1933, pp. 298–304.

[12] Ullmann, *Individual and Society in the Middle Ages*, pp. 53–98, "The Practical Thesis."

[13] George C. Homans, *English Villagers of the Thirteenth Century*. Cambridge: Harvard University Press, 1942, p. 331.

[14] Ullmann, *Individual and Society in the Middle Ages*, p. 59.

[15] Henri Pirenne, *Medieval Cities* (Frank D. Halsey, trans.). Garden City: Doubleday, 1956.

[16] Ullmann, *Individual and Society in the Middle Ages*, p. 105.

[17] Alfred Von Martin, *The Sociology of the Renaissance*. New York: Harper and Row, 1963, pp. 9–12.

[18] Ibid., p. 6.

[19] Ibid., p. 6.

[20] J. H. Parry, *The Establishment of the European Hegemony, 1445–1715*. New York: Harper and Row, 1961, p. 74.

[21] Ibid., p. 60.

[22] Von Martin, *The Sociology of the Renaissance*, p. 5.

[23] Ullmann, *Individual and Society in the Middle Ages*, p. 58.

[24] William Barclay Parsons, *Engineering in the Renaissance*. New York: Williams and Wilkins, 1939, pp. 280–282.

[25] Ibid., pp. 280–285.

[26] Roscoe Pound, ed. and trans., *Readings in Roman Law and the Civil Law and Modern Codes as Developments Thereof*. Cambridge: Harvard University Press, 1914.

[27] Ullmann, *Individual and Society in the Middle Ages*, p. 113.

[28] Parsons, *Engineering in the Renaissance*, pp. 67–96.

[29] Ibid. See especially Part III, "Mining Engineering in the Renaissance," Part IV, "Municipal and Governmental Engineering in the Renaissance," Part V, "Hydraulic Engineering in the Renaissance," and Part VI, "Structural Engineering in the Renaissance."

[30] See Erik H. Erikson, *Young Man Luther*. New York: W. W. Norton, 1958, pp. 223–250.

[31] Max Weber, "The Protestant Sects and the Spirit of Capitalism," in H. H. Gerth and C. Wright Mills, eds., *From Max Weber: Essays in Sociology*. New York: Oxford University Press, 1958, pp. 302–322.

[32] Von Martin, *The Sociology of the Renaissance*, pp. 72–92, and Guy E. Swanson, *Religion and Regime: A Sociological Account of the Reformation*. Ann Arbor: University of Michigan Press, 1967.

[33] Swanson, *Religion and Regime*, p. 251.

[34] Von Martin, *The Sociology of the Renaissance*, p. 91.

[35] Michael Walzer, *The Revolution of the Saints*. Cambridge: Harvard University Press, 1965.

[36] See Perry Miller, *The New England Mind: The Seventeenth Century*. New York: Macmillan, 1939, p. 491.

[37] George L. Haskins, *Law and Authority in Early Massachusetts*. New York: Macmillan, 1960, pp. 15, 61.

[38] Perry Miller, *The New England Mind: From Colony to Province*. Boston: Beacon Press, 1961, pp. 68–81, 114.

[39] Miller, *From Colony to Province*, pp. 82–92.

[40] See, concerning the trial of Anne Hutchinson, the summary by Kai T. Erikson, *Wayward Puritans*. New York: Wiley, 1969, pp. 71–107.

[41] Miller, *From Colony to Province*, p. 37.

[42] Ibid., p. 307.

[43] Haskins, *Law and Authority in Early Massachusetts*, pp. 21–42.

[44] Ibid., p. 186.

[45] Ibid., pp. 43–65.

[46] Kai Erikson, *Wayward Puritans*, p. 135.

[47] Miller, *From Colony to Province*, pp. 40–52.

[48] Haskins, *Law and Authority in Early Massachusetts*, p. 186.

[49] See Elliott A. Krause, "The Lawyer's Mandate in Colonial Massachusetts," Northeastern University, mimeo, 1969.

[50] John Langdon Sibley, *Biographical Sketches of Graduates of Harvard University in Cambridge, Massachusetts*, Vols. 1–3. Cambridge: C. W. Sever, 1873. Clifford K. Shipton, ed., *Sibley's Harvard Graduates*, Vol. 4. Cambridge: Harvard University Press, n.d.

[51] Miller, *From Colony to Province*, pp. 345–366.

[52] Oliver W. Larkin, *Art and Life in America*. New York: Holt, Rinehart and Winston, 1949, p. 147.

[53] Daniel H. Calhoun, *Professional Lives in America*. Cambridge: Harvard University Press, 1965, pp. 1–19.

[54] Ibid., pp. 60–61.

[55] A. Whitney Griswold, *The Lawyer in America.* Cambridge: Harvard University Press, 1965, p. 20.

[56] Joseph F. Kett, *The Formation of the American Medical Profession.* New Haven: Yale University Press, 1968, pp. 108–109.

[57] Ibid., pp. 156–164.

[58] Christopher Jencks and David Riesman, *The Academic Revolution.* Garden City: Doubleday, 1969, p. 13.

[59] Jurgen Kuczynski, *The Rise of the Working Class.* New York: McGraw-Hill, 1967, pp. 137–225.

[60] Stephan Thernstrom, *Poverty and Progress: Social Mobility in a Nineteenth Century City.* Cambridge: Harvard University Press, 1964, p. 87.

[61] Ibid., pp. 138–165.

[62] Arthur Mann, *Yankee Reformers in an Urban Age.* Cambridge: Harvard University Press, 1954, p. 195.

CHAPTER TWO, THE BIOGRAPHICAL APPROACH

[1] Talcott Parsons, "The Superego and the Theory of Social Systems," in *Social Structure and Personality.* New York: Free Press, 1964, p. 28.

[2] David C. McClelland, *The Achieving Society.* Princeton: Van Nostrand, 1961.

[3] See, for example, the discussion of attitudes toward work in Elliot Liebow, *Tally's Corner.* Boston: Little, Brown, 1967, pp. 29–71, "Men and Jobs."

[4] John Scanzoni, "Socialization, Achievement and Achievement Values," *American Sociological Review* 32 (June, 1967), pp. 449–456.

[5] Erik H. Erikson, "The Healthy Personality," in *Identity and the Life Cycle, Psychological Issues, Monograph 1.* New York: International Universities Press, 1959, p. 86.

[6] For a review of this program, see Sar Levitan, *The Great Society's Poor Law.* Baltimore: Johns Hopkins Press, 1969, pp. 133–164.

[7] Anne Roe, "Personality Structure and Occupational Behavior," in Henry Borow, ed., *Man in a World at Work.* Boston: Houghton Mifflin, 1964, pp. 196–214.

[8] Melvin L. DeFleur, "Occupational Roles as Portrayed on Television," *Public Opinion Quarterly* 28 (Spring, 1964), pp. 57–74.

[9] Eli Ginzberg et al., *Occupational Choice.* New York: Columbia University Press, 1951.

[10] William P. Kuvlevsky, "Occupational Aspirations and Subsequent Attainment: A Longitudinal Study of Young Adults," *Proceedings of the Southwest Sociological Association* 16 (1966), pp. 205–220.

[11] Robert R. Sears, Eleanor E. Maccoby, and Harry Levin, *Patterns of Child Rearing.* Evanston: Row, Peterson and Co., 1957.

[12] George Psathas, "Toward a Theory of Occupational Choice for Women," *Sociology and Social Research* 52 (January, 1968), pp. 253–269.

[13] R. R. Dale and S. Griffith, *Down Stream, Failure in the Grammar School.* London: Routledge and Kegan Paul, 1965.

[14] Angus Campbell and W. C. Ackerman, "What People Think About College," *American Education* 1 (February, 1965), p. 30.

[15] Talcott Parsons and Winston White, "The Link Between Character and Society," in *Social Structure and Personality,* p. 211.

[16] James S. Coleman, *The Adolescent Society.* New York: Free Press, 1961.

[17] J. Eugene Haas, Marvin Taves, and David Shaw, "Primary Group Influence on Vocational Choice," *Sociological Quarterly* 2 (April, 1961), pp. 87–96.

[18] Talcott Parsons, "The School Class as a Social System," in *Social Structure and Personality,* pp. 129–154.

[19] Aaron V. Cicourel and John I. Kitsuse, *The Educational Decision-Makers.* Indianapolis: Bobbs-Merrill, 1963.

[20] Ibid., p. 145.

[21] Edgar Z. Friedenberg, *The Vanishing Adolescent.* Boston: Beacon Press, 1960.

[22] Walter L. Slocum, *Occupational Careers.* Chicago: Aldine, 1966, p. 209.

[23] Christopher Jencks and David Riesman, *The Academic Revolution.* Garden City: Doubleday, 1969.

[24] Bruce K. Eckland, "Academic Ability, Higher Education, and Occupational Mobility," *American Sociological Review* 30 (October, 1965), pp. 735–746.

[25] Morris Rosenberg, with the assistance of Edward A. Suchman and Rose K. Goldsen, *Occupations and Values*. New York: Free Press, 1957.

[26] Burton R. Clark, "The 'Cooling Out' Function in Higher Education," in A. H. Halsey, Jean Floud, and C. Arnold Anderson, *Education, Economy, and Society*. New York: Free Press, 1961, pp. 513–527.

[27] Archie O. Haller, "Planning to Farm: A Social Psychological Interpretation," *Social Forces* 37 (March, 1959), pp. 263–268; and "The Occupational Achievement Process of Farm-Reared Youth in Urban-Industrial Society," *Rural Sociology* 25 (September, 1960), pp. 321–333; Raymond Payne, "Development of Occupational and Migration Expectations and Choices Among Urban, Small Town and Rural Adolescent Boys," *Rural Sociology* 21 (March, 1956), pp. 117–125; and Lee Burchinal, "What About Your Daughter's Future?" *Iowa Farm Science* 14 (June, 1960), pp. 9–10.

[28] Murray A. Straus, "Personal Characteristics and Functional Needs in the Choice of Farming as an Occupation," *Rural Sociology* 21 (September and December, 1956), pp. 3–4, 257–266.

[29] J. Janicki, "Z Badan Nad Aspiracjami Zawodowymi w Polsce w Latach 1958–1959" ("Inquiries into Occupational Aspirations in Poland, 1958–1959"), *Stud. Socjol.* 1 (1961), pp. 217–225; Stefan Nowak, "Egalitarian Attitudes of Warsaw Students," *American Sociological Review* 25 (April, 1960), pp. 219–231.

[30] V. N. Shubkin, V. I. Artemov, N. P. Moskalenko, N. V. Buzokova, and V. A. Kalmyk, "Kolichestvennye Metody v Sotsiologicheskikih Issledovaniyakh Problem Trudoustroistva i Vybora Professii" ("Quantitative Methods in Sociological Studies of Problems of Job Placement and Choice of Occupation") in A. G. Aganbegian, et al., eds., *Kolichestvennye Metody v Sotsiologii* (*Quantitative Methods in Sociology*). Moscow: Nauka, 1966. English translation of Part 1 of article in *Soviet Sociology* 7 (Summer, 1968), pp. 3–24.

[31] E. Jacques Brazeau, "Language Differences and Occupational Experience," *Canadian Journal of Economics and Political Science* 24 (November, 1958), pp. 532–540.

[32] Harold L. Sheppard and A. Harvey Belitsky, *The Job Hunt*. Baltimore: Johns Hopkins Press, 1966.

[33] Jean-Rene Treanton, "Le Concept de 'Carriere' " ("The Career Concept"), *Revue Francaise de Sociologie* 1 (January–March, 1960), pp. 73–80.

[34] Harold L. Wilensky, "Orderly Careers and Social Participation: The Impact of Work History on Social Integration in the Middle Mass," *American Sociological Review* 26 (August, 1961), pp. 521–539.

[35] Bennett Berger, "New Stage of American Man: Almost Endless Adolescence," *The New York Times Magazine* (November 2, 1969), p. 32.

[36] Rhoda Baruch, "The Interruption and Resumption of Women's Careers," *Harvard Studies in Career Development*, No. 50. Cambridge: Harvard Graduate School of Education, September 1966.

[37] David Gottlieb, *Processes of Socialization in the American Graduate School*, Doctoral Dissertation, University of Chicago, Department of Sociology, May 1960.

[38] Oswald Hall, "Types of Medical Careers," *American Journal of Sociology* 55 (November, 1949), pp. 243–253; Joseph H. Fichter, *Religion as an Occupation*. Notre Dame: University of Notre Dame Press, 1961.

[39] Howard S. Becker and James W. Carper, "The Development of Identification with an Occupation," *American Journal of Sociology* 21 (January, 1956), p. 290.

[40] Fred E. Katz, "Occupational Contact Networks," *Social Forces* 37 (October, 1958), pp. 52–55.

[41] Lee Braude, *The Rabbi: A Study of the Relation of Contingency Situations to Differential Career Structures*. Doctoral Dissertation, University of Chicago, Department of Sociology, February 1964; Lawrence B. Lamson, *The Protestant Minister in Chicago*. Doctoral Dissertation, University of Chicago, 1955; Julius Roth, "How Nurses' Aides Learn Their Job," *American Journal of Nursing* 62 (August, 1962), pp. 54–57.

[42] Earl Bogdanoff and Arnold J. Glass, *The Sociology of the Public Case Worker in*

an Urban Area. Master's paper, University of Chicago, Department of Sociology, March 1954.

43 L. Wesley Wager, *Career Patterns and Role Problems of Airline Pilots in a Major Airline Company.* Doctoral Dissertation, University of Chicago, Department of Sociology, May 1956.

44 Some scientists handled this issue by becoming "political" representatives of their field; see Leo Szilard, "Reminiscences," in Donald Fleming and Bernard Bailyn, eds., *The Intellectual Migration.* Cambridge: Harvard University Press, 1969, pp. 94–151.

45 Theodore N. Ferdinand, "On the Obsolescence of Scientists and Engineers," *American Scientist* 54 (March, 1966), pp. 46–56.

46 Fred H. Goldner, "Demotion in Industrial Management," *American Sociological Review* 30 (October, 1965), pp. 714–724.

47 Howard S. Becker, "The Career of the Chicago Public School Teacher," *American Journal of Sociology* 57 (March, 1952), pp. 473–477.

48 William H. Whyte, Jr., *The Organization Man.* New York: Simon and Schuster, 1956, pp. 173–185.

49 Paul C. P. Siu, *The Chinese Laundryman: A Study of Social Isolation.* Doctoral Dissertation, University of Chicago, Department of Sociology, May 1953.

50 William Hodge, "Navaho Urban Silversmiths," *Anthropological Quarterly* 40 (October, 1967), pp. 185–200.

51 George K. Floro, *The City Manager in the State of Michigan: A Case Study of an Itinerant Professional.* Doctoral Dissertation, University of Chicago, Department of Sociology, 1954.

52 Samuel E. Wallace, "Reference Group Behavior in Occupational Role Socialization," *Sociological Quarterly* 7 (Summer, 1966), pp. 366–372.

53 David V. Tiedemann, "Career Pattern Studies: Current Findings with Possibilities," *Harvard Studies in Career Development, No.* 40. Cambridge: Harvard Graduate School of Education, July 1965.

54 Anne Roe, "Factors Influencing Occupational Decisions: A Pilot Study," *Harvard Studies in Career Development, No.* 32. Cambridge: Harvard Graduate School of Education, July 1964, p. 19.

55 Eileen Morley, "The Career Crisis of Losing One's Job," *Harvard Studies in Career Development, No.* 53. Cambridge: Harvard Graduate School of Education, April 1967.

56 Everett C. Hughes, "Career Advancement and Learning the System in Career Development in Industry," *Harvard Studies in Career Development, No.* 53. Cambridge: Harvard Graduate School of Education, March 1968, pp. 67–68.

57 Mason Griff, *Role Conflict and the Career Development of the Commercial Artist,* Doctoral Dissertation, University of Chicago, 1958.

58 Søren Kierkegaard, *Fear and Trembling & The Sickness Unto Death* (Walter Lowrie, trans.). Garden City: Doubleday, 1954.

59 Howard S. Becker, "Notes on the Concept of Commitment," *American Journal of Sociology* 66 (July, 1960), p. 32.

60 Blanche Geer, "Occupational Commitment and the Teaching Profession," *School Review* 74 (Spring, 1966), pp. 31–47.

61 Oscar Grusky, "Career Mobility and Organizational Commitment," *Administrative Science Quarterly* 10 (March, 1966), pp. 488–503.

62 William Kornhauser, *Liberal and Radical Political Careers,* Doctoral Dissertation, University of Chicago, Department of Sociology, 1953.

63 Everett C. Hughes, "Personality Types and the Division of Labor," in his *Men and their Work.* New York: Free Press, 1958, pp. 11–22.

64 Hughes, "License and Mandate," in *Men and their Work,* pp. 78–87.

65 Hughes, "The 'Gleichschaltung' of the German Statistical Yearbook: A Case in Professional Political Neutrality," in *Men and their Work,* pp. 145–156.

66 Hughes, "Mistakes at Work," in *Men and their Work,* pp. 88–101.

67 Hughes, "Personality Types and the Division of Labor," in *Men and their Work,* pp. 23–41.

68 Robert K. Merton, George S. Reader, and Patricia Kendall, eds., *The Student-*

Physician: Introductory Studies in the Sociology of Medical Education. Cambridge: Harvard University Press, 1957; Howard S. Becker, Blanche Geer, Everett C. Hughes, and Anselm Strauss, *Boys in White*. Chicago: University of Chicago Press, 1961.

[69] Becker et al., *Boys in White*, pp. 137–157; Howard S. Becker and Blanche Geer, "The Fate of Idealism in Medical School," *American Sociological Review* 23 (February, 1958), pp. 50–56.

[70] Hall, "Types of Medical Careers," pp. 243–253.

[71] Kurt W. Back, Robert E. Coker, Thomas G. Donnelly, and Bernard S. Phillips, "Public Health as a Career in Medicine: Secondary Choice within a Profession," *American Sociological Review* 23 (October, 1958), pp. 533–541.

[72] Eliot Friedson and Buford Rhea, "Processes of Control in a Company of Equals," *Social Problems* 11 (Fall, 1963), pp. 119–131.

[73] Howard S. Becker, "Contingencies of the Professional Dance Musician's Career," *Human Organization* 12 (Spring, 1953), pp. 22–26.

[74] Blanche Geer, Jack Haas, Charles ViVona, Stephen J. Miller, Clyde Woods, and Howard S. Becker, "Learning the Ropes, Situational Learning in Four Occupational Training Programs," in Irwin Deutscher and Elizabeth J. Thompson, eds., *Among the People*. New York: Basic Books, 1968, pp. 228–229.

[75] Alvin Gouldner, "Cosmopolitans and Locals: Toward an Analysis of Latent Social Roles," *Administrative Science Quarterly* 2 (December, 1957), pp. 281–306.

[76] Whyte, *Organization Man*, pp. 225–265.

[77] Barney Glaser, *Organizational Scientists: Their Professional Careers*. Indianapolis: Bobbs-Merrill, 1964. See also the preface by Anselm Strauss, p. ix.

[78] Howard S. Becker and Blanche Geer, "Latent Culture: A Note on the Theory of Latent Social Roles," *Administrative Science Quarterly* 5 (September, 1960), pp. 304–313.

[79] Becker and Geer, "Latent Culture," p. 308.

[80] Geer et al., "Learning the Ropes," p. 229.

[81] Max Weber, "Bureaucracy," in H. H. Gerth and C. Wright Mills, eds., *From Max Weber: Essays in Sociology*. New York: Oxford University Press, 1958, pp. 196–244.

[82] Robert K. Merton, "Bureaucratic Structure and Personality," in his *Social Theory and Social Structure*. New York: Free Press, 1957, pp. 195–206.

[83] Peter Blau, *The Dynamics of Bureaucracy*. Chicago: University of Chicago Press, 1965, p. 108.

[84] Fritz J. Roethlisberger and William J. Dickson, *Management and the Worker*. Cambridge: Harvard University Press, 1949, p. 522.

[85] Whyte, *Organization Man*, pp. 184–185.

[86] Bogdanoff and Glass, *The Sociology of the Public Case Worker in an Urban Area*, p. 130.

[87] Karl Marx, *Economic and Philosophical Manuscripts of 1844* (Martin Milligan, trans.). London: Lawrence and Wishert, 1959.

[88] Nancy C. Morse and Robert S. Weiss, "The Function and Meaning of Work and the Job," *American Sociological Review* 20 (April, 1955), pp 191–198.

[89] George C. Homans, "The Cash Posters: A Study of a Group of Working Girls," *American Sociological Review* 19 (1954), pp. 724–733.

[90] Hughes observed their process in an area where the black group was a *large* minority, which may account for some of the "mixing" he saw. See Everett C. Hughes, "The Knitting of Racial Groups in Industry," *American Sociological Review* 11 (1946), p. 517.

[91] Edgar Z. Friedenberg, "Truth: Upper, Middle, and Lower," in *The Dignity of Youth and Other Atavisms*. Boston: Beacon Press, 1965, pp. 23–36.

[92] Eli Chinoy, *Automobile Workers and the American Dream*. Garden City: Doubleday, 1955.

[93] Elliott A. Krause, "Trust, Training, and the School Dropout's World View," *Community Mental Health Journal* 4 (1968), pp. 369–374.

[94] Erich Fromm, *Escape From Freedom*. New York: Holt, Rinehart and Winston, 1961.

CHAPTER THREE, THE DIVISION OF LABOR: STRUCTURE AND FUNCTION

[1] Émile Durkheim, *The Division of Labor in Society* (G. Simpson, trans.). New York: Macmillan, 1933.

[2] Ibid., pp. 68–69.

[3] Ibid., pp. 109–110.

[4] George Orwell, *Animal Farm: A Fairy Story*. London: Secker and Warburg, 1945.

[5] For the early discussion of alienation, see Karl Marx, *Economic and Philosophical Manuscripts of 1844* (Martin Milligan, trans.). London: Lawrence and Wishart, 1959.

[6] Georges Friedmann, "La these de Durkheim et les formes contemporaines de la division du travail," *Cahiers Internationaux de Sociologie* 19 (July–December 1955), pp. 45–58.

[7] Talcott Parsons, *The Social System*. New York: Free Press, 1951, pp. 160–161.

[8] Ibid., p. 178.

[9] Talcott Parsons and Neil Smelser, *Economy and Society*. New York: Free Press, 1956, pp. 114–123.

[10] Ibid., pp. 85–97.

[11] Robert K. Merton, *Social Theory and Social Structure*. New York: Free Press, 1957, pp. 19–82.

[12] Wassily Leontief, *Input-Output Economics*. New York: Oxford University Press, 1966.

[13] The point should be made here that the boundaries between occupational fields are always imposed by the analyst, that is, they are arbitrary. See the concluding chapter, comparing analyst-drawn lines with occupational group-drawn lines.

[14] Floyd K. Harmston and Richard E. Lund, *Application of an Input-Output Framework to a Community Economic System*. Columbia: University of Missouri Press, 1967.

[15] Jane Jacobs, *The Economy of Cities*. New York: Random House, 1961, pp. 85–121.

[16] United States Department of Labor, *Dictionary of Occupational Titles*. Bureau of Employment Security, United States Employment Service, Third Edition. Washington, D.C.: United States Government Printing Office, 1965.

[17] Leontief, *Input-Output Economics*, pp. 44–48.

[18] Karl Marx, *Capital: A Critique of Political Economy. Vol. I. A Critical Analysis of Capitalist Production* (Samuel Moore and Edward Aveling, trans.). Chicago: Kerr, 1887.

[19] In 1880 Marx worked with Jules Guesde to determine the grounds on which to base the platform of the French Labor Party. Several welfare state measures were included.

[20] Kingsley Davis and Wilbert Moore, "Some Principles of Stratification," *American Sociological Review* 10 (1945), pp. 242–249.

[21] Raymond Aron, *Dix-huit leçons sur la société industrielle*. Paris: Editions Gallimard, 1962.

[22] Alex Inkeles and Peter Rossi, "Social Stratification and Mobility in the Soviet Union," in Alex Inkeles, *Social Change in Soviet Russia*. Cambridge: Harvard University Press, 1968, pp. 170–171.

[23] For a discussion of these issues, see Raymond Aron, *Democratie et totalitarianisme*. Paris: Gallimard, 1965, pp. 322–338.

[24] This power, since it is essentially irresistible, eventually becomes perceived by citizens as legitimate. See Alex Inkeles and Raymond A. Bauer, *The Soviet Citizen: Daily Life in a Totalitarian Society*. Cambridge: Harvard University Press, 1959, pp. 289–290.

[25] Friedrich A. Hayek, *The Road to Serfdom*. Chicago: University of Chicago Press, pp. 88–100.

[26] For a description of this system, somewhat modified, see Oscar Lewis, *Village Life in Northern India*. Urbana: University of Illinois Press, 1958, pp. 55–88.

[27] Morris Janowitz, *The Military in the Political Development of New Nations*. Chicago: University of Chicago Press, 1964, pp. 49–58.

[28] Ibid., pp. 35–36.

29 Peter Blau and Otis Dudley Duncan, *The American Occupational Structure*. New York: Wiley, 1967.

30 F. Theodore Malm, "Patterns and the Functioning of Labor Markets," *Industrial Labor Relations Review* 5 (July, 1952), pp. 507–525.

31 Orme W. Phelps, "A Structural Model of the U.S. Labor Market," *Industrial Labor Relations Review* 10 (April, 1957), pp. 402–423.

32 This is a consequence of automation and problems of unemployment, not of a trend toward democratization. For the position of 1950, see Inkeles and Rossi, "Social Stratification and Mobility in the Soviet Union," p. 173.

33 See Kaare Svalastoga, *Social Differentiation*. New York: David McKay, 1965, pp. 23–25.

34 Bureau of the Census, United States Department of Commerce, *Consumer Income in the United States*. Washington D.C.: United States Government Printing Office, 1967.

35 Gross, "Plus ça change. . . . ? The Sexual Structure of Occupations Over Time," *Social Problems* 16 (Fall, 1968), pp. 198–208.

36 Alva Myrdal and Viola Klein, *Women's Two Roles: Home and Work*. London: Routledge and Kegan Paul, 1956; Maria L. Forniciari, "Osservazioni sull' andamento del lavoro feminile in Italia negli ultimi 50 anni" (Observations on the Course of Female Labor in Italy in the Last 50 Years), *Revue Internationale des Sciences Sociales* 17 (May–June, 1956), pp. 222–240.

37 C. E. V. Leser, "Trends in Women's Work Participation," *Population Studies* 12 (November, 1958), pp. 100–110.

38 Herman D. Bloch, "The Employment Status of the New York Negro in Retrospect," *Phylon* 20 (Winter, 1959), pp. 327–344.

39 E. P. Hutchinson, *Immigrants and Their Children, 1850–1950*. New York: Wiley, 1958.

40 Christopher Jencks and David Riesman, *The Academic Revolution*. Garden City: Doubleday, 1969, p. 66.

41 Everett C. Hughes, "Work and the Self," in his *Men and Their Work*. New York: Free Press, 1958, pp. 49–52.

42 Svalastoga, *Social Differentiation*, pp. 29–30.

43 Ibid., p. 25.

44 Raymond L. Gold, "In the Basement—The Apartment-Building Janitor," in Peter L. Berger, ed., *The Human Shape of Work*. New York: Macmillan, 1964, pp. 11–14.

45 See, for a criticism of the validity of this type of approach, Pitrim Sorokin, *Fads and Foibles in Modern Sociology and Related Sciences*. Chicago: Henry Regnery, 1956.

46 T. B. Bottomore, *Elites and Society*. New York: Basic Books, 1964, p. 46.

47 Theodore Geiger, *On Social Order and Mass Society*. (Selected papers edited by Renate Mayntz; Robert E. Peck, trans.). Chicago: University of Chicago Press, 1969

48 The literature on the definition and measurement of occupational mobility is complex and extensive. See Blau and Duncan, *The American Occupational Structure*, or Svalastoga, *Social Differentiation*, for critical reviews of this literature.

49 Blau and Duncan, *The American-Occupational Structure*, pp. 152–161.

50 For a criticism of "reformers" who accept the American educational system, see Edgar Z. Friedenberg, "Sentimental Education," *New York Review of Books* (November 21, 1968), pp. 18–22.

51 Blau and Duncan, *The American Occupational Structure*, pp. 10–18.

52 Ibid., pp. 401–440.

53 Ibid., pp. 405–406.

54 Stephan Thernstrom, *Poverty and Progress: Social Mobility in Newburyport 1850–1880*. Cambridge: Harvard University Press, 1964, pp. 115–137.

55 Thernstrom, *Poverty and Progress*, p. 111. But the Irish never got far in Newburyport. The mobility of the Irish, both occupationally and politically, was higher in Boston than in Newburyport, according to the historical record, especially in the area of politics.

56 As far as recent statistics are concerned, the last three years may signal a second upturn in black mobility. In general, we would agree with Blau and Duncan that "Equitable treatment in terms of universalistic standards is not sufficient for a seriously

underprivileged and deprived group to catch up with the rest, or, for that matter, to keep abreast of their progress. It requires a helping hand," p. 425.

[57] Thernstrom, *Poverty and Progress*, pp. 225–239.

[58] Seymour Martin Lipset and Reinhard Bendix, *Social Mobility in Industrial Society*. California: University of California Press, 1959, p. 72.

[59] Alexander M. Carr-Saunders and P. M. Wilson, *The Professions*. Oxford: Oxford University Press, 1933, pp. 284–287.

[60] Hughes, "Work and the Self," in *Men and their Work*, pp. 54–55.

[61] Hughes, "Professional and Career Problems of Sociology," in ibid., pp. 157–168.

[62] Hughes, "License and Mandate," in ibid., pp. 78–87.

[63] See, for example, Walter Wardwell, "Limited, Marginal, and Quasi-Practitioners," in Howard E. Freeman, Sol Levine, and Leo G. Reader, eds., *Handbook of Medical Sociology*. Englewood Cliffs: Prentice-Hall, 1963, pp. 213–240.

[64] Hughes, "License and Mandate," pp. 85–87.

[65] Corinne Gilb, *Hidden Hierarchies: The Professions and Government*. New York: Harper and Row, 1966; Geoffrey Millerson, *The Qualifying Associations: A Study in Professionalization*. London: Routledge and Kegan Paul, 1964.

[66] William Barclay Parsons, *Engineering in the Renaissance*. New York: Williams and Wilkins, 1939, p. 282.

[67] Ernest Greenwood, "Attributes of a Profession," *Social Work* 2 (July, 1957), pp. 44–55.

[68] The idea of the basis of a profession being scientific or value-based is discussed by Dietrich Reuschmeyer, "Doctors and Lawyers: A Comment on the Theory of the Professions," *Canadian Review of Sociology and Anthropology* 1 (February, 1964), pp. 17–30.

[69] Raymond Aron, *Dix-huit leçons*, p. 361. The two intelligentsia referred to are the engineering-technical-scientific elite and the "media experts" in the mass communications industry.

[70] Max Weber, "Bureaucracy," in H. H. Gerth and C. Wright Mills, eds., *From Max Weber: Essays in Sociology*. New York: Oxford University Press, 1958, pp. 228–235, and the Introduction by the editors, pp. 70–74.

[71] Ibid., pp. 235–239.

[72] Hannah Arendt, *Eichmann in Jerusalem: A Report on the Banality of Evil*. New York: Viking Press, 1963.

[73] Mark Field, "Structural Strain in the Role of the Soviet Physician," *American Journal of Sociology* 58 (March, 1953), pp. 493–502.

[74] Marjorie Taubenhaus and Roy Penchansky, "The Medical Care Program of the United Mine Workers Welfare and Retirement Fund," in Roy Penchansky, ed., *Health Services Administration: Policy Cases and the Case Method*. Cambridge: Harvard University Press, 1968, p. 157.

[75] Michel Crozier, *The Bureaucratic Phenomenon*. Chicago: University of Chicago Press, 1964.

[76] George Homans, *The Human Group*. New York: Harcourt, Brace, 1950, pp. 369–413.

[77] Ibid., p. 398.

[78] Barney Glaser, *Organizational Scientists: Their Professional Careers*. Indianapolis: Bobbs-Merrill, 1964, pp. 128–129.

[79] William H. Whyte, Jr., *The Organization Man*. Garden City: Doubleday, 1957, pp. 238–253.

[80] Erwin O. Smigel, *The Wall Street Lawyer*. New York: Free Press, 1964.

CHAPTER FOUR, THE DIVISION OF LABOR: CONFLICTS OF INTEREST

[1] For a critical discussion of Marx's "inevitability" thesis, see Raymond Aron, *Main Currents in Sociological Thought*, Vol. I. Garden City: Doubleday, 1968, pp. 149–165.

[2] Concerning class consciousness as a form of ideology, see Aron's discussion, ibid., pp. 217–220. Concerning ideology as a factor in the political process, see Elliott A. Krause, "Functions of a Bureaucratic Ideology: Citizen Participation," *Social Problems* 16 (Fall, 1968), pp. 129–143.

[3] C. Wright Mills, *White Collar: The American Middle Classes*. New York: Oxford University Press, 1956, pp. 301–323.

[4] Ibid., pp. 240–249.

[5] Harold L. Wilensky, "The Professionalization of Everyone?" *American Journal of Sociology* 70 (September, 1964), pp. 137–158.

[6] We do not intend by this illustration to suggest that factors other than deliberate development of occupational consciousness did not enter the picture. What we do suggest is that occupational consciousness is necessary to capitalize upon the opportunity that is often created by these other factors.

[7] Karl Marx and Friedrich Engels, *Manifesto of the Communists*. New York: Schaerr and Frantz, 1883, p. 1.

[8] For a historical study of the bitter rivalry between the AFL and the CIO in the area of meat processing and butchering, see David Body, *The Butcher Workmen: A Study of Unionization*. Cambridge: Harvard University Press, 1964, pp. 216–240.

[9] The recent upswing in right-wing political action by some workers, such as the construction workers of the United States in 1970, should not be overestimated, as the evidence on voting patterns from the last national presidential election did not demonstrate a major swing to the right by the worker or blue-collar group, in spite of predictions of this occurrence.

[10] For a discussion of the political affiliations and behavior of British workers, see John H. Goldthorpe, David Lockwood, Frank Bechhofer, and Jennifer Platt, *The Affluent Worker: Political Attitudes and Behavior*. Cambridge: Cambridge University Press, 1968.

[11] Stanislaw Ossowski, *Class Structure and the Social Consciousness* (Sheila Patterson, trans.). New York: Free Press, 1963, pp. 110–118.

[12] The enforcibility of such laws is a major issue, as the subsequent discussion will indicate.

[13] Krause, "Functions of a Bureaucratic Ideology," p. 132.

[14] Eliot Friedson and Buford Rhea, "Knowledge and Judgment in Professional Evaluation," *Administrative Science Quarterly* 10 (June, 1965), pp. 107–124.

[15] Don K. Price, *The Scientific Estate*. Cambridge: Harvard University Press, 1965, pp. 16–17.

[16] See Sidney Fine, *Laissez Faire and the General-Welfare State*. Ann Arbor: University of Michigan Press, 1956.

[17] Ibid., pp. 98–125.

[18] For a brief historical review of the Taylorist movement, see Georges Friedmann, *Industrial Society*. New York: Free Press, 1955, pp. 37–66.

[19] Ibid., pp. 365–372.

[20] Eventually, over the protests of the American Medical Association, the Medicare legislation was passed. See Richard Harris, *A Sacred Trust*. Baltimore: Penguin Books, 1969.

[21] C. Wright Mills, *The Power Elite*. New York: Oxford University Press, 1956. The actual phrase "military-industrial complex" is, however, that of President Eisenhower in his formal final address as president.

[22] This is not to say that employment would necessarily fall as a consequence of a cut in military spending. Leontief calculates that it would, instead, rise. See Wassily Leontief and Martin Hoffenberg, "The Economic Effects of Disarmament," in Leontief, *Input-Output Economics*. New York: Oxford University Press, 1966, pp. 167–183. In 1968, in the South Carolina Congressional District of Mendel Rivers, there was a billboard listing all the defense plants in the area, and a slogan "Rivers Delivers."

[23] Marc Pilisuk and Thomas Hayden, "Is There a Military-Industrial Complex Which Prevents Peace? Consensus and Countervailing Power in Pluralistic Systems," *Journal of Social Issues* 21 (July, 1965), pp. 98–99.

[24] Jean Meynaud, *Technocracy* (Paul Barnes, trans.). New York: Free Press, 1964, p. 30.

[25] Ibid., p. 32.

[26] See Michael Young, *The Rise of the Meritocracy, 1870–2033*. Baltimore: Penguin Books, 1961.

[27] Meynaud, *Technocracy*, pp. 71–144.

[28] This is the ultimate conclusion of Azrael concerning the degree to which Soviet technocrats can oppose the wishes of the state. See Jeremy R. Azrael, *Managerial Power and Soviet Politics*. Cambridge: Harvard University Press, 1966.

[29] Samuel P. Huntington, *Clientalism, A Study in Administrative Politics*. Doctoral Dissertation, Harvard University, 1951.

[30] John McDermott, "Technology: The Opiate of the Intellectuals," *New York Review of Books* 13 (July 31, 1969), p. 27.

[31] Meynaud, "Themes of Technocratic Ideology," in *Technocracy*, pp. 207–247.

[32] Ibid., p. 207.

[33] McDermott, "Technology: The Opiate of the Intellectuals," pp. 32–35.

[34] Krause, "Functions of a Bureaucratic Ideology," pp. 142–143.

[35] The original work by Nader was on automobile safety. In recent years research groups by Nader and others have been gathering evidence that can be used for class-action suits.

[36] This is markedly not the case for *public* employees in white-collar work, where the very low salaries make organization more possible; in areas such as schoolteaching, unionization is extensive as of 1970.

[37] See, for a case example of this breakdown in confidence in union leadership, Alvin W. Gouldner, *Wildcat Strike*. Antioch: Antioch Press, 1954.

[38] The new laws on the collective bargaining rights of federal employees, passed under the Kennedy administration, should not be confused with laws giving such employees the right to strike. On the other hand, since bargaining without the threat of a strike is almost meaningless, federal employees, such as the men in the postal service, have gone out on strike illegally, and have not been punished, as their leverage was too great at the particular time and places chosen.

[39] It should be clearly noted that not *all* professors, probably only a minority, in fact, support the radicalization of professional training. The more common sentiment among senior faculty is probably more closely represented by Sidney Hook, *Academic Freedom and Academic Anarchy*. New York: Cowles Book Co., 1970.

[40] One might also note that many of the community activities of such groups as the Black Panther Party have been in the area of community health care and social services, in spite of the image that the mass media have given of such organizations. The black community, however, has been tending in recent years to operate as a racial political block and not through existent national organizations that are integrated, both because they are not local enough in orientation and because they are integrated and therefore might have divided loyalties.

[41] For a discussion of relations between the "professional" and the "union-oriented" groups in the politics of the teaching field, see Alan Rosenthal, *Pedagogues and Power: Teacher Groups in School Politics*. Syracuse: Syracuse University Press, 1969.

[42] As Moynihan points out, this may not have the intended consequence. If cooptation is an inevitable result of this style of management, then the direct relation of a city government to its people can become blurred by this intermediate group that is really not representative of either. Conflict may be deferred but not confronted by such an approach. See Daniel P. Moynihan, "Toward a National Urban Policy," in Daniel P. Moynihan, ed., *Toward a National Urban Policy*. New York: Basic Books, 1970.

[43] This procedure has always been part of the traditional work pattern in the medical profession, and thus can hardly be considered a "radicalization" of the law firm's approach.

[44] Raymond Aron, *La lutte de classes*. Paris: Gallimard, 1964, p. 359.

[45] This is not to say, obviously, that small groups from either category are not extremely vociferous and politically quite active.

[46] Ida Russakoff Hoos, "When the Computer Takes Over the Office," *Harvard Business Review* 38 (July–August, 1960), pp. 102–112.

[47] Manfred Stanley, "The Negative Impacts of Technology," Fourth Annual Report, Harvard Program on Technology and Society, 1967–1968, pp. 17–18; Manfred Stanley, "Technology and Its Critics," Fifth Annual Report, Harvard Program on Technology and Society, 1968–1969, pp. 14–17.

[48] Zbigniew Brzezinski, "American Transition," *New Republic* 157 (December 23, 1967), pp. 18–21. For a somewhat modified position, without so many of the totalitarian implications of the original article, see his *Between Two Ages: America's Role in the Technetronic Era*. New York: Viking Press, 1970, pp. 1–23. It is interesting to contrast this book with Meynaud's.

CHAPTER FIVE, THE HEALTH FIELD

[1] Charles Singer and E. Ashworth Underwood, A *Short History of Medicine*. New York: Oxford University Press, 1962, pp. 3–8.

[2] The instruments for skull surgery were present in ancient Egypt, and physical anthropologists date the operation of trephination of the skull from the Neolithic period. Ibid., p. 2.

[3] Ibid., p. 28.

[4] Ibid., pp. 29–34.

[5] Ibid., pp. 55–59.

[6] For an overview of the role of universities in medieval society, and thus of the role of medicine taught in universities, see Hastings Rashdall, *The Universities of Europe in the Middle Ages* (3 Vols.). Oxford: Oxford University Press, 1936.

[7] Singer and Underwood, *A Short History of Medicine*, pp. 56–59, note that the Romans developed the model of the hospital which is the present one, one which was also adopted by Charlemagne, as the Holy Roman Emperor.

[8] Ibid., pp. 73–76.

[9] Ibid., pp. 80–84.

[10] W. S. C. Copeman, *Doctors and Disease in Tudor Times*. London: Dawson's 1960, p. 5.

[11] In fact, sometimes the clergymen, for religious rather than scientific motives, but with some medical training, were ahead of the time. See, for example, Cotton Mather's defense of vaccination in Boston, in the 1720s, in Perry Miller, *The New England Mind: From Colony to Province*. Boston: Beacon Press, 1953, pp. 345–366.

[12] See Joseph F. Kett, *The Formation of the American Medical Profession, The Role of Institutions* 1780–1860. New Haven: Yale University Press, 1968, p. 110.

[13] Ibid., pp. 106–107.

[14] Ibid., pp. 107–116.

[15] Ibid., p. 169.

[16] Daniel H. Calhoun, *Professional Lives in America. Structure and Aspiration* 1750–1850. Cambridge: Harvard University Press, 1965.

[17] Richard H. Shryock, "Medical Practice in the Old South," in his *Medicine in America: Historical Essays*. Baltimore: Johns Hopkins Press, p. 64.

[18] Richard Dunlop, *Doctors of the American Frontier*. Garden City: Doubleday, 1962, pp. 131–155.

[19] Abraham Flexner, *Medical Education in the United States and Canada: A Report to the Carnegie Foundation for the Advancement of Teaching*. New York: The Carnegie Foundation for the Advancement of Teaching, 1910.

[20] Howard S. Becker, Blanche Geer, Everett C. Hughes, and Anselm Strauss, *Boys in White: Student Culture in Medical School*. Chicago: University of Chicago Press, 1961, pp. 221–238.

[21] Howard S. Becker and Blanche Geer, "The Fate of Idealism in Medical School," *American Sociological Review* 23 (February, 1958), pp. 50–56.

[22] For a review of the literature that is still relevant, although it does not go past 1963, see Robert N. Wilson, "Patient-Practitioner Relationships," in Howard E. Freeman, Sol Levine, and Leo G. Reader, *Handbook of Medical Sociology*. Englewood Cliffs: Prentice-Hall, 1963, pp. 273–295.

[23] Becker, Geer, Hughes, and Strauss, *Boys in White*, p. 422.

[24] Natalie Rogloff, "The Decision to Study Medicine," in Robert K. Merton, George G. Reader, and Patricia L. Kendall, eds., *The Student Physician*. Cambridge: Harvard University Press, 1957, pp. 109–130; Werner Thieleus, "Some Comparisons of Entrants to Medical School and Law School," in ibid., pp. 131–152.

[25] Stuart Adams, "Trends in Occupational Origins of Physicians," *American Sociological Review* 18 (August, 1953), pp. 404–409.

[26] Ronald G. Corwin and Martin J. Taves, "Nursing and Other Health Professions," in Freeman, Levine, and Reader, *Handbook of Medical Sociology*, pp. 193–196. Esther L. Middlewood, "Why Do Students Drop Out?" *American Journal of Nursing* 46 (December, 1946), pp. 838–840.

[27] Sandy F. Mannino, "The Professional Man Nurse: Why He Chose Nursing and Other Characteristics of Men in Nursing," *Nursing Research* 12 (Summer, 1963), pp. 185–186.

[28] Basil Sherlock and Alan Cohen, "The Strategy of Occupational Choice: Recruitment to Dentistry," *Social Forces* 44 (March, 1966), pp. 303–313.

[29] D. M. More and Nathan Kohn, "Some Motives for Entering Dentistry," *American Journal of Sociology* 66 (July, 1960), pp. 47–53.

[30] The last three studies quoted agree on this, with minor exceptions.

[31] Footnote 20, same section.

[32] The Case-Western Reserve plan involves more than just the field training; major curriculum reform, with teaching by body system rather than academic discipline, is another reform, one which has not caught on at other schools to the same extent as the early field experience. The major problem with curriculum reform, at any school, is the vested interest of academic departments.

[33] Becker, Geer, Hughes, and Strauss, *Boys in White*, p. 435.

[34] This is standard procedure in the Case-Western Reserve plan, for example.

[35] Renee Fox, in Merton et al., *The Student Physician*.

[36] Howard S. Becker and Blanche Geer, "Medical Education," in Freeman, Levine, and Reader, *Handbook of Medical Sociology*, p. 178.

[37] Ibid., pp. 367–383.

[38] Ibid., pp. 135–157.

[39] National Advisory Commission on Health Manpower, *Report of the National Advisory Commission on Health Manpower*, Vol. 1. Washington, D.C.: U.S. Government Printing Office, 1967, p. 14.

[40] Stephen J. Miller, *Prescription for Leadership; Training for the Medical Elite*. Chicago: Aldine Publishing Company, 1970, p. 11.

[41] Ibid., p. 51.

[42] Ibid., pp. 56–89.

[43] Emily Mumford, *Interns: From Students to Physicians*. Cambridge: Harvard University Press, 1970, concluding chapter.

[44] Alan F. Blum and Larry Rosenberg, "Some Problems Involved in Professionalizing Social Interaction: The Case of Psychotherapeutic Training," *Journal of Health and Human Behavior* 9 (March, 1968), pp. 72–85.

[45] Kurt W. Back, Robert E. Coker, Jr., Thomas G. Donnelly, and Bernard S. Phillips, "Public Health as a Career in Medicine: Secondary Choice Within a Profession," *American Sociological Review* 23 (October, 1958), pp. 533–541.

[46] Oswald Hall, "The Informal Organization of the Medical Profession," *Canadian Journal of Economic and Political Science* 12 (1946), pp. 30–44.

[47] Personal communication from a medical relative of the author.

[48] Ronald G. Corwin and Marvin J. Taves, "Nursing and Other Health Professions," in Freeman, Levine, and Reader, *Handbook of Medical Sociology*, pp. 200–203.

[49] See Anselm Strauss, "The Structure and Ideology of American Nursing: An Interpretation," in Fred Davis, ed., *The Nursing Profession*. New York: Wiley, 1966, pp. 60–108.

[50] Corwin and Taves, "Nursing and Other Health Professions," p. 200.

[51] A conflict is being created by the increasing demand for nurses, on the one hand, and the actions by college schools of nursing to end the hospital training schools, as "second-class" institutions. Unfortunately, many lower-middle-class and poor girls cannot go to college in order to become a nurse. And on the other hand, the college nurses just aren't getting the nursing experience they need to work in hospitals. See Fred Davis, Virginia L. Olesen, and Elvi Waik Whittaker, "Problems and Issues in Collegiate Nursing Education," in Fred Davis, ed., *The Nursing Profession*, p. 173.

[52] Cynthia Krueger, "Do 'Bad Girls' Become Good Nurses?" *Trans-action* 5 (July–August, 1968), pp. 31–36.

[53] See Hans O. Mauksch, "The Organizational Context of Nursing Practice," in Davis, *The Nursing Profession*, pp. 109–137.

[54] Walter I. Wardwell, "Limited, Marginal, and Quasi-Practitioners," in Freeman, Levine, and Reader, *Handbook of Medical Sociology*, pp. 213–214.

[55] As with nurses, the manpower problem in health increases the bargaining position of marginal professionals such as osteopaths. In some states, such as California, they may practice medicine with the rights of the standard physician.

[56] See especially Miller, *Prescription for Leadership*, pp. 155–165, "Exchange with Subordinates."

[57] Anselm Strauss, Leonard Schatzman, Danuta Ehrlich, Rue Bucher, and Melvin Shabshin, "The Hospital and its Negotiated Order," in Eliot Friedson, ed., *The Hospital in Modern Society*. London: Collier-Macmillan, 1963.

[58] Blanche Geer, Jack Haas, Charles ViVona, Stephen J. Miller, Clyde Woods, and Howard S. Becker, "Learning the Ropes, Situational Learning in Four Occupational Training Programs," in Irwin Deutcher and Elizabeth J. Thompson, eds., *Among the People*. New York: Basic Books, 1968, pp. 228–229.

[59] For a discussion of the problems in health manpower, as well as present proportions, see *The Report of the National Advisory Commission of Health Manpower.*

[60] See, for example, Elton Rayack, "The Supply of Physician's Services," *Industrial Labor Relations Review* 17 (January, 1964), pp. 221–237.

[61] In terms of the manpower issues for special research, see Dale L. Hiestrand, "Research Into Manpower for Health Service," *Milbank Memorial Fund Quarterly* 44 (October, 1966), pp. 146–181.

[62] Everett C. Hughes, *Men and their Work*. New York: Free Press, 1958, p. 107.

[63] See the descriptive photo essay, "Costly Machines that Save Lives," by the Editors of *Fortune, Our Ailing Medical System, Fortune* 81 (January, 1970), pp. 92–95.

[64] Personal communication from Mark Field, April 1970.

[65] For a discussion of the comparison between the Soviet Union and the United States on allocation of resources for manpower on the one hand and for technology on the other, see Mark Field, *Soviet Socialized Medicine*. New York: Free Press, 1967.

[66] Osler L. Peterson, Leon P. Andrews, Robert S. Spain, and Bernard G. Greenberg, *An Analytical Study of North Carolina General Practice*. Evanston: Association of American Medical Colleges, 1956.

[67] Parker G. Marden, "A Demographic and Ecological Analysis of the Distribution of Physicians in Metropolitan America," *American Journal of Sociology* 72 (November, 1966), pp. 290–300.

[68] See Eliot Friedson, *The Profession of Medicine*. New York: Dodd, Mead, 1970; and his forthcoming work, *Professional Dominance: The Social Structure of Medical Care.*

[69] Hall, "The Informal Organization of the Medical Profession." See also two other articles by him which are still pertinent to the vicissitudes of patients: Oswald Hall, "The Stages of a Medical Career," *American Journal of Sociology* 53 (March, 1948), pp. 327–336; and "Types of Medical Careers," *American Journal of Sociology* 55 (November, 1949), pp. 243–253.

[70] For a discussion of the conflicts of interest represented by this form of health service, see Joseph W. Garbarino, *Health Plans and Collective Bargaining*. Berkeley: University of California Press, 1960.

[71] Peterson et al., *An Analytical Study of North Carolina General Practice*, pp. 9–17.

[72] Ibid., pp. 143–147.

[73] Personal communication of a point to be made in a forthcoming publication by Mark Field.

[74] Eliot Friedson, *Patients' Views of Medical Practice*. New York: Russell Sage, 1961.

[75] Singer and Underwood, *A Short History of Medicine*, pp. 191–204.

[76] See Ruth B. Freeman, "Public Health Nursing," in Alfred H. Katz and Jean Spencer Felton, eds., *Health and the Community*. New York: Free Press, 1965, pp. 466–473.

[77] Jean Spencer Felton, "Preventive Medicine," in ibid., pp. 428–430.

[78] For a discussion of the issues, see Russell R. Monroe, Gerald D. Klee, and Eugene B. Brody, eds., *Psychiatric Epidemiology and Mental Health Planning*. American Psychiatric Association, Psychiatric Research Report No. 22, Washington, D.C.: American Psychiatric Association, 1967.

[79] This distinction is less true for the late 1960s than previously, as the Veteran's Administration is not getting the funds proportional to the need for care for Vietnam veterans that they received previously for veterans of World War II and Korea. In all cases, state and local salaries are nowhere near competitive, except in special projects, which are usually federally funded.

[80] This trend was once fought, but now is being used instead as the rationale for hospital expansion in the areas of community clinics or "outposts." But this in turn is an invasion of the "market" of the community practitioner. See the conflict-of-interest analysis in this chapter.

[81] For a further discussion, see John Knowles, ed., *Hospitals, Doctors, and the Public Interest*. Cambridge: Harvard University Press, 1965.

[82] Ray Elling, "The Shifting Power Structure in Health," *Milbank Memorial Fund Quarterly* 46 (January 1968), pp. 119–143.

[83] Miller, *Prescription for Leadership*.

[84] For the British experience, see William J. Curran, "Nationalized Health Services: The British Experience," in Roy Penchansky, ed., *Health Services Administration: Policy Cases and the Case Method*. Cambridge: Harvard University Press, 1968, pp. 332–373.

[85] For a discussion of the complex issues here, see Robert M. Cunningham, Jr., *The Third World of Medicine*. New York: McGraw-Hill, 1961, pp. 183–254.

[86] One critical aspect of the third-party relation lies in the power that each of the parties has to dissolve the relation. See the last section of this chapter.

[87] Georg Simmel, "The Triad," in Kurt H. Wolff, ed. and trans., *The Sociology of Georg Simmel*. New York: Free Press, 1950, pp. 143–169.

[88] For the general recruitment pattern for higher education in the Soviet Union, see Nigel Grant, *Soviet Education*. Baltimore: Penguin Books, 1964, pp. 109–131.

[89] Humboldt University, *Medizin und Sociologie: Materialen des 2 Internationalen Symposions 1–3.12.1966 in Berlin*. Berlin: Humboldt University Press, 1967, p. 282.

[90] Field, *Soviet Socialized Medicine*, p. 110.

[91] Ibid., p. 111.

[92] Personal communication.

[93] Field, *Soviet Socialized Medicine*, p. 111.

[94] Ibid., p. 115.

[95] Ibid., p. 121.

[96] See David Mechanic, "General Medical Practice in England and Wales, Its Organization and Future," *New England Journal of Medicine* 279 (September 26, 1968), pp. 680–689.

[97] Ibid., pp. 684–686, which documents the British government's inability to get government-run local health centers going, centers which would of course compete with the hospitals. The hospital physicians, being more elite in social standing, appear to have more political influence on the administration of the health service than do the community-based physicians.

[98] See John Z. Bowers, *Medical Education in Japan*. New York: Harper and Row, 1965, pp. 46–58.

[99] Ibid., pp. 102–134.

[100] Ibid., pp. 55–58.

[101] For a discussion of medical manpower problems in Turkey, see Carl E. Taylor, Rahmi Dirican, and Kurt W. Deuschle, *Health Manpower Planning in Turkey*. Baltimore: Johns Hopkins Press, 1968.

[102] See, for example, Bowers, *Medical Education in Japan*, pp. 53–54: "The Japan National Railways . . . operates a chain of hospitals in the major cities on its right of way; essentially every major industry operates its own hospital system, which, with low-cost housing, pleasure resorts, and semiannual bonuses, are important fringe benefits to bolster the comparatively low salary levels."

[103] Mark G. Field and Jason Aronson, "Soviet Community Mental Health Services and Work Therapy: A Report of Two Visits," *Community Mental Health Journal* 1 (Spring, 1965), pp. 81–90.

[104] It is important to note that access to the Soviet special medical facilities is restricted to those of a certain political group (high Party officials and their families) whereas access to service in elite medical facilities is on a basis of wealth in the British, Japanese, and American systems, although in many cases there are class distinctions within hospitals serving all. In the American system, there are the charity wards and the semi-private wards, with the former for the poor and often in a different part of the hospital with a different degree of service.

[105] Bowers, *Medical Education in Japan*, p. 49. Each citizen is required to be a member of *some* health insurance plan, which in each case is related to a hospital.

[106] Mechanic, "General Medical Practice in England and Wales," pp. 685–686; Bowers, *Medical Education in Japan*, p. 51.

[107] Thomas L. Hall et al., *Health Manpower in Peru*. Baltimore: Johns Hopkins Press, 1969, pp. 19–31.

[108] Richard Harris, *A Sacred Trust*. Baltimore: Penguin Books, 1969.

[109] Robin F. Badgeley and Samuel Wolfe, *Doctor's Strike: Medical Care and Conflict in Saskatchewan*. New York: Atherton Press, 1967.

[110] See Roy Penchansky, Beryl M. Safford, and Henry Simmons, "Medical Practice in a Group Setting: The Russelton Experience," in Roy Penchansky, ed., *Health Services Administration*. Cambridge: Harvard University Press, 1968, pp. 182–218; and Beryl M. Safford, "Changing a Community's Pattern of Medical Care: The Russelton Experience," in ibid., pp. 219–259.

[111] Garbarino, *Health Plans and Collective Bargaining*, p. 178.

CHAPTER SIX, THE LEGAL PROFESSION

[1] Max Rheinstein, ed., *Max Weber on Law in Economy and Society* (Edward Shils and Max Rheinstein, trans.). Cambridge: Harvard University Press, 1954, pp. 198–223.

[2] Ibid., pp. 72, 212.

[3] Ibid., p. 213.

[4] For a history of the legal profession, see Roscoe Pound, *The Lawyer from Antiquity to Modern Times*. St. Paul: West Publishing Company, 1953.

[5] Ibid., pp. 35–58.

[6] Ibid., pp. 87–94.

[7] On the contrast between the role of law and law experts on the Continent and in England, see Walter Ullmann, *Individual and Society in the Middle Ages*. Baltimore: Johns Hopkins Press, 1968, pp. 91–92.

[8] In addition, the Puritans were familiar with the simple law that was relevant to the daily life of the early colony. See George L. Haskins, *Law and Authority in Early Massachusetts*. New York: Macmillan, 1960, p. 186. Puritan writers in England, under the Stuarts and in the Interregnum, constantly expressed their distrust of lawyers.

[9] Ibid., p. 145.

[10] For a description of the decline of the Puritan state, see Perry Miller, *The New England Mind: From Colony to Province*. Cambridge: Harvard University Press, 1953.

[11] See Erwin N. Griswold, *Law and Lawyers in the United States*. Cambridge: Harvard University Press, 1965, pp. 11–12. Almost half of the signers of the Declaration of Independence and a majority of those who attended the Constitutional Convention were lawyers.

[12] Ibid., p. 12.

[13] Ibid., p. 16.

[14] Ibid., p. 23.

[15] Ibid., p. 23.

[16] Ibid., p. 23.

[17] On the other hand, there are financial limits to this kind of activism. The Office of Economic Opportunity, which funded many of these programs in the late 1960s, has come under attack from powerful groups for their funding of "antiestablishment" legal action.

[18] Griswold, *Law and Lawyers in the United States*, p. 58.

[19] Ibid., pp. 58–59.

[20] Ibid., p. 59.

[21] Ibid., pp. 59–60.

[22] Ibid., p. 60. For more detailed information, see *Lawyers in the Making*, Report No. 96, National Opinion Research Center, University of Chicago, December 1963.

[23] Dan C. Lortie, "Laymen to Lawmen: Law School, Careers, and Professional Socialization," *Harvard Educational Review* 29 (Fall, 1959), p. 367 *fn.*

[24] Idem.

[25] See Jerome Carlin, *Lawyers on Their Own: A Study of Individual Practitioners in Chicago*. New Brunswick: Rutgers University Press, 1962; and Jack Ladinsky, "Career of Lawyers, Law Practice, and Legal Institutions," *American Sociological Review* 28 (February, 1963), pp. 47–54.

[26] David Riesman, "Toward an Anthropological Science of Law and the Legal Profession," in *Individualism Reconsidered*. New York: Free Press, 1954, pp. 440–466, especially pp. 452–456 for the following points in the text.

[27] See *The Harvard Law Record*, especially the issues from January to May of 1969.

[28] Haskins, *Law and Authority in Early Massachusetts*, pp. 25–42, and John P. Dawson, *A History of Lay Judges*. Cambridge: Harvard University Press, 1960.

[29] The following discussion is based primarily on the extensive study of the English legal profession and court system by Brian Abel-Smith and Robert Stevens, *Lawyers and the Courts: A Sociological Study of the English Legal System 1750–1965*. Cambridge: Harvard University Press, 1967.

[30] Ibid., pp. 460–461.

[31] Alex Inkeles and Kent Geiger, "Critical Letters to the Soviet Press," in Alex Inkeles, *Social Change in Soviet Russia*. Cambridge: Harvard University Press, 1968, pp. 302–303. (First published in *American Sociological Review*, December 1952 and February 1953.)

[32] For an extensive discussion of the Soviet legal system, see Harold J. Berman, *Justice in the USSR: An Interpretation of Soviet Law*. Cambridge: Harvard University Press, 1963. For the "education" function, see Chapter 12, "The Educational Role of the Soviet Court."

[33] Personal communication from a former Soviet bloc lawyer. For a series of cases, see Boris A. Konstantinovsky, *Soviet Law in Action: The Recollected Cases of a Soviet Lawyer*, Harold J. Berman, ed. Cambridge: Harvard University Press, 1953.

[34] Carl A. Llewellyn, quoted in Griswold, *Law and Lawyers in the United States*, p. 32.

[35] See Carlin, *Lawyers on Their Own* and Jerome E. Carlin, *Lawyer's Ethics: A Survey of the New York City Bar*. New York: Russell Sage Foundation, 1966.

[36] Erwin O. Smigel, *The Wall Street Lawyer: Professional Organization Man?* New York: Free Press, 1964.

[37] Geoffrey C. Hazard, Jr., "Reflections on Four Studies of the Legal Profession," in *Law and Society*, supplement to the Summer 1965 issue of *Social Problems*, p. 53.

[38] Personal communication from a former law professor in an Eastern European nation.

[39] The career pattern in the legal profession is thus in marked contrast to that in medicine, where virtually all of those trained practice in their field.

[40] For example, President Nixon went from a career in politics to a Wall Street law firm, then back into politics and into the presidency, where he appointed one member of his former law firm as a cabinet member in his administration.

[41] As Durkheim notes, contracts (and thus the need to have experts in them) exist in all complex societies, whether traditional or modern, but in those with modern, organic division of labor they are likely to be more overt and specialized, paralleling the specialization in division of labor. See Émile Durkheim, *The Division of Labor in Society* (George Simpson, trans.). New York: The Free Press, 1947, pp. 203–217, 226–229.

[42] To my knowledge, Merton has not applied the manifest versus latent function to whole occupational groups, in terms of their systems function in the society. For his

general discussion, see Robert K. Merton, *Social Theory and Social Structure*. New York: Free Press, 1957, pp. 19–82.

[43] There is a difference between a bureaucratic career in a *lawyer's* bureaucracy (Smigel's Wall Street law firm) and a career in a government bureaucracy with legal functions, such as the Justice Department or OEO Legal Services. In the former, the bureaucratization is by lawyers for lawyers, but not necessarily in the latter.

[44] Griswold, *Law and Lawyers in the United States*, p. 57.

[45] In a study of the bar in a small Midwestern city, Handler noted that as we go toward the present, many of the commercial aspects of the expertise of lawyers are replaced by experts in economics, city planning, and business development; the degree of influence wielded in commercial areas may decrease as a result, in all but large city areas with large city firms. See Joel F. Handler, *The Lawyer and His Community: The Practicing Bar in a Middle-Sized City*. Madison: University of Wisconsin Press, 1967, pp. 151–154.

[46] Abel-Smith and Stevens, *Lawyers and the Courts*, pp. 1, 115, 258.

[47] Talcott Parsons, "A Sociologist Looks at the Legal Profession," in his *Essays in Sociological Theory*. New York: Free Press, 1954, pp. 370–385.

[48] Ibid., p. 383.

[49] On the other hand, in contrast to the actions of Ralph Nader in this area, as one working solo with no interest in profit, there are, in the early 1970s, apparently to be a few law firms which will specialize in mass action suits, and if the numbers sueing and the award is large enough, a cut of the award could be at least moderately profitable to the lawyers or firm involved.

[50] Erwin N. Griswold, "Intellect and Spirit," Address at the Sesquicentennial Celebration at Harvard Law School, in Cambridge, September 23, 1967.

[51] Interview with John G. Bonomi, member of New York City Bar Discipline Committee, by Bloom in Murray Teigh Bloom, *The Trouble with Lawyers*. New York: Simon and Schuster, 1968, p. 175.

[52] Ibid., pp. 192–220.

[53] Ibid., p. 316.

[54] Ibid., p. 316.

[55] For figures on probate work, see ibid., p. 204.

[56] Leon Friedman, "Legal Gouging," *The New Republic* 160 (February 1, 1969), p. 40. (Review of Bloom, *The Trouble with Lawyers*.)

[57] Robert E. Keaton and Jeffrey O'Connell, *After Cars Crash: The Need for Legal and Insurance Reform*. Homewood, Ill. D. Jones-Irwin, 1967.

[58] Bloom, *The Trouble with Lawyers*, p. 185.

[59] Bloom suggests action by the press, by citizen groups, and by high-ranking state and federal judges, in ibid., pp. 336–346.

[60] Ibid., pp. 109–124.

CHAPTER SEVEN, THE CLERGY

[1] Émile Durkheim, *Elementary Forms of the Religious Life* (J. W. Swain, trans.). London: Allen and Unwin, 1915.

[2] Alfred Balk, *The Religion Business*. Richmond: John Knox Press, 1968, p. 13.

[3] For a discussion of the role of prophets as against the role of official priests, see Max Weber, *Ancient Judaism*, trans. and ed. by H. H. Gerth and D. Martindale. New York: Free Press, 1952.

[4] Marvin T. Judy, *The Multiple Staff Ministry*. Nashville: Abingdon Press, 1969, pp. 20–21.

[5] See Thomas M. Lindsay, *The Church and the Ministry in the Early Centuries*. London: Hodder and Stoughton, 1902.

[6] Walter Ullmann, *Individual and Society in the Middle Ages*. Baltimore: Johns Hopkins Press, 1966, pp. 18–21.

[7] Ibid., pp. 37–40, 130–133, where Ullmann shows that the "divine right" idea gave the king potential possession of any layman's land, but conversely, the church had a greater right to *its* land than the king had to his.

[8] See Frederick Eby, *Early Protestant Educators: The Educational Writings of Martin Luther, John Calvin, and Other Leaders of Protestant Thought*. New York: McGraw-Hill, 1931.

[9] For an interesting perspective on this, see Martin Luther, *Martin Luther's Reply to King Henry VIII* (E. S. Buchanan, trans.). New York: (no press), 1928.

[10] See Perry Miller, *Orthodoxy in Massachusetts, 1630–1650*. Cambridge: Harvard University Press, 1933.

[11] Perry Miller, *The New England Mind: From Colony to Province*. Boston: Beacon Press, 1961, pp. 126–127.

[12] Ibid., p. 127.

[13] Richard L. Bushman, *From Puritan to Yankee: Character and Social Order in Connecticut, 1690–1765*. Cambridge: Harvard University Press, 1967, pp. 147–234.

[14] Daniel H. Calhoun, *Professional Lives in America: Structure and Aspiration, 1750–1850*. Cambridge: Harvard University Press, 1965, pp. 88–177.

[15] James Kavanaugh, *A Modern Priest Looks at His Outdated Church*. New York: Trident Press, 1967, p. 19.

[16] Ibid., p. 21.

[17] Conversely, the more liberal the doctrine, such as Unitarianism, the more likely that the majority of the church members will not have been born into the faith.

[18] Christopher Jencks and David Riesman, *The Academic Revolution*. Garden City: Doubleday, 1969, pp. 210–211.

[19] Concerning trends in seminary education, see Walter D. Wagoner, *Bachelor of Divinity*. New York: Association Press, 1963.

[20] Ibid., pp. 42–52.

[21] Harvey G. Cox, "The 'New Breed' in American Churches: Sources of Social Activism in American Religion," in William G. McLaughlin and Robert N. Bellah, eds., *Religion in America*. Boston: Houghton Mifflin, 1960.

[22] Kavanaugh, *A Modern Priest Looks at His Outdated Church*, p. 24.

[23] Gerald J. Jud, Edgar W. Mills, Jr., and Genevieve W. Burch, *Expastors*. Philadelphia: Pilgrim Press, 1970.

[24] Ibid., p. 60.

[25] The spread of dissension through other age ranges especially characterizes the later 1960s.

[26] Jud et. al., *Expastors*, pp. 48–50.

[27] For example, Harrison's comment, "The Baptists are unwilling to confer authority upon their leaders and are equally unwilling to recognize that they have attained power apart from authority." See P. M. Harrison, *Authority and Power in The Free Church Tradition*. Princeton: Princeton University Press, 1959.

[28] Samuel W. Blizzard, "The Minister's Dilemma," *The Christian Century* (April 25, 1956), pp. 508–510.

[29] Wallace Denton, *The Role of the Minister's Wife*. Philadelphia: Westminster Press, 1962.

[30] Talcott Parsons, "Mental Illness and 'Spiritual Malaise': The Role of the Psychiatrist and the Minister of Religion," in Parsons, *Social Structure and Personality*. New York: Free Press, 1964, pp. 229–324.

[31] Richard V. McCann, *The Churches and Mental Health*. New York: Basic Books, 1962.

[32] Judy, *The Multiple Staff Ministry*, pp. 209–219.

[33] James M. Gustafson, "The Clergy in the United States," *Daedalus* 92 (Fall, 1963), p. 727.

[34] Idem.

[35] Joseph Fichter, *Religion as an Occupation*. South Bend: University of Notre Dame Press, 1961. See also Fichter, *Parochial School*. South Bend: University of Notre Dame Press, 1958.

[36] For a review of this struggle, consult *The Soviet Encyclopedia*.

[37] See, for example, Alex Inkeles, "Family and Church in Postwar USSR," in his *Social Change in Soviet Russia*. Cambridge: Harvard University Press, 1968, pp. 222–223.

[38] Ibid., p. 225.

[39] Hans Lamm, "Jews and Judaism in The Soviet Union," in William Fletcher and Anthony J. Strover, *Religion and the Search for New Ideals in the USSR*. New York: Praeger, 1967.

[40] Nino LoBello, *The Vatican Empire*. New York: Trident, 1958.

[41] See Chapter Ten in LoBello, "The Vatican in Politics."

[42] In Israel, the issue centers around the "law of the return," which states that one who is *born* to Jewish parents can be a citizen just by immigrating, but one who converts to another faith is in a more complicated position if he wishes citizenship.

[43] Marx claimed that religion was *one* form, but not the only form, of "false consciousness."

[44] There is a controversy as to whether he deliberately intended this end, as well.

[45] Eugene Carson Blake, Preface to Balk, *The Religion Business*.

[46] Martin A. Larson, *Church Wealth and Business Income*. New York: Philosophical Library, 1965, p. 71.

[47] LoBello, *The Vatican Empire*, p. 135.

[48] Arthur Mann, *Yankee Reformers in the Urban Age: Social Reform in Boston 1880–1900*. New York: Harper and Row, 1966, pp. 73–101.

[49] Cox, "The 'New Breed' in American Churches."

[50] Ibid., p. 368.

[51] Ibid., p. 369.

[52] E. Q. Campbell and T. F. Pettigrew, "Racial Crisis and Moral Dilemma: A Role Analysis of Little Rock Ministers," *American Journal of Sociology* 64 (1959), pp. 509–516.

[53] Ibid., p. 515.

[54] Cox, "The 'New Breed' in American Churches," p. 375.

[55] The facts regarding population growth are interesting in this connection, since the nations with the greatest population problems are non-Catholic, or Catholic with the problems of malnutrition concentrated in a half-native, half-Catholic culture complex, such as the native interpretations of Catholicism in Mexico. Pope Paul's stand on birth control may be modified in the coming years, and is overtly being opposed in the United States and Holland, by many parish priests.

CHAPTER EIGHT, THE MILITARY FIELD

[1] Robert G. Albion, *Introduction to Military History*. New York: The Century Co., 1929, p. 95.

[2] Ibid., p. 96.

[3] Ibid., p 97.

[4] Ibid., p. 97.

[5] Lynn White, Jr., *Medieval Technology and Social Change*. London: Oxford University Press, 1962, pp. 93–98.

[6] Alfred Vagts, *A History of Militarism*. New York: Free Press, 1967, p. 42.

[7] William Barclay Parsons, *Engineers and Engineering in the Renaissance*. New York: Williams and Wilkins, 1939, pp. 43–50.

[8] Albion, *Introduction to Military History*, p. 99.

[9] Samuel P. Huntington, *The Soldier and the State*. Cambridge: Harvard University Press, 1967, p. 21 *fn*.

[10] Michael Walzer, *The Revolution of the Saints*. Cambridge: Harvard University Press, 1965, p. 276.

[11] Huntington, *The Soldier and the State*, pp. 20–28.

[12] Vagts, *A History of Militarism*, pp. 116–128; Huntington, *The Soldier and the State*, pp. 39–42.

[13] Huntington, *The Soldier and the State*, pp. 55–58.

[14] Ibid., pp. 194–195.

[15] Ibid., pp. 198–199.

[16] Morris Janowitz, *The Professional Soldier*. New York: Free Press, 1960, pp. 79–103.

[17] Ibid., pp. 100–101.

[18] John P. Lovell, "The Professional Socialization of the West Point Cadet," in Morris Janowitz, ed., *The New Military*. New York: Russell Sage Foundation, 1964, p. 135.

[19] Max Weber, "Politics as a Vocation," in H. H. Gerth and C. Wright Mills, eds., *From Max Weber: Essays in Sociology*. New York: Oxford University Press, 1958, pp. 77–128.

[20] Janowitz, *The New Military*, p. 108.

[21] Morris Janowitz and Roger Little, *Sociology and the Military Establishment*. New York: Russell Sage Foundation, 1959, p. 49.

[22] Recent decisions of the United States Supreme Court, as of 1970, make moral objection to a given war possible for those who do not belong to a pacifist religion. This in part has been a consequence of the pressure mobilized originally by the draft resistance movement.

[23] Especially as in the Korean and Vietnamese conflicts, when total mobilization of the population has not occurred.

[24] See Harold Wool, "The Armed Forces as a Training Institution," in Eli Ginzberg, *The Nation's Children*, Vol. 2. New York: Columbia University Press, 1959, pp. 158–185.

[25] Janowitz and Little, *Sociology and the Military Establishment*, p. 44.

[26] For changes in the socialization process for the West Point cadet, see Lovell, "The Professional Socialization of the West Point Cadet," pp. 142–145.

[27] Janowitz and Little, *Sociology and the Military Establishment*, p. 55.

[28] Mayer N. Zald and William Simon, "Career Opportunities and Commitments Among Officers," in Janowitz, *The New Military*, p. 273. See also Gene M. Lyons and John W. Masland, *Education and Military Leadership: A Study of the ROTC*. Princeton: Princeton University Press, 1959.

[29] This approach is running into trouble when it encounters politically sophisticated college graduate draftees who received their political education on the campuses of the late 1960s.

[30] Roy L. Grinker and John P. Spiegel, *Men Under Stress*. Philadelphia: Blakiston, 1945; Eli Ginzberg et al., *The Ineffective Soldier*, 3 vols. New York: Columbia University Press, 1959.

[31] Samuel Stouffer et al., *The American Soldier: Studies in Social Psychology in World War II*. Princeton: Princeton University Press, 1949.

[32] Roger W. Little, "Buddy Relations and Combat Performance," in Janowitz, *The New Military*, pp. 195–223.

[33] See Zald and Simon, "Career Opportunities and Commitments Among Officers," pp. 257–285. See also, especially for the academy versus non-academy distinction at top ranks, John W. Masland and Laurence I. Radway, *Soldiers and Scholars*. Princeton: Princeton University Press, 1957.

[34] Masland and Radway, ibid., Chapters 15–19 ("Senior Military Education").

[35] The increase in commitment to the military career is highest for those in the OCS group; that is, as time goes on, those who have internal mobility out of enlisted status develop higher commitment to officerdom than those who started at this rank (except for academy graduates). See Zald and Simon, "Career Opportunities and Commitments Among Officers," p. 272.

[36] Kurt Lang, "Technology and Career Management in the Military Establishment," in Janowitz, *The New Military*, p. 76.

[37] The calculation of leaving versus staying in a role is itself a step in the direction of disengagement. For a discussion of retirement problems, see Albert D. Biderman, "Sequels to a Military Career: The Retired Military Officer," in Janowitz, *The New Military*, pp. 287–336.

[38] Zald and Simon, "Career Opportunities and Commitments Among Officers," pp. 266–276; Lyons and Masland, *Education and Military Leadership*, concluding chapter.

[39] Lovell, "The Professional Socialization of the West Point Cadet," pp. 126–131.

[40] Ibid., p. 127; Janowitz, *The Professional Soldier*, p. 264.

[41] Huntington, *The Soldier and the State*, p. 79.

[42] Idem.

[43] Janowitz, *The Professional Soldier*, p. 164, and the entire section, "Adaptive Career Experiences," pp. 165–171.

[44] Lang, "Technology and Career Management in the Military Establishment," p. 46. The distribution in the general labor force is strikingly similar.

[45] Masland and Radway, *Soldiers and Scholars*, p. 519.

[46] Ibid., p. 514. Italics mine.

[47] For an analysis of the role of the CIA in foreign affairs, see Fred J. Cook, *The Warfare State*. New York: Macmillan, 1962.

[48] Alfred Vagts, *The Military Attaché*. Princeton: Princeton University Press, 1967.

[49] Isidore F. Stone, *In a Time of Torment*. New York: Random House, 1967.

[50] For a discussion of the role of university-based defense research centers in the military-industrial complex, see Seymour Melman, *Pentagon Capitalism: The Political Economy of War*. New York: McGraw-Hill, 1970.

[51] Weber, "Bureaucracy," in Gerth and Mills, *From Max Weber: Essays in Sociology*.

[52] Janowitz and Little, *Sociology and the Military Establishment*, pp. 66–74.

[53] For the need for such skills in the military, see Janowitz, *The Professional Soldier*, pp. 38–53.

[54] Note that by "hierarchical" here is meant only the possession of all elite positions by academy men, not possession by, for example, enlisted men or civilians.

[55] Janowitz, *The Professional Soldier*, pp. 347–371.

[56] Harold Lasswell, "The Garrison State and Specialist on Violence," *American Journal of Sociology* 46 (January, 1941), pp. 455–468.

[57] Roman Kolkowitz, *The Soviet Army and the Communist Party: Institutions in Conflict*. Santa Monica: RAND Corporation, 1966, p. vii.

[58] Ibid., p. v.

[59] Ibid., pp. 181–215.

[60] R. L. Garthoff, *The Role of the Military in Recent Soviet Politics*. Santa Monica: The RAND Corporation, 1956, pp. ii–iii; and Kolkowitz, *The Soviet Army and the Communist Party*, pp. vii–xi, 500–513.

[61] Kolkowitz, *The Soviet Army and the Communist Party*, p. ix.

[62] Ibid., pp. 455–475.

[63] Morris Janowitz, *The Military in the Political Development of New Nations: An Essay in Comparative Analysis*. Chicago: University of Chicago Press, 1964, p. 1.

[64] Ibid., pp. 6–7.

[65] Ibid., pp. 75–77.

[66] Vagts, *Military Attaché*, p. 249: "It is this modern concept of the 'national interest' which the accusatory 'merchant of death' literature usually ignores, overlooking the fact that keeping national war industries on a standby basis in peace time is one of the aims of the service attachés and the military and naval missions to underdeveloped countries, who act as salesmen for the international armaments industries."

[67] Janowitz, *Military in Political Development*, pp. 35–36, 69.

[68] Ibid., p. 100.

[69] Eugene V. Walter, *Terror and Resistance: A Study of Political Violence*. New York: Oxford University Press, 1969.

[70] Janowitz, *Military in Political Development*, pp. 18–23.

[71] Janowitz, *The Professional Soldier*, p. 264.

[72] Masland and Radway, *Soldiers and Scholars*, pp. 511–512.

[73] Huntington, *The Soldier and the State*, pp. 437–440.

[74] Going by educational level of entrants at different ranks, and per cent of Negroes. See Lang, "Technology and Career Management in the Military Establishment," pp. 54–62.

[75] Huntington, *The Soldier and the State*, pp. 163–192.

[76] Marc Pilisuk and Thomas Hayden, "Is There a Military-Industrial Complex Which Prevents Peace? Consensus and Countervailing Power in Pluralistic Systems," *Journal of Social Issues* 21 (July, 1965), pp. 98–99.

[77] The political values of modern youth are an element here. See Theodore Roszak, *The Making of a Counter-Culture*. New York: Doubleday, 1969.

CHAPTER NINE, BUSINESS AND INDUSTRY

1 Stephan Thernstrom, *Poverty and Progress: Social Mobility in a Nineteenth Century City*. Cambridge: Harvard University Press, 1964, pp. 68–70.

2 Ibid., pp. 138–165.

3 Ibid., p. 114.

4 Theodore Caplow, *The Sociology of Work*. Minneapolis: University of Minnesota Press, 1954, p. 188.

5 David Brody, *The Butcher Workmen: A Study of Unionization*. Cambridge: Harvard University Press, 1964, p. 129.

6 Louis Adamic, *Dynamite: The Story of Class Violence in America*. New York: Chelsea House, 1931, p. 350.

7 Idem.

8 Brody, *The Butcher Workmen*, p. 217.

9 Peter F. Drucker, *The Concept of the Corporation*. New York: New American Library, 1964, pp. 238–240.

10 Ibid., p. 241.

11 Harry Levinson, *Executive Stress*. New York: Harper and Row, 1964, p. 147.

12 For an overall discussion of prestige rating, see David Riesman, *Constraint and Variety in American Education*. Lincoln: University of Nebraska Press, 1956.

13 William H. Whyte, Jr., *The Organization Man*. Garden City: Doubleday, 1957, pp. 225–238.

14 Theodore N. Ferdinand, "On the Obsolescence of Scientists and Engineers," *American Scientist* 54 (March, 1966), pp. 46–56.

15 Michel Crozier, *The Bureaucratic Phenomenon*. Chicago: University of Chicago Press, 1964, p. 101.

16 See the discussion of training at "Kard Business-Machine School" in Blanche Geer, Jack Haas, Charles ViVona, Stephen J. Miller, Clyde Woods, and Howard S. Becker, "Learning the Ropes. Situational Learning in Four Occupational Training Programs," in Irwin Deutscher and Elizabeth J. Thompson, eds., *Among the People*. New York: Basic Books, 1968, pp. 211–214.

17 Elliot Liebow, *Tally's Corner: A Study of Negro Streetcorner Men*. Boston: Little, Brown, 1967, pp. 29–71.

18 Quoted from the Harvard Business School Catalogue, in Charles D. Orth, 3rd, *Social Structure and Learning Climate: The First Year at Harvard Business School*. Cambridge: Harvard Business School, Division of Research, 1963, p. 53.

19 Ibid., p. 47.

20 See Howard S. Becker, Blanche Geer, Everett C. Hughes, and Anselm Strauss, *Boys in White: Student Culture in Medical School*. Chicago: University of Chicago Press, 1961, Part Two ("Student Culture in the Freshman Year"), pp. 65–184. Becker and Geer were consultants to Orth's project.

21 Orth, *Social Structure and Learning Climate*, pp. 210–220.

22 Whyte, *The Organization Man*, pp. 132–138.

23 Richard C. Hodgson, Daniel J. Levinson, and Abraham Zaleznik, *The Executive Role Constellation: An Analysis of Personality and Role Constellations in Management*. Cambridge: Harvard Business School, Division of Research, 1965.

24 C. Jackson Grayson, *Decisions Under Uncertainty: Drilling Decisions by Oil and Gas Operators*. Cambridge: Harvard Business School, Division of Research, 1960.

25 Ibid., p. 3 of the abstract prepared by the Division of Research, Harvard Business School, Brighton, Massachusetts.

26 Everett C. Hughes, "Career Advancement and Learning in the System," in *Career Development in Industry*. Harvard Studies in Career Development, No. 59. Cambridge: Harvard Graduate School of Education, March, 1968, pp. 67–68.

27 Whyte, *The Organization Man*, pp. 173–185.

28 David Allison, "The Industrial Scientist," in his *The R & D Game: Technical Men, Technical Managers, and Research Productivity*. Cambridge: M.I.T. Press, 1969, p. 26.

[29] Ibid., p. 23.

[30] Barney Glaser, *Organizational Scientists: Their Professional Careers.* Indianapolis: Bobbs-Merrill, 1964.

[31] Allison, "The Industrial Scientist," p. 25. He is quoting Jack Morton of Bell Labs.

[32] Elinor Langner, "The Women of the Telephone Company," *New York Review of Books* 14 (March 26, 1970), p. 14; and see Elinor Langner, "Inside the New York Telephone Company," *New York Review of Books* 14 (March 12, 1970), pp. 16–24.

[33] Langner, "Women of the Telephone Company," p. 16.

[34] William H. Form and Delbert C. Miller, "Occupational Career Pattern as a Sociological Instrument," *American Journal of Sociology* 54 (January, 1949), pp. 317–329.

[35] Peter Blau and Otis Dudley Duncan, *The American Occupational Structure.* New York: Wiley, 1967.

[36] Personal communication.

[37] Alvin W. Gouldner, *Patterns of Industrial Bureaucracy.* New York: Free Press, 1954, pp. 105–115.

[38] Martin Meissner, *Technology and the Worker: Technical Demands and Social Processes in Industry.* San Francisco: Chandler, 1969.

[39] Georges Friedmann, *Industrial Society: The Emergence of the Human Problems of Automation.* New York: Free Press, 1955, pp. 129–155.

[40] Fritz J. Roethlisberger and W. G. Dickson, *Management and the Worker.* Cambridge: Harvard University Press, 1939, p. 388.

[41] Donald Roy, "Quota Restriction and Goldbricking in the Machine Shop," *American Journal of Sociology* 57 (1952), pp. 427–442.

[42] Abraham Zaleznik, *Worker Satisfaction and Development: A Case Study of Work and Social Behavior in a Factory Group.* Cambridge: Harvard Business School, Division of Research, 1956.

[43] Crozier, *The Bureaucratic Phenomenon,* pp. 189–191.

[44] Park's observations referred to geography, as this referred to social group membership in the urban residential pattern.

[45] Abraham Zaleznik, *Foreman Training in a Growing Enterprise.* Cambridge: Harvard Business School, Division of Research, 1951.

[46] Crozier, *The Bureaucratic Phenomenon,* pp. 190–192.

[47] Alvin W. Gouldner, *Wildcat Strike: A Study in Worker-Management Relationships.* New York: Harper Torchbooks, 1965, pp. 89–105.

[48] Levinson, *Executive Stress,* pp. 144–155; Crozier, *The Bureaucratic Phenomenon,* pp. 112–118.

[49] Louis B. Barnes, *Organizational Systems and Engineering Groups: A Comparative Study of Two Technical Groups in Industry.* Cambridge: Harvard Business School, Division of Research, 1960.

[50] Richard E. Walton, *The Impact of the Professional Engineering Union: A Study of Collective Bargaining Among Engineers and Scientists and Its Significance for Management.* Cambridge: Harvard Business School, Division of Research, 1961.

[51] However, the men in Crozier's study were *mechanics* and far less trained than the ones in Walton's study, who were engineers. But the occupational group leverage phenomenon is relevant to both groups.

[52] See C. Wright Mills, *White Collar: The American Middle Classes.* New York: Oxford University Press, 1956, pp. 312–314; and Langner, "Women of the Telephone Company," pp. 18–21.

[53] Arthur N. Turner and Paul R. Lawrence, *Industrial Jobs and the Worker: An Investigation of Response to Task Attributes.* Cambridge: Harvard Business School, Division of Research, 1965.

[54] Crozier, *The Bureaucratic Phenomenon,* pp. 237–269.

[55] Shmuel N. Eisenstadt, *Absorption of Immigrants in Israel.* London: Routledge, 1954.

[56] Crozier, *The Bureaucratic Phenomenon,* p. 138.

[57] Alex Inkeles, "Industrial Man: The Relation of Status to Experience, Perception, and Value," *American Journal of Sociology* 66 (July, 1960), p. 18.

[58] Ibid., p. 12.

[59] Project Description, *Sociocultural Aspects of Social Change*. Alex Inkeles, Project Director. Harvard University: Center for International Affairs, mimeo, no date, p. 4.

[60] Idem.

[61] This statement is based on the author's own understanding of project results, checked with Professor Inkeles.

[62] Olatunde Oloko, *Some Social and Psychological Factors Affecting Commitment to Industrial Employment in Nigeria*, Doctoral Dissertation, Harvard University, 1970.

[63] Rowan Ireland, *The Factory as a School for Social Change*. Doctoral Dissertation, Harvard University, 1969.

[64] Manning Nash, *Machine-Age Maya: The Industrialization of a Guatemalan Community*. Chicago: University of Chicago Press, 1967.

[65] Raymond Aron, *Dix-huit leçons sur la société industrielle*. Paris: Editions Gallimard, 1962, p. 50. (My translation.)

[66] Wassily Leontief, "The Structure of Development," in his *Input-Output Economics*. New York: Oxford University Press, 1966, pp. 50–51.

[67] Aron, *Dix-huit leçons*, p. 359.

[68] Kurt Borchardt, *Structure and Performance of the U.S. Communications Industry: Government Regulation and Company Planning*. Cambridge: Harvard Business School, Division of Research, 1970.

[69] Stephen S. Cohen, *Modern Capitalist Planning: The French Model*. Cambridge: Harvard University Press, 1969; John H. McArthur and Bruce R. Scott, *Industrial Planning in France*. Cambridge: Harvard Business School, Division of Research, 1969.

[70] Cohen, *Modern Capitalist Planning*, p. 198.

[71] David Granick, *The Red Executive*. Garden City: Doubleday, 1961, pp. 129–140.

[72] Jerry F. Hough, *The Soviet Prefects: The Local Party Organs in Industrial Decision-Making*. Cambridge: Harvard University Press, 1969, pp. 306–317.

[73] Jeremy R. Azrael, *Managerial Power and Soviet Politics*. Cambridge: Harvard University Press, 1966, p. 173.

[74] Marshall E. Dimock, *The Japanese Technocracy: Management and Government in Japan*. New York: Walker/Weatherhill, 1968.

[75] Cohen, *Modern Capitalist Planning*, p. 198.

[76] Ibid., p. 199.

[77] Stanislaw Ossowski, *Class Structure in the Social Consciousness* (Sheila Patterson, trans.). New York: Free Press, 1963, p. 154.

[78] Emily C. Brown, *Soviet Trade Unions and Labor Relations*. Cambridge: Harvard University Press, 1966, pp. 202–238.

CHAPTER TEN, SCIENCE AND THE ARTS

[1] Arnold Hauser, *A Social History of Art*, Vol. 1. New York: Random House, 1951, p. 36.

[2] Ibid., pp. 81–100.

[3] Walter Ullmann, *Individual and Society in the Middle Ages*. Baltimore: Johns Hopkins Press, 1966, pp. 100–151.

[4] A. C. Crombie, *Medieval and Early Modern Science, Vol. I: Science in the Middle Ages—V–XIII Centuries*. Cambridge: Harvard University Press, 1967, p. 61.

[5] Hauser, *A Social History of Art*, Vol. II, pp. 60–61.

[6] Ullmann, *Individual and Society in the Middle Ages*, p. 105.

[7] Betty Burroughs, ed., *Vasari's Lives of the Artists*. New York: Simon and Schuster, 1946.

[8] Bernard Barber, *Science and the Social Order*. New York: Crowell-Collier, 1962, p. 82.

[9] A. C. Crombie, *Medieval and Early Modern Science, Vol. II: Science in the Later Middle Ages and Early Modern Times—XIII–XVII Centuries*. Cambridge: Harvard University Press, 1967, p. 288.

[10] Robert K. Merton, *Social Theory and Social Structure*. New York: Free Press, 1957, p. 584.

[11] Ibid., p. 579. See also Robert K. Merton, "Science, Technology, and Society in Seventeenth-Century England," OSIRIS, IV, Part 2. Bruges, Belgium, 1938.

[12] Oliver Larkin, *Art and Life in America*. New York: Holt, Rinehart and Winston, 1949, pp. 18–19.

[13] William J. Baumol and William G. Dickson, *Performing Arts—The Economic Dilemma*. Cambridge: M.I.T. Press, 1966, p. 63.

[14] See, for example, Lawrence Kubie, *Neurotic Distortion of the Creative Process*. New York: Noonday, 1961; and Robert S. White, *Ego and Reality in Psychoanalytic Theory*. New York: International Universities Press, 1963 (Psychological Issues Monograph No. 11), pp. 24–43.

[15] Anne Roe, *The Making of a Scientist*. New York: Dodd, Mead, 1953; and Bernice T. Eiduson, *Scientists: Their Psychological World*. New York: Basic Books, 1962.

[16] Jonathan Kozol, *Death at an Early Age: The Destruction of the Hearts and Minds of Negro Children in the Boston Public Schools*. Boston: Houghton Mifflin, 1967; and John Holt, *Why Children Fail*. New York: Dell, 1964.

[17] Robert N. Wilson, "The Poet in American Society," in Robert N. Wilson, ed., *The Arts in Society*. Englewood Cliffs: Prentice-Hall, 1964, pp. 24–32; see also Spencer Klaw, *The New Brahmins: Scientific Life in America*. New York: William Morrow, 1968, pp. 15–43.

[18] Mason Griff, "The Recruitment of the Artist," in Wilson, *Arts in Society*, p. 73.

[19] Idem.

[20] Griff, "The Recruitment of the Artist," p. 81; and Bernard Rosenberg and Norris Fliegel, *The Vanguard Artist: Portrait and Self-Portrait*. Chicago: Quadrangle Books, 1965, pp. 103–137.

[21] Rosenberg and Fliegel, *The Vanguard Artist*, p. 126.

[22] Klaw, *The New Brahmins*, pp. 15–43; and Theodore Caplow and Reece McGee, *The Academic Marketplace*. Garden City: Doubleday, 1958, pp. 68–79.

[23] Carol Pierson Ryser, "The Student Dancer," in Wilson, *The Arts in Society*, pp. 95–121; Rosenberg and Fliegel, *The Vanguard Artist*, pp. 65–100.

[24] James D. Watson, *The Double Helix*. New York: Antheneum, 1968.

[25] Caplow and McGee, *The Academic Marketplace*, pp. 87–90.

[26] Rosenberg and Fliegel, *The Vanguard Artist*, pp. 208–209.

[27] Watson, *The Double Helix*, pp. 164–171.

[28] See Howard S. Becker, "Contingencies of the Professional Dance Musician's Career," *Human Organization* 12 (Spring, 1953), pp. 22–26; Rosenberg and Fliegel, *The Vanguard Artist*, p. 205.

[29] Merton, *Social Theory and Social Structure*, pp. 552–561.

[30] Renato Poggioli, *The Theory of the Avant-Garde* (Gerald Fitzgerald, trans.). Cambridge: Harvard University Press, 1968, pp. 8–12.

[31] Norman W. Storer, *The Social System of Science*. New York: Holt, Rinehart and Winston, 1966, p. 160. See also Norman W. Storer, "Basic Versus Applied Research: The Conflict Between Means and Ends in Science," *Indiana Sociological Bulletin* 2 (October, 1964), pp. 34–42.

[32] C. P. Snow, *The Two Cultures and the Scientific Revolution*. New York: Cambridge University Press, 1959.

[33] Andrei D. Sakharov, *Progress, Coexistence and Intellectual Freedom*. London: Deutsch, 1968.

[34] Not all Western writers have commercial success, of course, nor have hacks necessarily starved in Eastern Europe or the United States.

[35] Poggioli, *The Theory of the Avant-Garde*, p. 79.

[36] Merton, *Social Theory and Social Structure*, p. 556.

[37] Don K. Price, *The Scientific Estate*. Cambridge: Harvard University Press, 1965, pp. 126–162.

[38] Baumol and Dickson, *Performing Arts*, pp. 137–160.

CHAPTER ELEVEN, ILLEGAL OCCUPATIONS

[1] Harry Benjamin and R. E. L. Masters, *Prostitution and Morality*. New York: Julian Press, 1964, pp. 40–41.

[2] Ibid., p. 59.

[3] Ibid., p. 61.

[4] The Jews were often barred from other occupations, and thus usury became an ethnic speciality. When the Christian position on usury changed, primarily as a consequence of the Protestant Reformation, usury became an acceptable occupation for them as well.

[5] Walter Muir Whitehill, *Boston: A Topographical History*. Cambridge: Harvard University Press, 1963, pp. 7–8.

[6] Edwin H. Sutherland, *White Collar Crime*. New York: Holt, Rinehart and Winston, 1949, pp. 257–266.

[7] Benjamin and Masters, *Prostitution and Morality*, p. 91.

[8] Robert K. Merton, "Social Structure and Anomie," in Hendrik M. Ruitenbeek, ed., *Varieties of Modern Social Theory*. New York: Dutton, 1963, pp. 364–401.

[9] Edwin H. Sutherland, ed., *The Professional Thief, By a Professional Thief*. Chicago: University of Chicago Press, 1937, pp. 140–153.

[10] See Elliott A. Krause, "The Gluecks and Sociology: Evolution of a Controversy," Paper delivered at the 1969–1970 Annual Meeting, American Association for the Advancement of Science, December, 1969.

[11] August Aichhorn, "On the Technique of Child Guidance," in Otto Fleischmann, Paul Kramer, and Helen Ross, eds., *Delinquency and Child Guidance: Selected Papers by August Aichhorn*. New York: International Universities Press, 1964, pp. 170–171.

[12] See William F. Whyte, *Street Corner Society*. Chicago: University of Chicago Press, 1955, pp. 111–146.

[13] Benjamin and Masters, *Prostitution and Morality*, pp. 88–107.

[14] Sutherland, *Thief*, p. 23.

[15] See Howard S. Becker, "Notes on the Concept of Commitment," *American Journal of Sociology* 66 (July, 1960), p. 32, and Blanche Geer, "Occupational Commitment and the Teaching Profession," *School Review* 74 (Spring, 1966), pp. 31–47.

[16] Whyte, *Street Corner Society*, p. 145.

[17] Sutherland, *Thief*, p. 56.

[18] For a discussion of organized crime as a social system, see Donald A. Cressey, *Theft of a Nation: The Structure and Operation of Organized Crime in America*. New York: Harper and Row, 1969, pp. 221–247. See also Peter Maas, *The Valachi Papers*. New York: Bantam Books, 1969.

[19] Sutherland, *Thief*, p. 38.

[20] For a description of the legal, social, and occupational issues here, see Lawrence Lader, *Abortion*. Boston: Beacon Press, 1966. As of June, 1970, however, the AMA has come out in favor of legalized abortion in hospitals, performed by physicians, for "economic and social" reasons, as well as for medical reasons.

[21] Sutherland, *Thief*, pp. 38–41.

[22] Everett C. Hughes, "Work and the Self," in *Men and their Work*. New York: Free Press, 1958.

[23] For a research investigation of this hypothesis, see Kai T. Erikson, *Wayward Puritans*. New York: Wiley, 1966, pp. 161–205.

[24] This issue is part of the overall consideration which the Soviet Union has given to the family. See Alex Inkeles, *Social Change in Soviet Russia*. Cambridge: Harvard University Press, 1968, p. 5.

[25] See Jimmy Breslin, *The Gang Who Couldn't Shoot Straight*. New York: Viking, 1969. Mario Puzo, *The Godfather*. New York: Putnam's, 1969.

[26] Cressey, *Theft of a Nation*, p. 162.

[27] Ibid., p. xi.

CHAPTER TWELVE, THE FIELD OF EDUCATION

[1] E. B. Castle, *Ancient Education and Today*. Baltimore: Penguin Books, 1961, p. 64.

[2] Ibid., pp. 45–48.

[3] Ibid., p. 129.

[4] Alexander M. Carr-Saunders and P. N. Wilson, *The Professions*. Oxford: Oxford University Press, 1933.

[5] For a history of Harvard, see Samuel Eliot Morison, *Three Centuries of Harvard, 1636–1936*. Cambridge: Harvard University Press, 1946.

[6] Wilson Smith, "The Teacher in Puritan Culture," *Harvard Educational Review* 36 (Fall, 1966), p. 409.

[7] David Tyack, "The Kingdom of God and the Common School," *Harvard Educational Review* 36 (Fall, 1966), pp. 447–469.

[8] Richard Hofstadter, *Anti-Intellectualism in American Life*. New York: Alfred A. Knopf, 1963, p. 79.

[9] Christopher Jencks and David Riesman, *The Academic Revolution*. Garden City: Doubleday, 1969, p. 3.

[10] Idem.

[11] Ibid., pp. 12–20.

[12] James B. Conant, *The Education of American Teachers*. New York: McGraw-Hill, 1963, p. 74.

[13] Ibid., pp. 73–111.

[14] Myron Brenton, *What's Happened to Teacher?* New York: Coward-McCann, 1970, p. 109.

[15] Herbert R. Kohl, *The Open Classroom*. New York: Random House, 1969, p. 103.

[16] Howard S. Becker, "The Career of the Chicago Public Schoolteacher," *American Journal of Sociology* 57 (March, 1952), pp. 473–477.

[17] For a discussion of the hiring process, see Theodore Caplow and Reece J. McGee, *The Academic Marketplace*. New York: Basic Books, 1958.

[18] This type of appointment is often part of the bargaining for new jobs, by well-known "grantsmen" thinking of switching schools.

[19] This last factor is not considered extensively by Caplow and McGee in part because this attention to the law of supply and demand, across the entire field, was not extensive.

[20] Alvin W. Gouldner, "Cosmopolitans and Locals: Toward an Analysis of Latent Social Roles," *Administrative Science Quarterly* 2 (December, 1957), pp. 281–306.

[21] Talcott Parsons, "The School Class as a Social System," in his *Social Structure and Personality*. London: Collier-Macmillan, 1964, pp. 129–154.

[22] Talcott Parsons and Winston White, "The Link between Character and Society," in *Social Structure and Personality*, pp. 183–235.

[23] Aaron V. Cicourel and John I. Kitsuse, *The Educational Decision-Makers*. Indianapolis: Bobbs-Merrill, 1963, p. 145.

[24] Brenton, *What's Happened to Teacher?* p. 36.

[25] Perhaps the downturn in applications to graduate school is in part attributed to this motivation, although draft eligibility changes and the job market situation may also be factors here. It is still true, however, that radical Harvard Ph.D.'s go to Berkeley, and not Mississippi State, for their first job.

[26] Paul Goodman, *Compulsory Mis-Education and the Community of Scholars*. New York: Random House, 1966, pp. 323–339.

[27] Harmon Ziegler, *The Political Life of American Teachers*. Englewood Cliffs: Prentice-Hall, 1967, pp. 127–143.

[28] Alan Rosenthal, *Pedagogues and Power: Teacher Groups in School Politics*. Syracuse: Syracuse University Press, 1969, pp. 1–2.

[29] Ibid., pp. 71–93.

[30] Peter Schrag, *Village School Downtown*. Boston: Beacon Press, 1967; David Rogers, *110 Livingston Street: Politics and Bureaucracy in the New York School System*. New York: Random House, 1968; Henry S. Resnik, *Turning on the System: War in the Philadelphia Public Schools*. New York: Pantheon, 1970.

[31] James Ridgeway, *The Closed Corporation: American Universities in Crisis*. New York: Ballantine Books, 1968, p. 193.

[32] Nigel Grant, *Soviet Education*. Baltimore: Penguin Books, 1964, pp. 23–31.

[33] Ibid., pp. 32–37.

[34] Personal communication.

[35] Paul Goodman, *Utopian Essays and Practical Proposals*. New York: Random House, 1962.

[36] Charles Muscatine, Chairman, *The Muscatine Report on Higher Education at Berkeley*. Berkeley: University of California Press, 1968.

[37] Anthony Oettinger and Sema Marks, *Run, Computer, Run: The Mythology of Educational Innovation*. Cambridge: Harvard University Press, 1969.

CHAPTER THIRTEEN, PUBLIC SERVICE OCCUPATIONS

[1] For a history of Egypt with respect to this issue, see Marcel Brion, *Histoire de l'Egypte*. Paris: Fayard, 1954.

[2] See, for example, Alvin W. Gouldner, *The Hellenic World: A Sociological Analysis*. New York: Harper Torchbooks, 1965.

[3] Walter Ullmann, *Individual and Society in the Middle Ages*. Baltimore: Johns Hopkins Press, 1966, pp. 11–12.

[4] George C. Homans, *English Villagers of the Thirteenth Century*. Cambridge: Harvard University Press, 1942, p. 337.

[5] See the regulations concerning the mason's guild which were passed in a few years by the King of France, in William B. Parsons, *Engineer and Engineering in the Renaissance*. New York: Williams and Wilkins, 1939, pp. 643–645.

[6] See Alfred Von Martin, *The Sociology of the Renaissance*. New York: Harper and Row, 1963.

[7] Michael Young, *The Rise of the Meritocracy, 1870–2033*. Baltimore: Penguin Books, 1958.

[8] The legal system of the English village was the basis for the Puritan colony's laws; its approach to public service naturally followed from this. See George L. Haskins, *Law and Authority in Early Massachusetts*. New York: Macmillan, 1960, pp. 43–69.

[9] Sidney H. Aronson, *Status and Kinship in the Higher Civil Service: Standards in the Administration of John Adams, Thomas Jefferson, and Andrew Jackson*. Cambridge: Harvard University Press, 1964.

[10] But this "dedication" may interfere with responsible and responsive work in public service. See F. William Howton, *Functionaries*. Chicago: Quadrangle Books, 1969.

[11] For an evaluation of ethnic groups in public service, see Nathan Glazer and Daniel P. Moynihan, *Beyond the Melting Pot*. Cambridge: M.I.T. Press, 1963; and Peter Schrag, *Village School Downtown: Boston Schools, Boston Politics*. Boston: Beacon Press, 1967.

[12] Max Weber, "Bureaucracy," in H. H. Gerth and C. Wright Mills, eds., *From Max Weber: Essays in Sociology*. New York: Oxford University Press, 1958.

[13] James Q. Wilson, *Varieties of Police Behavior: The Management of Law and Order in Eight Communities*. Cambridge: Harvard University Press, 1968.

[14] Howton, *Functionaries*, p. 44.

[15] For an extensive discussion of the technocratic attitude, see Jean Meynaud, *Technocracy* (Paul Barnes, trans.). New York: Free Press, 1969.

[16] In Boston, for example, the city services almost shut down during the last week before the election.

[17] Daniel P. Moynihan, *Maximum Feasible Misunderstanding: Community Action in the War on Poverty*. New York: Free Press, 1969.

[18] Lewis Coser, Comment at the 1966 Annual Meeting, Society for the Study of Social Problems, Miami, Florida.

[19] Howton, *Functionaries*, pp. 122–140.

[20] Ibid., pp. 128–132.

[21] Ibid., pp. 132–136.

[22] Morris Titmuss, *Essays on the Welfare State*. London: Routledge and Kegan Paul,

1969; Elliott A. Krause, "Functions of a Bureaucratic Ideology: Citizen Participation," *Social Problems* 16 (Fall, 1968), pp. 129–143.

23 Elliott A. Krause, "Structured Strain in Marginal Professions: Rehabilitation Counseling," *Journal of Health and Human Behavior* 6 (Spring, 1965), pp. 55–62.

24 Martin Anderson, *The Federal Bulldozer*. New York: McGraw-Hill, 1967.

25 Thomas B. Bottomore, *Elites in Society*. New York: Basic Books, 1965.

26 For a description of the peasant's point of view, see John Womack, Jr., *Zapata and the Mexican Revolution*. New York: Knopf, 1969.

27 On the Cuban experiment, see Maurice Zeitlin, *Revolutionary Politics and the Cuban Working Class*. Princeton: Princeton University Press, 1967.

28 Piet Thoenes, *The Elite in the Welfare State* (J. E. Brigham, trans.). London: Faber and Faber, 1966.

29 The problem with this legislation lies precisely in the giving of rights which cannot be protected without the one device—the strike—that gives them reality as rights.

CHAPTER FOURTEEN, THE CAREER ACTIVIST

1 Michael Walzer, *The Revolution of the Saints*. Cambridge: Harvard University Press, 1965.

2 Ibid., p. 159.

3 See Kai Erikson, *Wayward Puritans*. New York: Wiley, 1966, pp. 71–106.

4 Frederick Jackson Turner, *The United States, 1830–1850: The Nation and Its Sections*. New York: 1935.

5 Chester McArthur Destler, *American Radicalism 1865–1901*. Chicago: Quadrangle Books, 1966.

6 For a discussion of Gompers' role in the Populist-Labor alliance, see Destler, *American Radicalism*, pp. 29, 174, 182–183, 200, 223.

7 See James W. Hulse, *Revolutionists in London: A Study of Five Unorthodox Socialists*. Oxford: Clarendon Press, 1970.

8 Marion K. Sanders, *The Professional Radical: Conversations with Saul Alinsky*. New York: Harper and Row, 1970, pp. 68–69.

9 Stokely Carmichael and Charles V. Hamilton, *Black Power*. New York: Random House, 1967, pp. 58–84.

10 Robert Michels, *Political Parties* (E. and C. Paul, trans.). New York: Free Press, 1949.

11 Erik H. Erikson, *Young Man Luther*. New York: W. W. Norton, 1958.

12 Sanders-Alinsky, *The Professional Radical*, p. 26.

13 Peter Matthiessen, *Sal Si Puedes—Escape If You Can: Cesar Chavez and the New American Revolution*. New York: Random House, 1969.

14 Sanders-Alinsky, *The Professional Radical*, p. 35.

15 Matthiessen, *Escape If You Can*, pp. 123, 307.

16 For an extensive biography of Huey Long, see T. H. Williams, *Huey Long*. New York: Knopf, 1969.

17 See Jerry Rubin, *Do It*. New York: Simon and Schuster, 1970; and Abbie Hoffman, *Revolution for the Hell of It*. New York: Dial, 1968.

18 Max Weber, "Politics as a Vocation," in H. H. Gerth and C. Wright Mills, eds., *From Max Weber: Essays in Sociology*. New York: Oxford University Press, 1958, pp. 77–128.

19 Sanders-Alinsky, *The Professional Radical*, pp. 30–33.

20 Edward C. Banfield and James Q. Wilson, *City Politics*. Cambridge: Harvard University Press, 1963.

21 Sanders-Alinsky, *The Professional Radical*, p. 49.

22 Carmichael and Hamilton, *Black Power*, pp. 77–84.

23 Lewis A. Coser, *The Functions of Social Conflict*. New York: Free Press, 1956.

24 Sanders-Alinsky, *The Professional Radical*, p. 73.

CHAPTER FIFTEEN, THE POLITICS OF SKILL

1 Harold D. Lasswell, *Politics: Who Gets What, When, How*. Cleveland: World Publishing Co., 1958.

2 Robert K. Merton, "Manifest and Latent Functions," in *Social Theory and Social Structure*. New York: Free Press, 1957, pp. 19–84.

3 Lasswell, *Politics*, pp. 97–112.

4 This research needs to be carried out in a career or biographical perspective, in order to gain an understanding of the critical places where intervention is needed.

5 The Editors of *Fortune*, "American Youth: Its Outlook Is Changing the World," *Fortune* 79 (January, 1969), entire issue.

6 The interest-based nature of this argument is often clear when one observes the different positions espoused by groups such as The Automation Institute or The Socialist Worker's Alliance.

7 Sebastian DeGrazia, *Of Time, Work and Leisure*. New York: Twentieth Century Fund, 1962.

8 David Riesman, "The Ethics of We Happy Few," *University Observer* 1 (1947), pp. 19–28.

INDEX TO NAMES

Numbers in parentheses refer to the numbers of footnotes.

INDEX TO SUBJECTS